MEMOIRS OF A MBORORO

Cameroon Studies

General Editors: *Shirley Ardener, E.M. Chilver* and *Ian Fowler*, Associate Members of Queen Elizabeth House, University of Oxford.

Volume 1
Kingdom on Mount Cameroon. Studies in the History of the Cameroon Coast, 1500–1970 – Edwin Ardener. Edited and with an Introduction by Shirley Ardener.

Volume 2
African Crossroads. Intersections between History and Anthropology in Cameroon – Edited by Ian Fowler and David Zeitlyn.

Volume 3
Cameroon's Tycoon. Max Esser's Expedition and its Consequences – Edited by E.M. Chilver and Ute Röschenthaler.

Volume 4
Swedish Ventures in Cameroon, 1883–1923. Trade and Travel, People and Politics – Edited and with Commentaries by Shirley Ardener.

Volume 5
Memoirs of a Mbororo. The Life of Ndudi Umaru: Fulani Nomad of Cameroon – Henri Bocquené, translated by Philip Burnham and Gordeen Gorder.

MEMOIRS OF A MBORORO

The Life of Ndudi Umaru: Fulani Nomad of Cameroon

HENRI BOCQUENÉ

Translated by Philip Burnham and Gordeen Gorder

Berghahn Books
New York • Oxford

First published in 2002 by **Berghahn Books**

www.berghahnbooks.com

© 2002 English Language Edition, Berghahn Books
© 1986 Éditions KARTHALA, Paris
Originally published as *Moi, Un Mbororo: Autobiographie de Oumarou Ndoudi: Peul nomade du Cameroun*

Library of Congress Cataloging-in-Publication Data

Bocquené, Henri.
   [Moi, un Mbororo. English]
   Memoirs of a Mbororo : the life of Ndudi Umaru, Fulani nomad of Cameroon / Henri Bocquené ; translated by Philip Burnham and Gordeen Gorder.
    p. cm. -- (Cameroon studies ; v. 5)
   ISBN 1–57181–844–8 (cloth : alk. paper)
    1. Bororo (African people)--Biography. 2. Bororo (African people)--Social life and customs. 3. Ndoudi, Oumarou, 1945- I. Ndoudi, Oumarou, 1945- II. Title. III. Series.

DT571.B67 B6313 2002
967.11`00496322--dc21   2002018426

British Library Cataloguing in Publication Data
A catalogue record for this book is available from the British Library.

Printed in the United States on acid-free paper

ISBN 1–57181–844–8 hardback

Table of Contents

List of Illustrations

Preface to the English Translation

It is with mixed emotions that I write this preface. I am very happy finally to be making available to English-language readers this fascinating account of Ndudi Umaru's life and the rich cultural setting in which he lived. But I am very sad that neither Ndudi nor his interlocutor Père Henri Bocquené, both of them my close friends, lived to see its publication. Père Henri and I first met in northern Cameroon in 1968 when I was engaged in social anthropological research in the Meiganga region (now called the Mbere Department). Our friendship grew over the course of the next few years, during some nine months of which my wife and I were his neighbours, living in and around the town of Djohong where his Catholic mission station was located. It was at Djohong, in 1973, that he introduced me to Ndudi Umaru, and I soon became just as captivated as Père Henri by Ndudi's lively spirit and exceptional life history.

In her preface to *Moi un Mbororo*, the original French edition, Christiane Seydou rightly stresses the influence of Père Henri's outsider's curiosity and gaze in stimulating the progressive development of Ndudi's critical interest in his own society. However, even in the earliest days of their friendship, it was apparent to me that Ndudi possessed a degree of insight into his own society which was original to him and quite exceptional in my experience of the nomadic cattle-herding Mbororo Fulani people. Used to living by his wits, having dwelled in many different social environments during his long search for a cure for his leprosy, Ndudi occupied the unique position of being both on the inside and on the outside of his own society – a double perspective born of marginality. At the same time, due to his skill as a raconteur and player of the *garaya*, the one-stringed banjo, Ndudi was ever-sensitive to his audience and had an outgoing personality, which one more usually encountered among non-Mbororo professional praise-singers or other performers than among the notoriously reserved Mbororo.

The collaboration of Ndudi and Père Henri has given us a privileged view into the world of the Mbororo and the complex and ever-changing social mosaic of West African savanna societies through which these cattle herders move. For the western public, the Mbororo have often been the photogenic subjects of 'disappearing world' documentary films or glossy coffee table volumes. Like other nomads, their life style and customs are seen as exotic or even mysterious by their sedentary African neighbours, not to mention western urban dwellers like ourselves. In this regard, it is not the least of Ndudi's and Père Henri's achievements to have rendered 'the exotic' comprehensible, even almost familiar at times, preserving the cultural authenticity of Ndudi's account while at the same time making this unique world more accessible to outsiders.

Père Henri and I began discussing the idea of an English translation of *Moi un Mbororo* even before the French edition appeared in 1986, for I felt certain that this was a book that deserved the widest possible circulation. However, other work intervened, and it was from an unexpected quarter that help appeared in the form of a draft translation of the text by Mrs Gordeen Gorder, a missionary then working in Nigeria. In the end, this English translation represents a joint effort between Mrs Gorder and myself, with my contribution being chiefly in the area of ensuring accuracy regarding cultural detail and specialised vocabulary. I have also attempted as far as possible to preserve the character of the oral narrative style of the original seventy-eight hours of tape-recorded material, the tone of which I was familiar with from many discussions with Ndudi.

For anthropologists like myself, *Memoirs of a Mbororo: the Life of Ndudi Umaru* will be of much use as an ethnographic document, and we can only regret that Père Bocquené was obliged for commercial reasons to truncate the original 1,100 pages of Ndudi's oral account. The lay reader might indeed have found it difficult, for example, to plough through extended passages on Mbororo cattle remedies and other ethno-veterinary practices, but the wealth of cultural detail embodied in Ndudi's original text is a monument to his concern to record the knowledge and practices of his own people. But perhaps more than its worth as an ethnography is the value of this book's portrayal of a richly layered life experience – in parts a marginal, tragic life, the life of a gambler and a trickster, but also the life of a seeker after knowledge as a source of personal fulfilment and identity. While some western anthropologists are fond nowadays of describing their ethnographies in fashionable terms as attempts to discover one's Self via a relationship with the Other, Ndudi's work makes a similar journey via a different route, including some reflexive detours stimulated by the long friendship between nomad and missionary.

The subject of this book, then, is an autobiographical account of the first thirty years of Ndudi's life. It begins in north-eastern Nigeria, where he was born and spent his early years, and moves to north-central Cameroon, where he encountered Père Henri and began recording his life story. Progress on the joint project was slowed by Père Henri's serious health problems, which necessitated several medical evacuations to France and soon caused the two collaborators to move from the very rural setting of Djohong to the city of Ngaoundere, with its better medical facilities. During periods when Père Henri's health was stabilised, Ndudi and he were able to travel quite widely. Together, they visited many of the places mentioned in Ndudi's narrative, both in Cameroon and Nigeria, and met some of Ndudi's relations and acquaintances who live scattered throughout this zone. At Ngaoundere, from the early 1980s, Ndudi settled into a more stable lifestyle in which the practice of Islam played an increasing part. In addition to the salary he received from Père Henri, he would often supplement his income by selling the herbal and other remedies which he had learned from his father and other acquaintances, as described here and there in this book.

When the French edition of this book was published in 1986 by Editions Karthala, it enjoyed an immediate success, as much with the general reading public as with academia. Among the many tributes and favourable reviews the book received, Père Henri particularly valued the letter he received from Claude Lévi-Strauss, a facsimile of which was included in the second French edition which soon followed.[1] Père Henri ensured that all the royalties of the book were paid to Ndudi in the form of cattle, which allowed him to accumulate a modest herd and later to build himself a house at Ngaoundere.

At Ngaoundere as well, Ndudi continued his romantic adventures, first marrying and then divorcing Tobi, a Fulbe woman from Tcheboa who also suffered from leprosy. He then married Mairama, a Mbororo woman who, one might say, was the love of his life despite their tempestuous relationship, during which they divorced twice only to remarry each time. Finally, Ndudi married Fatou, a young disabled woman from his own clan, as a second wife. Ndudi was overjoyed when Fatou soon gave birth to his first child, Ai, followed three years later by a second daughter, Hawa.

Another important part of Ndudi's life from the early 1980s was his involvement in the work of Lisbet Holtedahl, social anthropologist and film-maker from the University of Tromsø in Norway. Ndudi's gifts as an interviewer came to the fore in this context, and he had a key role in the production of several documentary films. He also participated actively in the research projects of the Ngaoundere-Anthropos programme, an academic collaboration between Norwegian universities and the University of Ngaoundere. In the midst of so much dynamism and positive achievement, it therefore came as a devastating shock to Ndudi's family and friends when, in February 1994, we learned of his sudden death in a road accident while he was walking in Ngaoundere.

By this time, Père Henri's state of health had already necessitated his permanent repatriation to France, and the news of Ndudi's death came as a crushing blow. Nevertheless, as his strength permitted, he continued to work on his voluminous Mbororo archive, including the verbatim transcripts and translations of Ndudi's oral account, right up to the time of his death, in August 2000.

Père Henri made arrangements with his literary executor, Lisbet Holtedahl, for all his material to be deposited in a Bocquené archive, which is to be accessible via the Ngaoundere-Anthropos programme at the University of Ngaoundere. I have also arranged for a collection of related material on the Mbororo and other peoples of Adamawa to be made available on the Internet, through the University of Kent's 'Experience-Rich Anthropology' initiative (http://lucy.ukc.ac.uk). All royalties from the present book will be paid to Ndudi's family, who continue to live in Ngaoundere.

Philip Burnham
University College London

1: See the next page for the text of Claude Lévi-Strauss's letter.

Letter from Claude Lévi-Strauss

30 September 1988

Dear Father,

Your Mbororo are certainly very different from mine (except perhaps in their taste for self-ornamentation). But that hasn't prevented me from reading your book with enchantment: this is life, this is the reality. Without belonging to the profession, you have produced one of the masterworks of ethnographic literature. Rich and precise information, accompanied by penetrating insights, emerge from each page – not in the form of arid data but integrated with the unfolding of an individual existence. One feels a little bit Mbororo after having read your book.

With thanks for your gracious letter and package, Father, please accept my warm regards.

Claude Lévi-Strauss

Preface to the French Edition

This book is the fruit of a friendly collusion between two men over some fifteen years. Although their backgrounds could scarcely have been more different, from the moment of their first meeting they implicitly recognised each another as partners in a privileged encounter. From then on, throughout their shared journey, and whatever its rhythmic alternation of agreements and disputes, they could not but fulfil the promise of their unexpected meeting.

Presumably, it was their shared situation of marginality that drew together the French missionary and the young Mbororo leper from the very outset. The first was living on his own in the middle of Cameroon among already Islamised nomadic and semi-nomadic herders. The second, who had been left to his own devices early in life, was living in town far from his kith and kin to obtain treatment for his disease. For it was among such settled people that the young leper had traded his nomadic life for that of an itinerant, even a vagrant, to the point that he risked gradually losing his identity. Eventually, as he confesses himself, he came to 'feel a bit the stranger' even in his own uncles' camp.

One can also presume that what propelled these men towards each other was the same need to 'find themselves' which was at the heart of their sense of marginality. The first needed to learn from the other how to enter wholeheartedly into the life of those who had welcomed him and, by being fully attentive to things and to people, to become open to a reality they could share. The second also needed to situate himself in relation to those around him but, above all, he needed to relate to his own self and to a life which, up to that point, had tossed him from one country to another, from one family to another, from one way of life to another, and from one adventure to another.

Finally, and more than anything, it was probably their mutual curiosity, as attentive as it was friendly - in a word, their openness of heart and mind - that led them to get to know and understand each other. Better still, it led each of them to know and understand himself: one in his destiny as a missionary, the other in his destiny as a Mbororo herder. This is where the unique quality of their relationship really lies.

Recalling his first encounter with the man he would call the *Para*, the young Mbororo Ndudi Umaru recognises how neatly the invitation to accompany the Para to his home in Djohong coincided with his own wish to leave his uncles who, as he says, had never really accepted him. Seeking to explain the probable grounds for their rejection of him, he launches into self-criticism. His hands, impaired by leprosy, prevented him from accomplishing most of the tasks of herding, making him a useless mouth to feed. His excessive taste for strong drink and neglect of the daily prayers showed his disregard for Islamic precepts. Finally, his escapades and the bad company he kept only accentuated the unfavourable impression he had made on his paternal relatives. Tired of feeling 'in the way' and unappreciated, Ndudi had left his uncles and cousins once before. Without telling them he was going, Ndudi had spent several months in the Central African Republic. Besides the hope of immediate material security it held out, Ndudi's departure to live with the *Para* must have struck him as simply another opportunity to resume his penchant for adventuresome wanderings.

Certainly Ndudi could not have foreseen that his flight from his family and their pastoral life would be the prelude to a re-rooting in his native culture: a culture which he now knows more expertly than the men of the Ringimaji and other clans – sons of the first generation to arrive in the Country of the Mountain – who have gradually allowed themselves to be so influenced by the sedentary Fulbe lifestyle that some are even ashamed to be called Mbororo. This re-rooting was the happy – though not a little paradoxical – outcome of Ndudi's meeting and collaboration with this *Para* who, nonetheless, displayed all the characteristics of 'a foreigner': origin, language, culture, status, religion. This is indeed the most interesting aspect of the human adventure lived by these two men.

Far from trying to take advantage of the 'marginality' of his new friend by tempting him into his own cultural universe, the *Para* (motivated, it seems, as much by a healthy intuition as by a considered ideological stance) established the principles of their association from the very outset. Ndudi would introduce him to this other world, that of the Mbororo, and guide him towards a deep understanding of it. In return, he – the European, the White, the Nazarene – would initiate the illiterate Ndudi into a new world, the world of writing. At least, the *Para* would be happy to teach Ndudi to write his own language, Fulfulde.

At first glance, this exchange might appear unequal: for one, access to the whole of a foreign culture; for the other, acquisition of an elementary technique for transcribing the sounds of his language into written signs! Ndudi himself often scolded the *Para* for not teaching him French, the language which is believed, at least by those who cannot speak it, to confer status on its adepts in the so-called francophone countries of Africa. Yet this was the *Para*'s real wisdom: his refusal to 'produce' one of those 'educated persons' for whom access to writing and to basic French is seldom more than an open door to an acculturation aggravated by disillusionment.

The situation of this Para also seems quite paradoxical. On one hand, he expected Ndudi to help him learn all aspects of Mbororo culture while, on the other, he assumed the role of professor, teaching this same Ndudi not only how to write his own language but much more – its structures and rules, in a word, its entire grammar. And yet it was this apprenticeship in grammar and writing – plus his detailed recounting of the life of his community, its habits and customs, its beliefs and practices – that brought Ndudi back to himself, writing himself back into his life and personality as a Mbororo. This is not the least of the merits of the common adventure which bound Ndudi and the *Para* together.

Surely it was this outsider's perspective, and the minute and exacting curiosity of the *Para*, which sensitised Ndudi to his own culture, to his own society, and finally to himself. It permitted him to understand what had made him the way he was and how to recover his place in the society to which he belonged. It sent him back to the world from which he had first been distanced, then separated, by the fortunes of life. In discovering himself and returning to his own people, Ndudi became aware not only of the originality but also of the profound values and coherence of his ancestral culture which, henceforth, he was able to contemplate with a keener eye and a mind both more perceptive and more free. By recounting everything that made up his universe, Ndudi reconquered it, making it his own through words that simultaneously surrendered that world to others.

As for his acquisition of the orthography and grammar of his language – quite aside from the unquestionable value such knowledge has for an almost-spontaneous grasp of or insight into the deep mental mechanisms of each culture – it endowed Ndudi with a two-fold wealth. It is a tool which allows him now to act as a collector and preserver of the traditions and oral literature of the Mbororo, which has long been his goal. It also establishes his 'literate' status, which gives him worth in his own eyes, as well as those of his brothers.

Thus we see a reversal of the unequal exchange we questioned above. His daily meetings with Ndudi, and Ndudi's active and loyal friendship, gave the Para a more intimate understanding of the Mbororo people and of a Mbororo world that had become his own adopted homeland. Yet was it not even more important for Ndudi to find himself through this friendship: to return to his roots and rediscover his true worth? From that point on, he assumed the task of handing down all those traditions which are the foundation of the Mbororo world he comes from.

Together with his translator and accomplice Henri Bocquené, Ndudi Umaru offers the reader something that is still rare in African studies: a rich ethnographic experience that has been lived from the inside, an intimate marriage between an autobiography and a monograph. This is all the more interesting because it is an experience related by someone who has never been subjected to a 'western' education, which might have imbued him with the modes of thought or criteria of evaluation of outsiders.

For us, this text – autobiography, ethnography and intimate monograph – is a rich document in more than one way. It offers information that enables us to grasp Mbororo society and culture as objective structures and general modes of functioning, but it also conveys the subjective dimensions of a lived human reality, that of a man who is at once the spontaneous product of his culture and an involuntary producer of it. Even more than this, thanks to the new lucidity he gained through being reflected in the gaze of an outsider, Ndudi set himself the task of also observing like an outsider, and he has conscientiously reproduced for us what he saw. What we welcome here is thus the testimony of an indigenous ethnographer, in the etymological sense of that word.

As for the interpreter's role which fell to Henri Bocquené in transmitting this work to the western reader, we can easily imagine the problems it entailed and the difficult choices it demanded. Henri Bocquené explains these in his own introduction. With this translation of Ndudi Umaru's autobiography, he has completed the shared task to which each of them brought his own contribution at different levels, at different moments, and in different forms. Thus, after having been the link between Ndudi and his rediscovered ancestral culture, Henri Bocquené made himself the 'interpreter' – in the original sense of that term – between Ndudi's world and our own, between the words of a Mbororo herder from Adamawa and the ears of every reader who may be a stranger to this world but who is curious about other people and other lives.

Christiane Seydou
National Centre for Scientific Research,
Paris, 1985

Introduction

It was in the summer of 1962 that I first became seriously interested in the Mbororo. It would not be accurate to say that I had never heard about them previously. They had already vaguely pricked my curiosity, but certainly not to the point of impinging on my concerns as a missionary. So it was a big surprise for me when, after six years as a military chaplain in Algeria, I was asked to live with them.

Since I knew so little about them, my first instinct was to wander through the anthropology shelves of several Parisian libraries. Searching through one card catalogue after another, I finally found a reference to 'Bororo' (as the name is often spelled in French). But when I looked more closely, I quickly discovered those Bororo were not mine – they lived in South America!

At the library of the Musée de l'Homme, I finally found under the listing 'Mbororo' the notation 'see Fulbe'. When I found 'Fulbe', I saw the notation 'see Peul'. Those references, which annoyed me at the time, seem well-founded to me today. But how could I have known then that '*Fulbe*' was the plural of *Pullo*, which became *Peul*, or even *Peuhl* in French (and *Fulani* in English) or that the *Mbororo* (or '*Bororo*') were a nomadic segment of the eastern Fulani?

That same week I had the pleasant surprise of seeing a documentary called *Nomads of the Sun* at a cinema. This film was about the Wodabe of Niger, an important group of nomadic Fulani who will be mentioned frequently in this book. The filmmaker, H. Brandt, also had had the excellent idea of compiling some of the best and most representative of the pictures into a book of the same title.

This was my first 'visual' contact with this unknown world. My search for information also led me to the author of a study which had just been published about the Muslims of black Africa, Professor J.-C. Froelich. If I no longer remember what I learned from him about the degree of Islamisation of the Mbororo, I will always remember the phrase he used to give me some idea about these people: 'If you believe they are black, you will find them white; if, on the other hand, you expect them to be white, they will seem black.' That hardly shed any light on my future hosts for me!

That was the extent of my sketchy knowledge when, several days after my arrival in Douala, Cameroon in December 1962, I had the opportunity of meeting my first Mbororo milk-seller as I stopped at Garoua Boulai, on the road between Yaounde and Ngaoundere. I still have a very vivid memory of that first meeting. With a large calabash of milk sitting in front of her, the woman squatted at the door of a Syrian merchant. She was rather white.

Nine years later another meeting awaited me, which was even more memorable. This was the meeting I had with Ndudi Umaru, son of Koyne, at the home of his uncle

Ardo Gauja in Djohong where I had lived since 1962. Ndudi was about twenty-five years old. That meeting, which might have been only a fleeting instant in our two lives, was – on the contrary – the beginning of a privileged relationship and a long and fruitful collaboration which continues today.

It is difficult for me to analyse the feelings I had in those days and to remember what attracted me to Ndudi. It must have been an 'emotional moment' for him too. How can I explain the sudden and unexpected proposal which I made to him? 'Come with me. You'll teach me your language, and I'll teach you to read and write it.'

His response was equally quick and spontaneous and, that very night, carrying a simple blanket and the guitar that accompanied him everywhere, Ndudi arrived at my house. The next day on my veranda, I began to teach him to hold his first ball-point pen between his fingers, the first joints of which had been eaten away by leprosy.

Ndudi has put this episode into his autobiography. 'For me,' he says, 'writing was only a game, something unimportant, something with no future, a white-man's business.' As for me, on the other hand, I realised right away what a precious opportunity it was for me to have such a companion by my side.

While teaching him to draw lines and to spell his first words, I gave him a job to do right away. Since my arrival in Cameroon nine years before, I had tape-recorded a large amount of material, especially stories and conversations of adults about their habits and customs. I listened to them again with Ndudi in order to benefit from his explanations and interpretations. But I quickly saw that he was impatient to tell me his own stories, to describe the experiences he'd had with his family. He liked to answer my questions and was happy to satisfy my curiosity.

I remember my first problem: 'But what are the *ginaji* – spirits, genies, jinns? – which seem so familiar to you Mbororo? What are they?'

Without a doubt, Ndudi was surprised by my ignorance of that subject because he answered, 'We Blacks believe the Whites are always in contact with the Spirits. It's only through contact with them that the Whites are able to build big bridges over rivers, make airplanes fly, and make radios talk. We believe these Spirits make themselves visible to Whites. We also think it's directly because of God and not the Spirits that the Whites succeeded in going to the moon. The Spirits would not have been able to do that.'

He spoke while sitting deep down in a rattan armchair and, gradually during the conversation, my confidence grew. His explanation seemed to me to be a good omen.

In this way, over the course of time, Ndudi helped me to review the subjects and themes I had taped. But, intrigued by the game, he was quick to become the one asking the questions, going to interview a certain old healer or a renowned story-teller. For him, every occasion was a good one for using the microphone. The time and the place did not matter: at the side of the path wherever he met someone, on a riverbank, in a corner of a marketplace with the noise of the crowd in the background, in the courtyard of a *sare* (family compound), in the midst of the cackling of hens, in the car when stopped or moving, and – of course – around the fire in the evenings with the silence of the night broken only by muffled lowing.

More than once we used our imaginations to dream up a ruse so we could meet some women who otherwise would have been suspicious of our sudden contact and would have run off. Over the years, many tape recordings accumulated.

In 1976, after spending two years at the National Institute of Oriental Languages and Civilisations in Paris, where I mastered the transcription and grammar of Fulfulde (the language of the Fulani) that I had just learned, I began studying those documents together with Ndudi, who had not wasted any time during my two years' absence. Wasn't it time to begin our big project? We were in agreement; our decision was made. But what was this project?

Ndudi was very clear about it and explained our joint venture in these terms: 'I understood that the *Para* was waiting for me to help him write this book about the Mbororo: who are we? how do we live? what is our life as nomads like?'

As for myself, my original intention was to write a book about the Mbororo in their own language. Over the years, Ndudi had acquired a reliable knowledge of spelling and a very refined perception of the problems of the transcription and grammar of his language. Besides Ndudi's personal qualities, his facility in writing his language can be attributed to two factors. The first is the simplicity of the conventions adopted by the congress organised in 1966 in Bamako by UNESCO for the transcription of West African languages. The second is the fact that Ndudi, knowing no European language and having never gone to school, could learn to write his own language and master the system of equivalencies between speech sounds and their orthography without being bothered by interference from another system.

Ndudi, an ardent researcher, filled his school notebooks day after day with tales, stories, and all sorts of 'little things' which make up the daily life of the Mbororo. Furthermore, he decided he would record all the treasures of wisdom which the Elders had handed down through their advice, thoughts and proverbs. He wanted to serve as the memory of all those respected old men who have departed from this life without leaving the slightest written trace of their passage on this earth. However, while awaiting the completion of this long endeavour, we agreed - Ndudi and I - to record a long account of his life, which had been rich in events and adventures.

No rigid framework would be permitted to sterilise the spontaneity of this story. Our plan was simple: the life of Ndudi Umaru together with, as the story unfolded, all the details of Mbororo life – customs, beliefs, habits, etc. I was hesitant only about the method to follow. Should I go back to the notes that I had accumulated, which could furnish us with a lot of ethnographic information? I had indexed a large part of them and had already transcribed and translated them. Or would it be better to keep all that knowledge in the background and work with a much more immediate approach?

It was the latter method which prevailed. Focusing on the present, Ndudi himself agreed to disregard everything he had already told me: episodes of his life and many other things. To affirm our decision and our method, we transformed our recordings into archives. They were bound up in packets and placed at the bottom of a trunk that was locked with a key.

So, the only thing I had to do then was listen to Ndudi. For fifteen months of daily meetings, I recorded what was to become Ndudi's 'book'. This narrative, in a spontaneous and oral style, was recorded on fifty-two cassettes. I began transcribing the seventy-eight hours of narration in Fulfulde. Mid-way through this long and arduous task, I opted for 'simultaneous' translation. So, sentence after sentence – just as an interpreter would do – using the controls of my tape-recorder and the keyboard of my typewriter, I soon found myself facing 1,100 pages of French text.

The task remained of reducing the volume of this autobiography to a 'reasonable' size for publication. This was the first problem I had to solve. Concerned about preserving Ndudi's style and the quality of his lively story – translating a man and a culture – I could not imagine making either a résumé or a digest. I had to make a choice in the least subjective way possible. I decided that what would guide me would be my initial objective: to obtain as close a glimpse as possible of the Mbororo world. To my regret, I had to delete certain episodes from the life of our hero in order to preserve an equilibrium between the anecdotes of his life and the illustrative account he provides us of the Mbororo people and their culture.

I also had to leave aside certain technical subjects – for example, women's finery, food, or traditional veterinary art – which would have made the story move too slowly and which, besides, could form the basis of separate publications. Most of Ndudi's observations about other ethnic groups (though they are interesting in the Cameroonian context) were also set aside, since they doubtless would not always have interested other readers.

From a very long discourse about common Muslim beliefs and practices, I kept only the part where Ndudi related the impact of Islam on the mind of the Mbororo, as he experiences it and interprets it. As for the wide variety of folktales (which Ndudi never tires of), I had to make a selection which could exemplify both his personal preferences and the various types of stories which reflect the behaviour and ideas of his society.

I want to stress the hesitations I have had during the long task of shortening the text. I worry that I may not have maintained an equilibrium between the anecdotal and the thematic.

The anecdotal - these are the things that happened to Ndudi Umaru, the son of Koyne, the funny and the inane or the sad and the painful. I had to omit many tales of his leprosy, his contacts with a wide variety of other ethnic groups, his adventures with charlatans, his stays in prison, and so on, which if collected together, would make a complete book, or indeed two.

The thematic - these are the ways and customs of the Mbororo, all those ancient traditions which sustain their mode of life and which allow them to maintain their identity in spite of their travels and the changes of modern times.

Very often I felt the urge to rethink the single-minded 'plan' which we had adopted and which we expressed in the vocabulary of weaving – the warp and the weft. The warp of time, such as our hero lived it; the weft of customs. The event and the abiding order, the personal and the social, psychology and ethnography. But this concern always evoked the same response: 'Maintain the equilibrium.'

For honesty's sake, I owe it to the reader to explain my position in the Mbororo world. I was sent to Cameroon as a missionary by an order which, paradoxically, had been known up to that time for its missionary work in the Great Canadian North and whose members were renowned as 'specialists in difficult missions' - the O.M.I. (the Order of Mary the Immaculate).

When I arrived in Cameroon, I had no special training in anthropology or linguistics for confronting this 'difficult mission'. If in the past such training may have been considered unnecessary, that time has changed. More and more, there are missionaries who reinforce their 'field experience' with studies in those two disciplines. On one hand, those studies serve as a natural diversion, helping missionaries to keep their personal equilibrium; on the other hand, they provide a deeper understanding of their 'exotic' neighbours. Moreover, such study is necessary for those missionaries without parishioners, without direct pastoral activity. Their only role can be that of witnesses who show an attitude of respect and esteem for those 'human brothers' who welcome them. We cannot help but think here about Father de Foucauld and his impressive works on the Targui language.

As for me, my aim was to listen in on this Mbororo world where my missionary destiny had taken me so I would be a better witness to that world and a better witness of that world when I returned to my own people. As a missionary in the midst of Muslims, I could profit (more than many others) from having free time to study carefully the language of my hosts. In addition, I was determined to follow the advice of one of my uncles - also a missionary. He had begun roaming the snows of the Mackenzie before the war of 1914-1918 and – though he was born in 1884 – was 'still breathing' in 1984, as the Mbororo say!

On the evening of my departure for Cameroon, my uncle had said to me, 'From the very beginning, write down everything you see. Very quickly it will all seem very familiar and natural.' That is what I did. Then I met Ndudi. He encouraged me all the more to continue the task of observation which I had begun before I met him.

In order to present this account of the Mbororo world, I have chosen to use the words of the Mbororo Ndudi (who, as he himself says, 'belongs to the world of cattle by birth') in order to assure absolute authenticity. I only have to be responsible for the risks of betrayal in the translation. This was obviously the second problem I faced in my task.

Perhaps throughout this story I should have stuck more closely to the narrator's words, respecting the details of his language. In place of 'months', I could have spoken of 'moons'; 'years' could have been 'rainy seasons'; 'calf' might have been 'child of the cow'; etc. By being concerned to make the spirit of the language explicit, I could have exaggerated the syntactical characteristics of Fulfulde by stressing the chopped rhythm of its speech and by giving the reader in this way a sort of a copy, rather than an interpretation. However, was it not preferable for me to translate instinctively the words of someone who I felt so close to from the first time I met him, someone who spoke to me about the things and people I always wanted to know more about?

This was a feeling that came from my heart, and it seemed better not to subject it to the constraining directives of reason or academic principles of translation. I felt so close to this young 'nomadic herder' that I could not bind myself to any style of translation other than that of the affinity and delight I felt in pursuing this task. For me personally, this offered a promise of success. Perhaps I will give readers the impression that I have been a spokesman for Ndudi rather than a translator. That is for them to judge.

Of course, I could have set myself the task of fully transcribing the fifty-two recorded cassettes and then proceeding to do a translation that was faithful to the written text. However, such a translation, even if it had greater scientific exactitude, would have seemed lifeless and dull to me. I preferred to preserve (as far as my capabilities permitted it) the quality of immediate translation – from mouth to ear – because the man who speaks does so with his whole person. The tone of voice, some mimicry, a gesture, a simple silence more or less prolonged – all these aspects carry meaning. A simple hesitation at the beginning of a sentence has a semantic value and gives an attentive listener information that the written sentence would not suggest.

The reader will perhaps be surprised that he will never find in Ndudi's mouth certain vulgar expressions which we have become accustomed to finding in some African literature written in French. The reason is simple: Ndudi is not a French-speaker. He says this, he repeats it, he regrets it . . . and he scolds me about it. But that's the fact of the matter: we have never exchanged a single word in French. Why then should I amuse myself by putting into his mouth those 'black Sambo' expressions (intending no pejorative connotation) which he has never heard and which, personally, are not very familiar to me? It is equally useless to search my translation for any examples of Africanisms.

In the preface to their novel *La Randonnée de Samba Diouf*, the authors J. and J. Tharaud express their surprise to their friend André Demais who had been their interpreter in Senegal. They congratulate him for speaking Mandinka and Wolof with the same ease as the dialect of the Perigord. 'Why, dear friend,' they added, 'your Blacks actually express themselves like academicians!'

'My goodness,' their interpreter friend responds, 'what would you have me do? I translate what they say word-for-word. This proves their languages are flexible and rich and able to express the most subtle nuances, demonstrating the value of their civilisation.'

The reader will perhaps discover some discrepancies in the translation. I will not deny it. I had this impression myself when I re-read it. I was not surprised and, undoubtedly, I would have tried to remedy them if I had not listened to Marguerite Yourcenar make this statement on the radio: 'For me, style is a matter of adapting to the subject being discussed.' That idea really impressed me and, in the end, it guided me in my work. I cannot say that I made this an absolute principle, but she certainly reassured me. On the other hand, I take responsibility for certain technical terms which even a long periphrase would not have translated correctly.

Whenever one is dealing with a shift in language, one must keep in mind the starting point and the ending point. At the outset, there is the nomadic Fulani herder, someone who rather lives 'on the edge'. The final destination is the western reader who runs the risk of being fatigued and discouraged by a constant literary, as well as cultural, bewilderment. Moving between one and the other is the uncomfortable task of anyone who wants to be the interpreter of the message.

At the end of this adventuresome endeavour, there are still some points which leave me dissatisfied and uncomfortable. For example, I was constantly bothered by the conventions and orthography that I was forced to adopt concerning the spelling of Fulani words. If I did this, it was for the benefit of the reader. I did not want to put a lot of words in parentheses or use a special typeface.

Furthermore, because of the knowledge I had accumulated during the long months of conversations, tapings, transcriptions and translations, I had the strong desire to verify everything Ndudi told me and to see for myself the reality of every subject he discussed, just as I had done during the first years.

Another subject of dissatisfaction: this is the near-total lack that I feel today of discussion of common experiences with other people who have done research among the Fulani and who are much more qualified than I am in anthropology and sociology. I admit that I also stayed away from anything that had been written and presented by way of books or articles about the Fulani. I feared I would be too much influenced by their way of seeing things, which would not necessarily be the way I would see things nor the way Ndudi would – so great is the impression I have of the enormous variety which is found under the name of 'pastoral Fulani'. These herders have moved over such vast areas for so many centuries that it is completely natural that they do not form a homogeneous cultural unit. Their language has diversified into numerous dialectical forms, and that variety sometimes causes a near-break in communication. Is this not an indication that their culture must also be varied?

I would have been very happy to have been able to put the final touches on this work in Ndudi's presence so I could have put some facts into perspective, de-emphasised certain events, verified certain numbers and concealed some proper names. I can see myself discussing grammar with him almost as an equal, finding new verbal roots or giving significance to some rare syntactical form. This is an appealing thought, which would have led me to a better comprehension of the text and led Ndudi to mastery of Fulani grammar, probably the only person in this region of Africa to have discovered the structure without having had to compare it to another language learned in school or at a university. What a fascinating thought! But alas, to speak as Ndudi would, the good Muslim that he is: 'God had planned it differently.'

The more I progressed in my translation, Ndudi's 'book' seemed to me more and more difficult to complete because there was so much material. Encouragement and precious help permitted me to bring this work to an end. Thanks to one and all.

Finally today, in spite of all the reservations that I could express, I feel great joy to be the interpreter between you and this Fulani herder, a nomad and a leper. I think you will appreciate the lively and truthful way he has of letting us penetrate the society which is his and to which he has always been faithful.

How have I – the missionary, his friend – carried out this task? Should I respond as a missionary, with all that term implies in the background – at least for some people – about the concern for evangelisation? Should I simply respond as a man concerned about his fellow human beings? I let each person interpret my role as he understands it, providing he respects my constant effort to be sincere and truthful, encouraged as I have been by Ndudi himself.

Of course, if everything Ndudi describes is true, not everything conforms to strict historical truth. I will explain myself by referring to Victor Hugo. In the last chapter of his book *Quatre-vingt-treize*, Hugo writes as follows: 'History has its truth, legend has its own. Legendary truth is a fabrication which results in reality. Besides, history and legend have the same goal: to paint the eternal man beneath the mortal man.'

As Ndudi gradually revealed to me his ephemeral being, I discovered in him timeless man. Man; simply that. Man beyond his language and his culture, beyond his health and his sickness, and – I can say – beyond his religion.

Henri Bocquené
Paris, 1985

Preliminary Note

'My uncle – may God protect you – I want to know how many rainy seasons I've lived.'

Uncle Magaji, the older brother of Ndudi's father, put his hand into the deep pocket of his robe and brought out his string of big, flat prayer beads. He held the beads in both hands and began to count them while mumbling very short names which seemed to me to be the names of villages. He stopped on a last bead which he held between his thumb and forefinger, picked up the string of beads again, and counted the beads once more, stopping at the last number: thirty-two. 'You have had thirty-two rainy seasons, my son.'

That number surprised Ndudi. Very astonished, he turned to me and then to his uncle and said, 'But, my uncle – may God bless you – I thought I was thirty-five years old! That's what I told the *Para* yesterday.'

I nodded. His uncle did not contradict him. He simply picked up his beads again and began mumbling and running through them a second time, before concluding, 'Yes, my son, you're right. You're the one who is telling the truth.'

Ndudi looked at me, satisfied. I was also satisfied. From now on I could solidly anchor his autobiography in time. He was born in 1945.

Based on that date, it would have been possible for me in this book to have fixed the dates of his travels through the eighty-nine villages which he has enumerated for me. But why should I have done that? What interest would such historical precision have had for a reader who is only concerned with anthropological or psychological topics?

As for the location of Ndudi's travels, the accompanying map will permit us to follow him on his journeys. This map shows the northeastern part of Nigeria from Selem, where he was born, to the Cameroon border. It also includes the area of Cameroon from Garoua to the southern part of Adamawa.

From this point on, all the words in this book are Ndudi's. He has assured me many times that he had decided to speak with freedom and frankness about his own people and about other people, without leniency toward himself.

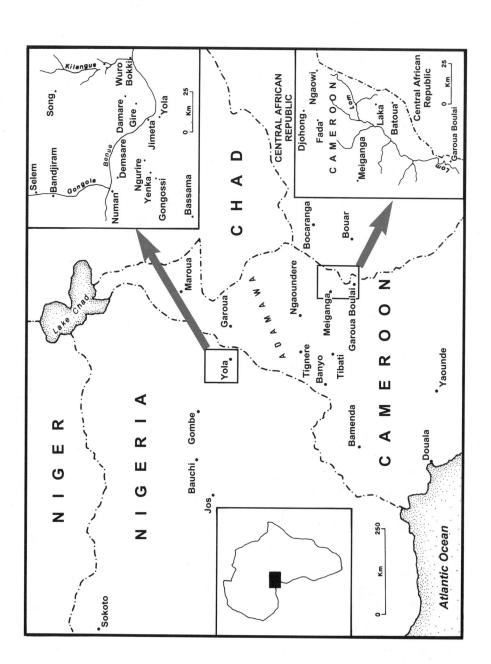

CHAPTER 1

My First Memories of Childhood

The earliest memories I have of my childhood are of the games we played, the cruelty of my stepmother, the hunger we experienced, and the beginning of my leprosy.

Our Games

Without a doubt, the favourite game of all young Mbororo is playing with toy cows made from clay or forked sticks. Some days we boys would go looking for clay in the riverbeds, but the best clay came from termite hills.[1]

Sometimes it might take us a long while to find an active termite hill with soil that was still moist. And sometimes a termite hill which we'd found several days earlier – wet and fresh to perfection – would be completely dried up when we returned. The termites had gone somewhere else. So we would go somewhere else too. We'd search and search. The day might pass without finding anything. At other times luck would smile on us. When that happened, each of us would have plenty of clay. We'd carry huge lumps into the shade and sit there on the ground with our legs spread.

There were some boys who could quickly shape ten or even twenty animals. Once the cows were formed, they were left in the sun to dry. While the first cows were drying, we'd make more and more. Soon all the cattle were there together, a real herd. We'd work for an hour, but it wouldn't take more than ten minutes for the figures to dry. Then we'd take the animals and begin to play. We'd make very small bundles of grass to put on the backs of some of them; those were our pack oxen. We would crouch on all fours so it would be easier to move the animals. We traced furrows in the dirt; for us, they were rivers where we could lead our cows to water. Kneeling down, we'd move our hands from one cow to another.

We played another cattle game with small forked sticks. These cows were called *gogue*. They were made with the same small sticks that our mothers used for beating sour milk. All along those sticks were small parallel branches that were slightly curved. We imagined those protrusions to be humps, navels and horns. After getting rid of some of the extra branches, we'd add a little wood which we carved with our teeth so as to make ears. With a quick bite, we'd remove a bit of bark so the horns would be white. Then we'd change some details here and there.

We'd twist some horns so our cattle would look the way we wanted them to and sharpen the horns as much as possible. Then we'd face each other, with one cow battling against another. Because of the sharp horns, our hands were always bloody. Today there was blood, tomorrow scars. No one paid any attention.

Our games usually lasted until the beginning of the afternoon, the time when Muslims pray, called *jura*.[2] Actually, it was really hunger that made us go back home – whether or not it was time for the *jura* prayer.

My Stepmother

In every Mbororo house, there is always some gruel waiting for the children, which the mother prepares before leaving for the market. Often it's served by an older sister or a grandmother. When the grandmother sees her grandchildren coming, she always says, 'Come quickly and drink your gruel.' They come running. She ladles out the gruel from a large calabash and then distributes it.

The gruel is very liquid and is drunk. It's made from millet and boiling water which are stirred together on the fire. It's what remains from the Mbororo breakfast. The mother always makes a lot so that some will be left over. She mixes the left-over porridge with the sour milk from the evening before, a sort of liquid yoghurt which gives the porridge a sour taste. Then this gruel is set aside. Anyone who wants some can come drink it, including the herders when they return from the pastures.

In the dry season when there's not enough milk to add to the morning gruel, our mothers use pods from the *jabbi*[3] tree or pulp from the baobab fruit. They soak one or other of these fruits until it ferments. Then the whitish liquid is strained off and added to the gruel, giving the sour taste we love.

All our young playmates would find this refreshing and nourishing gruel waiting for them when they went back home. But not my brothers and I – because we no longer had a mother. Our mother had been dead for a long time, before I could walk. She died from leprosy. In her place, we had a stepmother, a widow who our father had married. Her deceased husband had given her two sons: Garga and Yunusa. She had kept them with her. They were the only ones that counted. We didn't exist for her. For example, in the morning when she left to sell milk, she took gruel to the house of one of her friends and said it should only be given to her own children. The neighbour, who was also mean, would do exactly as she had been told. When we all came in together, she'd take Garga and Yunusa aside and lead them into her house so that they could drink the gruel. When they were full, she brought them back so we could keep a watch on them while they played.

Sometimes when we were really hungry, we'd get bold enough to follow them to her house, hoping she'd give us a little. But when she'd see us, she'd chase us away. Dumbfounded, we'd leave and look for somewhere else to go. Usually we went to the home of one of our playmates.

Certain women took pity on us and would invite us to drink their gruel. Whether our stomachs were empty or not, we would wait at our house for the herd to return. It was absolutely necessary to be there so we could tie up the calves and keep them from going to their mothers for milk. We tied them to the long calf rope that had short ropes attached to it. They could be slipped around the calves' necks. Then we'd play a little more until the adults returned.

You must understand that, every morning, Mbororo villages are deserted. Everyone goes away to spend the day elsewhere. Some go to the surrounding markets; others, who are older, gather far off – sometimes at the horizon, at the foot of a big tree. The most able go with the herd to pasture. They pass the day there, watching their animals, perhaps forty of them. In those days, there was a lot of disease and many herds had fewer than thirty animals: a bull, several milk cows, some heifers, some old cows and some calves.

At sunset when the herd had returned, we'd wait for our parents. It is always a joy for children to see the silhouette of their mother coming far in the distance. On her head there's always a calabash. She is returning from the market, and she always brings many good things: fresh manioc tubers, peanut sticks, bananas and perhaps doughnuts. But my brothers and I knew we had nothing to wait for. Our stepmother never had anything for us. Everything was saved for her own children. And besides, when she gave them something, she did it in secret inside her house, and she forbade them to come share anything with us. If we risked peeking in through the open door, she'd jump up to chase us. 'You will be in for it if you don't get out of here, you greedy dogs! Ever since I came home, you've been following at my heels like dogs. You can see very well I didn't bring anything home! Look in my calabash. Don't you see it's empty?'

All during this time we could hear her children munching peanut sticks right behind her on their bed.

Because I was smaller than the others, I'd slip behind the straw hut and, without raising my voice, call through the straw wall, 'Garga! Yunusa! Come and play!' My stepmother would shout, 'Who's there? Go away. They aren't coming out.' I wanted Garga to come out with his peanut stick; he'd surely give me a bite. But seeing that neither brother would come out, I'd wander off somewhere else.

My brothers and I would stop at the doors of some huts where the women felt sorry for us. 'Look at these poor children; their mother came back from the market and did not bring them anything!' Some women would give us a peanut stick. We'd share it among the five of us when Mori was with us. Think about the small bit each of us had: a peanut stick is no bigger or longer than a school pencil! We'd nibble it so it would last as long as possible.

What we waited for was the return of our father – we, that is, Maje, Musa and my oldest sister Gogo. But I must not forget to mention Mori, our half-sister. All five of us had the same father, but Mori had a different mother. Her mother had only been married a short time to our father when they were divorced. Mori was born to that marriage, and we loved her very much.

Since Mori was very young at the time of the divorce, she naturally had gone with her mother because she was still being nursed. But when she had been weaned, my father took her back. She should have stayed and lived with us. But because of the cruelty of our stepmother (who was also her stepmother), my father had pity on Mori. He let her pass long visits with her mother, who treated her well. But my father could not stop himself from taking her back from time to time. She was, first of all, his daughter.

The cruelty of our stepmother never let up. Every minute she was thinking about how to annoy us. She deprived us of food; she forbade us to enter her house, to sit next to her, and even to play with her children. But on the other hand, she knew very well how to turn to us when it was time to sweep the house or clean up the babies' messes. She never gave us a minute of peace. She always found good reasons to make us do chores.

But as we got older, we learned how to get back at her, even right before our father's eyes. We stood up to her to the point that the day came when we'd reproach her ten times for every scolding she gave us. When she'd try to send us on errands, we'd pretend not to hear her. We'd finally got her where we wanted her. We had learned to measure out our effort and our help in proportion to the food she gave us. No food, no work. What more could she do? Nothing. And we knew it. We preferred doing small errands like gathering wood for the little old women who knew how to repay us with some food. Whatever our stepmother did and said made no difference to us. No matter how often she ordered us to do something, we refused to obey. We openly disobeyed her. We insulted her.

But we were careful! One day at sunset, my brother Maje saw that she had gone to a neighbour's house to pound peppers for sauce. He took advantage of the moment to slip into her house. He really wanted some milk. But she returned unexpectedly. Maje was caught in the act. And how she slapped him and strangled him! She hit him violently on the back with her fist, 'Pim!' We heard her hitting him from our hut. Maje lost his breath. He couldn't cry or speak. He came back to us and lay down, unable to say a word. He could hardly moan.

We quickly ran to tell our father, who was sitting with the men in their usual place, at the *dado*.[4] 'Come quickly, Papa. Look at Maje. Hari hit him. This is what he's doing; this is how he looks!' Papa came immediately and realised what had happened. He was completely shattered. He turned toward his wife and hit her as hard as he could. Five days later, Maje died. He never really regained his breath.

The cruelty of our stepmother never slackened. On the contrary, at certain times she was worse. This was the case when two of the other children from her former marriage came to visit. One was named Manga, the other Adamu. When their father died, they had, of course, been taken by a paternal uncle. This is what happens in such cases. However the mother always has the possibility of seeing her children again and of having them stay for some days in her new home. The only way a widow can keep her children is to marry a younger brother of her dead husband.

At fairly regular intervals we saw our stepmother's two children, Manga and Adamu. When they were with us, her cruelty toward us doubled.

There certainly were days when our stepmother had every reason to be angry with us: sometimes we took pleasure in being as mean as possible to her. For example, when she was away, we encouraged the calves to stomp on her clay pots and calabashes,[5] which had been put out in the sun to dry. Or if the calves did this on their own, instead of chasing them away, we watched them do it. We took malicious pleasure in spoiling some of her things. We sprinkled the millet with lots of water so that it fermented and was good for nothing but to be thrown away. We spilled flour on the ground and blamed it on the chickens. Before Garga and Yunusa could talk, we blamed many things on them.

Before our stepmother went to the market, she always said to us, 'Don't forget to gather wood for tonight.' We didn't say no, but we never did anything. When she returned at sunset, there was no wood for cooking and no water either. She had to go find those things herself. And we sat there and watched her. We didn't move. Yes, we knew how to be mean too.

We slept in our own hut, all five of us. Normally I would have slept in my mother's hut, like all children under age seven, near my mother, in her bed or on another bed just at her side. But with my stepmother, there was no possibility of that. She only took her own children to her side.

If rain threatened, our father would hurry to build us a shelter of branches and straw wherever we stopped late in the afternoon. He'd arrange a place for us to sleep. Sometimes it was a 'bed': four forked stakes fixed in the ground which held a straw frame or a mat. He did this in the rainy season to protect us from the wet ground. In the dry season, he'd put a mat on the ground and our bed was made. I always stretched out near my sister Gogo. Often I slept between her and Mori, at least when I was little.

My Father

In fact, our father was like a mother to us. He was our father; he was our mother. He watched over us at night. He also paid attention to our food. He never returned in the evening from the place where the men gathered for their common meal without bringing us something. The other men, who knew our situation very well, would say to him, 'Take what's left to your children. Everyone knows their stepmother doesn't give them enough food.'

'It's true,' our father would say sadly. 'It's not a secret to anyone.' We'd wait until he returned, and this hope kept us awake. How would we have been able to sleep when our stomachs gnawed with hunger?

We always waited very impatiently for his return from a trip or from the market. We'd go a long way off to meet him. He'd give us his hat which he carried on his back and which served as a bag for his provisions. Then we'd go off and sit in the trees, taking our time to eat what he'd brought us.

Some evenings when he didn't see us, he'd hang his hat on a branch of a certain tree. When he'd find us, all he had to do was point his finger in that direction for us to understand that he hadn't forgotten us. Then we'd run to find our tree and his hat. When we'd get back home – with full stomachs – we wouldn't care whether or not our stepmother had given us anything to eat that night.

In the evenings our father would come to unroll our mats and in the mornings, he'd take them, often wet with urine, out to dry in the sun. Later, when our sister was older, he gave this task to her.

My father had a special tenderness for me: I was the youngest of my siblings and I wasn't healthy. He gave me more attention than he gave the two children my stepmother had given him, even though they were younger. He surely had pity for me. We were always seen together. I followed him everywhere. Even when he was sitting with the Elders, I was with him. When I grew older, I accompanied him every day to the pastures from morning until evening. He taught me to recognise plants. He'd say to me, 'Do you see this plant? It's good for the cattle. This is how you use it. Make it into powder and throw it on the embers to make smoke. It's good for upset stomachs.' He taught me to distinguish between plants that are used for people and plants that are used for animals. A snake bite is treated differently for a man than for a cow.

My father spent his time looking for medicines for me and for my brother Maje. Everywhere he went to spend a day, the first thing he asked people was, 'Who knows a good medicine for leprosy? Two of my children have it. Soon it will carry them off, like it took their mother. They've reached the point that we can't understand them when they speak.'

Sometimes someone would say to him, 'Yes, I have what you need at my house.' My father would follow him, even if he had to go a long way and he'd return no matter what time of the day or night. Sometimes they'd give him recipes: 'Dig up this root … etc.' I remember three of these formulas. There's nothing I haven't swallowed; I thought it was for my own good. Sometimes the things were repulsive, like the droppings of a chicken, or of a vulture, or the excrement of a new baby. What disgusting things I ate!

Sometimes my father went on long trips for ten days or so. Someone had simply said to him, 'There's a certain person who I lived with long ago. Now he is living with such-and-such a clan, in such-and-such a direction. Go see him; he has what you need.' My father would go and come back with a new formula, but it had no effect on us. Maybe it would have if we'd been able to follow the diet which was always prescribed for such a case. But this was never possible because of our cruel stepmother. My father suffered from this. He could do nothing about it, but he kept searching unceasingly.

My First Education

During the years of my youth which I am reliving with you, I had no idea about God or about the fear he should have inspired in me. Our older brothers never prayed; neither did our father or mother. When they reached the age that their beards began to grow, sometimes one or another of my brothers would perform the gestures of Muslim prayer. But it seemed they were only practising. They didn't want to look too awkward when the day came that they'd have to pray with the *Fulbe*.[6] Otherwise, they risked not being accepted in a Fulbe home. If they were considered to be atrocious 'pagans', how would they eat when they travelled?

Under such conditions, religion had no part in our lives as children. On the other hand, from the time we were very young, we understood that the weight of what we call *pulaku*[7] was upon us. To practice *pulaku* is to live like a true Fulani, to have honour. It's like a code of manners. It belongs only to us, the Mbororo of the bush. The Fulani of the towns and villages don't follow it any longer. Even more excluded from the practice of *pulaku* are all those non-Fulbe, whom we disdainfully call the

Kado.[8] *Pulaku* applies to all the details of our daily life, both within the family and with neighbours and strangers alike.

Sometimes our neighbours' cattle would come to natron licks we had set up at the foot of a tree. Certainly we could chase the cows away, but only after taking many precautions. This was our father's responsibility. He did it gently – with his hand, without being cruel, without even lifting his voice. 'It's nothing,' he would say to the owner who came with many excuses. 'Anyway, isn't my cows' food the same as yours?' This is the way to act like a Fulani.

We have a joking relationship with our grandparents. It's all right to laugh about our grandfather's beard, his little eyes, or his big ears. We can say anything we like when we talk to him. But, of course, we can't become too bold in our jokes. And we can't tease him when he's with important people. But in private, we don't annoy him when we say, 'Your beard is like the hair of a billy-goat.' 'You have got the eyes of a jackal.' 'Your hat is as dirty as a farmer's.'

Sometimes I would approach my grandfather while reading the lines in my palm. 'I had a dream last night, Jumba. You have only got two more days to live. You're close to death. Haven't you noticed all the wrinkles on your face?' He would laugh, or he'd grab his staff and chase us.

When I'd see my grandfather beginning to fall asleep, I'd slip up close to him, grab a hair from his beard, pull it, and run away. He'd jump up, looking for the person who had dared to do that. Very proud, I'd run toward my father. 'Babale, look at the hair I just pulled from Jumba's beard.' Then my father would take his turn chasing me, shouting, 'Little imp!' When Jumba was around, I was happy. I'd stay with him day and night. I never stopped playing tricks on him. This is how *pulaku* tells us to behave.

It was the same with our grandmother. I'd amuse myself by saying to her, 'Look, Grandmother, all your hair is gone! You can't even do it up any more. The beauty of your youth is finished!'

Sometimes I'd come running with my hands held out in front of me. 'Look at this thread: it's beautiful and fine.'

'Come closer so I can see it.' She brought her hands toward mine so she could grab it and then I'd pretend the wind had blown it away.

When she'd go to the spring, we'd drink her milk and steal small bits of meat from her. When we felt sleepy during the day, we'd go to her house and stretch out on her mat. We had the right to take anything in her house.

From the time we Mbororo are very young, we learn to distinguish between our various uncles and aunts. We are very respectful of our paternal uncle (*bappanyo*), our father's brother. We always greet him by crouching down, never standing. There are never any jokes with him! He has the same rights over us as our father does. He can strike his nephew if the boy doesn't follow the right path.

Our paternal aunt (*gogo*), our father's sister, is also given great respect. We always maintain a certain reserve toward her. We boys can't help thinking that someday she may be our mother-in-law. Who can say whether we might not marry one of her daughters sometime later?

Our attitude toward our mother's brother (*kao*) is one of veneration. These feelings are similar to those we have for our own mother but with much more reserve.

If we see our *kao* coming, we have to take another path. This uncle is also greeted by crouching down. But when the greetings are finished, we keep our distance from him. We can't pronounce the name of this uncle, or even the name of a person who shares his name. In him we see a future father-in-law. It's from this uncle that a boy receives his first heifer. Only after this uncle has made this first gesture can the other uncles offer gifts. A maternal uncle can never strike his nephew. This would bring him great misfortune, such as the loss of his herd. Anyway, he loves his sisters' children too much to do that!

We show the same reserve for our maternal aunt (*yapendo*). We take care so as not to meet her on the road or at the marketplace. If we were about to cross her path while walking in the countryside, we'd hide ourselves in the tall grass so that she would not see us. Our parents never stop warning us against thoughtless actions which children can so quickly do.

We also know how to distinguish between our parallel cousins and our cross cousins.[9] We can play whatever jokes we want on our cross cousins *dendirabe*. But sometimes the fun is pushed very far, too far. Because of this relationship, a robust fellow can catch his little cousin and strangle him until he is nearly dead. The cousin is tied up, smeared with cow dung, and left to bake all day in the sun. Or someone may jump up behind his cousin and push him into a thornbush!

One day, one of my cousins, the son of an aunt on my father's side, found us all alone. There were no adults around. The best thing he could think of was to tie us up with the calf ropes. There were four of us: our half-sister Mori, Musa, my oldest sister Gogo and myself. Being stronger than any of us, he tied up our feet. He joined our hands and feet, binding them very tightly. Then he attached us to the calf rope. He rubbed our heads and coated our bodies with cow dung. Content with what he'd done, he left for the market. We shouted ... but no one was there! Many hours later, our grandfather found us like that when he returned home with his goats. He understood immediately that only that imbecile Ori could have played such a mean trick on us.

Another time this same Ori crept up without making any noise. He found Mori drinking her gruel. He pushed her away, took her bowl, and drank the gruel. Then he put a cord around Mori's neck and pulled it. Her eyes popped out of their sockets. She vomited the gruel she'd just drunk. Then Ori left just the way he'd come.

You can see the jokes between cross cousins (*dendirabe*) can go very far. You can take the pants off a small cousin who isn't strong enough to defend himself, light a fire, and burn them; or if he's proud of his hair and his beautiful braids, you can shave his head! If a victim were to become angry and insult the parents of the cousin who caused his misery, he would disgrace himself. He would have gone beyond the bounds of *pulaku*.

On the other hand, with our parallel cousins *derdirabe* our attitude is completely different. Certainly, when we're young, we play and have fun together. But as we grow up, we come to understand that we have the same concerns. Their father is mine. My father is theirs. Therefore it is only natural we should help each other. The troubles of one are the troubles of the other. There's no question of practical jokes. We always try to show consideration and real kindness toward each other.

We feel the weight of *pulaku* on us from the time we're very young. There are precise rules that must be followed. The rules are numerous and they touch all aspects of life. Nothing in our life, from morning to night, escapes *pulaku*.

If we forget the rules, we know we've done wrong. But, on the other hand, *pulaku* doesn't forbid us from having a good time with a girl. For us, there's nothing wrong with that. That's all there is to it!

Figure 1.1: A young herder

Figure 1.2: Boy drinking fresh milk

CHAPTER 2

From Day to Day

Children and Herds

All Mbororo children are interested in the world of cattle and sheep. You should see them on mornings when their father or older brother doesn't want to take them along to guard the herd during the day. They cry and stamp their feet in rage. They refuse to go back home, and they follow along in secret. The herder brings them back. They escape again. They're brought back again and again until the herd disappears over the horizon. They have to be punished before they'll sit quietly and accept the fact that they have to stay and play in the village.

Those children are never really happy until they hear their father say, 'Catch the calves. Tie them up!' Now the children are really doing what they want to do! They try to run down all the calves that are frisking about. Sometimes they bother the calves so much they make them nervous and wild. Only children are able to approach them. Sometimes there's such a bond between a calf and a child that only they can touch the calf. Some cows only allow these children to touch their calves.

Tying up the calves occupies the children for a good part of the day. They take one calf after another, leading each one to a long rope that's tied between two stakes. At regular intervals along the rope are small cords which end with an open collar. At one end is a loop; at the other, a knot about as big as a piece of candy. The herder comes with his calf that he's pulling as much as he's pushing. When he gets to the right place, the cord is passed around the calf's neck and the knot is nimbly put into the loop. The herder makes sure the calf is properly tied up: not so tight that he chokes himself and not so loose that he escapes. The children pay attention because their parents never stop warning them.

A young apprentice quickly learns why the calves are tied up. The reasons vary according to the time of day. In the morning when the herd leaves for its long walk, the calves are tied up so they do not follow. They'd never be able to keep up with the herd. There are holes where they could disappear. There are hyenas and other wild animals that could eat them. Sometimes the cattle suddenly bolt and run off, and the calves would risk being trampled.

Late in the afternoon when the cows return from pasture, the calves must be tied up again so they won't run away during the night, and especially so they don't go to the udders of their mothers. A herdsman must always think about milk. Isn't milk the whole life of a Mbororo? There's a different reason for tying up the calves every hour of the day. And, if the calves are still tied up during the dry season when the cows have no milk, it's simply out of habit!

But some cows are tricky. Since their calves are forbidden to come to them, they go to their calves so the calves can suck. In the morning when the herder wants to milk a certain cow, he can tell immediately what's happened. When he unties the calf and calls the mother by name, the calf does not move. The mother does not move either. The herder quickly understands what the two of them did during the night.

Among us, it's the man who milks the cows. This is how he does it. As I said, he begins by untying the calf and calling the mother by name, 'Hey, Red One!' The cow moos softly and gets up to come toward her calf. The calf runs to his mother. He's allowed to suck a little. When foam appears around the calf's muzzle, the milker gets in position, squatting on his heels with a calabash held between his knees. But the calf is never happy about this and so he must be tied to the right leg of the mother or a cord must be put around his neck so he can be attached to a tree, a stump, or even a big clump of grass. Often it's a boy or a girl who is given the responsibility of holding the troublesome calf at a distance.

When the milking is finished, the child who has helped his father receives a good portion of milk as his reward. His brothers and sisters do not waste any time in arriving. They're still sleepy. In their idle hands, they hold bowls which the father fills with foamy milk. But the children do not drink the milk of just any cow; they have their favourite cow. Some even refuse to drink milk that's a mixture from many cows.

The children drink greedily until their stomachs are full. There's foam everywhere: around their mouths, at the ends of their noses, on their bulging stomachs if they're only wearing loin cloths, or on their well-soiled clothes. Then there's nothing more to do than to squat down and wait for their millet gruel. On cold mornings in the dry season, they all form a circle with their hands stretched out toward the fire.

Their mother has her own fire between three hearthstones. There she heats water and when it boils, she pours in the millet flour which she or her daughter has just pounded. She mixes it, stirring it all together with her cooking stick. The gruel must not get thick. She adds some fresh milk. Then all she has left to do is to pour it into several bowls which are carried to the various groups that are crouched on their heels in circles. The bowl is passed from hand to hand. A calabash ladle floats on top of the gruel – only one ladle, which everyone puts to his mouth. When he's drunk some, he puts the ladle back on top of the gruel; then the bowl is passed to the next person, and so on. After the bowl has made one round, it's passed around a second time. When the first calabash is empty, it's replaced by a second. Each person only drinks one ladle-full at a time. For the children, the calabash is placed in the middle of their circle since they can't pass the heavy bowl. But they too have only one ladle which they pass from hand to hand.

After the gruel is finished, everyone leaves for their daily tasks. But before this, at first light, many have already eaten what was left over from the previous night: millet porridge crumbled up and re-heated in last night's sauce.

The Mbororo do not prepare a meal at noon. At that time of day, they're all scattered. It's only in the evening that they come together again to eat porridge.[1] Everyone uses their fingers to pull off a small lump and then dips it into the sauce before putting it into their mouth.

In the season of high grass when it rains nearly every day, it's the children who watch over the herd during the day. They are the only ones around. Their brothers and fathers have gone to various markets in the area or to another Mbororo village. The boys and girls are trusted with the herd at this time when it's not necessary to go very far in order to find good pastures.

Many children wait impatiently for this season. This is their chance to prove they're good herders. They only have to be seven or eight years old before they're given complete responsibility for the herd. They're very proud of this.

Other children prefer to stay in the village to play. But after a while, even they decide to go with the herd so they don't have to stay with the little children and can be with their playmates.

When we'd leave the camp in the morning, our father would always go with us for a little way. He'd always give us instructions. 'Be sure you don't go in that direction; there are too many fields. You'll have arguments with the farmers. They're really nasty here. So go toward the Little Red Mountain. The grass is good there. Be careful of the mud when you cross Barkehi Creek.'[2] For the Mbororo, each place has a name so it can be easily found. Our father would also say, 'Don't try to find your friends, especially not Ndotti's gang! When you're together, you only think about playing. You no longer pay attention to your cattle, and let them do what they want.' We'd promise our father to follow his orders. But as soon as he was gone, we'd do what we wanted!

It is true that sometimes you find a young herder who does not let his animals out of his sight. He never looks for his friends. He only meets them when he goes to the watering hole with his herd, but he does not stay with them very long. He quickly goes to the head of the herd and leads the animals away, all by himself. Even though he's very young, he is not afraid. When he sees that all is well and that there's plenty of grass, he climbs a tree and begins to sing praises to his steers and cows. He makes a litany, passing from one cow to another. He describes their most beautiful characteristics. Or he sings the songs that he's learned from his elders, insulting imaginary enemies. In my case, I'd try to seek out company. But when I was alone, I was never bored. I've spent hours watching battles between termites and ants.

I'd see termites with enormous heads that had ants in their mouths which they could bite in two. However, it seemed to me the ants killed more than the termites did. Around the ants were cadavers, more cadavers, piles of cadavers. In their battles, you'd see some fall here and some fall there. Sometimes I was so busy watching them I forgot my animals. I'd watch and I'd not think about anything else. The ants continued their massacre. They chased the termites right into their hole. And inside the hole, the ants certainly continued to destroy the termites because it wasn't long before I'd see the ants coming back out. They'd pull or push out the bodies of the termites that had been killed in the war. Some pulled four at a time. They just kept coming out! The bodies piled up, piles of bodies, piles everywhere!

I also saw ants that had been killed in combat carried back to their own holes by other ants. Isn't that incredible? Just like people! Yes, the surviving ants carried back to their village those ants that had lost their lives in battle. It was really marvellous to watch these battles when they took place in the open – on a tree trunk or near dried cow dung, a spot the termites particularly liked.

I'd watch, I'd observe, and during that time my herd would wander further away. I learned how to distinguish between different types of ants and termites. There's the little white termite that's fragile and not very strong. When ants attack it, it only makes one mouthful. There are red termites which are very strong. They have big heads and are always looking for a fight. There are wood termites. As for the ants, there are so many different types!

I was especially happy to leave camp and be alone when I'd see that a cow was going to calve. I knew my father would say, 'Today it would be better if I came with you. There's a good chance Blacky will have her little one.'

'Maybe, but you don't have to come with me. I know what to do. I can take care of things by myself.'

'What are you saying?' my father would respond. 'When you're busy with her, who will take care of the rest of the herd?'

What joy to be alone in the bush when a calf was born! How proud I was! I'd take hold of the calf. I'd lay him on the ground. The mother would follow me. I'd hold the calf again and try to get him to stand up. He'd fall down. I'd stand him up again. And in the evening when I returned home with the young calf on my shoulders, I could not have had greater joy. Everyone came to see him and to say something. I'd sit there, acting very important, breathing heavily. 'Oof! I'm on my last legs! I carried him all the way from the Red Mountain. Can you imagine that? I kept him on my shoulders all the time!'

And people would say, 'You know, Ndudi, there aren't many others who would have been able to do what you did. How many others would have left the mother and the calf in the middle of the bush.' And some would add, 'This boy's really brave, this Ndudi. He's really the son of his father!'

When I heard these praises, I forgot all about being tired. But they had not seen how I'd spent all my time pestering the little calf: I'd grabbed hold of him and stood him up, but he couldn't stand on his feet. I'd forced him to suck when he didn't want to! And I'd put him back under the nose of his mother so she could lick him once more. And the mother had accepted all that! It was amazing she didn't butt such a herder with her horns. A question of habit on both sides. We knew each other too well![3]

However, not all cows are so docile. There are some that won't allow the calf to be touched, especially if the calf is born in the bush, and particularly if it's a heifer with her first calf. In that case, it's better if the father accompanies his son. But on the other hand, when a cow has already had several calves, you can do what you want with her. It's sort of like with your grandmother. You can sit next to the cow and watch her lick her calf. She accepts that very well.

Some days I'd escape from solitude. When I'd arrive at the pastures, just as soon as my father had turned his back, I'd quickly look for another herd in the area, and I'd go in that direction. Once I was with my friends, I'd only think about playing. So what about the animals! It did not matter to me whether or not they filled their stomachs.

One of our favourite pastimes was seeing our cattle fight head to head, horns against horns. It was a sight we never tired of. We'd stand and watch, cheering them on. We each identified with our own bull.

'You see that; I'm stronger than you!'

'Look, now I'm pushing you back!'

'Look! You're going to run away soon. Oh, you coward!'

And, when the battle was over, the winner would say to his friend, 'That's it. I won. I made you run away.'

So that the fight would be more violent, we'd sharpen the horns of our cattle. We'd do this with the help of another boy. We'd ask him to caress the sexual parts of the animal with a stick or with his hand so the animal would be calm. All Mbororo know how to do this operation and do it regularly. While the animal was calm, we'd work to make the ends of the horns more pointed. We'd use a knife or a pumice stone, often both of them. Actually we were only interested in just one of the two horns. We had watched our bull. We'd paid attention to which one of his horns he used the most. Usually it was the left one. So we wouldn't touch the right one. Our father never failed to notice when we'd sharpened the horns. In the evening he'd call us to the middle of the herd that had gathered together for the night. 'Did you sharpen this horn, you little imp? Come closer.' And he'd beat us there in the field. Then he'd arrange to have the point disappear. He'd always take away our knives. He knew we did not have any need for them. Even if it were necessary for us to cut the throat of an animal that was in difficulty so the meat could be saved, he couldn't count on us, knife or not. So he'd take our knives away. But we'd always manage to get one of those sharpening stones which the Mbororo use to take calluses off their heels.

What our father feared happened once, right before my eyes. That day the battle was unusually violent. The two bulls charged, gaining speed as they approached each other. All of a sudden, the stronger bull threw his rival to the ground and gored him mercilessly. His guts were spread all over. Nothing could be done. We let him die. We were only children; we would not have been able to cut his throat with our little knives. Because he died in that way, he became carrion, unclean for anyone.[4] Eating that meat was unthinkable! Selling it was forbidden! It was only prey for vultures or for farmers with whom we did not have the right to exchange it for a few measures of millet.

The child who was the son of the bull's owner started to cry. He cried hot tears when he got back to his camp.

'And where's our big bull?'

'He's dead!'

'What? How did that happen?'

'He fought with the bull of someone. He was gored. We saw his guts spill out.'

'Well, it's just what I feared,' said the father. 'But haven't I told you many times not to mix our cows with those of our neighbours? But you only do what's in your head. You only think about playing.'

And the blows rained down on the poor boy who cried until he lost his breath. But on the other hand, no formal complaint was made by the aggrieved owner of the bull. Nor were there any harsh words. This was in the name of *pulaku*. When our fathers met, they'd only say, 'My friend, did you see what our worthless children did?'

'It was like an accident, a misfortune.'

'What is there to say,' the other would say. 'There's nothing to be done. Even if my bull had not fought, he would have died in some other way! This was fated to happen. The fight had nothing to do with it. May God give us better luck! It does not matter. Let's let the matter drop.'

This is what was said by the man who suffered the loss. The matter was never spoken of again. And we continued to amuse ourselves just as before.

Hunting for Birds

Having fun – some children never really think about anything else! Sometimes guinea fowl are abundant where we pasture our cattle. Then we have no other thought than to steal their eggs. Stick in hand, we poke around everywhere – pushing the stick into the bushes and separating the tall grass. We go here; we run there.

When there aren't any guinea fowl, we look for all sorts of other birds. The eggs we find are put right on the fire to roast. We don't cook them in water. The little birds which we take from their nest are also put directly on the fire. We grill them.

We do not eat eggs that have black streaks on them. They would bring us bad luck. That's also true for the eggs of all black birds. But it is especially true for the eggs of the bird we call the *saruandu*.

We call all black birds by the same name, *bale-bale*. They're the subject of one of our little songs: 'Bale-bale, you fart, you stink. Send your black stench over there.'

This is what we sing when a child farts in our midst. We say, 'Who farted?' We pick up a little dust from the ground. We throw it in the air and notice what direction the wind is blowing. That tells us which child is guilty. 'It's you who farted!' and we repeat our little song for him: 'Bale-bale, you fart, you stink. Send your black stench over there.'

Then all of us turn toward the stinker and applaud. Upset, he does not waste any time getting angry. He quickly grabs one of us. And then there's a fight! No, there's nothing in this world that would make us touch the eggs of black birds, especially if they have streaks on them.

I spoke about the *saruandu*. Ah, the Mbororo hate to see them! They're constantly bothering the animals. They are always there, on the animals' backs, always reopening sores the animals have on their skin. The sores enlarge when they're pecked. When the birds are there, the sores never heal. It's impossible for them to graze in peace. When we succeed in trapping one of those birds, we really torture it. We cut off its claws and clip off its beak right at the edge of its nose. Then we make it fly away, knowing it won't go far because it has no claws for perching and no beak for eating. We steal their nestlings; we break their eggs; we smash them to pieces, swearing to do everything possible to make their species disappear forever from the face of the earth.

On the other hand, we feel very attached to egrets, those beautiful white birds which follow our cows step-by-step. We respect them. You'll never see a herder raise his stick against one of them. I've never seen their eggs. They never bother an animal while grazing. They do not peck them. They're happy to follow the animals step-by-step in order to eat insects that they stir up as they walk. If need be, they're bold enough to peck off a tick if it's near a hoof. Sometimes they swoop down to attack a large insect and swallow it. They disappear when the animals return to camp for the night. But the next morning they'll be there again, faithfully making their rendezvous. Where do they spend the night? We do not know.

When we want to cook eggs, we take great pains in making the fire. Sometimes you see someone take out of his pocket the *jinadire* which he took from his father. This is a small sack made of thick, rough leather which contains three things: an iron bar the blacksmith has shaped like a 'U', a flintstone (the Mbororo have no trouble distinguishing flintstones from other stones), and a little cotton. Actually, it's not the real cotton that's planted in the fields, but the cotton which is found on certain trees. It's mixed with charcoal dust. It was so white, and it becomes so black! This lights very quickly. Each of these three things – the u-shaped bar, the flintstone and the fibre – has its own compartment in the little leather sack. When we want a fire, we use the stone to make a spark which lights the fibre. It's not too difficult.

If someone hasn't 'stolen' fire-making equipment from his father, there's something else he can do. He must hunt around and find a certain type of light bamboo, the kind the Fulbe use to make the mats they put on their beds. From one stem, two pieces of equal length are cut. One piece is shaped like a pencil; the other is laid on the ground over a little pile of fluff, which is actually the fringe from the edge of a garment or the little bits of rag that are found in the bottom of your pocket. With a knife, a hole is made in the bamboo strip that's lying on the ground. Dry crumpled grass that has been rubbed until it's nearly powder is put there alongside it. The point of the other stick is placed in the hole.

One boy takes that bamboo stick and holds it between the palms of his hands. He concentrates and begins to roll it between his hands. It must be done quickly, very quickly, without stopping. One boy can't finish the job by himself; there must be a relay. The relay must work flawlessly; even the slightest delay in changing hands will slow the work down. Gradually, the hole gets bigger and the point penetrates deeper. All heads are bent over the bamboo. All eyes are fixed on the point which digs in deeper and deeper. Watch it! Quick! Quicker! The most nimble boy almost flies to grab the bamboo stick which is released by the boy who was holding it.

'That's it! It's time!'

The bamboo on the bottom is pierced. And a little wisp of smoke rises, barely perceptible. All movement stops. Someone lies on his stomach and blows very softly. Everything can still fail. The smoke gets a little thicker. The boy blows again, and there's a spark. Hands appear with small bundles of dry, crumpled grass and the big pieces of bamboo are pulled out of the fire. Then twigs are brought. The fire starts. What luck!

It's not always like that. There are days when we try and try to start a fire, but nothing happens! And during all that time, our cows wander about. We round them up. We go back to our little sticks. We begin again. We try over and over. Nothing. Our hands are red. Here and there you see blisters. In spite of that, the fire does not start, and then we have to throw away the birds we'd wanted to grill. But it's rare that we have to give up. Generally children have enough patience to get the job done. Usually they succeed if they really want to. And their hands are agile, which is not the case with men. I don't think a man could succeed. Women, maybe, but I have never seen them do it.

Grilling birds and cooking eggs on the embers are not the only reasons we work so hard to make a fire from a flintstone or from wood. There are also the palm rats or squirrels, those heroes of our folk tales. If one of them has the misfortune of venturing into our midst, it's too bad for him! Between him and us, there's a crazy race. Sometimes our dogs help us.

But a squirrel can quickly go down a hole. If it's an anteater's hole, we consider the squirrel lost. But if it's a squirrel hole, we quickly scurry to find all the holes that are linked together. We plug up some of them. We leave the others open, and each of us stands guard. Then we make a fire over the hole where the squirrel disappeared. With lots of leaves, there's lots of smoke! Someone takes a deep breath and blows the thick smoke into the hole. With sticks in our hands, we watch all the other holes. Suddenly, someone pricks up their ears! 'I hear it coming,' says someone with his ear to the ground.

Choked by the smoke, the squirrel must try to escape from one hole or another. 'There he is!' The stick falls: 'Pim!' The squirrel lies still.

Stormy Encounters

Some days we'd happen to meet the herds of the Bodi clan. We knew what would happen then. We were happy about that. The Bodi are part of a large clan[5] that for us, the Jafun, have always been our opponents in the *soro*.[6]

We'd say among ourselves, 'Have you heard the Bodi cattle mooing? They're the same ones we met last week. Today we're in luck; there will be a *soro* . . . ! We climb trees and insult the Bodi – not just any way, but with the songs of the *suka*,[7] our brothers who are several years older than us. We imitate them.

Then the Bodi do the same. From far off they respond to our insults with other insults. We push our herds in their direction. We approach each other. Then one of us leaves our group to act as our spokesman. In his mouth are nothing but words of provocation. We advance toward them. We're face to face, eye to eye. Then one of us says to them, 'What do you want? What about all these insults? Do you think you can scare us? If it's the *soro* you want, then let's begin!'

They answer, 'Let's have a *soro*.'

'OK, we will go find some *soro* sticks.'

We leave our herding staves behind and go cut flexible sticks about the thickness of a finger. Maybe they are not thick, but they're strong and pliable. Then we ask, 'Who'll start?' having decided to have a real *soro* – not a practice *soro* – even a bloody *soro*, like our older brothers, the *suka*, have. Sometimes our brothers come home with their bodies striped with cuts. I will explain more about that later.

When we return to our camp, the more scars we have across our stomachs or on our chests the prouder we are. But it is not done to show off the scars too much. We just scratch ourselves a bit, as if it is nothing, and lift our shirts with blank expressions on our faces. But our older brothers are quick to catch on.

'Oh, you've had a *soro* today?'

'Of course,' we respond. 'We met the Bodi. You'd have done the same thing, wouldn't you?'

Soon everyone knows about it. Our fathers warn us again about such encounters which can turn out badly. But among the elders, there's always one who has not forgotten that he was once a child. 'You've done very well, my children. If you meet some little Bodi, do not be afraid. Certainly not. Do the *soro*. Hit them. That will shut them up. As for the Bodi girls, do not hesitate. Go right after them.'

Our fathers would always say, 'Oh please, Mr So-and-So, do not encourage the children to fight.'

'Look, my friend, isn't this what we've always done? Then do not forbid them to do it. Or you'll see what handsome cowards they'll make! It's better they begin to train themselves now. Yes, my children, if you meet little Bodi herders as you wander, do not be afraid of them. Do not be afraid of the Ba either. Never hesitate to do the *soro* with them. And get busy with their sisters!'

Personally, I had occasion to put this advice into practice. One day I met some Bodi girls. No boy was with them. I began by following their herd. Were their cattle going to the right? Then ours did too. Were they crossing a stream? So did ours. Before long we asked them frankly, 'Will you give it to us, the thing?'[8]

'No,' they answered, 'we don't want to.'

The only thing the girls knew how to say was, 'We don't want to.' Four of our boys were following the girls: Njauga, Ardo-Ina, Yidikau and Kiwo. With me, we were five.

It was time for us to water our animals at the river. When I saw the other four boys going toward the ford, I did not follow them. 'So,' they said to me, 'aren't you coming with us to water your animals?'

'No, not now,' I answered.

They understood very well that I did not want to be disturbed. They'd seen me following a little Bodi herdgirl. When they had gone, I went up to her. 'Don't you really want to give me your favour? Please give it to me.'

'No,' she answered, 'because I know you'll go and tell your friends right away.'

'Look, you don't know me. Do you think I'd be stupid enough to do that?'

And she let me have what I wanted. She must have been about eight years old, and I was too.

As soon as I got back to Njauga and his friends, I hastened to tell them all about my good fortune.

'Don't you think we knew what you were looking for when you didn't want to follow us?'

And the boys had nothing better to do when they met that girl than to ask her, 'Why did you refuse to give us what you gave Ndudi?'

Another time, I met four Bodi boys when I was alone. I came out of it with my head high, but my stomach and chest were a mass of stripes. There were swellings everywhere. I was proud of it. When I arrived back at camp, I met the man I thought of as a sort of second grandfather. He was the one who encouraged us to do the *soro*. 'Grandfather, today I met four Bodi when I was alone . Alone against four Bodi!'

'You're lying!'

'Look!' And I lifted up the side of my shirt.

He nodded his head, pensive and admiring. 'Bravo! This does not surprise me about you! I've always said you were courageous and that one day you'd be a tougher *soro* competitor than your oldest brother.'

'It's true, Grandfather. I'm not afraid of anything.'

'I also know your older brother always lets you drink the "courage potions" that serve him so well. Isn't that right?'

'It's true. He always lets me drink his secret concoctions.'

'Yes, yes, I understand. You know, no one becomes courageous without taking something. You've become courageous thanks to the medicine of your oldest brother.'

I agreed with him. Oh yes, I was proud!

It's a fact that many Mbororo benefit from preparations made by their older brothers who are at the *soro* age. When the older brothers boil their roots or bark, they always signal their younger brothers to come close. They want them not to know fear right from an early age. I myself watched how my brother did it. He crushed different barks and *borkonno* (peppers) and then added some very bitter roots – *bakurehi*[9] or *alali* roots[10] – and I don't know what else. There were many other things, but I've forgotten their names. This mixture of powders which he'd crushed and sifted was put into a little pot of water on the fire. Then he added some red natron and cooked it! And boiled it! Then, near the end, he added some millet flour. He took the pot from the fire and, with a stick, he stirred and stirred in order to make a gruel that was not too thick. Once the mixture had slightly cooled, he rubbed his eyes, made a grimace, and swallowed all of it with one gulp. It was bitter like Nivaquine (quinine)! He'd take this potion every morning and evening.

Big brothers would always give some to their younger brothers. But not too much. My brother explained things to me and shared his potions with me. And I would help. Often when I'd walk off at the head of my herd, he'd say to me, 'When you pass near a certain tree, bring me some of its roots' or 'I need some dirt from an ant hill.' I would bring him several handfuls.

In the end, we knew the formula for these preparations and we were able to make them by ourselves in secret behind the village. When we'd drunk the potions, we'd get worked up. We'd speak to imaginary enemies; we'd raise our voices to insult them. We'd provoke them. The potion was effective immediately.

'Oh God, make me courageous,' we'd say, 'May I not fear anyone in the world! Certainly not the sons of the Bodi. If they shoot an arrow in my right eye, may the left one not even blink!'

You can see boys who stop an instant when they put the bowl to their lips in order to make invocations and oaths: 'I intend to drink this potion. This is the potion of the *soro*.'

With the bowl raised in a sign of prayer, others say: 'May I be courageous! Even if I am sitting on an ants' nest, keep me from moving. An arrow in my eye, may I not speak! If they burn my stomach, keep me from moving or speaking!' And so on. Each person specifies his intentions, says what he has to say, and then drinks. Then we see him begin to shake more and more violently. He's excited. He's irritated. The effect is achieved. No fear can come to him. Now no one better risk speaking even a word to him that he might take exception to! He can burst into anger for no reason at all.

Figure 2.1: Attaching calves to the calf-rope

Figure 2.2: Family setting up dry season camp

Figure 2.3: Wet season camp

CHAPTER 3

And the Seasons Pass

The Rainy Season (*Ndungu*)

During the rainy season,[1] when the herd is our responsibility, we children have many different pleasures, amusements and games.

But there are days that aren't fun. When it rains, the cattle scatter and start to run away. They don't like rain hitting their eyes. They run in the opposite direction from the rain, even if the rain drives them far away from their grazing! It's hopeless trying to stop them. Some herders weep with rage, but there's nothing that can be done! And there are usually sheep along with the herd. You have to keep your eye on them. Watch out for the wild dogs! We talk about them every day.

I remember one of my friends. We were grazing our cows near each other. He'd lost his sheep. 'Don't be too upset about it,' we told him. 'They must have gone back to camp.' He didn't know a band of wild dogs had come upon the sheep. They had killed fifteen sheep and eaten several. Only four of the sheep returned to my friend's parents' camp. And during all that time, my friend continued to play with me. Yes, when it rains, you have to be doubly careful. There can be a calamity if the cattle gallop off in one direction and the sheep in another.

The rainy season is also the time of violent storms, at least at its beginning. Lightning can bring misfortune. I saw what happened to a young herder from the Ba clan. He was very young, very small. He'd joined us while his animals grazed. An enormous storm came up. He took refuge, like we sometimes did, under the stomach of a cow. There he was, keeping very dry. Lightning hit a nearby tree. It killed fifteen animals. Among them was the cow that the small boy had used for protection. He was killed instantly. I was in the vicinity. It's not unusual for such misfortune to befall the Mbororo during the rainy season.

On the other hand, we know how to protect our herds from lightning when they're gathered at camp. If we're in a woody spot, this is what we do. One man who is armed with a machete circles the area that's reserved for the herd, not forgetting the place where the calves are tied to the calf rope; he nicks the trees he finds along his path. Then we can sleep in peace; we know that lightning won't touch those trees which have the mark of iron. We don't do anything except nick the trees. We aren't interested in the bark. This is not a 'medicine'; it's a magical practice, *yafi*.[2] It's always effective.

Sometimes the water rises quickly enough to cause a drowning. We go with our herd to pasture on the other side of a valley. At the bottom of the valley, there's usually only a little trickle of water. But we know that sometimes there's a risk that a little stream can swell because of a storm. We keep this in mind. We avoid going too far away. But it can happen that we let ourselves go further away than we had intended. And then a storm comes up! When we return, we find a real river in front of us. We hesitate, but we take a chance crossing it. The herder looks for his calmest cow, holds onto her tail, and follows her into the water. The herder holds tightly and crosses the river, without dropping his heavy raincoat, the *kabidowu*, the Mbororo raincoat, if possible. A little calf may stay back on the other side; some sheep may drown. Never mind!

One of my nephews, Musa, my sister's son, lost his life that way. He was only seven years old. He had gone out all alone to take his herd to pasture, just like an adult. The area where he went was marshy, it is true, with several low places that seemed insignificant. It started to rain – a terrible storm. His parents had gone to the Garoua market.

When they saw the sky looking so black, they thought right away about their young herder and they hurried back. They went out to meet the herd. All the animals were there, none were missing. But no Musa. Anxiously, they went out in the direction the herd had come from. They could not find him. They continued to look until very late in the night. Nothing. At dawn the next morning they found him wedged into a big clump of grass. They understood right away that he had tried to hold on to the clump. But the water had been too strong. Rain had transformed the valley into a raging torrent. But when they found his body in the clump of grass, there wasn't even a trickle of water left. However, their child had drowned.

There's another thing which causes us children a lot of trouble. It's *karfa*. The Mbororo use it and abuse it. These are mixtures we make in order to give 'energy' to our animals. Because of these treatments, cattle are able to bolt away quickly, even in the middle of the night, to escape anything following them. *Karfa* is what makes the animals nervous when a farmer approaches. Thanks to *karfa* they become sensitive to the slightest danger. An aeroplane flying over which is a little noisy makes them flee – even if the aeroplane is flying very high. And once they've started to panic, just try to stop them! Some herders run out of breath. And it's not unusual to hear young herders blame their parents. 'I don't know what my father gives our cattle for *karfa*[3] but, the day before yesterday, all they would do was run. They wouldn't stay in one place. It started after an aeroplane flew over. Did you see it too?'

And another will say, 'As soon as mine saw a farmer passing nearby, they scattered in all directions. It was impossible to stop them. Really, my father goes too far with his *karfa*. I will tell him if he continues to treat them with it, I won't herd the cattle any more.'

And one after another, the young herders try to outdo each other with their complaints about *karfa*.

Their complaints are very justified. Wasn't *karfa* the reason a young Mbororo herder was lost one day? He had gone rather far into the bush. His animals saw a farmer. They disappeared at triple gallop. The child was alone, completely lost in an area that was new to him. Which direction should he take? He had absolutely no idea. He wandered for two days without meeting anyone. During all that time his worried parents were out looking for him. They found him two days later in a Daneeji encampment where he'd been looked after.

That night there was a lively meeting of the elders. Some reproached others for making the *karfa* too strong. 'The *karfa* we give our animals is much too strong. Some day one of our children will be lost for good.'

And some grandfathers insisted, '*Karfa* is not as necessary as it used to be. We're rarely attacked. Here the herds are able to rest and fatten up peacefully. Let's not make the task too difficult for our children!'

The Season at the End of the Rains (*Yamnde*)

We're happy to see the rains diminish in intensity and frequency. But we know we're beginning a difficult season: the harvest season. At this time all the grass has reached maturity. Everything men have planted is ripe. The heads of millet are open and beginning to yellow. The cattle herding can no longer be left to the children. Only men are able to do that job. And they should not do it alone.

The grass is very high. A herder can only penetrate the grass by walking behind his animals. They have to make a passageway for him. No one can walk at the head of the herd because he can't make a path. Anyone who tries will be surrounded in all directions. Before him is a wall, a barrier. Only the cattle can make a path.

At this time all herders must keep their eyes open. If the animals get away from them, even for a short time, they can't be sure the cattle won't go into a millet field. When the smell of millet enters their nostrils, they put their noses in the air and sniff. They run toward the millet which has caught their attention. When that happens, the cows clean out the field very quickly. That costs the Mbororo a lot. To escape such a problem, a Mbororo is capable of telling all sorts of lies. He'll lie shamelessly to the owner of the field, even if the cattle were caught in the act and even if the farmer himself brings the animals back to camp. Right up to the last minute, the herder will disown the cattle, swearing they aren't his and that he doesn't even know who owns them. As for him, he never uses pastures in that direction; he always goes the opposite way.

When the herder sees himself trapped by a farmer who has too much proof against him, he moves away with great speed during the night. In the morning the camp is empty. Some farmers, fearing that trick, do not hesitate to stay at the camp all night. They wait patiently for the real proof: the cattle dung. The wronged farmer watches the cattle attentively. If he doesn't find any grains of millet in the dung, he doesn't insist. He goes away. But if he finds some, he shouts, 'Come, look at this. Aren't these millet grains?' Very happily he picks up some dung and wraps it in his shirt tail. Then, content and feeling very clever, he goes off to make a complaint to the village chief. 'Chief, the cattle of so-and-so have eaten my millet field. It's a Mbororo. He's camped at a certain spot. Let's go.' The farmer takes one or two policemen with him and they set off.

When they get there, the police take note: it's true that there are grains of mil-let in the dung. They have seen it. That's enough. They won't even go evaluate the damage in the field. Why bother? The Mbororo will pay whatever the chief decides. It's understandable that, under these conditions, the herd can't be left just in the hands of children. Their role becomes less important: they accompany the men and look after the sheep.

The Cold, Dry Season (*Dabunde*)

The harvest season doesn't last long, thank goodness. It's followed very quickly by the dry season. All the grass has turned yellow. There are bush fires here and there which burn off the vegetation. Soon the wind comes, a very cold wind on certain mornings. It's hard for the children to pull themselves away from the blan-kets that have protected them from the cold during the night. When they come out-side, the cold grips them because they only wear rags and filthy little cloths. But the children are needed. They do not even have time to warm themselves near the fire where the women are busy. The children are the ones responsible for taking the herds out first thing in the morning into the nearby pastures.

A child is often obliged to follow his father on these long walks which last the whole day. It's not surprising that some of the children get thin. And the children are dirty because they have neither the time nor the courage to bathe. You can see what looks like scabs on their necks. When they scratch themselves, their finger-nails leave marks on their skin. Their loin cloths are falling apart. As for their lit-tle shirts, they stand up by themselves because of the dirt. The children never bathe, and their mothers don't wash them either. They must wait for the swimming season before they get near water.

The time of gathering for feasts is finished: marriage, the name-giving cere-mony, awarding the title of *mallam* at the end of Koranic studies. There are no more meetings at the marketplaces. There's only one thing to think about: fatten-ing the herd. This is still possible at the beginning of the dry season because there's sufficient grass. But there's misfortune in store for the herder who 'misses' this season! His animals must face the difficult period that follows in an under-nourished state. They risk getting thin and suffering. This is why the Mbororo are eager to leave their rainy season camps. They hurry to find new pastures where the grass is still nourishing.

So this is a period of frequent moving. We never stay long in the same place. Today here, tomorrow several kilometres away. The children love these days of walking in the bush. Some wish, however, that they did not have so much to carry in their arms or on their shoulders: chickens, lambs . . .

When the farmers have finished gathering the heads of millet from their fields, they leave the stalks behind. In the evenings the Mbororo family heads go to talk with the people of the area: 'Have you finished harvesting your field that's near my camp?'

'Yes, my millet's been harvested. My stalks are for sale. If you want them, they're yours.'

They go to see the field and make an agreement. Once the sale has been made, one could say that the field belongs to the Mbororo. No one else has the right to let his animals enter there. Cattle love millet stalks, and this exceptionally good nourishment allows the cattle to fatten up for the rigors of the following months.

The Hot, Dry Season (*Sedu*)

Little by little, the mornings are not so cold. The wind stops. The sun is brighter. The leaves have fallen from nearly all the trees and are covering the ground like a thick carpet. Anything that has not been burned by the sun has been burned by the hands of men. There are ashes everywhere, which turn the herder the colour of a charcoal maker. Grass is so rare that leaves must be used for food. The cattle eat by stretching their necks, but it is especially the herder who must provide for them.

During this period, the herder always moves with his machete in his hand. If he sees a tree that never loses its leaves, he climbs it. But he only does this if someone else is on the ground. As soon as the cows hear the first strike of the machete, they run quickly to the tree. What a fight if no one's there to keep them away! The further, the better! When the cattle are freed, they run toward the branches and eat them, knocking their horns together.

Ponds, even if they're muddy, are a precious help. But when the herder arrives, he must watch carefully. Sometimes it takes hours before the herder can quench the thirst of his animals. Because they're always famished, they aren't strong. They drag along as they walk. We say their tails get longer. Their bones stick out from their skin. But watch out! When they see a little green grass beside the water, their fatigue disappears. It's almost impossible for the herder to hold the cattle back. There's trouble if one of them goes too far into the pond. The cow quickly sinks in the mud. When she tries to get out, she may tire herself and, in the end, fall over. And if there's enough water, she'll drown. The strongest herder will find he does not have enough strength to pull the cow out.

There's only one solution: call everyone around. Soon people come running from all directions. Five or ten men arrive, each bringing a long rope coiled on his shoulder. All of the men work together to pull out the foolish cow.

If such a thing befalls an old cow that's in bad condition, pulling her out will permanently injure her. She'll hardly have a chance to survive that dry season, especially if the camp is in a riverbed. Sand is difficult for old cattle. They often fall, and one morning they'll no longer have the strength to get up again. A herder will look for help. But when he returns, the cow is dead. That's how old Mbororo cattle die.

In some regions, we fear the edge of ponds for another reason: crocodiles. Sometimes a crocodile catches a cow or a calf. The crocodile waits until the cow stretches her neck to the water before grabbing her by the muzzle. It drags the cow in while it swims away. There's nothing that can be done about this kind of accident. An onlooker will have to be content to tell his frightening story to the others. There are also crocodiles – very, very old ones – which, it is said, have vegetation covering their backs; yes, grass has grown all along their dorsal spines. A cow will be tricked into going toward this appetising little islet. The cow is easy prey for the crocodile, which only has to pull the cow under water. This is absolutely true.

People are carried off by crocodiles too. The Mbororo often speak about this. When that happens, they always mention something strange: worms appear immediately at the place where the crocodile's teeth bit into the flesh – just as if they came from an old infection. Several cases of this are known. I know this happened to a Bata farmer whose thigh was gashed by a crocodile.

The Hot, Stormy Season (*Guleli*)

Now we come to the hottest time of year, the season we call *guleli*. You can smell the storm. Some clouds appear; they become heavier and stormier. But we do not complain about them. They bring hope. The idea that rain will soon come from these clouds helps us endure the heat which kills animals and people. When the sun is at its peak, we don't know where to go. Sometimes even the nights do not cool off.

But we have the consolation of seeing buds reborn on the tips of twigs. The bushes become green again and regain life. Everywhere, but especially on the burnt ground, little shoots of grass pierce through the earth. Green spaces enlarge. The animals get a little stronger. And then, one evening, we hear a clap of thunder in the distance off to the south. Everyone claps. Everyone rejoices. We know everything will change soon.

But we have to be patient. This is the most difficult time of year. In the evenings, the old people harp on about their miseries. They talk only about their debts. There's hardly any milk in the women's calabashes. Nevertheless, they continue to carry them on their heads when they go to market. There's no market for livestock either. They're too thin. They would not be worth much. And the villagers have enough meat with all our old or injured cows that we've sold them at very low prices. Cows that die are automatically the property of the 'pagans' because a good Muslim does not even have the right to give away such a beast.

Women can only feed their families by having recourse to the purse of the head of the family, who is always recalcitrant. When was the time they used to feed the whole family just by selling milk? For everything – for measures of millet,[4] for greens for the sauce, for all ingredients – they must ask their husband to put his hand into his pocket.

What can be done with the few drops of milk that the cows give so parsimoniously? Some women save the milk and add it to the milk of the evening before, of the evening before that, and sometimes to milk that's ten days old. It's sour. They add a mixture made from baobab pulp, pour in water, and whip it all together. Soon their calabash is full to the brim. They go to the farmers and exchange it for some measures of millet or manioc flour.

Happily, this season does not last too long. Even before the first stormy rains, some new leaves appease the appetites of our animals. Milk begins to flow again … a little! We must economise and save it all to be sold. It's useless for the children to say, 'Give me a little, just a little bit to taste.'

Their mother will push them away with her hand. 'May leprosy carry you off! Don't you see we don't have anything left to eat? We get a little milk and you want to drink it! Think a little about the others!'[5]

The Return of the Rains (*Seto*)

One day we hear real thunder. All at once the sky becomes black. It doesn't always rain, but we smell a sudden freshness. Certainly it's rained somewhere, not far away. We already feel a little better. And then one beautiful afternoon, it rains. We rejoice perhaps more for our animals than for ourselves. We're happy to see them lift up their nostrils and inhale the air.

As the rains become more regular, we're on the alert for news which passes from one family to another. 'Have you heard about so-and-so who's come from the south? He says there have been big storms on the Mountain of the Hyena. What are we waiting for before going there?'

So the next morning one of the men takes his bow and quiver, and off he goes. He wants to go to see for himself what it's like in that place. He plans to return that night. No one sees him go; at least that's what he thinks. The next day someone may ask him, 'It seems you were walking south yesterday. Did you see anything?'

He'll answer, 'No. You know the best place is still right where we are. It is no better anywhere else. Just the opposite in fact.' He lies shamelessly because, in the south, he'd seen that all the ponds were full. The vegetation was much greener there. But he does not want to say that; at this time of year, each herder prefers to go his own way.

All the large groups split up. Everywhere little groups form that hide from each other. An adult married son leaves with his wife. He goes east. But as soon as he's out of sight, he turns toward the south where he'd already scouted out the land several days earlier. These are the days when the Mbororo move a lot. They watch, they spy, they tell lies. Each man for himself!

'You go that way. I'll go in the other direction.'

An older brother separates from his younger brother. The two have already separated their herds from the herd of their father. One does not know where the other has gone, or he pretends not to know. Actually, each man secretly goes to see if the conditions of his brother are better than his own. If they are, he'll move toward his brother; and the next day they'll notice that, completely by accident, they're close to each other.

'Oh my, we didn't know you were so close!'

'Oh yes, we meet again!'

You should see us children play in the first rains. We go out nude. No more loin cloths for the boys; no more wrapper-skirts for the girls. We run in all directions.

Dripping wet, we lift our hands to the sky as if we are praying: 'May God give me luck like we have in *seto* (the first day of the rainy season)! May God give me *barka*![6] We refuse to take shelter. This is real joy: we think of the milk we'll soon be able to stuff ourselves with. We think of the imminent meetings with our cousins where we can continue our games. For long months we'll be together. Our work as herders will be nothing but pleasure with grass right at our door and the beautiful cows growing fat.

The women are thinking that, thanks to the milk which will bring them money,[7] they'll no longer have to depend on the wallets of their miserly husbands. The children will no longer cry with hunger.

The young *suka*, those adolescents of the age for *soro*, will pass on all their work as herders to the younger children. Only one thing will count for them now – the *soro* – where they'll try to make themselves shine. They go to a certain woman's camp to have their hair combed into one hundred braids trimmed with copper. They'll chase the girls day and night. They're already on the lookout for their girlfriends who they've agreed to meet behind the village for a romantic conversation. Nothing will stop them, certainly not distance.

The young girls think about their clothes, their make-up and their tattoos, which make them beautiful. They'll dance. And they'll stretch out the long evenings of dancing until the early morning hours. They're ashamed when they think about the sloppy clothes they've worn until now. They had completely neglected their hair-dos. But they'll make up for that now. They have decided to let themselves be courted by the handsome boys.

The *kori*, those young men who have left adolescence but have not yet entered into adulthood, are excited.[8] They're happy they'll soon meet again all the girls they've already had adventures with. Youth must have its day! Most of the young men are married and have children. But that does not matter.

The adults will be able to go back to visiting the markets without any worries. They'll find their friends again and exchange news.

The old people are also happy to see the end of the season that tires them out digging wells and watering their animals. They will be able to sit quietly, making cords and calf ropes. Those who are still healthy will go off to the markets.

I, Ndudi, also have great joy in seeing the return of this new season where everything is easy. But my joy isn't complete. I know I'm suffering from leprosy.

Milk in abundance? Yes, for the others, but not for me: I'm forbidden to drink it. I was then being treated with 'black medicines', 'bush medicines'.[9] These were accompanied by certain tabooed foods. I was forbidden to eat hot pepper or salt and certainly not fresh milk. All day long people kept telling me, 'Don't eat that. Don't eat peanuts. Don't eat peanut sticks. You mustn't drink milk. No butter!'

Almost everything was forbidden to me. And I no longer had a mother. So my joy in seeing the arrival of this season of abundance and of grand gatherings could not be as great as it was for my little friends.

Figure 3.1: Mbororo women

Figure 3.2: Women and their calabashes

CHAPTER 4

Passing the Evenings

A Mbororo never goes to bed without taking part in the evening gatherings. On moonlit nights when we children got together, I was the drummer of the 'heart drum'. I was not the only one who could beat the dance rhythm for my friends, but they said I was the best. That pleased me and I never got tired of tapping my hands on my chest, beating the rhythm – *diring! diring! diring!* But when the dance was very long, someone would come to relieve me. Nearly every day our mothers would interrupt our dances by calling us a hundred times, 'Come eat!' Actually they really wanted us to carry bowls of food to their husbands.

We boys borrowed our songs from the boys of the next older age class, that of the adolescents, the *suka*. The little girls did the same by copying their older sisters. In these songs, the *suka* insult their imaginary enemies and praise themselves. The one who stands out is the one who is the most scornful toward others and the most boastful of themselves. They also sing praises of their fathers: 'I, so-and-so, the son of so-and-so, who should I fear? Certainly not you, you're only good-for-nothings.' And the insults would come down like rain!

Young girls have only praises on their lips for the boys, who do not even listen to them because they are so busy praising themselves and insulting their adversaries. They all try to shout the loudest, 'I fear no one, especially not so-and-so, the son of so-and-so. Just let him provoke me when it's time for the *soro*. He'll see what I'm capable of!' Everyone sings about the same thing, and all at the same time.

During this time, the little girls make up couplets in honour of the boys: 'So-and-so, the son of so-and-so, there's no one more handsome. Look at his hair; one might think it's the hair of a white man. When he's dressed up and has put on his *soro* apron, no one can be compared to him. He's full of health. His limbs are strong. No girl can look at him without "swallowing a tooth."'[1] And the praises get better: 'Look how straight his nose is, and how well-shaped his mouth is, and his ears . . .' One by one, each feature is described in detail.

Ignoring the girls, we boys would continue to mock our opponents. We especially have it in for the Bodi, insulting them without stop. We claim they are evil.

Since each boy sings his song, all singing at once while trying to shout the loudest, it's not surprising that it's difficult to understand what's being sung. The girls' song is a little more orderly because they have a lead singer. She begins with the name of a certain boy, and the other girls join in the chorus. But since each girl wants to add the name of the boy she prefers, the singing ends up in great commotion.

In spite of all this, the songs and the insults are accompanied by the rhythm of the same drum, which everyone tries to follow. The drum also accompanies our dance: the dance of the *suka*.

For this dance, the girls stand next to each other in single file, east of the dancing area. We boys make a line also, to the west, facing the girls. At the sound of the 'heart drum', one girl – either alone or with her neighbour whom she holds by the waist – moves forward into the space between the two lines. The girls advance together. They sway lightly to the rhythm of the drum while humming in accompaniment. They do not hurry. When they get near the boys, one girl 'chooses'. She makes a sign to one boy. He immediately detaches himself from his group. He pursues the girls as they dance backwards with little steps toward their own group. The 'elected' boy continues and, when it's his turn – he signals a girl who takes a step forward. Then dancing – or rather skipping – she goes toward the boys where, in turn, she chooses the boy she likes.

There are boys who are never chosen because they're dirty, or ugly, or simply because they have no masculine charm. Weary of waiting, they leave the game and sit on the sidelines. Then they come back to try their luck. Finally, tired of being neglected, one of these boys advances on his own toward the girls as if he'd been chosen. He's shouted at. The others make fun of him: 'Oh, no! You're stealing your turn! Who chose you? Get back in line. We don't like anything about you!'

As for us, we boys also ignore any girl who's ugly or who has snot in her nose. Eventually she goes to join the little children. Everyone makes fun of her.

Some *kori* are there as spectators. They cheer us on. They keep egging on the boy who is liked by the girls more than the others.

'Oh, son of so-and-so, the girls have eyes only for you. What will it be like when you're grown up!' The boy who's the centre of attention in the dance is proud. He knows he has 'blood', as we say. When a boy 'chooses' his partner of the moment, he does it very nonchalantly – 'with nothing on his face' – even with a certain disinterest. To choose her, he is content to point his toe toward her. He backs this up with a sly wink. He never motions with his hand.

Some dancers are really cruel. They seem to be going toward one girl, but at the last minute they change direction and pick another. There are some girls who do not like that little game at all. And so, some boys take all the more pleasure in making them angry. These boys prolong their play-acting. There's every reason to think that so-and-so will be chosen. She waits; she looks for the little sign. At the last second, another girl is chosen. When the boy picks her rival, the girl has a twinge of heartbreak as she sees the dancers go to the centre of the dance ground and do their little number. Then they take their places again in the lines of dancers.

When the dance is over, we only think about one thing: gaining favours from the girls. This is what adults do, so naturally it's what we do too. We speak to one of our partners and ask the question, always the same question: 'Will I get your favours[2] today?'

She may answer, 'No, tonight it's not possible!'

We insist, 'Look, be nice. Don't be like that!'

Sometimes she persists in her refusal – she really does not like you.

'No, not today. I must go home.'

Hardly has she left you before she's stopped by another boy.

'Can I have your favours today?'

She does not hesitate to respond, 'All right, let's have what we both desire.'

And you'll see the two of them going off together. The only thing left for you is to try your charm on someone else.

I remember my first rendezvous with Mayrama, and with Afsatu. At our age, such meetings do not have any importance. But we repeat certain expressions we've heard. We use certain gestures. It's only when we're older that we learn to distinguish these childish amusements from those that risk leading to real consequences. We Mbororo have the reputation of knowing how to set our own limits. It's rare that we step beyond those limits with young girls who do not yet have husbands. A mother who hears a suitor come behind her house to 'click his fingers' understands this very well. She is not opposed to her daughter accepting such an invitation. In fact, she encourages it. She has confidence. She knows they'll stay within the limits, within the boundaries of Fulani custom. We're less reserved when we're younger, less prudent, but this has no consequence.

We Mbororo children learn about life very naturally. All year long we live with our cows and our sheep. We know what happens. However, it seems to me we're taught even more by listening to the words of our older brothers. I'm thinking here about our brothers in the *kori* age class. At their age, the worst rudeness is permitted. They enjoy talking bluntly about very crude things, even in front of children. You could say they even do it on purpose. On *soro* days, they point their fingers at the first woman who passes by and say shamelessly, 'Here's the woman I slept with last night. Yes, she's the one I "knocked over"; I know her. There's no doubt about it!' Then the Fulbe and all the people watching start to laugh and clap their hands! We children hear all this and we come to think of that kind of talk as ordinary. They teach us … things we don't find in books!

When we were alone, we'd try to put into practice what we'd learned. We did not see anything wrong with that; just the opposite in fact! So it was natural for us to brag about our successes as though we'd done something good! Hadn't we had fun? Well, then?

However, we couldn't boast too much in front of our parents even though we boys knew they wouldn't say anything to us. But the girls were really afraid of their mothers and aunts. The women are afraid that when their daughters get older they'll continue to run after the boys and then 'misfortune' will befall them. This is the only reason they're anxious and disapproving.

But no blame will be put on the boys. Some parents are even proud of them: 'When our son grows up, he'll be a handsome *suka*. He'll have lots of success with women. He has the blood!' Not much good is expected to come from a boy who doesn't seduce girls when he is young. It's not a good sign for his future. So fathers are proud and mothers tend to joke about it.

However, there are 'scenes' from time to time. This always happens when boys are angry because they did not get the favours they counted on. Egged on by jealousy, they rush home and say, 'So-and-so and so-and-so slept together. Yes, over there under that tree.'

The girls do the same thing. Because some girls are never approached by the boys, they're angry when they return home. If they're asked, 'Where's your cousin who left with you?' the response will be, 'Do you want to know where she is? Then go down there, behind the bushes. You'll see her sleeping with so-and-so!' The girl speaks loudly so everyone can hear her. The old people, sitting on their mats, smile. The women look at each other and shake their heads.

When the girl returns, her mother always demands an explanation. The girl is first taken into her mother's hut. And then there are storms of tears. 'What did I hear? If I ever catch you doing this again, I'll take away your desire for it by rubbing pepper in a certain place I have in mind. Do you understand?' And we hear shouting and crying. But this does not stop the girl from doing it again at the first occasion. That's how it happens.

But it's true that as the girls grow older, they calm down and become prudent. They're really afraid of becoming pregnant! And they have good reason! If it happens to one of them, it means expulsion from the family and from the clan. The girl must leave the region. It's even said that certain fathers have not hesitated to sacrifice a daughter who gave birth to a bastard. I do not think that would still happen today. The world is changing. But an illegitimate child continues to be the object of general disapproval and the greatest scorn. How much longer will this last? Here and there, some illegitimate children seem to be accepted, at least in the Adamawa region, the Country of the Mountain.

Anyway, year by year our passion only grows; our demands do too. But it's less and less easy to satisfy ourselves. Our companions, the girls, also become more and more difficult as they get older.

On the whole, the Mbororo have a sense about what is allowed and what is forbidden in these matters. That there are some people among them who descend to shameful acts, is this surprising? Such things happen everywhere in the world. As for me, I've sometimes heard talk about homosexual relations. That's sinful. They do it, I'm told, to enrich themselves. I don't understand what it means 'to enrich themselves', but I know what they do is very bad. Those who do it are condemned by our Book to have their throats cut. But a tribunal of men would be less severe, at least the kind of court the Whites have brought us. I've never heard of such a case among the Mbororo. But it is not uncommon to hear that some herders who are isolated in the bush and deprived of women do this with their cows.

This is what I saw one day. The man was not a Mbororo. Some children had surprised him when he was coupling with an ass. Because there were many of them, the children jumped on him. They bound his hands and feet and painted him blue with blueing that's found in markets for washing clothes. Then they paraded him through the little streets of their village. They shouted out what he'd done. I joined their parade. Little by little as we walked on, other children joined in.

'What's going on?' asked the people. 'Have you caught a robber?' 'No,' shouted the children. 'We surprised him when he was with an ass.'

'Allah! It's not possible!'

And we went on. Finally he was released and did not waste any time disappearing.

What a surprise when I bumped into him again in a small town, at Meiganga. He was in the marketplace, sitting there selling kola nuts. When he saw me, he turned his head and pretended he had not noticed. But I said to him, 'Oh good, Yamsa, so you're here now?'

'I'm here, as you see.' He seemed embarrassed and hung his head. He remembered.

To tell the truth, it should be said that we children sometimes got up to the same sort of foolishness. We're rather ashamed of this now. Some evenings, under various pretences (such as sharpening the horns for example), we'd go out together to one of our herds. And there we played bull with our cows. We would invite each other to 'visit' our cows. One day the men saw us. What a thrashing we got! It was our oldest brother who had discovered us. Because he was suspicious about something, he slept one night among our animals and he waited. You can imagine our surprise and confusion when, all of a sudden, he got up to chase us, cursing all the while: 'May leprosy take you! Don't you have any shame? With the cows! And this isn't the first time!' We scampered away fast and reached the bush. And no one ever spoke of it again. Some nights our animals wander into the area where we're sleeping. Among the cows there are always some we call 'clothes eaters'. We knew which ones they are. They're irresistibly attracted to the odour of dirt on our clothes lying next to us: a mixture of salty sweat, urine and filth. We try to break them of this strange habit. We entice them with old rags that have been powdered with hot pepper. If the trap works, what fun we have seeing them lift their head, shaking it in all directions – left and right – until this passes!

We Mbororo dream a lot. Sometimes we hear voices in the night. The voice of a child: 'Watch out, watch out! You're going to break my cows!' There's no need to ask this boy what he's dreaming about. Or a cow's name is shouted out: 'Dagay! Dagay!' From time to time, we hear some snatches of a herder's song. What a nightmare when we dream that our cows have entered a farmer's millet field and completely destroyed it! Some begin crying. They're awakened. 'What's the matter?'

'The farmer caught me. He doesn't want to let me go!'

We tell him it was only a dream and he goes back to sleep reassured.

In the morning when we're together, we retell our dreams. There are children who always have something to tell. Often they just make it up .

When the women dream, they hurry to tell their dreams to the old women. They believe in dreams. 'Tonight I dreamed that all the milk I was cooking on the fire boiled over.'

Then the grandmother responds in a preaching tone, 'Well, my dear, it's that you are no longer generous to the people around you. You don't know how to give. Tomorrow, take the first milk that your husband brings and give it away. This gesture will be profitable to you. You will be doing something good, and a good action is always profitable.'

We always envy a Mbororo who, when he wakes up, says he saw the Black Bull[3] in his dream. What luck for anyone who dreams about this Black Bull of the spirit world, especially if the bull was seen covering one of our cows! That day, the man will present milk to everyone in order to bring blessings on his herd. Seeing cows come out of termite holes is also interpreted as a particularly good omen.

On the other hand, simply to see meat in a dream is deeply troubling. The man will think one of his animals will die in the coming days. 'Oh, last night I had an ungodly dream: I dreamed about meat!' Or else: 'Poor me! I had a dream about hunting!'

As for the *kori*, those who have left adolescence without yet attaining the age of full maturity, they always dream about women. They take pleasure in saying that they have slept with so-and-so. The youngest of them always says, 'Last night I dreamed that I went to the village of so-and-so. I asked for her favours, and I got them. Really, it was not difficult! But how dreams lie. Ah, it would be better not to have such dreams which, in the end, lead to nothing!' And everyone laughs. Yes, may God remove the lies from dreams!

Figure 4.1: Boy lighting the evening fire in the corral

CHAPTER 5

Our Grandmothers' Stories

Some evenings we'd go to find our grandmothers or other old women so we could hear their stories. We knew their tales by heart because we'd heard them over and over. Our grandmothers were very conscious of the fact that in teaching us these stories, they were teaching us how to speak our language correctly. Since we had no books, what else could be done? We were always happy to listen to the stories, happy to hear them and to learn them.

We'd all go together to one of our grandmothers and say, 'Tell us a story, Grandmother!'

Sometimes she'd say, 'Oh no, not tonight! Didn't I ask you this morning to get me some wood? You didn't do it, so you'll have no stories tonight.' And the next day we'd replenish her wood pile.

When Grandmother had decided to tell a story, we'd sit near her. Grandmother Jebu was nice. She'd start by asking us, 'Do you want stories or riddles? Long stories or short stories? Funny stories or scary stories?'

We'd argue among ourselves, 'Riddles, Grandmother, riddles!'

Others shouted louder, 'No, Grandmother, stories, stories . . . a real story that lasts a long time!'

She let us squabble, and then she'd decide for herself.

Some old women could hardly see any longer. Others didn't have any teeth. We laughed at them among ourselves. The grandmother would think we were laughing at her story, but we were laughing at her! Sometimes while she was telling a story, someone would bring her something to eat. We'd soon steal morsels from her plate, but she did not even see that. We'd laugh. Some stories never finished. We'd get tired. One after another, we'd sneak away. When Grandmother had finished, she'd sometimes ask us to repeat the story. If we'd heard the story a hundred times, we did not have any trouble retelling it.

But there were some stories which we got all tangled up. Then each of us would break in. 'Be quiet. I know it. Listen!' The most determined of us would start speaking and go through it right to the end. That made Grandmother very happy.

We thought we could repeat the stories any time at all. But when we tried to tell them to adults in the daytime, they'd cut us off. 'Stop your stories! You must only tell them at night or else your cows will never have calves!' This was like a 'taboo' imposed on us. It must be said that we more or less respected this rule.

To the great joy of my sister Gogo, who preferred scary stories, Grandmother Jebu loved telling stories about people who had two heads, or three, or even ten. Little by little as the heads multiplied, you'd see the children who were getting frightened move closer to Grandmother. Others would look toward the door and say, 'There they are! They're coming!'

The ones who were the most scared glued themselves to her and pleaded. 'Stop, Grandmother! I don't like stories like that! I'm sure I'll have nightmares tonight!'

Here's a story I remember very well. It's very long. It's the tale of 'The Child and the Monsters'. A family had set up its camp during the seasonal migration in the middle of the bush, far away from everything. There were three in the family: a man, his wife and their child. Only a single child. Each day the man left to hunt or to collect fibres from tree trunks for making rope. His wife went to nearby villages to sell her milk. They left their only child at home, all alone.

One day when each of them was involved in these daily tasks, an enormous monster came to the camp. It had huge eyes on the top of its head, like two glowing red embers. It approached the child. 'Where's your father?' it asked.

'He's off watching the cows.'

'Where's your mother?'

'My mother has gone to sell milk.'

'Where's the extra milk?'

'It's on the shelf.'

Then the monster went to the shelf, took the calabash in its hands, drank the milk and left.

One day the parents asked the child, 'Who drinks the milk we leave in the big calabash on the shelf? We know you're content with the gruel we make for you every morning. So who's drinking all the milk in the big calabash?'

The child answered, 'You know, when you're not here, I see scary "things". If you were here, you'd be scared, very scared! Please don't say I drink the milk. I'm happy with my gruel. But some day one of you should spend the day here with me. You'll see this strange thing that I see.'

One day the father decided to stay home. 'All right,' he said to his son, 'as soon as this strange thing comes, I'll shoot it with an arrow. Yes, whatever comes – beast or human or anything else – I'll shoot, and I won't miss! I'll sit in the granary with my bow and quiver so I can see everything.'

He sat down and waited. Right at noon the huge "thing" appeared. It came up to the child. 'Where's your father?'

'He's hunting.'

'And your mother?'

'She's selling milk.'

'Where's the big calabash of milk?'

'It's on the shelf.'

The big "thing" went to the shelf and drank the milk.

The father had parted the straw roof of the granary and peeked out. But when he saw the big red eyes, he jumped back and fell on his behind. He soiled his pants and ruined all the millet. He never thought about using his bow. He didn't shout. He didn't even open his mouth. The monster went away just as it had come.

When his wife returned, the father of the child was content to say, 'Oh, my! Today God showed me something scary. It's best if we break camp.' They left and set up a new camp, far away from everything. It wasn't long before the monster found their new place. It came again and drank the milk; but this time the monster took away the child, hid him and kept him at its home.

The child grew and grew and grew until he was the size of an adult. Then his abductor said to him, 'I really should introduce you to my family.' And that's what the monster did.

Who would have thought that in this family of monsters … yes, in this monster's family … only the last one had just one head! That's right, only Gaji – for that was the monster's name – was normal; all the others had several heads.

In the family, Gaji was considered a bastard. The others had a different parentage. Gaji embarrassed them. They would say that they had to get rid of Gaji, had to eat him. They'd argue about that. They had actually decided to do it, but their mother stopped them. And the little one was shrewd!

Well, so it was that, one day, this stranger appeared among them who also had only one head. They immediately said to each other, 'Today food will not be lacking. There's a one-headed creature in our village? This is not possible!' And one after another the monsters came home from the bush.

When the child saw a creature with two heads coming toward him, he said to it, 'Why do you have two heads?'

'Are you surprised? Just wait, you haven't seen anything yet!'

Soon Three-Heads came. The child exclaimed, 'How did this happen? You have three heads!'

Three-Heads said, 'You haven't seen anything yet.'

Then Four-Heads arrived. '… You haven't seen anything yet!'

Then came Six-Heads. 'You haven't seen anything yet! Wait,' he added. 'Many-Heads is coming right behind me. He isn't far off.'

And there came Ten-Heads and then Fifteen-Heads.

The kidnapped child was placed in the midst of them, and they all agreed they would eat him. So they put their heads together to figure out how to do it. The monster we know said to them, 'I agree that you can eat him. Go get some wood. While you're gone, I'll kill him. I know what to do.' And so that's what they did.

When they left, Gaji took the child and hid him. Then Gaji collected the fibres of a tree called *barkehi* and of another tree called *bobori*.[1] These are red fibres. Gaji cut them and tied them together in a bundle. Returning to the house, Gaji put the fibres into a pot full of water. He lit a big fire and the water began to boil. The others returned. 'You took a long time doing that task,' Gaji said to them. 'Our "thing" is nearly cooked. Add your wood and it will be ready. Then we can eat it.' They hurried to place their wood under the pot and to stir up the fire. Then our monster said to the others, 'Bah! Your little sticks don't help at all. Wait for me. I'm going to look for some big stumps so we can make a good fire. But please do not touch the pot.'

As soon as Gaji turned his back, Ten-Heads and the others began to fish around in the pot. And they chewed and they swallowed! 'Great God,' they said, 'the flesh of this "creature" is so bitter! Maybe it hasn't cooked enough.' However, they continued to eat. But as soon as they took a mouthful, they spat it out. 'Bloody hell! The flesh of this "creature" – the "creature" with one head – is really bitter! What fun is it going to be to eat our little brother? None at all.'

So they forgot about their idea of eating him. They were persuaded that the flesh of their last little brother Gaji would taste just as terrible as the flesh of the 'creature' who also had only one head.

And that's how the story ends. It's true, my grandmother could really tell stories. But it wasn't every day she told us scary stories like that one. My elder sister, Gogo, always wanted to hear stories like that. She only remembered that kind of story. But we didn't like her to retell them to us.

Gogo particularly liked the story of 'The Hyena That Became a Man'. It was about a young girl who said to anyone who would listen that she would not agree to marry a young man if he had even the slightest blemish. She'd examine every suitor who presented himself and she'd always find a little fault. One day Hyena transformed himself into a man, a faultless man. She accepted Hyena. He married the young girl and took her to his house. It was the home of a wild beast. All that could be seen inside were human skulls. There were skulls everywhere! The young girl quickly realised she would also be eaten. You can guess the rest …

Here's another tale that my sister loved.

One day Hyena transformed himself into a medicine man. He'd learned that a woman was worried about the health of her daughter whose breasts were starting to develop. This woman was not very clever. Hyena went to see her. 'I've heard that your daughter has a pussy boil. Let me do something about it. I'm a doctor. I know how to puncture the abscess and get the pus out.'

So they fixed up a straw house for him. He made the woman bring him salt, pepper and some other condiments . . . and the girl who was supposedly sick.

When night came, the 'doctor' began to cut off pieces of the young girl's body. The child cried. From outside her mother asked, 'What are you crying for? Do you hurt somewhere?'

It was the 'medicine man' who responded, 'I'd hardly touched her little string of beads before she thought I was eating her! … Ah! Such good red meat! With salt, oh-la-la, *fiyaou*! With hot pepper, oh-la-la, *fiyaou*!'

This word fiyaou means 'something good'. It caresses your ears like the wind. The were-doctor was quoting a phrase from a proverb. But the woman did not understand.

Then the woman came back again. 'Is it going better?' she asked.

'Oh, certainly, she's much better. If things continue like this, she'll be better very quickly. I think she can return home tomorrow.'

Hyena ate the girl until there was nothing left, absolutely nothing. The 'doctor' left his house and went to the home of the mother to say goodbye. 'It's finished, but wait a little longer. I gave her some sweet-smelling plants. She's taking her last fumigation. Wait a bit more before going to get her. As for me, I've finished my work.' And he disappeared. As foreseen, the mother went to find her daughter. What did she find? Not even the smallest bone!

Many of these scary stories teach a lesson: 'Never leave a child alone in the house.' 'Mothers, don't be upset when you see your young daughters growing up and developing.'

The characters that appear time and again in our tales are animals. Among them, the most important is the hyena. Simply mentioning his name calls to mind envy, gluttony and fear. Next come the squirrel (*jire*), the shrewd one who can always get out of a tight spot; the rabbit or the hare, who's never at the end of his wits; and the majestic lion, who settles the disputes that are brought before him with a single swipe of his paw. Their adventures never end.

When my grandmother was not around, I'd turn to the little old women who I liked helping. They had a special affection for me because they knew the way my stepmother treated me. My illness made them have pity on me. They'd give me food. Very often I went to their homes and spent the evening there along with their grandchildren. Some evenings I fell asleep there and spent the night with them. Sometimes my father would come to take me home to my brothers and sisters.

Most of the stories I know are those the old women taught me. But when we got older, they tried to 'preach' to us more often. I noticed that the older they got, the more they prayed, even when they did not know how to do it. I'm sure when they were younger, that was the last of their worries but . . . as death approaches! Eventually they'd reach the point of saying they'd forgotten all their old stories. They only remembered one tale, the one about 'The Marketplace of the Hereafter'.

To understand this tale, you must know the gesture that many of our grandmothers make – or it would be more correct to say 'made' – at the beginning of meals. They would take a small ball of porridge, the size of a mouthful, from the plate and, rather than putting it in their mouth, they would give it to the woman next to them. That woman tastes a little and passes it on. It's only when each woman has had her share that the grandmother starts to eat. Doing this constitutes an act of charity (*sadaka*).[2] If you ask her why she does it, she'll give you the following explanation. For her, it's not a folktale, but a real sermon. Here it is.

There once was an old woman known for her lack of generosity. She never gave away anything. Just once, she had thrown a bone to a dog – and that was a bone she'd already gnawed and sucked on. The dog took the bone and went away. One day as this woman was passing near a termite hill, she felt she was being approached by someone, by something. It was a big snake and it swallowed her. This snake was one of the 'people of the other world'. We do not know where it took her. But after a long trip, they came out at a place where there were lots of people who resembled people back here on earth. All around there were big houses like we see in our towns. But the snake, having transformed itself into a good old woman, said to her, 'You see, we're here in the other world.' The woman was afraid. Everywhere she saw women sitting next to their calabashes. She saw people coming and going. They put everything imaginable into those bowls: money, cloth, meat, doughnuts; in short, everything you can give away. The people who were coming and going were like angels. There were even some who'd give a cow and the calabash that had been used for milking it.

The old woman watched. No one brought anything to fill the calabash that was sitting next to her. At last she heard a bone fall into her calabash. A dog had brought it. A beautiful bone, all clean and neat, without even a trace of meat on it.

When she returned home that evening, she asked her companion for an explanation. 'Why are markets like this in your town? People don't buy anything; they don't sell anything.'

The old snake woman answered, 'I will explain it to you. Everyone you saw receiving something without paying was getting exactly what she'd given others when she was on earth. And so it was with you. Think about what you gave away when you were living on earth.'

The woman thought about that. 'Oh yes! One day I gave a bone to a dog.'

'Well, this is the same bone the dog came to throw into your calabash!'

The old woman, who was not very proud of what she'd done, became afraid. All she could do was say 'Bah!'

During this time – which lasted for some years – the people of the woman's village wondered what had become of her. Was she lost? Had she drowned? Had she been eaten by wild animals? Who could say? And then one day she reappeared in her village.

'Where have you been?' was the question everyone was asking her.

She responded, 'I was in the other world.'

'In the other world? And what happens there?'

And she told them all about it.

That same day the woman, who was very rich, collected everything she had. Her possessions were many, especially cows. She brought everything together and then she distributed it.

There are some stories – those of my childhood – which every real Mbororo must know. 'The Butter Girl' is one of them.

There was a woman who could not have children. Nothing helped her. God did not give her descendants. One day an old woman said to her, 'Take some butter. Make it into a lump and put it in a pot. Wait a long time without touching the pot. When you open it, you'll see.' She did as the old woman had told her. When she opened the pot, she found the butter full of worms. She went to tell the old woman, who said to her, 'Go back to the pot. Shut it and wait.' That's what she did. When she opened the pot again, she found a child. It was a girl. She was beautiful. The child grew up. People talked a lot about her beauty, saying, 'It's not a poor man that will have this girl in marriage. He will have to be a king.' And that's what happened …

There isn't a Mbororo who doesn't know the ending of the story. The other wives of her husband and her mother-in-law were jealous. They made this beautiful wife pound all the millet out in the sun. When they came back from the market, she had melted!

Often people say our folktales are 'lies'. But the stories are fictions which always teach a lesson. The lesson depends as well on who's listening. That's how it was for me when I heard the story of 'The Stepmother and the Orphan'. I could not help but think I was in the same situation. It was the same for my brothers and sisters. We no longer had a mother and her replacement, our stepmother, was mean. My grandmother liked to tell us this sad story. There once was a great chief who had two wives. Each one had a child. When one of the wives died, it was only natural that the chief showed a great tenderness toward the little orphan girl. One day he left on a trip or went off to a war. Before his departure, he ordered the remaining wife to take care of the child. 'Don't give her work that's too hard. Pay careful attention to her.'

The stepmother reassured him. But as soon as her husband had departed, she began to insult the little girl, 'May the plague strike you!' And she gave the girl the heaviest chores: carrying water and collecting wood. The girl had to pound the millet and start the fire. She had to wash the clothes, take care of her little brother, clean him up and so on. And she did that all day long. One day when the step-mother had sent the girl to draw water, she had the girl pushed into the pond by an evildoer. The girl disappeared; but even though she was deep in the water, she did not die.

A short time later, the great chief returned, accompanied by his retinue. At the first sound of the trumpets, his wife had the trunk of a tree cut down and a hole carved in it. She buried the trunk and made the place look like a grave. When the *lamido*[3] passed in front of the pond, a child's voice could be heard. It was a song, but I've forgotten the tune and the words. Then one of the slaves said to his master, 'Master, may God bless you! I hear your child's voice coming from the pond.'

The chief replied, 'That's ridiculous! Would my child be speaking from the pond? Kill this man for me!' And he was killed.

A little further on, the voice was heard again. Another slave said, 'There's no doubt about it. I hear your child's voice too.'

The chief was very angry. 'What's this? You're all crazy! Kill him!' And he was killed.

And again the voice was heard. Someone told the chief. That slave was killed too. And this went on until there was only one slave left.

When it was his turn, the last slave spoke to his master. 'Oh may God bless you! If you want, kill me. But I hear your child's voice in the pond too.' The chief listened carefully and heard the voice. He ordered the drum to be sounded. All the slaves from the surrounding villages came running. He ordered them to empty the pond. They emptied it. There they found his child alive. Roots were starting to grow on her. The slaves cut off the roots and pulled out the orphan. They cleaned her up and fixed her hair. Then, after wrapping her up, they carried her on their heads like someone carries a heavy load.

When the chief arrived back home, he took his place in the entry house. He called the stepmother and his child. It was the stepmother's own child who came. The chief said to the child, 'Where's your sister?'

The child responded, 'I don't know.'

The father continued, 'Go get your mother. Tell her to come!'

The child went away. The mother arrived. 'Where's so-and-so?' the chief asked her.

'So-and-so? . . . Just this instant I sent her on an errand. She'll be back in a moment.'

They waited and waited . . . Nothing! The husband asked his wife again, 'Where's so-and-so?'

'So-and-so . . . just left to draw water from the spring.'

The people who had gone to carry water returned. He did not see his child. Astonished, he asked again, 'Where's so-and-so?'

'She went to wash the dirty plates. She followed the people doing the dishes.'

The dishwashers came back. But the child still was not there. The man asked again, 'Where's so-and-so?'

'I saw her follow those who went to gather wood.'

The people gathering wood came back. She was not with them. 'Where's so-and-so?' asked the great chief again.

Then his wife said to him, 'So-and-so? . . . I don't want to hide the truth from you any longer . . . So-and-so, soon after your departure . . . I don't know what sickness she had . . . but in a few days, she was dead! Her grave is over there!'

He gave an order to his slaves: 'Go dig open the grave and bring me her remains! I must see!'

The slaves went, opened the grave, and found nothing but a tree. That's all.

The stepmother never imagined that the child was wrapped in one of the packages that was lying on the ground. The chief then spoke to his wife, 'Well! You've killed her. Yes, I know it! How did you kill her? Where's her body? Did you drown her in the river or what?'

He'd already asked his child, 'What do you want me to do with your stepmother?'

She'd responded that she wanted to be hidden in the midst of some pieces of cloth. And she had added, 'Tell her that she should come choose all the pieces of cloth she likes. Then at the right moment, I'll scratch her eyes out.'

The woman came forward and began to choose the cloth she wanted while inside the bundle the orphan was holding a needle in her hand. 'I'll take this piece, and this and this . . .' Then the stepmother discovered the child who quickly gouged out her stepmother's eyes. The stepmother jumped back and fell down. The chief killed her and, at the same time, he killed the child of that stepmother too.

This story, which makes people cry, teaches women to treat the children of their co-wives well and not to show hatred toward them. For the women, it's a reminder to have pity so that meanness will be done away with.'

One might think that some of our stories are only the recitation of various events. Maybe that was their origin. But they've become real folktales today. They are lessons for us. So it is with 'The Milk Seller and Her Baby Eaten by Hyenas'. This tale is for women and it reminds them not to linger in the villages and return too late. There could be a calamity.

'The Hyena That Became a Man', the story loved by my sister Gogo which I've already told you, is a lesson for young girls. Mothers want to use it to put their girls on guard against foolishness and to make them listen to experienced adults who know the origins of our people.

Other stories of our grandmothers teach other lessons. I'm thinking of 'The Young Man and the Bird'. It teaches that each person must be allowed to eat what he likes. You should not scorn the food of others. We find the food of the Whites or of the Fulbe to be tasteless, and we cannot eat it. However, it's good for them. We'd prefer to die of hunger rather than to swallow meat that has been smoked by farmers. But would they be happy with our sauce made from baobab leaves and a bit of hot pepper?

I spoke of food but I could just as well have given you a story about houses, clothes or bedding. We Mbororo are happy with huts made from branches or from straw. We find these houses to be very satisfactory. When the Fulbe insult us about this, we reply, 'Your substantial houses! We couldn't sleep in them. We stifle in them, we can't get any air, and we're too hot!' But when they come to sleep in our houses, they prefer to sit up rather than to lie down on our beds which, for them, do not even deserve the name.

Everyone lives with his heritage, with the things he's become accustomed to. What's good for one is not necessarily good for others. We find all this in our tales. But they are told especially in order to teach us how to live as real Fulani in every circumstance of life. We can learn something from each story. We only have to pay a little attention while we listen. Some tales are for children, others for adults. Herders have their own stories. They show examples of courage: a person who leads a herd to the pastures does not fear the bush or anything he meets there.

I used to know many herders' stories, but now I only remember a couple of them. Here's one: 'The Herder and the Python'. A herder left early in the morning to walk with his herd all day. The time came to water the animals. The water of the pond where he'd led them had turned into blood. The cows did not want to drink it; they turned back. The herder led them back again. This time the water had become black like ebony. Once again the cows refused to drink and turned away. The herder brought them back again. The water was now white . . . white like milk that comes from a cow's udder. The animals did not want to drink it and they ran away. The herder gathered them up and led them back to the pond.

Then a monster appeared which looked like an enormous snake. 'Tell me, herder,' the snake said, 'you don't seem to be astonished by the marvels which I'm performing right before your eyes. Who do you think you are?'

'Say what you like,' replied the herder. 'But my animals must drink and they will drink.'

'Good! I'll make the water drinkable; but, I warn you, they won't drink it.'

The young herder said, 'They'll drink it.'

The monster replied, 'They won't drink it.'

The water went back to its natural state. The herder urged his animals to the bank. At that moment, the monster swept away the water with one powerful breath. The cows scattered and disappeared. But the herder did not move.

'From what I can see, I think you're looking for a fight,' said the monster.

'Perfect,' responded the young man. 'In any case, I'm not afraid of you. Let's go!'

And the fight began. The herder grabbed his stick and struck the monster a blow, who fell down. The monster got up and violently struck the herder with its tail. The herder fought with his stick, the monster with its tail. The fight continued. Hours passed. They'd started in the morning and now it was noon. The monster said to the boy, 'Can't you look at the sun to find out how long it's been since we started our battle?'

The young man responded, 'I won't lift up my head. My people don't look at the sun. If you want to, lift up your head and look at it.'

The monster got up and looked at the sun. The herder unsheathed his sword and cut off the monster's head. The monster fell. It was dead.

The young man could then water his herd. All went well. Walking at the head of the herd, he returned to his camp singing, 'I'm not afraid of anyone or anything! The bush does not frighten me. When a farmer comes to pick a quarrel with me, we'll see what we'll see!'

These herders' tales explain the mentality and behaviour of a Mbororo very well. Shrewd and proud, a Fulani does not give in to a farmer. His cattle eat up a field; so he knocks the farmer who owns the field on the head and decamps. What can he do? He has no other solution.

All these Mbororo stories are known by us, right down to the smallest details, at least those stories that form a part of the traditions of our family. However, we always listen to them as if we do not know them. The interest we have in hearing these tales in the evenings depends on the way they're told. Each person tells them differently, but with words that are the same. In that sense, a story is always new.

CHAPTER 6

Illness

My Leprosy

I haven't spoken much to you about my leprosy[1] except to say that my father spent his time looking for medicines for us, for Maje and me. What I haven't told you was how much I suffered. I'd watch my friends on the nights we had dances. They'd jump, turn and leap; I would be out of breath after ten minutes. I couldn't dance any more. While they danced without taking a minute's rest, I soon had to sit down off to one side. I had to be content to be a spectator.

I suffered even more when I saw boys and girls scatter as I approached them. I'd hesitate, stuck, all alone. When I'd try again to join them, they'd run away again and insult me, 'Look, you're a leper. Do you want to touch us? Our mothers have told us not to let you come near us.' And, indeed, I knew their mothers did say, 'Be careful. Do not get too close to Ndudi, especially if he's sweating. You could become a leper like him.'

Those words made me angry. I'd respond the only way I could and a fight would quickly develop. I was always ready to fight. What would happen if I were watching the cows and I met someone who spoke to me that way? I'd have a go at him, whether he wanted to or not, and we'd fight.

I remember one day I hit a child on the head and gashed his scalp. His mother complained to my father. But the complaint did not go further because of Fulani good manners. 'These are just children's affairs, of no importance,' responded the elders who were consulted. My father simply gave me a look, but he scolded one of my cousins who'd been with me and who'd been quick to encourage me to hit the boy.

I'd never let an insult go by without answering back. I'd never let anyone say 'dirty leper' to my face.

In the evenings, I could never act like my friends did toward the girls. No matter how I tried to obtain the favour of one of the girls, I was always refused. If I'd insist, she'd respond, 'Oh no. Don't you realise you're a leper? Anyway, I don't like you. I don't want anything from you!' And I'd return home, all alone and very sad. Occasionally I'd receive a better welcome from a girl who was more compassionate. But because of the refusals and rejections, I felt sorry for myself. I'd sit and think for long periods.

This sickness that is leprosy has different names, one of which is 'foreign body'. It takes several forms. The Whites say my leprosy is called lepromatous leprosy. It can never be completely healed. I saw my fingers swell up and their ends turn white as if they were full of pus. They were simply drying up. The blood didn't circulate in them any more. They got smaller. Doctors cut away part of my flesh to prevent the sores from becoming larger and deeper.

My mother was a leper. This is what I've learned about her. My mother had gone to the market at Numan. She bought some thin slices of grilled meat. Fearing it was goat meat, which the Mbororo are forbidden to eat, she confronted the merchant about it. He reassured her, 'Don't worry about anything. This really is beef.' She had confidence in the merchant, but he was lying.

Right away her face became full of pustules. They were everywhere, right up to her ears. Some days when she spoke, she could hardly be understood. The illness got worse and she died from leprosy. They say she did not pay much attention to her sickness. Her many pregnancies did not help, and neither did the boiling hot water which Mbororo women use to wash their bodies for forty days after each birth.

During her illness, she had continued to breast feed me. When she died, I was given cow's milk. There's every reason to believe the leprosy germs came to me through her milk. But it was only when I was about three years old that the first signs of my illness were noticed on my shoulders.

My older brother, Maje, had the same disease. His body had many more marks of it than mine, and they showed up much earlier. People would say, 'Look at this contagious thing which his mother has passed on to him.' They talked a lot, 'You must do this; you must do that.' But they did nothing! Soon my leprosy was as bad as my brother's.

And then the same sores that my brother and I had appeared on the face of our older sister, Gogo. She also had them above her breasts. Our grandfather, our father's father, was upset. 'This thing,' he said, 'if we don't pay attention, will end up taking away all our children. We must find a remedy.' And finding a remedy, as I've already told you, was the only thing our poor father thought about.

My grandfather met someone who told him about a new way to treat leprosy, at least at the beginning of the disease: burn the affected part with a hot coal of a certain tree. My grandfather himself did the cauterisation. Blisters appeared some time later. He broke the blisters, took off the skin and rubbed the spot with a powder made from the charcoal of the same wood. This wood was *gabdi*.[2] After the powder had been applied three times, the sore dried up. Soon the only thing left was a scar, which can still be seen on my sister's body.

It was impossible to give this treatment to Maje and me: we had too many sores. They were everywhere: on our faces, all over our backs and on our buttocks. Our ears were thick. We had big noses that were always blocked. Our lips were also swollen. Our necks were big. Our heads were full of sores.

Maje and I did all we could to get rid of the disease. I remember a remedy our father had taught us to make for ourselves. It was made from the *sabuli gorki*.[3] We pulled up the roots in order to take off the bark, which we let dry. Using a mortar, we pounded the bark into powder. Then we diluted the powder in water and drank it. It took a long time to prepare this medicine. Sometimes we'd even chew the roots right at the foot of the tree in order to save time. The next day when we'd wake up, we'd look at our bodies. We'd say, 'It's true, the roots we chewed yesterday have helped a lot.' We were glad to maintain that illusion. 'Did you see? The redness is almost gone from here. We must continue to take this remedy.' And we'd go back to our *sabuli gorki*. We had such a desire to be well so we'd be like the other boys, so we could play with them and do as they did. We were forbidden to play with them, even right at our own doorsteps!

My brother Maje was sicker than I. At least, it seemed so to me. I've told you how he died. One morning I wanted to wake him up. He did not move. He said nothing. I went to tell my father, 'I tried to wake up Maje, but he doesn't move.' My father came immediately, but he realised Maje was dead. My father went to the neighbouring village to look for a Fulbe who would bury Maje according to Muslim custom. The first rains came soon after Maje's death. For us, this was the time of moving almost daily. I've forgotten the name of the small village where our clan stayed during that rainy season. On the other hand, I still have the name 'Bassama' in my ears, the place where we were forced to settle during the long weeks of the harsh dry season that followed.

My Circumcision

Bassama … we children, those of my age, we were frightened to arrive there. Actually, we'd overheard our parents saying, 'This year, when we get back to our camp at Bassama, we must get the children together who are to be circumcised and do the operation.'[4]

When we'd meet together, we'd not fail to discuss the news: 'Did you hear? It's to happen this year. It will be at Bassama. We won't escape!'

One among us had this to say: 'So much the better for us! Strong as we are, shouldn't we already be circumcised?'

Another added, 'The sooner we do it, the sooner we can sleep with girls!'

That's how we talked among ourselves. But to tell the truth, we were scared. We thought about it often.

When we arrived at Bassama, we had to wait for Ramadan to finish. Then someone overheard the men who were coming back from the market saying, 'We saw the barber Yakubu. He's agreed. He'll come tomorrow.'

Actually it was the evening of the next market day that we saw someone named Yakubu arrive. He spent the night at our camp. We looked at him with suspicion. We were not really sure he was the man. Our parents had not said anything to us, but we had heard from our older brother that this was him! He knew the man well. 'He's the one who circumcised me. Believe me, I know him!' So we were on guard. The next morning we even planned to go and hide. Our parents, who saw we were nervous, tried to reassure us; but they said neither 'yes' nor 'no'.

There was a problem about me. Should I be circumcised? People said, 'Ndudi's a leper. Will the wound ever heal?'

Everyone gave his opinion. My father was less pessimistic. 'There's no reason it won't heal. The wind in the dry season will quickly dry up the wound. Can you imagine letting him go his whole life without being circumcised?'

In fact, this stranger by the name of Yakubu really was the man. He was the barber of Bassama who would cut off our foreskins.

That same morning when the men had finished milking the cows, they called us to say, 'It's best if we do the circumcision today.'

Our hearts sank, but we responded, 'Yes, all right!' But we were shaking all over. We looked at each other; looking one way and then the other . . . Then the men took us with them. Walking ahead, they led us under a big tree, west of the cattle enclosure.

We took our clothes off, and they washed our entire bodies. Then they said to us, 'Come!' They made us sit down with our legs spread apart and our penises lying above little holes they'd dug in the ground. Sitting right next to one another, we were scared to death.

I felt someone behind me put his hands over my eyes. I saw nothing more. They did not want me to see the knife that was already in the barber's hand.

He started with me. I felt him take my penis and prepare it by pulling the skin. He was looking for the exact place where he would pass his knife. He had long fingernails, long and sharp. It passed through my mind that he could have used them instead of his knife! He pressed hard. I felt a slight movement and thought that was the cut. I thought it was over. Not at all! That was simply his fingernail making the mark. Then he made the real cut, but he did not succeed in cutting all the way. There was still a bit of white skin that he tried to catch hold of in the midst of the flowing blood. He'd already thrown into the hole the black part of the foreskin that had come off with the first cut. It was at that moment I felt pain. But I did not move. And I cried even less. I think my leprosy made me less sensitive. Then one of the assistants washed my wound. He used water in which the barber had put some powder made from the pods of the tree called *gabdi*. Every barber always has some to hand. I felt a burning sensation. Then they told me to slap my thighs to help the flow of blood which was dripping into the hole.

Then it was Ardo Inna's turn. While I was slapping my thighs, I looked toward him. I wanted to watch. As soon as he felt the pressure of the fingernail, he let out a small groan. Nothing had been done yet. That made me want to laugh. Then the knife cut for real. Ardo Inna moved. His father held him tightly. 'Coward! Did Ndudi cry or make a move? And yet you assured me you would not say anything! If you go on like this, you'll never be able to do the *soro*!' Ardo Inna calmed down, and the barber moved on.

Next was Nga Iya. The knife cut cleanly. Nga Iya cried loudly. His father insulted him. They washed his wound and then passed on to the next boy. It was Nagambu's turn. The knife cut cleanly for him too. But he leaped up and let out a fart. The assistants burst out laughing. His father was furious.

When they saw that no more blood was flowing, they made us get up; and it was at that moment we saw Nagambu had fouled himself. Someone said jokingly, 'Oh, so that's how he did it!' We were then led under a shelter which had been prepared especially for us, right next to my father's house, near the calf rope.

While we were in the hands of the barber, our mothers had prepared a big cal-abash of *sobal*,[5] which had been crushed into sour milk and a nice plate of buttered couscous. Our aunts came to bring us all sorts of good things to eat: butter and chicken. My stepmother, as usual, was totally indifferent and offered me nothing.

But I was forbidden to touch chicken. All day long, I was told that if I ate it, I'd never get well. I could eat couscous, but without butter. I saw my friends stuff themselves with meat. They aroused my appetite. As soon as my father turned his back, I'd ask them, 'Please, give me a little piece.' They gave me some. After-wards I was careful to rub my hands in the sand and wipe my mouth well so my father would not notice anything.

We spent the night together, under the surveillance of my father who'd been put in charge of us. We slept on the ground with a thin bed of straw under our backs. We slept in a circle around the fire, which the cold nights of that season made nec-essary. The feet of one boy nearly touched the head of the next. The men placed reeds between our knees; they were about half as long as an arrow. That was to keep our knees apart during the night. The ends of the reeds were wrapped with rags so they would not hurt us. If we wanted to turn over during the night, one of our knees had to stay up in the air so that our thighs could not touch each other and squeeze our penises.

There were also three small bits of reeds which had been placed in a triangle around our organs. Each was about the length of a finger. They were tied together at the angles with thread. This was all kept in place by a string that went around our waists. We were never without this support, not even during the day. We remained nude, day and night. And it was in this outfit that we went into the bush to play with our bows and arrows.

Too bad for the little girls we'd run into! We accused them of following us in order to get a close-up look at the effects of our circumcisions. We'd also chase away our little brothers who had not yet been circumcised by shooting arrows at them that had small balls of wax on their tips.

The girls, even older ones, were afraid of us. All they had to do was see us and they were in a state of panic. Throwing down their calabashes which were full of water, they'd run off screaming into the bush. But once they got far enough away to feel secure, they'd turn around to make fun of us. 'Big circumcised fools!' they'd shout at us. Their insults would make us angry. We'd try to take revenge in every possible way. Hiding in the grass, we'd set an ambush along the path to the spring. We'd jump up without warning, barring their way, and really thrash them.

Even before our return, their mothers had already complained: 'Look what that band of circumcised boys did; they wouldn't let our daughters carry water from the spring! And don't you know they broke all their calabashes?'

After several days, we were feeling better. We could even watch our fathers' calves that we were responsible for. We were still nude and very dirty! Even before our circumcision, we didn't wash ourselves. You can imagine how dirty we'd got since we'd been sleeping on our simple straw beds.

During the day when we felt itching around our scars, our father told us to put our organs in the hot sand. The ground was like a fire in this season. We followed his advice. He wanted to prevent us from scratching ourselves with our hands.

Food was not lacking. We were totally pampered by our families who would bring us only the best things. We felt better and better. The first boy allowed to go back to his home was Ardo Inna, then Nagambu and finally Nga Iya. As for me, I was at my father's house so there was no question of my having to go elsewhere. During our convalescence – which each of us continued at his own home – we loved to get back together to play.

During those days there was a feast in a nearby village for the return of a woman who had gone to her mother's house to deliver her baby. After three years absence, she was coming back with her baby to take up her life with her husband. This was like her second marriage. The young woman was named Inani. Our little group went to the marriage too. We stayed by ourselves all day long; and when it was time to eat, we were served separately.

As night fell, we had a conversation and decided it was absolutely necessary that we not leave the feast before we'd 'rinsed' ourselves - or as we also say 'washed' ourselves – to employ the language of the shameless *kori*. Weren't we healed? Yes, we decided it would be today. Moreover, we had been encouraged to do so by the old man I've already told you about, who really understood young people and who always had a word to make you laugh: 'When your wound has healed, go after the girls. Hurry to rinse yourselves. That will bring you happiness. If you do not rinse yourselves immediately, you'll never have success with the women. Maybe you won't find anyone to marry. Your organ will waste away.'

Actually our wounds were not completely healed. But spurred on by his advice, we all went together to find girls our age to ask for their favour.

'What? Aren't you still healing?' they asked. 'Aren't you worried about it!'

'What? Not healed?' we responded. 'Look!' And since we were nude, it was easy to link gesture to word. We were careful to add that our fathers would not scold us. To the contrary, it was our fathers who'd told us, 'If you have the opportunity, don't miss out!'

But the girls refused.

There was one girl who slept at her grandmother's. I followed her. I pressed myself on her. 'Please, don't refuse what I ask.'

Then she said to me, 'Wait until my grandmother's really asleep. Be patient.'

The grandmother, who could no longer see, got drowsy, while muttering a few words in her half-sleep, and stopped talking. Her granddaughter judged that the moment had come. Actually the evening concluded with an act of no importance, as might be expected.

But that did not prevent me from running back to find Nagambu's gang. 'It's done. I've rinsed myself!'

Those boys who'd obtained nothing hurried to tell my father. When I got home, he scolded me. To make me afraid, he assured me that my wound would never heal and that he'd castrate me just like a steer. One might say that his curse came true. My wound, which had nearly disappeared, reopened. My friends had already started wearing their loin cloths for a long time whereas I had to keep wearing the bit of rag tied around my waist.

Once we were well, many of our relatives and friends came, even from far away, to congratulate us and offer gifts. They wanted to show that they were happy to see we'd left childhood behind and entered into adolescence. The gifts included heifers. You can imagine our joy when we saw the animals arrive several days later! We were so happy to look at them and to tell ourselves that they were really ours, no one's but ours.

The Miraculous Waters of Jimeta

Soon after my circumcision, my father heard about the miraculous waters of Jimeta. He took me with him and, after a long trip in a truck, we arrived at that place. Why the trip?

For several days there had been a rumour that water had suddenly sprung out of the ground. It healed people. It made lepers healthy. Blind people who washed their eyes in the water recovered their sight. The deaf who sprinkled water in their ears began to hear. Sterile women also went there in hope of having a baby. When he heard about all these miracles, my father decided to take me there. So after one day in a truck, we were in Jimeta.

When we arrived, we learned that this water had suddenly sprung up near the grave of someone who'd been dead a long time. His name had been forgotten, and no one there had really worried about the grave because it was in the middle of a field of manioc. Was this a holy man? No doubt he was, but I do not really know much about him. Anyway, it was impressive to see such beautiful water, clear and cool, spring up in this place. The terrain was rocky. We were in the middle of the dry season. So when a farmer pulled up a manioc root and saw this beautiful water gush forth, it was a miracle.

The people made the hole larger. Water quickly filled it. So everyone said, 'This is miracle water! This is water from God!' People started to drink it. They washed their faces with it. Some saw that it helped them. News of it spread through the neighbourhood and even farther afield because the radio reported it. This is how the news reached my father's ears. But, unfortunately, a few days before we arrived, the people of that area began to turn the water into a business. Before that, visitors drank as much as they wanted, praying in the manner they'd heard about. Now people spoke about money. My father could only have the water if he paid for it.

He rubbed mud all over my body. I lay down in the sun so the mud would dry more quickly. The hairs of my body stuck to this mud. It hurt. Even before the dried mud starting coming off, I asked my father to wash me with water that could be found a little further away, water he did not have to pay for. That's what he did. He took off the mud that had transformed me into an earth-coloured statue with my eyes sticking out.

Our stay in that place lasted five days. There were many people. However, we did not see any blind man recover his sight or any lame man walk. But in spite of that, people continued to arrive: children whose arms were paralysed, older people who could not move except when carried in a blanket, blind people, many blind people. A huge number of people slept at the edge of the village where they could buy some food. Night and day there were doughnuts to eat. Some people bought doughnuts to offer as alms to their neighbours. Before leaving, the rich even gave away money, always in the spirit of almsgiving. In general, anyone who drank from the spring felt obliged to give alms in one way or another.

Our return did not go unnoticed. All the Mbororo around knew that Koyne and his son Ndudi had gone to the miraculous water of Jimeta. And some neighbours had gone with us – another leper and a woman to whom God had not yet given a child.

People were waiting impatiently for us. 'How did it go? Is Ndudi better?' they asked my father. 'Certainly!' responded my father. 'He's much better than before. There's no doubt about it.' I said the same thing. But actually nothing about me had changed. Absolutely nothing. It was like adding water to water. Does that change anything? Nothing! It was just the same for me. This 'better' that my father was speaking of is what they refer to as being 'better like a Fulani'.

In fact, I should explain that when someone asks about the health of a sick person, a true Fulani can only answer, 'He's better.' He can't give any other response, even if the sick man is at death's door. I too had already learned that custom. It's part of our heritage. Therefore my response was the same as my father's: 'Thanks to God, I feel better!' But it was not true.

Saying a sick man is worse is to complain, to moan. Complain to whom? Complain about whom? He who believes that everything comes from God - good health, sickness, death – must accept whatever comes without complaining. Even when he's dying, a real believer will say, 'I'm getting better.' And he'll even add, 'I thank God.'

To be honest, it must be said that some people see this attitude as Fulani pride, which has nothing to do with religion. As for me, I do not know what to think.

'Black Medicines'

So it was to Bassama that we had returned after our pilgrimage to the waters of Jimeta. The hottest season had just begun. The animals were so thin that we had to stay where we were. So we went back to Bassama. Moreover, there was every reason to remain at that place, especially with its big pools to water our herds.

It was there in Bassama, I remember, that my father began to teach me about the 'black medicines', bush medicines which are mainly made from plants: from leaves, bark and roots. His knowledge, which was very broad, was handed down from his father, from his grandfather and from his great-grandfather. Among all his children, I was the one he'd chosen to receive this heritage. He could not teach the others about them because he was always very reserved toward them. I was the first of his children he had spoken to by calling his name.

When we'd walk in the bush, he'd stop and say to me, 'Look closely at this plant. This is what I bring you for your illness. You must be able to obtain it, even if I'm not here.' He also showed me plants that were for the herd. He knew which plants would help the cows to be fertile, others which would protect them from illnesses. He knew which plants would keep him safe from accidents and from the evil doings of chiefs of the area.

He made sure I remembered certain details: 'Look at this bark,' he'd say to me. 'If you want to use it, you must take certain steps. In the evening of the day before, put some millet seeds at the foot of the tree you want to take the bark from. The next day if you see that all the seeds have been removed by termites, then, but only then, strip off the bark. Notice which direction you're facing. Put the powder you obtain into some water. If you drink it, you'll be able to face the gravest dangers.'

My father would also dig up some wild onions. He'd cook them with some real onions. 'With this,' he said, 'the chiefs will have no power over you. If you're accused of something, you're bound to win out, even if everything is against you.'

I always watched my father prepare the *karfa* which made the cows wild and dangerous when necessary. He'd spill a powder on the glowing red embers. The smoke would blow toward the herd. Thanks to *karfa* the animals would take flight immediately at the first alert. They would be on guard against the approach of a farmer, especially if he had bad intentions toward them. One vulture head – dried, crushed and sifted - was part of the formula of this powder.

The knowledge he gave me allowed me to treat myself and to be of service to people of the villages where I lived. It was seldom that they did not give me some money in exchange. Today I still remember ten or so formulas. First to come to mind are the love potions made to attract the love of women. And I know how to cure upset stomachs and how to treat the 'clap'. I know what needs to be taken in order to become invisible in time of danger. I was also shown how to make 'the medicine of iron' which prevents iron in all its forms – knives, spears, bullets – from penetrating the body. But I've never practised making it. Would it work? I don't know because I've never tried it.

On the other hand, I can still today prepare the formula made from scented plants to make people friendly. I use it before starting out on a trip. I can also put evil curses on people I do not like. And I know some tricks of sleight-of-hand, which are based simply on dexterity or guile. We call this *sidabaru*.

If I were in the North – north of the River Benue – where even today all the plants you need can be found, I could make a formula that shoots needles into a person's body or another formula which extracts them. It was not my father who taught me that, but certain villagers from northern Nigeria.

Ever since I was a child, I've known how to make charms, particularly those carried as a protection against fear. My father had not gone to Koranic school. But at his house he kept many sheets of paper carefully arranged in a leather sack. They were pages of writing taken from our Holy Books. He did not know how to read, but when he felt the need, he'd go see a marabout. My father would ask the marabout to copy one of those pages on his wooden slate, explaining why he wanted it done. The marabout chose from among the pages spread in front of him the page which was most suitable. Then he'd write it, wash off the slate and give my father the water to drink. Sometimes my father would save that water in a bottle and pour it on the natron which he gave the animals to lick.

But, as I've told you, my father's speciality was 'black medicines' which he made himself. That's why he always had around him piles of bark, roots, parasitic plants, berries, dried fruits and bush figs. All that was ready to be pounded. At the bottom of the mortar, under the pestle, those ingredients were transformed into a thick paste. The paste was spread out or crumbled on a mat and left to dry. In the evening when the paste was really dry, my father would pound it again. But, he told me, in order for some powders to be effective, he had to wait to pound them until after the herd had returned to the paddock. When he'd sifted the powder very finely, he'd put it into a square rag. He paid great attention to the knot he tied: it enabled him to identify the powder again. Then he'd throw all his different coloured rags into one pouch. Sometimes he slid a small stick into the knot.

All day long visitors flocked around. Some came from far away. After the usual greetings, some people made a sign to my father that they wanted to whisper in his ear. Others made no bones about it and would ask directly: 'Koyne, I have a cow with a swollen foot, and the swelling is spreading to the top of its leg. Couldn't you come to see her and tell me what you think?'

My father would go there. Quickly he'd say, 'Good, I have what you need. Come, follow me.'

Once back in his *buteru*,[6] my father would signal for me to bring his big sack. He'd put everything out on his mat and begin to search through it. He'd take out one of those little packages, open it, close it again, open another and then close that one. He'd hold one up to his nose and look closely at the knot of another. You could hear him thinking aloud. I'd watch him do that, and sometimes I found what he was looking for before he did. 'Papa,' I'd say proudly, 'isn't this the one?' Then when a new client came to see him later that day, he showed his confidence in my powers of observation and my good memory.

Money was never talked about. My father never sold anything. He never took a penny for his powders.

My father also had the reputation of being able to heal eyes. He treated this sort of illness with incantations. Did someone have an eye complaint? People would say to him, 'Go see Koyne. He knows many formulas.' These incantations did not come from the Koran. They were not taken from any book. They had been handed down from father to son. I knew a certain number of them, but I've forgotten them all.

This is how he worked. He'd take a string made of palm leaf fibres. He'd tie a knot and spit on it; then he'd continue to make knots and spit. He knotted; he spat. Then he'd give the cord to his visitor and tell him to put it around the neck of the sick man. Three days later, if God were willing, the eyes of the sick man would be healed. People also consulted him about burns. And he was known for treating the children's illness called 'bush sickness'. For that, he used smoke in addition to spittle.

No sick person ever stayed at our house. And I never saw a mentally ill person at our compound. My father would treat them, but always through an intermediary.

Figure 6.1: Cooking meat for a feast

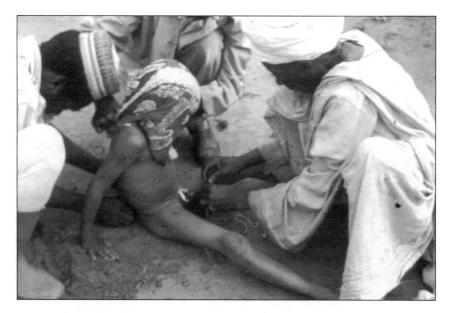

Figure 6.2: Circumcision

CHAPTER 7

Seasonal Migration and the Wet Season Camp

At Bassama, where we met up with our family again after our trip to the waters of Jimeta, we stayed about two more months, the most difficult months of the season. Our bony animals stumbled about lamentably. They hardly had the strength to walk down to the pools where a little bit of water had escaped evaporation by the sun. We were in a hurry to leave, to go somewhere else.

To leave! That idea brought joy to the hearts of my friends. They waited impatiently for the time when we would move daily. The oldest already imagined themselves walking at the head of the herd.

I too, a nomad at heart, was happy we'd soon be walking again on the bush trails. However, I was apprehensive. I did not have a lot of strength. I often asked myself if my health would bear the long walks. Each morning as I woke up, I saw my leprosy spreading. I often thought about the fact that this disease had killed my brother. My mother had also died of leprosy. I too would be taken by it. I thought about that day and night.

But travelling in the bush[1] in search of greener pastures is our life as Mbororo. It's part of our heritage, whether it pleases us or not on certain days. There's never a question of quitting this kind of life and building houses like the villagers do. This is the way we differ from the Fulbe. We all know – from the youngest to the oldest – that we are not like the others. We are Mbororo, that is to say, people of the bush. We do not complain about this. We accept this situation and we like it.

The Movement of the Herd

Goodbye, Bassama!

It's the height of the sun and the strength of its rays that fix the moment of departure. Everything's ready. The young man who'll walk at the head has already picked up his quiver and bow. He holds a stick in his hand. On his head he has a large-brimmed straw hat. Hanging everywhere on him are small bottles and flasks of medicines.

And so he leaves, followed by several sturdy young girls. Together they form the lead group. The cows follow. Little by little, their line stretches out.

The mother has not yet finished her preparations for the departure. She's busy with the bundle she'll carry on her head. The young children chase the chickens, which are given to the grandmother, who carries them on her back as if they were babies. The children carry some, which hang head down from their shoulders. Two children sit astride a donkey, carefully tied together with a thick rope.

It's this group which brings up the rear – many women and children, but also the elderly; sometimes there's an old woman on a horse.

At the head of the group, the young men, accompanied by the young women who may be their wives, continue walking rapidly. They do not worry too much about what's going on behind them – even if there's a shout from far back that one of the pack-oxen is losing its load. A group that slows down is sometimes passed by a family that has followed on its heels since morning. Without slowing down, the families just exchange the usual greetings.

During these seasonal migrations through the bush, not every day is the same as the next. Some days it's a pleasure to walk; you do not feel the fatigue. But other times things happen to slow us down. It's often the old men and women who cause the delay or the children who are hungry and sulk, or a calf born along the route that must be carried, or some other bother. There are many happenings which I'll tell you about later.

But when the group is made up of young people in the prime of life – strong men, vigorous girls, older children, cows without young calves – there's no greater pleasure than walking at a good pace, especially if the animals have been treated with *karfa*. How proud the herder is when, all alone at its head, he leads the herd in his wake! He runs. The animals are on his heels. He can practically feel their horns in his back. Sometimes he must slow them down with his stick.

And when other Mbororo who are already encamped see him pass so rapidly, everyone sings his praises. 'Ah! Here's someone who knows how to take care of his animals! Look how they stick to him! But isn't that so-and-so, the son of so-and-so? Well there's nothing surprising about that; doesn't his father have the reputation of knowing about *karfa*?'

The Gongola River

The bush became green bit by bit. Our animals gained weight and the calabashes were full of milk. However, we could not linger very long in one place. We'd quickly use up the new pastures. Each day we'd advance toward the place where we'd planned to make our rainy season camp.

To reach there, we had to cross the Gongola River. 'We must hurry to get to the other side of the river,' some of the elders would say. 'The first rains quickly swell the river and make it overflow. By lingering here, we risk not being able to get to the other side this year. Let's plan to cross next Saturday'

So that day, just after sunrise, we found ourselves gathered at the edge of the river. It was full. The current was rapid and there were eddies. The cows and sheep would certainly have to fight against the current. As for us, the only thing we could do was talk to the boatmen. They were already there, waiting for customers.

A good swimmer crossed to the other side of the river. Once there, he sat on a big branch overhanging the water and called out his refrain. He did not stop repeating: O-le! O-le! This was to call the cow at the head of the herd. She made her decision and resolutely entered the water. All the others followed, spreading out in a large arc. The current would carry them fairly far downstream, but eventually to the opposite bank. However, some weak animals were carried very far from the herdsman.

We lost one ox. He had rushed into the water before anyone had taken the baggage off his back. The heavy load prevented him from swimming, and he was carried far downstream by the current. When he was found, he'd been dead a long time. For us, because the ox had not been slaughtered according to ritual, it had become 'vulgar carrion'.[2] We could not even sell it to recover a few pennies. Our religion even forbids giving the carcass away, and certainly we cannot exchange it for any services. So when the boatmen, who knew very well they would get the meat, suggested we could have free passage, all of us Mbororo said unanimously, 'The meat's for you, but we cannot accept anything in exchange, not even free transport. We'll pay our passage as always.'

The boatmen continued their coming and going. In their canoes, they loaded people, sheep and goats, pell-mell among the bundles. For a donkey they tied a rope around its muzzle before it entered the water; then, while the donkey swam, one man held its head out of the water while his companion manoeuvred the canoe with a pole.

The first herders who crossed with the majority of the animals did not wait for the rest of us. They continued on ahead. Once they'd set up camp for the night, some came back to help us. When the peasants had brought the last of us over, they hurried to skin the steer they'd already hauled up on shore. You can imagine the welcome they'd receive in the village!

Sometimes it becomes necessary to cross a deep river without either boatmen or canoes. Not all Mbororo know how to swim. Sometimes we have to rely on the people who live along the river, usually fishermen-farmers. They're accustomed to carrying people across the river on their backs. Then one must endure the spectacle – which is not very enjoyable for a husband, of seeing his own wife being carried on the back of one of those awful pagans! You'll hear the woman complaining, 'Poor me! What misery! Look at me on the back of this awful farmer! But what else can I do?' And when they've crossed the river, the swimmer takes a deep breath as he straightens up his back and then pretends he's being carried away by the current. He goes further out, returns and then circles around. The breasts of the young woman really excite him! When he finally puts her on shore, he quickly goes back to the other side, thinking about the next woman.

On the other hand, when he has to carry an old woman, he uses a calabash. He asks her to lie down with her stomach on the calabash and to hang on tight. Then, swimming with one hand, he holds her with the other as he moves forward. But if a young woman wants to be carried that way, he'll protest, 'Oh no! Not you! You aren't heavy enough. You won't stay on top of the water. I'd better carry you on my back.' Oh, those pagans! They really know the ropes. And we even have to pay to watch this sight!

But we're even more afraid of bridges. There are trails in the bush where we cannot avoid them; we must cross them. In general, the bridges are tree trunks, joined together by vines and covered with earth. If there are houses around the bridge forming a village, as often happens, we're ready to walk several days out of our way in order to avoid such spots.

When a donkey sees a bridge and he hears the noise of his hoofs as he starts to cross it – *kata, kata, kata!* – he refuses to go forward. He turns around. Our horses become nervous. Our cows run away. They'd settle down if we Mbororo were by ourselves. But the villagers come to watch. They look on and make fun of us. There they are, surprised to see us carrying all sorts of baggage on our heads. They laugh at our old women who carry chickens on their backs like babies. They make remarks about our women who have their wrapper-skirts drawn up over their knees, about the milk which is running down their backs, about the children whose noses are full of snot and whose eyelids are stuck together with caked dirt. 'Ah, these Mbororo! What on earth do they look like? They're filthy!'

This is why we do everything possible to avoid towns and villages. For us, it's the bush. We know nothing else. But when we stop for the night, all these incidents are material for jokes; they are even exaggerated. The men laugh openly as they sit on their mats; while the women, who are in their shelters, hide their laughter, not daring to raise their voices. We chatter and have a good time.

We've laughed a long time about the adventure of one brave old man who was crossing the Gongola River. He and his wife had no children and only a few animals. Usually they joined a larger group. But this particular day – since his wife was no longer as hardy as her husband – they had fallen quite a distance behind the others. They had no real pack-oxen, but only some bull-calves that were flighty and poorly trained. And those young animals jumped, galloped and wildly shook the bundles on their backs. Then one bundle fell to the ground. It was too heavy for the old man to put on the animal's back by himself. He waited for help, but there was no one on the horizon. Finally he saw a farmer coming toward him. It's well known that cows do not like the bad odour of pagans, so the cows all scattered when they smelled him. His wife had all the trouble in the world in barring the cows' path. Finally, with great effort, the old man managed to put his belongings on the back of the bull-calf. They started walking again – the man in front, his wife behind. She walked along with a donkey that had its flanks covered with chickens hanging upside down. She had a lot of trouble following, the poor lady, especially because she was herding three sheep in front of her, one of which had a limp.

When they arrived at the river, no one was there. The boatmen had gone back to their village. But the cows, seeing the tracks of the herd that had gone before them, were nervous and seemed tempted to follow. The old man thought there was no possibility of doing that. There was the donkey, his wife and the three sheep. Tomorrow it would be daylight. Other Mbororo would certainly be crossing the river too. There would be boatmen. It was better to spend the night on this side.

That's what the man was thinking when the animals went into the water all by themselves. He hesitated to go himself. But what could he do to stop them? Anyway, it was too late. He heard the old woman shout. 'The cows are on the other side, and you're here. Don't you see they'll destroy the farmers' manioc fields?'

The man could only answer, 'What do you want me to do? You know the water's deep. You won't gain anything if I drown.'

'You drown? There's no question of that. There isn't as much water as you think.'

The old man, who remembered there were hyenas in the area, made his decision. But he was hardly in the water when the current carried him off. And so he drifted away. His wife saw him disappear, come back to the surface and then disappear again. Then she did not see him any more.

The man was wearing wide, baggy pants held up by a long cord. And this strong cord, made with a long wick of a kerosene lamp, had caught on a root at the bottom of the water. He thought he was being held by a hippopotamus. He struck at it with his hands when he wasn't swallowing water. But it was impossible to get free! His wife did all she could to scare the supposed hippopotamus. All of a sudden the cord finally came loose. After swimming a few strokes, the man succeeded in getting caught in a thornbush. He escaped by the skin of his teeth.

Once out of the water, he ran after his cows, caught them and led them back toward the river bank. His wife was still on the other side, but he did not have enough courage to go back in the water and join her. He saw her there with her donkey, sheep and chickens. The poor chickens, which had not been on the ground since morning, were stretching their necks toward the ground to try to peck. The unperturbed donkey did not move a muscle.

Before the end of the day, God happened to send a farmer passing by. The old man promised the farmer two *pam*[3] if the farmer would bring his wife across the river. The man waved the bills which he held in his hand. 'Allah! God is my witness that I'll give these to you.' The farmer grabbed the money, took off his clothes, untied an old rotten canoe and crossed over. He brought the wife, the donkey, the sheep and the chickens back to the other side.

At last the man and his wife were reunited. They camped on high ground, and the next day they rejoined the group they'd been travelling with.

The Rainy-Season Camp

Two days later it would not have been possible for us to have crossed the Gongola River because it had started to rain so hard. We'd have had to do what some other groups did: turn back; and for long months we'd have found ourselves cut off from our relatives and friends who had crossed at an opportune moment.

Little by little we saw an increase in the number of herds grazing near us; they were on the right, they were on the left. There were cows on the hills, and more cows in the valleys. Everywhere there were spots of red, black and even white moving on the green.

And so it happened that, quite naturally, here we were together, with several families living one next to the other. You can imagine the joy the children had in meeting their cousins again! But this still was not the final gathering. Our parents had put too much care into building their huts; surely they wouldn't make our rainy-season village in this place, we wondered. In fact, the very next day we heard the adults discussing which place should be chosen for the camp. Some claimed last year's huts were still in good condition. We would only have to give them a sweep with a broom. 'Sweep and enter', as we say in such a case. Others had noticed that donkeys had been in the huts and ruined them. Several of the roof poles had also been taken away by neighbouring farmers.

It was finally decided we would not go back to the same camp. We'd move a little away from the village of the local people. We'd settle west of this village with the strange name of Wuro Ginaji, that is, 'Village of the Spirits'. There, it was said, was a beautiful sandy plain where we would not have to walk in mud.

The centre of the village of Wuro Ginaji was occupied by some Fulbe called the Witi. Pagans who spoke different languages lived in the surrounding countryside. There were the Bura, Kananku, Lungundu and Tangalé. There were no other Mbororo except us, the Jafun; only here and there were a few Kiri, Kessu and Kitaku who led lives similar to ours, spoke the same language, but refused to be called Mbororo. There were no Wodabe families there at that time. However, on a hill near ours, there were some Bodi.

It was to this village that our women went every day to sell milk so they could bring back all the things necessary for making meals: millet, leafy vegetables and various condiments for our sauces. We showed our friendship toward the Fulbe by selling them our injured animals at a low price. Like all Muslims, they only accepted animals that had been slaughtered by cutting their throats. Among those Fulbe were many cattle herders. They were waiting until they had enough cattle so they could return to the bush and lead the kind of life we did. They did not farm unless they'd lost their animals, in an epidemic for example. They used their income to buy cattle so they could go back to nomadic life. The hope of becoming herders again gave them strength to work as farmers.

Considering them similar to ourselves we invited them to all our feasts: to celebrate marriages, name-giving ceremonies and the end of Koranic studies. One of their marabouts buried our dead and presided over all our religious ceremonies. We had more confidence in their religious knowledge than in our own.

We hired the pagans to do some of our hard work. Among them, many of the Bura were Muslims. The Tangalé and the Kananku were more apt to be attracted to the mission, the religion of the Nassara.[4]

At that time when I first heard talk about the mission, I did not really know what that meant. I used the word, but I did not understand it. I saw that those who were part of it met under a straw shelter. Seated on tree trunks which had been placed on the ground, they had little books in their hands. They listened to someone who spoke something like a 'sermon'. I noticed they dressed better on Sundays than on other days. And they all gathered together – men, women and children. They sang. They had a big feast every year which they called *Kirsimet* (Christmas).

But in the families of those farmers, religion divided the people. Some joined the mission, others were Muslims, but most of them stayed just as they had always been. Why change? You could recognise this last group by the way they dressed: the men were often nude, with a simple cover over their penises; the women had a bunch of leaves in front and in back, like a loin cloth; up to a fairly mature age, the young girls continued to go nude, their bodies covered with shea nut oil.

Someone called *Pasto* circulated from one village to another. He came from the town of Numan to invite the pagans to join the mission. He travelled right up to the mountain villages. But up there, no one wanted to follow him. They even insulted him. He was a Bata and did not understand what they said, but he had someone with him who translated everything into the Hausa language. You'd hear the venerable old men stand up against the religion of the Whites. 'Do we need to follow this new religion? Everything the Whites say is a lie. As for us, we've learned other things.'

In one of the villages, one market day, the Pasto came, accompanied by a White. That was the first time the people had seen a white man. It was the first time for me too. Everyone looked at him as though he were a strange beast. We heard all sorts of remarks. Someone said, 'Did you see his hair? And his eyes? They're grey like cat's eyes. How can he see with them? And his fingernails? Did you see them?'

People talked and talked. Some even said Whites do not die. Others added that Whites never need to go to the toilet. It was especially our old women who spoke. 'Yes,' they said, 'they're never sick. They don't die. They can make whatever they like, even living things. Nothing is impossible for them. They make things that fly, and even more – everything that passes through their heads!' I heard all these remarks.

Each year when we came back there during the rainy season, we noticed the mission was making progress among the people. They had received a lot of money to construct a large house of prayer. Later there was a school which the pagans and the Muslims would have wanted all their children to go to, both boys and girls. The Pasto also came to see us. From time to time, he was accompanied by Whites who came to take photos. The children hid. They were really afraid.

The 'Watered' Bodi

That year during the wet season, the camp closest to ours belonged to the Bodi clan. Their young people are always full of belligerence when they meet us at the *soro*.

Our proximity to the Bodi worried our parents, who warned us once more to be on guard against them. 'Watch out, little ones! If you play with Bodi children, there are words which you must never pronounce in front of them; for example, monkey, pig,[5] hot pepper, dog ****. If you insult them, never tell them they have the teeth of warthogs or the a*** of monkeys. When you say those words in front of them, they throw themselves on you and do the worst sorts of things. You know why!'

We reassured them, 'Don't worry. We know what you mean. We know their customs.' Our parents alluded to the custom which the Bodi have of 'watering' their children. But we did not know any more about it!

One day we found ourselves together, Jafun children and Bodi children. We quickly decided to have a *soro*. We were five against ten. The game was not equal, but it began calmly. It degenerated quickly. We shouted insults at each other that were more and more crude. What a good occasion for us to throw in their faces those forbidden words that made them furious! But we did not dare insult them too much because we realised the insults would come back on us. All of a sudden, without our knowing why, some of them began to moan and then to howl like wild beasts. They dropped their *soro* sticks in order to arm themselves with their large herdsman's sticks they'd left at the foot of a tree. There was a moment of confusion among them, and then they divided into two camps: those who had been 'watered' and the others. This last group seemed calm, but the others – both boys and girls – all screamed at once and fell on top of each other.

They ran toward us, threatening us with their raised sticks. What could we do except run away? The Bodi who had not drunk the potion shouted to us, 'Run towards the east! Turn quickly toward the east! the east! the east!' We followed their advice. At that moment, all the children chasing us fell down.

We were told later that if we had continued to run toward the west, they'd have caught us and we'd have been doomed to certain death. However, running to the east paralyses them and makes them lose their senses; they fall down and remain still as if they were dead.

When I was a little older, I asked my father for an explanation. This is what he told me: 'As far as I know, the children are forced to swallow a potion: some water in which the most repugnant things you can imagine have been soaked – excrement of pig and monkey, large caterpillars, millipedes, snails, itchy plant burrs, new-born baby's excrement, the afterbirth of a cow that has just given birth, etc. All this soaks for weeks and months in a large pot. They add hot pepper and bits of pig they have bought in secret from the farmers – a bit of its tail and its scrotum. They know all this has a satanic stench which is offensive to the Muslim spirit. This explains why the people they attack are saved by running toward the east, the direction of Mecca, the direction dear to men who pray. Certainly this custom is pagan; they know it. But it's deeply anchored in their tradition, and they do not want to stop it.'

Later someone else gave me the following details. From time to time a certain number of children who have reached the age to be 'watered', as they say, are presented to the elders of their clan. The council makes a selection: some are too young or too puny, and others still do not have their parents' permission. The elders discuss the choices.

In the end, they agree on certain names: some boys, but also some girls.

On the appointed day, they grab these children without making any noise. Some of the children really try to escape, but they're caught and forced to go to the place that's been prepared. A large pot is brought, stinking and swarming with worms. Some of the assistants wear wild pig skins made into aprons, which have been passed from one generation to another for this abominable ceremony.

The children are there, attached to a long rope. You might think they were calves! Someone takes a bow string and makes a slip knot, which he passes around the neck of the first child. While he pulls, another person armed with a big wooden spoon full of this awful mixture is waiting. When the child who is choking tries to breathe, he opens his mouth; at that moment the contents of the spoon are poured into his mouth. The rope is loosened, and the assistants move on to the next child.

Once the children are 'watered' like this, they lie there, stretched out, incapable of getting up. Those who try to stand up fall down again and lie prostrate. The assistants sit near them, impassive. They wait. From time to time, an assistant bends over to look at the body of one of the little ones. 'He seems dead,' he says, turning away toward the others. Sometimes there are deaths. The children may lie prostrate for hours. For about ten days, they do not eat or drink. They all have diarrhoea. Much later, there are some who still are not completely well. Some are so shocked they do not recover. There are always two or three out of ten who react very badly. In these cases, after several weeks they're given an antidote to drink, which will counteract the effect of the first potion.

When I discovered these secrets, I thanked God I was not born into one of the Bodi clans – and not the Geroji or Ba clans either – which put their children through such miseries. I asked my father if we'd done the same thing in times past. 'Never,' he told me. And I've always heard it said that when one of our family groups is incorporated into one of those clans, the family would never want to adopt this custom of 'watering', the exact name of which I've forgotten.

But we Jafun children, those of our age, were merciless. Many times during our games we got angry and made the Bodi children explode. When they had fallen over, we hid ourselves so we could see their parents come. They'd take a medicine from their pockets, which they always carried for such cases. Then they came to complain to our parents about the naughty tricks we played on their children. 'Please, watch your children. You know our customs. If we had not arrived quickly yesterday, some of our children would certainly have died because of them. Punish them well!'

Our parents always taught us a lesson. They forbade us to do it again, but they knew us. Realising we would not pay any attention to them, they preferred to move camp and put a good distance between the Bodi and us.

Figure 7.1: Loading pack ox for seasonal migration

Figure 7.2: Following the herd on seasonal migration

Figure 7.3: Herds ford river during seasonal migration

CHAPTER 8

Family Festivals

The Name-Giving Ceremony

The rainy season is the season of reunions among the Mbororo. Therefore, it's the season of family feasts. Everyone has put off celebrating them until now. How could a large group be invited when families are so widely scattered, when there's no more milk, when food is lacking and the cows are thin?

Some days after our arrival at Wuro Ginaji, all the conditions were right. The first big family reunion of the year was the name-giving ceremony for the first-born of my maternal aunt Jabiya. She is dead now. God give her pardon! The baby was a girl.

I obtained permission from my father to attend. 'On condition,' he told me, 'that you stay near me. I don't want you running around with the other children. Yes, you'll have to stay with me. I'll watch so you don't eat fatty things or drink fresh milk. You know very well the medicines I give you have no effect if you don't follow your diet.'

The evening before, my father was busy preparing the clothes I would wear. He asked my older sister Gogo to redo my hair. That did not take long because I had very little hair. And anyway, with children, there is not much to do; they are not very difficult.

I also got my charm belt ready to wear, a belt like every boy wore around his waist. It was a girdle of leather, inside of which there were different charms: fibres of certain trees mixed with the hair of a mule and several amulets. It was my father who had prepared the belt for me. He had even explained to me everything he put inside. There were all sorts of powders, some for protection against snake bites, others against the effect of poison, and many other things which he alone knew the secret of. I rubbed my belt with butter to make it shine. My older brother Musa did the same; so did my friends.

Everyone was busy getting ready. Once our hair was fixed, we boys hurried off to be seen. 'Do you see how nicely my hair has been done?' We were happy to admire the silhouettes of our hair-do projected on the ground by the sun. Some admired themselves in tiny pieces of mirror they'd stolen from their sisters.

Everyone was busy preparing an ointment to rub on their faces on the morning of departure. This is how it was made: You gather some flowers from the tree we call *karehi*.[1] They are very fragrant. You put the flowers into a mortar and pound them and add some shea nut oil. Then you get some pieces of a broken mirror which are ground into very fine powder, using a millstone. Everything is mixed together to make an ointment, which is poured into a flask. Before leaving in the morning, we poured a few drops of this ointment into the palms of our hands to rub on our faces. Smelling good gave us confidence. Then we outlined our eyes with antimony powder. I asked my father to put some on me when he was putting on his.

The morning of the feast arrived. The women left first. On their heads were big calabashes full of milk. The children followed. I would have liked to join them. They signalled to me, but my father held me back. Once there, however, I was able to sneak away while he carried on a long conversation. I joined up with my friends. They'd put aside all the things I liked but was forbidden to eat: milk, couscous drowned in butter and fatty meat. At my age, these family reunions were mainly opportunities to play and eat.

But a name-giving ceremony (*inderi*) is held primarily to give a name to a child. This is done on the eighth day after the birth if conditions are favourable. A *mallam*[2] chooses the name, so on the eve of the 'baptism',[3] someone had gone to Wuro Ginaji to fetch him.

For the family who holds such a festival, it is not just an impromptu affair. Provisions must be on hand – millet, rice, tea, etc. – and kola nuts cannot be forgotten. Millet is poured into goat-skin sacks, which are very deep but not very wide; about ten sacks are filled, each containing about thirty bowls of millet. The sacks are carried to the homes of neighbours who are thereby, without ceremony, invited to participate in the preparations for the feast. Since these tall sacks almost stand up when they're left at the neighbour's house, we say we have gone to 'lean' them there. Everyone knows what that means.

After the women have pounded the millet at home, they make small millet balls which they carry to the host's encampment on the morning of the 'baptism'. When the balls have been broken into sour milk, they're presented to the guests. Early in the morning, at sunrise, people closest to the family gather west of the house, not far from the calf rope.

They begin by shaving the baby's head. A calabash is brought in which some *barkehi* leaves are floating on top of a little milk. The baby's hair is dampened with it. Then someone who's skilled at this task shaves the head. He uses a very sharp knife or – what's more often used today – a razor blade purchased at the market. The baby is held on its grandmother's knees.

The hair is not thrown on the ground but carefully put into the milk in the calabash. When the operation is finished, everything – the milk, hair and *barkehi* leaves – is poured on the roof of the mother's house, just over the doorway. In accordance with *pulaku* the mother is not present. She does not appear all day long. She takes refuge in a neighbouring village. She will not return until the evening after the guests have departed. The baby has no breast to suck on this day. He's only given a little cow's milk.

After this ceremony, the *mallam* is asked to proceed with choosing a name. He consults his papers. He determines the day of the birth. He looks for some correspondence between that day and certain texts. Then he knows what name must be given. A certain text, a certain day of birth, a certain name. On that day, the right name was Hawa. The *mallam* holds up his hands in front of himself and, looking at his palms as if they were books, he recites the proper phrases. He prays. All the guests raise their hands too. Everyone has a *barkehi* branch in one hand. The women, who stay on the doorstep of their house, do the same. The prayer finishes with a loud recitation of the *Alfatiya*,[4] said while passing both hands over the face, from the head to the chest. Then everyone, when he as a chance, blows on the child and says, 'May God make you grow! May you grow old enough to respond to the calling of your name!' Each guest then may take one or two kola nuts.

The guests then gather around a bowl of couscous, which has been prepared in a special way for this occasion and which has a special name. But before touching this food, the grandparents will have already chosen their own name for the child, a funny name or a nickname,[5] complimentary or not, in connection with some event. In my case, my major name, which was given to me by the *mallam*, is Umaru while my other name, Ndudi, was given in honour of a stranger by that name who was present at my name-giving ceremony.[6]

Many Mbororo children – both boys and girls – have the name Ser, in honour of the Ser (French *Soeur*: nursing sister) who was in charge of the maternity clinic where they were born. There are also some named Para in honour of the Mbororo Para (*Père*: priest).

For Hawa, the best nickname the grandmothers could find to give her was Atta. This is a Hausa word which means 'rich merchant'. They wanted to emphasise the great wealth of the baby's mother who had just inherited many cows.

After the name-giving, the men move toward the herd, which is still in the paddock. The grandmothers are invited to come and choose. 'I want five animals!' the first grandmother says. 'Yes, if we don't kill five, I won't pick any!'

'I choose this beautiful heifer!' says another. 'I know she's pregnant. So what! She's nice and fat!'

And so they continue joking like that. Someone finishes by saying, 'Look, let's be serious! Enough jokes!'

Finally the paternal grandfather closes the matter, 'It will be this steer … .'

The young people take hold of the steer. They begin by tying up the back legs with a long rope. The rope is pulled toward the head in order to tie it around the base of the horns. Then with some pushing and others pulling, the young people make the animal lose his balance and fall over, lying on his side. Someone takes the steer's head by the horns and fixes the two points into the ground.

The *mallam* takes his knife and gives directions so the head will be oriented correctly. With the knife in his hand, he waits for the neck to be positioned in just the right way, being sure nothing is in his way. Then he bends over and pronounces the words of the ritual: '*Bissimillahi*. In the name of God!' At the same time he stabs with the knife and cuts the length of the neck, leaving behind a deep slit. The blood starts to squirt at once. A packet of leaves, which has been prepared for this purpose, is thrown on the gaping wound. Water is carried to the *mallam* in a kettle so he can wash the wound. When he lets go of his knife, which is dripping with blood, he's reminded once again that he must lean his knife against something so the end of the handle is on the ground and the tip of the blade pointed upward. If he does not do it that way, our traditions tell us the meat will make us sick.

The young people go at once to take care of the second animal, which has been brought by the family of the baby's father. The same gestures and words are repeated. So two animals are stretched out like that on the ground. They're skinned and the meat is removed. Each family is busy around its own animal. Likewise, each family has its own fire. Each begins to divide up the meat. But both families must take big quarters of meat to the door of the house where the baby's mother lives. It's always the same parts of the animal which are kept for the women: the thighs, the loin and especially the stomach.

One must take care during the carrying of the meat, which is done with the help of the farmers, that all the pieces arrive safely at their destination. Thefts are frequent!

Before the butchering is finished, you might see a Mbororo setting aside one organ or another so they can perform some magic once they've returned home. In some families, the baby is brought and placed in the stomach of the slaughtered animal, which is still steaming. A large mark is made on the baby's face, from top to bottom, with the spilled blood. I do not know what they're thinking about when they do these things. I think it's to protect the baby from the sickness called *ndungu*, a disease of the rainy season. In their conception this is equivalent to what the Whites have brought us: vaccination.

But the main rite of this day other than the choosing of the name is the shaving of the hair. The hair is moistened with milk that's come from all the calabashes, from all the families; one could say, from all the cows together. This rite is so important that, at least in the past, the only persons who could claim the title 'Fulani of the bush' – that is, a Mbororo – were those who had been shaved with milk. It's like that for me. To assert my identity, I introduce myself as, 'I Ndudi, son of Koyne, shaved with milk.' And I often add, 'I Ndudi, the leper, for whom God has made life easier.'

After these ceremonies, the men erect the *galbal*. This is a long, solid pole which is placed on two forked stakes stuck firmly into the ground. Work like this is always given to the neighbouring farmers who are also asked to pile up a large quantity of wood for cooking. While some are busy with the firewood, others – some Mbororo – who are sitting near the quarters of meat, begin to cut all the pieces of meat into strips. It's really an art to prepare such a large quantity of meat in this way. These strips are as long as an arm and as big around as three fingers. They work in pairs to do this task: one holds the meat in his hands, the other adroitly wields the knife in order to obtain the longest strips possible. The strips are immediately hung on the pole which, little by little, becomes a curtain of meat. The strips are simply exposed to the air while the light smoke keeps the flies at a distance.

All this goes on under the vigilant eye of the person chosen by the family to be in charge. At the right moment, he'll give the order to light the big fire. He also watches over three or four pots of stew which are already simmering on other fires. From time to time, he uses a long stick to stir the sauce, which is swimming in fat. Sometimes he adds pinches of salt and hot pepper to season it.

The women have their own fire in their area where they cook the tripe in a heavily spiced sauce. Women also are in charge of preparing large plates of rice and millet porridge for the guests. The *kori* are busy all over the place. They're on the look-out for groups of young women and young girls who arrive in procession from all four directions. The women all have a calabash of milk or of *sobal* on their heads. When they're spotted, the *kori* shout out their traditional phrase: *njabani be!* which they quickly change to *njabi lebi!* The first is correct: 'Welcome them!' Not the second, which is a deformation: 'Welcome the pubic hair!' Oh, those awful *kori*!

Then another large group of women arrives. Seeing those women, the *kori* are careful not to shout jeers at them. The women, who walk in a straight line, come from the village of the parents-in-law. They accompany the mother-in-law. They don't come empty handed.

The sun climbs higher. The guests keep coming. They join those who are already there, sitting under trees or straw shelters. The neighbouring farmers come too. They're happy for the opportunity offered them to eat meat until they're stuffed. They quickly offer their help. They're given all the parts we do not like: the head, the tongue and some other pieces. They hurry to put this meat next to the fire on little sticks poked into the ground. Others wrap their meat in leaves and stash it in trees.

The Hausa and Fulbe merchants are also there. Each one sets up his merchandise on a mat placed in front of him or on a rickety table that he's carried on his head. There's soap, bottles of perfume, ointments, batteries, matches and candy. Kola nuts, which are being sold elsewhere, await buyers.

We children are always trying to get some coins from our parents so we can buy sugar cubes, candy or mints.

It's time for the prayer, called *jura*, at the beginning of the afternoon. All the men gather and line up in two or three rows, facing Mecca. A *mallam* is in front of them, well separated from the group. The men stand up straight, their arms by their sides. They bow deeply. They kneel, touch the ground with their foreheads, rise and then sit for several seconds on their heels. They repeat this series of positions several times.

When the prayers are finished, the meal is served. But do not think the guests are starving. Not at all! As soon as they arrived, they were offered milk to drink and some bits for nibbling. This is the time for the person in charge to throw on the fire the long strips of meat which have been hanging on the poles. He asks the *kori* to go to all the neighbouring houses and collect all the bowls they can find. When all these utensils are gathered, the 'master of the pole' sweeps the glowing embers with a large bundle of leaves. When the fine dust of ash has disappeared, he throws on several strips. The fire quickly produces a thick smoke, and the good smell of fat fills the air. The smoke tickles the nose and arouses the appetite. We joke among ourselves that at this moment the farmers inhale so much they do not need any sauce for their millet porridge!

The 'master of the pole', using a long stick, retrieves one piece of meat after another from the coals and puts them on the bundles of leaves which the *kori* have placed in front of him.

Then the *kori* carry the meat to different groups of guests who are seated according to their age. When it's a group of men of a respectable age, the *kori* put down the packets with deference, after taking off their shoes a certain distance away. Then, while the women fill the bowls, about ten *kori* join together and, at a signal from the person in charge of the distribution, shout their traditional phrase. Their hands rest on the shoulders of their neighbours in the circle and, with one mouth almost next to another, they shout, prolonging the words: *Lenyol mbadi yesso!* that is to say, 'Clansmen, come forward!' This call is repeated three times. At the end they say: *Min mbada dow lesso!* 'As for us, we're going to your beds!' One more saucy joke from the *kori* who are always on the lookout for the slightest confusion of words. 'As for us,' they mean, 'while you men are eating, we'll be busy with your wives!'

When the *kori* call, all the men get up. They form a line and place themselves two by two, facing each other. They squat down, carefully placing themselves in a line. The men try to imitate the 'calf rope'. For them, this is like a prayer offered as a benediction on those who have invited them. Everyone's absolutely quiet.

Among us Mbororo, there's a tradition that we always start with the white, that is, the *sobal*, the small white balls broken into the white milk. This whiteness reminds us of the 'whiteness of the heart', which we wish for ourselves and which we wish on behalf of the people who have received us. It is like a prayer.

Another tradition of *pulaku* insists that we must not get up one after another as we finish eating. That would be a serious breach of our tradition. If someone does get up, all the guests must stop eating; the remaining food is considered unfit for consumption. However, when someone's finished, he's free to move back from those who are still eating. But he must do this discreetly, while staying in a seated position. We wait for the most respected people to get up before we move.

The *kori* come to clean up and invite the men of the next age group to take their turn forming the 'calf rope' for their meal. Then the youths in the *suka* class have their turn. And finally, when all the others have had their turns, the *kori* themselves eat.

The Fulbe eat by themselves, according to their custom, without sitting in a line like we do. So do the farmers. But no sooner have the farmers been served than they've eaten everything! They ask the *makama*[7] for more food. There's a prank many of them play – they pretend they have just arrived and have not had their share. The *makama* is not fooled. He rebuffs them and calls them all sorts of names, but he promises to give them whatever remains when he's finished taking care of the Fulbe. The *makama* alone takes the calabashes of *sobal* back to the women, in addition to the food the women themselves have prepared. The women organise their own distribution.

As for the children, they're all put together around big plates of *sobal* with milk and bowls of rice with sauce. They're always served plenty. Left on their own, they waste a lot. They want to see who will eat the fastest, who will take the biggest handful of rice and who will spill the most on his stomach or on the ground! From time to time a woman tries to bring things to order but, when she scolds them, they do not pay any attention. As soon as the children have finished their plates, they're ready to start over. They go and find the *makama* and tell him their tall stories. Very kindly, he quickly satisfies their whims.

Goodbye to Adolescence

It was at this *inderi* that I saw for the first time the rite of passage at which a *suka* becomes a *kori*. The return of the herds from pasture is the signal. Some *suka* who are asked to come forward run away. Without a doubt, this is just play-acting because the others have no trouble grabbing them and bringing them back. The *suka* present themselves, willingly or not, to a man who's sitting off to one side on a mat. He holds a razor in his hand. His task is to cut off the braids at the back of their heads.

Jugal was the first to step forward. Then came Nyako. This man was already thirty years old but until now he had always refused at the last moment to have his braids cut. Duka, Ori, Okorni ... they all came. You could see they were a little sad about being obliged to say goodbye to their adolescence.

The man with the razor did not completely shave their heads. He was content to cut the braids off. The braids were then placed in a calabash full of milk. When the 'shaving' was finished, someone took the calabash and poured its contents into a hole that had been dug in the middle of the paddock, or even perhaps in a termite hole. This is a gesture of prayer. While the milk is being spilled, God is asked to make the herds prosper. Once the *kori* candidates have been shaved, they take cow excrement in their hands and cover their skulls with a thick layer of it. They make crowns of *barkehi* leaves and put the crowns on their own heads. They cover their bodies with the same leaves; they attach little twigs everywhere they can: to their arms and feet, around their waists. Finally each *kori* keeps one branch, which he holds in his hand. Disguised like this, the *kori* run all around the area, going into every village to drive off all the animals they find. They herd the cattle in front of them, making them run. No animal escapes. The *kori* always begin their crazy race toward the west.

People are waiting for them to pass. They're on guard. They've milked their cows earlier than usual so they would not be without milk for the day. Little by little as the new *kori* advance further west, the herd grows. At a certain point, they change direction, turning around, and move toward the east. Then they drive the herd to the north, and finally toward the south. As they do this, each *kori* prays to have for himself as many animals as there are in front of him now.

Tired out from running, the *kori* return to the villages they'd passed through and give back the animals they'd taken with them. In every home they find big calabashes of milk set out for them near the paddock. They drink until they're full and then spill some milk on their heads. Before leaving, each *kori* places some *barkehi* leaves over the door of the head of the household. These leaves are taken from the big branches which the *kori* have carried since morning and which they've never let go of. This is how they act everywhere they go, and sometimes their race takes them very far away.

During these days the young *kori* feel they have the right to do the worst things possible. The poor young women they meet on the path! The *kori* do not hesitate to rape them. Seen like that – nude torsos, heads covered with excrement, and all covered with leaves – who would not be afraid?

It's in this get-up that they go to the person they judge to be the most respected, and also the richest. They wait for him to give them his advice and a prayer of intercession: 'You're leaving your adolescence (*sukaku*),' he tells them. 'Ahead of you are some years of youth before you enter into the age of maturity. Until now you've made the most of your youth. May God give you as much joy in this intermediate age (*koraku*), even more if possible! May he make your herd increase!'

They all respond in unison: '*Amina!*'

Then a long litany begins in which the biggest herd-owners of the region are mentioned.

'May God give you as many cattle as so-and-so!'

'*Amina!*'

'And as so-and-so!'

'*Amina!*'

'And as so-and-so!'

'*Amina!*'

The enumeration with the resounding *amina* continues for a long time. Then the *kori* leave with joy in their hearts. 'Think,' they say among themselves, 'what a great day of blessing it is today! Think about it: such an important *ardo* has prayed for us! Who has a voice more agreeable to God?' Then the *kori* go around to each of their families. Everywhere couscous has been prepared for them.

This feast lasts several days. The new *kori* stay covered with *barkehi* leaves. They wait for the yellow leaves to fall off by themselves. At the place where their cattle are kept, the *kori* throw their leaves on the ground and burn them, whilst saying one last prayer.

Figure 8.1: Baby dipped in cow's rumen at its naming ceremony

CHAPTER 9

A Village Interlude

At the Village of Jembu

During these feasts, I had not looked after myself. I had not kept to my diet and my illness had worsened. I was very swollen up around my eyes and ears. My voice was muffled; I could hardly make myself understood.

Just at that time, when my grandfather Jumba was particularly discouraged about my illness, some good news came to us. A stranger passing by told us about a new medicine which cured lepers, a White-man's medicine which could be found at Jembu. He encouraged us to go there. My father did not have to be told twice. We'd just arrived at our rainy-season camp, and his presence at home was not so necessary. So he decided to take me to Jembu. He knew very well it was the last chance for me. He saw that, even if I managed to hold on until the end of the rainy season, I could never again walk the bush paths with all the others at the time of the big seasonal migration.

My father sold two steers so he'd have some money, and five days later we began the long trip which took more than a week. Leaving early in the morning, we were at Selem in time for the market. We spent our first night at Dikoa. We thought when we came to the big road we'd be able to take a truck. But we quickly learned it would be difficult to travel that way. Most drivers were Ibo,[1] whom we also call Nyamiri, and we knew they were really afraid of lepers and kept their distance from them. We were counting on finding a Hausa driver. One of them stopped and signalled for us to get on his truck. But the Ibo who were already in the truck told him that if he took us, they'd get out. So we were left on the side of the road. As we watched them drive away, we kept hoping another driver would take us. That never happened.

So we walked on. After an hour, I could not go any further. I could not stand the sun. I was always thirsty. I was willing to drink any water, even if it were yellow with mud; but my thirst was never quenched. Often we travelled at night by moonlight. We hardly ate anything. I had no appetite; neither did my father because he suffered so much to see me in such a state.

One night – near Missau – we arrived in a village lost in the bush. Someone gave us a corner at the entrance of his house. While we slept, a hyena crossed the room where we were lying. It had entered the courtyard to catch a goat. We were awakened by people shouting. The hyena became afraid and was able to escape through a hole in the straw fence. My father pointed out to me where the animal had threaded its way between the two of us! We learned later that hyenas were plentiful in that region.

The next day we were beside a river that was not too wide, but quite deep. The rains of the night before had flooded it. When the river receded, it had left behind muddy spots and there were large puddles of water on the path which led to the ford. My father advanced cautiously. He probed the holes with his stick; with his other hand he held on to me. All of a sudden I saw him disappear. He had just enough time to let go of my hand. He'd fallen into a deep hole filled with water. It took him some time to reappear . . . I often remember that scene. What would have become of me, all alone, if he had died? I do not dare think about it!

We did succeed in crossing the river. I'll always remember the village near the riverbank where we were welcomed. In my whole life, I've never seen or heard so many mosquitoes! It was awful. Surely the people who lived there were cursed by God. Day and night – whether sitting, standing or lying down – the people spent their time swatting mosquitoes.

'How can you live with all these mosquitoes?'

'Oh, we're used to them!' the people responded.

Thinking it would be better outside than in one of their huts, we had spread out our mats outdoors. Needless to say, we did not sleep that night. Besides the mosquitoes, we heard hyenas howling behind the houses.

After these adventures and many more, we finally arrived at Jembu.

Naturally my father did not know anyone in that village of sedentary people. He was wondering where to go when God helped him find an old friend. This was a Mbororo with whom my father had done the *soro* when he was young. His Mbororo friend had not had any luck; an epidemic had killed all his animals. He'd had to leave nomadic life and look for refuge in this village of Jembu, where he'd been given some fields to cultivate.

After greeting us, he offered to accompany us to the dispensary for lepers. Until then my father had thought that my treatment would only last a few days, or a week at the most. He was dismayed to learn that the treatment would take months, maybe even years! At a loss to know what to do, he was relieved when his old friend offered to keep me at his house. 'I'll take care of him as long as necessary.'

'What do you think, Ndudi?' my father asked me. 'Can you stay here alone, without me?'

'Sure,' I answered him. 'You can leave me without worrying.'

The next morning my father took me to the dispensary for lepers. It was a Saturday. They began by seeing the regular patients. They were all lepers. The men were waiting on one side, the women on the other. When the White arrived, his assistants started playing a *garmofon*,[2] one of the old *tourni-diski* which had a huge mouth. There was also some sort of black calabash cover which went round. We saw something move on top of it. From the huge mouth came songs and preaching in our language, Fulfulde. They said, 'Oh sick ones, may God make you well! And you who are well, may he continue to keep you in good health!'

We responded in unison: '*Amina!*'

The mouth also spoke Hausa. It was only after the prayer was finished that the lepers were called. Each one responded when he heard his name: 'Sa! (Sir!)' That must have been English. Each one who was called went up for his medicine.

After the medicine was distributed, one of the regular patients told my father this was the time to introduce me. The White was astonished when he learned how far we had come. He looked carefully over my whole body. He made a little cut on my ear to take a drop of blood that he spread on a piece of glass. He rubbed the inside of my nose to get some mucus, which he put on another piece of glass. Then he gave me three big tablets. My father took me back to the home of his friend, and the next day he began the trip home alone. I did not cry at all.

My landlord's house was four or five kilometres from the village. I went regularly to take my tablets. I quickly became accustomed to this white doctor, and I soon started to play with his children. We played on a swing. We spoke Hausa among ourselves.

My landlord had a daughter my age, Damana. Although he was a Mbororo, he was a farmer like the other people of this area, most of whom were Witi. Like them, he knew about only one thing: work. He was hard on Damana. He never made me go to the fields with him. However, I was quick to help Damana with her work, as much as I had strength to do.

Koranic School

At Jembu there was a Koranic school, which boys of my age attended. My landlord left it to me to decide whether or not I wanted to go. So each day I made up my mind according to my mood. However, I quickly began to like school and, encouraged by my progress and by the teacher, I became more and more regular in attendance. There were about twenty students in this Koranic school at Jembu, including one girl. Those who did not have relatives in the village were treated like the children of the teacher; they ate and slept at his house. In general, Koranic teachers make life hard for their students. If some teachers are honest, like the one in Jembu, there are more who think of nothing but profiting from their knowledge.

Children at Koranic schools are often pitiful to behold. They are dressed in rags, which hardly cover their stomachs. There's a thick layer of dirt around their necks. When they sweat and scratch, their fingernails leave marks on their skin. The water which spills down their backs as they carry jugs from the well streaks the dust that covers their bodies. They never take a bath. They always wear the same rags. That's how they sleep too, in their frayed, stinking blankets. Some children sleep on sheep skins, others on frayed mats. Sometimes they have beds without a mattress, balanced on four wobbly legs.

The students wake up early, long before sunrise. First they light a fire, a big blazing fire. By its light, they read Koranic passages written by their teacher, or by themselves when they're advanced enough. The texts are in Arabic which, of course, they do not understand. They chant very loudly, trying to see who has the loudest voice. In this confusion, you see someone stand up; he's lost the thread. He asks the teacher to find his place. If he does that again, he'd better watch out!

Then it's time for prayer, followed by manual labour: weeding the fields, watching the cows or domestic chores. In the evening the students come together for the big meal of the day, which is always the same: porridge bathed in sauce. Sometimes there are beans, which are eaten without forks or spoons.

The course of study takes three or four years. Boys often have a lot of trouble completing the course. Some of the religious teachers, who are not very conscientious, give out certificates well before studies are properly completed. Those teachers are simply in a hurry to receive the cow that the parents have promised as a payment at graduation. Students spend their time in class copying verses onto their slates and then washing them off. They work quickly in order to reach the end of the Koran and to obtain the title of 'mallam' as soon as possible! As a result, all the words have been seen but none are remembered. This does not hinder the teacher from going along to the parents and happily announcing that their son has completed his course. The teacher knows the agreed reward that awaits him.

In these schools, there's no recreation. There are never any games supervised by the teacher. The children compensate for that however they can when they go off to carry water or to collect wood. When they return to the mallam's house, it's fear that reigns. If the child's name is called, he trembles. Will he be hit? But if the mallam steps out for two minutes during class, the children begin to chatter, laugh and make an uproar. One of them acts as lookout. At the first alert, each student begins to chant something to give the impression that he's reciting his verse. But watch out if the teacher arrives unannounced! The students fall over each other scrambling for their slates!

There are some schools where students are obliged to beg in order to live. The teacher does not have enough to feed them. He sends them around the streets of the village two-by-two. People know the children and do not fail to call them when they pass by their doors: 'Almajiri! Come, over here, take this,' the villagers say as they offer a bit of porridge. 'Take the sauce too.' The children take everything they're given and mix it in the same bowl. With dirty hands, they knead their millet, manioc and corn porridge into one ball. To them, everything is good!

It is commonly said – it's even a proverb – that an almajiri never has a full stomach. No matter how much he receives, he never has enough. Often when he returns from his tour around the village, his bowl is as empty as when he left. He says he's had no luck because no one gave him anything! Empty stomach or full stomach, he must study: write the texts, read the texts and learn them by heart. Too bad for the blockheads and the wayward students! The mallam must work desperately on them. Sometimes their feet and hands are bound and they're put out in the bright sun for the whole day. The teacher never listens to their complaints. The more they cry, the more they're hit! They are only untied when they've learned the particular passage in question. Others are deprived of food when they do not remember their lessons. They have to watch the other students eat while they, with empty stomachs, rehearse the same verses.

Terrorised like that by their teachers, the students often lose weight. Even if they eat, how can the food do them any good in such conditions? How can they not be tempted to run away? This happens and more often than you'd believe. Those who flee often band together in a group of two or three to organise their flight. They're wary of returning to their own homes for fear of punishment, so they stay together in the bush as long as possible. Sometimes they stay for weeks. Because they're afraid of wild animals, they sleep in trees. Fearing they'll be followed, they change their direction each morning in order to conceal their path. They eat berries and wild fruits. Sometimes they venture into small isolated villages where people take pity on them and give them something to eat. Sometimes they get lost. Sometimes – so it's said – one of these runaways can be taken in hand by another Koranic teacher and develop a taste for studying. In accepting this new teacher, the boy is convinced it's a choice he has made for himself.

But it cannot be denied that there are some teachers who understand absolutely nothing about their profession. It's said they take pleasure in terrorising their students. Those teachers stifle the spirits of their charges, and their tongues too, by frequently beating them until they cry. Also, as we've seen, these teachers are not concerned about the children's food. They have no pity.

One teacher who was not like that, far from it, was the *mallam* of Jembu whose school I attended. I was happy there. He was a true Koranic teacher. He never thought of using his religious knowledge to exploit people! He never stopped warning us about sources of pollution and the risks of contact with our urine and excrement. 'If you touch the Koran, the Holy Book – or even your slates – with dirty hands, the most awful misfortunes await you: leprosy, insanity, etc.' He made us afraid. He always used fear to make us remember his instructions. As for our clothes, which were always dirty and ragged, he never stopped being uneasy about them. For him, all dirt was equal. The type of dirt did not matter to him.

To encourage us to study, he knew how to make his promises attractive. 'If you follow along to the end of your studies, you won't go to hell; neither will your parents. Your sins and theirs will be erased. The flesh of your body will be protected from the fire; or if you do go to hell, you won't stay there long. You'll quickly enter Paradise!'

He also said to us, 'Obey your parents like you obey me. I'm sort of a father to you. Fear God. Fear your parents. Respect the poor. Show your esteem for the elderly. Help the blind. Know how to have pity. Do not make fun of paralysed people and those who cannot see. It is a sin to do that. And certainly, children, do not say you cannot sin. That is false. You sin too.'

He hardly ever talked to us about what's forbidden in our religion, like abstaining from the meat of an animal which has not been properly slaughtered. Only once or twice he told us it was forbidden to eat pork.

He taught the older students how to recite the Koranic beads. He taught them to purify the various parts of their bodies before prayer. He showed them how to do the prostrations and described the positions of praying: standing, hands at their sides, prostrating themselves, touching their foreheads to the ground, sitting back on their heels. He taught them a certain number of Scriptures, those which are

given to people to drink to obtain a certain effect. He told them not to let themselves be distracted from their studies by chasing after girls.

His wives were in seclusion. The older students did not have permission to go
into the wives' quarters. When the older students went to draw water for the
wives, they had to leave the buckets at the compound entrance and let the younger
children carry the buckets further inside. One of the teacher's daughters was
among the students. Usually there are not many girls. Some of the girls who begin
studying do not finish the course because they are given in marriage before the
course is completed. Or else they're frequently absent. Their mothers need them
to make and sell doughnuts. First, people have to live!

'First, people have to live.' That was the reason I had to do the thing that is most
shameful for a Mbororo: beg.[3] How did that happen to me? My landlord was poor.
There were days when we did not get enough to eat. So he sent his children to look
elsewhere for what he could not give them. Very simply, I became accustomed to
following them. I did what they did. Like them, I was proud when I was lucky
enough to bring enough food back to the house for two days. I came to the conclusion that this had the good effect of making me feel unashamed of begging!

It was especially on market days that I begged. Alone or with Damana, I headed
toward the women who sold doughnuts. They never failed to toss some into our
greasy calabash. The two of us would go off to eat the doughnuts. Then we went
to the side where the Mbororo women sold their milk. There was always someone
who would crush a small ball of *sobal* into sour milk for us. Then we continued on
toward the candy merchants. It was more difficult to get them to have pity on us!

With our stomachs full, we went to visit the merchants, who sat on the ground
behind mats which were covered with the beautiful things we wished for. What we
wanted from them was not merchandise, but a few coins. One coin here, another
there. When we went back to the house, I'd take care to bury my coins in a hole
I'd made under my mat ... until the day Damana discovered my hiding place!

Most of my coins were from passengers sitting on the backs of trucks. I liked to
loiter where these vehicles were parked. At first I was really afraid of them, their
big eyes especially! I was in awe of the men I saw sleeping underneath them.
Really, they were courageous! But then I got bold enough to touch the trucks; just
like the men, I slid my hand over their smooth sides, caressing them. I went from
one to another. In some markets there were even ten of them!

Some passengers were accustomed to seeing me loiter like that, and they nearly
always tossed me some small coins. I was happy. I did not think any more about
shame. People really liked me. It's true that at that age I was without malice, trying to be nice to everyone. I never failed to share the extra I had. I was very happy
at Jembu. I was made for the sedentary life, with a 'permanent' house. Thanks to
begging, I always had a little money. I ate well. I was happy.

However, from time to time, I felt nostalgic about the life I'd had before. I
missed my brothers and sisters. And the milk too. I was eager to see our cows.
Cows ... certainly there were some in Jembu, but they were not ours! And I especially wanted to see again the cow that was my real friend, my cow Ole, a good
cow that I had sucked milk from in secret. I often thought of all that.

Then one day I learned that my father had come to see me. It was the end of the dry season. Someone came on his bicycle to tell me the news at the marketplace where I was just in the midst of begging. I rushed home. My father was there. He'd brought me some beautiful clothes. And he also gave some to my landlord's children. He was overjoyed when he saw I was improving.

He brought the sad news that my grandfather Jumba had died. I wept to hear this. He also told me all of our clan, the Diganko, would leave Wuro Ginaji so they could settle far away in the Selem region, near Yola, close to the Cameroon border. He added that although the family would be far away, that would not prevent his coming to get me the following year. But I did not want to stay in Jembu when my family was going so far away. I wanted to go back and live with them. He tried to insist, repeating that I should stay in Jembu for my own good, but I did not want to hear that. He could not get me to change my mind.

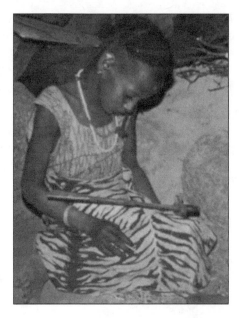

Figure 9.1: Evening Koranic study

Figure 9.2: Studying Koranic verses

CHAPTER 10

A Return to the Nomadic Life

A Carefree Shepherd

So we left Jembu, retracing the same path on the return journey but in better conditions. Here was the big Gongola River, then Selem and finally Wuro Ginaji. Right away I began to tend the cattle. That was necessary. Otherwise what would I have done all alone at the camp?

I had left Jembu with a little medicine, which I quickly used up. I started to use 'black medicines' again. They were less effective, and my illness got worse very soon. The nodules reappeared on my face. My voice was muffled again. Everything was just like it had been before.

In addition, with my grandfather gone, I found myself alone, with no one to protect me. In him I had lost my second father. I fell under the control of my mean stepmother once again. I could not hope for anything from the wife of my grandfather, who was still alive but who felt no relationship to me. She was also very mean. I could only count on pity from neighbours. What would I have done without my father who redoubled his attentions towards me? Unfortunately he was away more often than I would have liked. During the rainy season that followed, I took my turn at guarding the animals, just like all the others. And that year there was an event that I'll always remember.

From high up in a tree, I was watching my cows graze on beautiful grass. Sitting on a branch with my back against the trunk, I was playing my flute.[1] Because I was not paying attention, I began to daydream and I fell asleep. When I woke up, my herd was no longer there. Worried, I began to look for them. I ran here; I ran there. Not finding them, I took the path which the animals always followed to return home. In doing so, I passed by a millet field that I knew well. Maybe my cows were there? That would have surprised me because I'd noticed for several days that the stalks had been grazed on. Looking closer, I noticed that the tips of the stalks were already very yellow. And I did not see any fresh hoof prints, neither around the field nor in the field. I came to the conclusion that it was not my cows who had done the damage. While I was looking for my cows, a farmer who had seen my herd wandering about without a herdsman began to follow them everywhere they went.

As for me, I was tired so I sat down at the edge of the path. I waited for my animals to come. And soon they came, with full stomachs. I was very happy to find them – and in such good condition – so I sang a song of praise in their honour. I was certain I'd be praised. I went up to my favourite cow, Ole, like I had done every day since my return.

Then from behind me, I heard the deep voice of a farmer saying, 'Hello, friend!' Surprised, I felt the blood freeze in my veins. The farmer continued, 'Are these your cows?' Obviously I could not deny it. 'Do you know they ate my entire millet field?' And he followed me without adding another word.

I returned home. My father, seeing the stranger behind the herd, asked me, 'Ndudi, what's happened?' I acted astonished, pretending I did not understand what he was talking about. 'What about this farmer behind you?'

'Oh!' was all I said in response.

During that time, the stranger seated himself to the south of the paddock, at the place where we usually receive neighbouring people who are not Mbororo. Knowing that we do not like it if they come too close, they stop a good distance away. They signal their presence with a resounding *gafara!* (excuse me!). Squatting or standing, leaning on their spears, they wait for us to approach them. Before the farmer even opened his mouth, my father had already guessed what had happened. He repeated, 'And so, Ndudi?' I did not say anything.

First he finished milking a cow, then he went to the visitor. 'Is it a big field? Is there a lot of damage?' My father suggested he go see.

'See what?' asked the surprised farmer. 'Isn't it sufficient that you see me here in order to understand that your animals ate my whole millet field? I even caught them in the act.'

My father insisted he go to the place. The farmer obstinately refused. 'I want to be paid right away. If you don't pay me, I'll complain to the *lamido*.'

This pagan knew very well there's nothing in the world we fear as much as going to court. My father particularly. We're accustomed to working things out among ourselves on a friendly basis. My father asked him, 'How much do you want for reparations?'

'Thirty pounds (Nigerian).'

'That's a lot,' exclaimed my father. 'I'd be happy to pay, but not before seeing the field.'

'Then in that case,' the farmer said to my father, 'let's go before the *lamido*.'

So they went. There too, there was no question of going to verify the damage. My father had to pay. No one asked that I should be summoned. I know very well what I'd have said; I'd have told them to go see the tips of the eaten stalks which were already yellow from the sun. But what's the value of a child's testimony, especially of a Mbororo, to whom the villagers give no consideration?

When my father returned after paying the money, 1 had to control my anger. He told me that since my return from Jembu, I was only a villager who thought of nothing but playing, and that he would no longer trust me with the herd. These were just words in the air because the next day I left again to accompany the animals to pasture. From that day on, my father lengthened his list of recommendations. 'Watch out for this; pay attention to that.' He even went so far as to threaten to kill me if my cows did any more damage in a field. I can assure you I redoubled my vigilance!

However, I did not stop drinking milk from the teats of the cows. Some cows go to pasture together with their grown-up calves that are just about to be weaned. When I saw a calf beginning to drink milk, I'd shout to my friends, 'Hey, Yikao. Hey, Kiwo! I've got a calf drinking milk. Come quickly!' They'd come running. While one boy caressed the calf under the tail, the other took a teat and put it in his mouth. We left nothing for the calf, which we held far away from his mother! Among the Mbororo, you find some who only think about cheating by drinking milk that way. Others never consider it.

What I've said here also applies to our sisters and female cousins when they watch the cows. The boys know what it means to be invited by a girl to share the milk of her cow; it's a mark of great esteem. The boy feels privileged and always hopes to have something else as well . . . , while the two herds graze peacefully together!

'Diseases of the Spirits'

Sometimes I spent the whole day at the camp with Yunusa, Garga and Rua. I was the oldest so I was in charge of them. From time to time, other children - the neighbours - came to join us. Once we were alone and the people and animals had gone, we dreamed of nothing but having fun.

We built houses from branches. Each boy had a house for himself and for his 'wife'.

The 'wives' went to the bush to look for wild sorrel; then, on a real fire built west of the paddock, the 'wives' cooked a mixture of sorrel and flour in a little butter. We 'men' conversed in the shade of a tree, watching our forked sticks or our clay cows, which we were never without.

Kneeling to the ground like their mothers did, our companions came to put food at our feet. We ate. Then, after conversing again among ourselves, 'night' came. Each 'man' went into his house to join his 'wife' on a bed of grass and leaves. Then someone wasted no time in imitating a cock crowing. The day had begun! All the 'men', even the youngest, turned toward the east and tried to remember how their parents did their prostrations for prayer.

One day when we were all together playing house, something happened to little Yunusa. He was playing with his cousin Ida and his brother Yidikau. All at once Yunusa left them. He told them he wanted to drink some gruel back at home. Soon Ida came to tell us she did not know where Yunusa was. We began to look for him. We went from one house to another. We called. No Yunusa. He was only seven years old.

When our mothers returned from the market, they were surprised they did not see Yunusa with us. We had to tell them we had not seen him since the beginning of the afternoon. Maybe he was at the neighbours' house? But he was not there. A little later my stepmother, Yunusa's mother, went to throw out some garbage where she usually did. She found Yunusa there, stretched out on the ground. His eyes were rolling and his mouth was twisted. She shouted and then, taking Yunusa in her arms, she brought him back to her house and laid him on her bed. Soon everyone was there. Someone said, 'Yunusa's dead! Yunusa's dead!' But he was not dead. He was breathing.

Because all the men were gone, Yunusa's mother took care of him. She ran to get the flasks her husband had left in his house in case she ever needed them. She used them and enveloped Yunusa with smoke.

The men arrived. Dumru, Haroji and Tori's father were there; and others, like Jalel and two of my uncles. They were all there, bent over Yunusa. Some invoked Koranic verses or magic phrases by spitting over the child's whole body. Spittle and magic words followed one after the other.

After a long time, Yunusa tried to get up. But he couldn't. They made him sit up. He did not speak. His mouth was contorted and his lips were trembling. He was staring, always off to the same side. Everyone around him said, 'This is the work of the Spirits. Yes, it's the Spirits.' They made all the more smoke around him.

Then my father arrived. He tried ointments, then lotions, and from lotions he moved to fumigations. Certain kinds of smoke that were meant to chase away the Spirits smelled awful. Powder was thrown on embers in a pot. The pot was slipped under the blanket that covered the child. The night passed that way.

The next day a pot of very dirty, stinking water was brought. It had been left for a long time so all sorts of things could ferment, the one more disgusting than the next. Someone washed Yunusa with it. They even gave him some to drink. Then the fumigations resumed. The sessions became less frequent; however, they lasted a good week. There was an improvement. But Yunusa still could not talk. Then he started to say some words, though they were incomprehensible at first. One day he spoke almost correctly and he let us know he couldn't hear. And that's how it was: the day he could hear, he was mute; and the day he could speak he was deaf. One day like this, one day like that. But his walking had become normal.

A friend advised my father to find a certain praise-singer, a man who played the *garaya*, someone who had the reputation of having power over the Spirits. 'It's high time you did it,' he insisted, 'or Yunusa will be affected for the rest of his life.' We knew another praise-singer, also renowned, who was a family friend. He was a Witi named Doya, who had the confidence of all the Mbororo. They often used his services.

Doya came by horse one day in the late afternoon. He was accompanied by four people, including a praise-singer without any special gift and a woman. They were offered a meal, which they ate by themselves west of the paddock: barbecued mutton and couscous. When the meal was finished, night fell. They soon began to play their instruments. I listened to the praise-singer, who had a strong voice, recite the names of my grandfather, my father and many others, not forgetting the name of Yunusa. He sang praises to them.

Yunusa was lying on his mat inside the hut.[3] When his name was called, he did not move. Then Doya, the principal praise-singer, intoned a long litany. He listed a multitude of Spirits, invoking their names. Suddenly he happened on the name of the Spirit which was possessing Yunusa. At that exact moment, Yunusa shouted. The people who were there ran toward him. But he'd already leaped from his bed and was running toward them. They grabbed him. He escaped from them and threw himself down in front of the musicians. Stretched out on the ground, he thrashed about in every direction. Then he got up and began to dance frantically to the musicians' rhythm. We all stood around him watching.

Alerted by the continual beating of the drum, people arrived from all directions. Some of them collapsed in the midst of the spectators as soon as they arrived. They'd heard the song of the Spirit which had possessed them in the past. They stood up again, and when it was their turn, they entered into the dance. Soon there were about ten people dancing. The music lasted all night.

At dawn Doya intoned the last tune: 'After Sambo, there are no more Spirits.' All the dancers fell down. Stretched out on the ground, they remained immobile for several minutes as if they were sleeping. They all fell down, except for one or two who ran away. That song was the end of the session. The Spirits were gone. Not even one was left. Yunusa got up, returned to his house, stretched out on his mat and slept well. When he woke up, he was no longer the same. He spoke and he heard everything. There was no trace of his previous condition. None.

None, except this. In the future, whenever he heard his own tune, he had an irresistible urge to dance. He went into a state in which he did very strange things. For example, he would gather leaves from a tree, put them in his mouth and spit out coins! Sometimes he suddenly had an inspiration and he would make predictions concerning someone's life. Everyone concluded that his former Spirit had been transformed into the Spirit of a magician. People were surprised that such a young boy already possessed such a gift, the gift of the *boka*.[4]

What I'm telling you, I Ndudi, have seen with my own eyes!

Finally, you should know that these 'dancer' Spirits which I've been talking about are called *Bori* by the Hausa and *Girka* by some Mbororo clans in Nigeria. They only wake up in someone who is possessed by them when the sound of a guitar is heard.

Some years later in another region, my older sister Gogo was visited by the Spirits. I want to tell you about that now because her exorcism was very much like what we've just seen. This is what happened. She was about twenty years old. She'd been married several years, but she did not yet have a child. She had a beautiful voice and loved to sing. She knew many songs; she was our best leader when we sat around the fire in the evenings.

Her husband had been selected on the very day of her 'baptism'. He was her cousin, the son of one of our aunts. So this was a real kinship marriage.[5] My sister did not like that cousin. In spite of everything that was done to change her mind, she never liked him. However, she was obliged to accept the marriage. But later, because of her stubbornness, her family had no choice but to 'break' the obligation.

Then she married a certain Issa, the son of Jalel, an authentic Jafun from the Goranko clan, like us. One night when she was having fun singing and dancing, she crawled up on a termite hill. That was a mistake. But what was more serious was the fact that she was singing a tune which only praise-singers use when they're chasing away the Spirits. Her friends waited for the worst to happen. And that very night, as she went into her house, she fainted on her doorstep. People busied themselves around her and got out their traditional medicines, like they did for Yunusa. They tried everything: spittle, incantations, ointments, fumigations. My father sent his remedies, but he did not go and see her. It would have been indecent for him to go to her house. Such is our Fulani reserve.

She regained her senses, got up and continued her work almost normally. But from that day on, she refused to eat or drink. She rejected everything people brought her. In order to take a few mouthfuls, she demanded that her husband be present. But everyone knows a Mbororo woman never eats in the presence of her husband. Besides that, something unthinkable, she kept calling for him. His name was constantly on her lips. He responded and, with a breach even more serious, he went into his wife's house during the day. That was scandalous and absolutely unheard of during the first months of marriage. But that's what happened.

So that she would agree to eat, her husband tried all sorts of means, like you do for a child. On this meagre diet, she lost weight day by day. Finally Doya was called and everything was done as it had been for Yunusa. I remember the musicians worked even harder. The dances were quite varied. Some were funny: they had to dance on one foot with an arm curled up and an eye closed! Another dance was that of a woman selling milk: as many calabashes as possible were brought, and the women wriggled while they sang, 'Milk-butter! Milk-butter!' And there was the dance of the hyena: the dancer stealthily advanced and stole a child which he put at the feet of the praise-singers as if they had to eat the child. There were many different tunes.

During the last song, Gogo fell, lying immobile. When she woke up, she was normal again.

However later, each time she heard musicians play her Spirit's song, she could not keep herself from dancing. Whenever there were no opportunities to dance, she lost weight. Her family would send for a praise-singer musician who knew her well. Then she'd dance and regain her health.

The Big Migration[6]

When I left Jembu, I already knew that after that rainy season in Wuro Ginaji (where I had broken my arm), we would travel far off, very far. We would go to lands we had never seen. The farmers would be different there. We knew, however, there was an important Fulani chief there, a *lamido*. But what would the little chiefs of the pagan villages be like? Would food be plentiful? As for the grass, we already knew from relatives who were there that we'd have nothing to complain about. We also wondered how we would regard the people of the *bariki* and their chief, the *gomna*.[7] There were many unknown things. But none of these questions were very important to us nomads. What is it that always pushes us to look in other places, as if other places would always be better? Essentially there is only one answer: the cow.

Say ten families live together under the authority of the same leader. They've been together for many years. They live in a single big village during the rainy season, and they also live in a single village near to the pools when the tired animals can go no further. Then a large group of Mbororo with hundreds and hundreds of cows arrives, often coming from very far away. Those Mbororo might be complete strangers to the others. The herders from the two groups quickly arrive at a confrontation. They come to blows. One fears the worst. In this case, *pulaku* demands that those who have lived on the land for a long time give way. This is how the Fulani behave.

Or maybe some Mbororo leave the places where they've been camping because those places are more and more taken over by fields. There are fields everywhere, around our camps and on our migration paths. Every minute there are new conflicts about destroyed fields, about animals that have been wounded with an arrow or a machete, about herders who were attacked, injured or killed. It's no longer possible to live like that. The Mbororo must go somewhere else.

Or another case. Until now the region has been healthy. But recently disease-carrying flies have appeared. The pastures are invaded by ticks, which lodge in the hair of the animals and attack the skin. The calves have diarrhoea, their bodies become covered with long hair and they die. One would almost say that the 'bush' drives them away. The survivors gain no weight. Or perhaps there are no more calves because the cows are sterile. We discuss the problem: 'Wouldn't it be better to leave?'

'But will it be better elsewhere?'

The discussion isn't long when it's a question of a contagious disease. Then everyone wants to flee from such inhospitable regions. For those who can't, it's catastrophic. Sometimes they're reduced to cultivating the land.

There are other reasons for leaving: cattle tax, for example. Each year, it goes up. A family is taxed for one hundred head, but they do not have thirty, not even twenty. Sometimes it's necessary to sell five cows to settle the taxes on ten. If you do not pay, you go to prison. This real injustice pushes the Mbororo to think: 'This country is no longer worthwhile for me. They're "eating"[8] us and the *gomna* shuts his eyes!'

'But, my friend,' says another, 'don't have any illusions. Wherever we go, we will find the same problems with government people. Aren't they the same everywhere today? It's my opinion we should be patient and stay here.'

'No, I don't agree! We can't continue to be insulted and cheated. Let's go!' And so the group is divided in two.

Sometimes a family or a clan makes its escape from an area. This migration-flight has a name in the Fulani language. It is an unplanned departure, with nothing left behind, a departure precipitated by circumstances. Here's an example. Some Mbororo went to the market. They were insulted. A fight followed. A farmer was hurt, or even killed. This is what happens. As soon as the Mbororo return to their camp, no matter what hour of the day or night it is, the men alert the whole clan. Each one hurries about his business. The baggage is tied together any way possible, and it's thrown on the backs of the pack-oxen. Things that are a little too awkward are left behind. The Mbororo leave quickly with the intention of covering as much distance as possible before their first stop. They'll walk ten days in a row if they must, even at night, so great is their desire to make a quick getaway.

It's in such circumstances they're happy to have treated their animals with *karfa* so they will be wary and nervous. Too bad for the poor man who's neglected to give it to his animals! His flight will be disorderly. Too bad for the herder and the cows left behind. There will be a raid and he may be killed.

In times past when the Mbororo changed their location, they knew they would have a new *gomna*. But they weren't at all worried about knowing his name or about knowing the real name of the country. They didn't even know about certain papers that were necessary for people when they changed countries. After the Mbororo had moved, they simply waited for someone to come talk to them. Anyway – they thought – once they were settled somewhere, who'd come to bother them in this little corner hidden in the bush?

However, wherever they settled, people soon noticed their presence. It was the women, the milk sellers, who attracted the attention of the villagers to the new camp. Some people asked the women directly, 'Where are you staying? Where did you come from?'

They always received this response: 'We come from far away. It's only by chance that we're here. We're only passing by.'

But that was false. The chief of the village closest to the camp soon heard about the newcomers who were living on his land. He wasted no time in pestering them. He arranged to meet their leaders. 'Do you know,' he said to them, 'you're in our region without permission? This could cost you a lot if I report it to the *lamido*; he'll talk to the *gomna* right away. You risk paying big fines or maybe even going to prison. But don't be afraid. I can arrange everything. Do you have animals? Give me some, and tomorrow I'll go tell the *lamido* you've asked me to bring your greetings to him. I'll congratulate him on your arrival because this will increase his people and property.'

'All right,' said the Mbororo. From that time on, they were caught up in a system of gifts which never finished. Today things are a little different. The traditional chiefs have been replaced by the Animal Husbandry Service. Now a family can't cross a frontier with their cows and family members without permission from the Veterinary Service. They can't enter a new country until a veterinarian - now there are many of them - has come to see and inspect the herd. He comes. He looks … more or less! The Mbororo quickly understand. They know what they have to do to hear him say, 'You can enter. The authorities of my country authorise it.' Then everyone's happy.

In the last few years, a new kind of migration has appeared. A man sells his animals when he's moving away; and he amasses bundles of money, which he puts in his pocket. When he arrives at his destination, he uses that money so he can slowly buy a new herd of the breed that's dominant in the new region. These new migrations have caused the loss of many kin in big families. It's actually rare that everyone agrees to the move. Some stay, and one day the separation becomes permanent when the small group is absorbed into a larger group; the smaller group will adopt the larger group's clan name and its traditions.

As for my own case, I have relatives in all four directions. I have some at Gombe and Jimeta in northern Nigeria; there are others in the Garoua region, north of the Benue; others are in the Central African Republic, which we call the

Congo; and some are in Chad. The origin of this dispersion of the family was dissension at the time of a big move. Brothers didn't agree and separated; sons couldn't convince their fathers to follow them. This is how relatives are lost, particularly since those who move don't always go to the agreed-upon place. They move their camp. And some families blend together.

When uncles and aunts die, the nephews and nieces hardly consider each other as relatives. This is the case with me. One day I wanted to visit my father's two brothers in the Adamawa mountains of Cameroon. Our families had lived separately for twenty years. When I introduced myself to them, the children of those uncles – boys and girls – were totally indifferent to me. I was of no interest to them. It was as though there was no tie of kinship between us. I was a stranger.

It is marriages which permit a family that's been cut off from its clan to retain some contacts. At first there is a lot of coming and going between the families of the sons-in-law and daughters-in-law. But as the years pass, the visits become less frequent. From time to time, a new marriage arranged between kin by a messenger brings the families closer together. Then, nothing more.

In the realm of kinship, there are also customs which are being lost. My uncles' children, whom I just spoke to you about, no longer do the *soro*. They hardly understand what it meant to their parents. There's nothing in the world that would make them agree to go back to this 'fools' game', as they call it. As for us, their cousins in Garoua, we still fervently hold on to this custom.

We Jafun of the North – both boys and girls – have our hair in braids. We give the braids a shape and decorate them with pieces of aluminium and copper. Our relatives in the South laugh when they see our hair like that. They make fun of us and treat us as though we're 'crazy'. Our braids make them ashamed, to the point that they disown us and say they have no kinship with us.

One can say the same about the big Wodabe tribe, which is so well known for its dance called the *gerewol*. Many Wodabe families that have gone far off have lost nearly all contact with Niger. They don't even have the special costumes and rattles for the *gerewol* dance in their baggage. Unlike the real Wodabe who have stayed in Niger, they eat good things, dress well and no longer live immersed in magic. However, something always remains which sets them apart in their new surroundings; they are Wodabe.

It's a curious fact that when we migrate, we almost always go toward the east, away from the setting sun and toward the rising sun. When someone asks us about our origins, we raise our arm toward the west: we are from Mali.

Those who migrate can't remember very far back into their past. The history of their migration goes back one generation, maybe two, but they can't talk about the country of their origin. They don't have any. They're without land. No Mbororo can link himself either to a country or a flag that he would pass on from generation to generation. The Mbororo have no fatherland. So it isn't astonishing that everywhere they wander with their herds, the Mbororo are treated like people of no importance. They don't have the right to any consideration. The least of the farmers is not worried about saying to them, 'Why did you come here? You don't even have a country. And if you're chased from here, where will you go?'

Because the Mbororo are without a homeland, they are also without memories. None of them worry about knowing where their ancestors spent their lives. When they leave a place, they don't think about it any longer. Some young people have no idea where their great-grandfather might have been buried. They don't even try to learn where they themselves were born. In such conditions, who knows their history?

Can some traces of their history be found in the stories which have been passed down through the generations? Actually, the stories are usually about the origin of their cows! This subject really interests the children who don't forget to ask during the evening get-togethers, 'Grandmother, how did cows appear on earth?' Then the grandmother tells a wonderful story.

There was a little boy. His mother was dead. He was raised by another wife of his father; she was very mean. One day she abandoned the child in the middle of the bush in order to get rid of him. She hoped he would be eaten by wild animals. Lost, the little one wandered here and there. He didn't know which way to go. He met an old woman who said to him, 'Go to the edge of the pond which you see there. When you get there, turn your back to the pond. Then call out. When you hear something shaking behind you, don't turn around. Walk forward, forward, and never turn around!'

The child responded, 'All right!'

He went toward the pond. He stopped at the edge, turned his back and walked straight forward. He called, he called and he called! Behind him he heard a big noise: *Ri-di-di, ri-di-di, ri-di-di!* The earth shook. He was afraid and turned around in spite of himself. What did he see? A huge herd of animals was coming out of the pond. They came in waves. but the waves stopped before his very eyes. The last animal trying to get out was a black bull. The boy saw the black bull fall back into the water and disappear!

The grandmothers end their story by adding that if the child hadn't turned around, the bull wouldn't have fallen back into the water and no one in the world would be without cows.

The 'Black Bull'! This is what the Mbororo are searching for through their magic, to give fertility to the herd. This is *alfalu*. They thank God when they dream about the Black Bull. They stop to look at their cows on the edge of rivers or ponds. And if the Black Bull were to come out of the water? Who knows? Why not?

When the Mbororo have a black bull in their herd, it's a blessing. They know very well that it isn't the real Black Bull of the legend, but he has the right to special attention. He's left to die naturally. Or some say he can be sacrificed as a form of almsgiving. People also say about these jet-black bulls that it's enough to rub them on a dark night to make sparks shoot up and see their backbones glow!

The Mbororo, who have so little to say about their own origins, are inexhaustible when they talk about the origins of their cows. Cows are everything to the Mbororo. It's a fact that no one can deny: in past times the Mbororo attached more importance to a cow than to a human being; for them, the life of a cow had more value than that of a child. If they had to choose, there was no hesitation. An exaggeration? Maybe, but it's certain there were such cases. Still today you can hear a Mbororo say, when speaking about his favourite cow, that he would rather die himself than see his cow die.

What is important to understand is that for a Mbororo – who knows nothing about commerce or agriculture – the cow is his means of survival. The cow is his life.

A Note on the Spirits

Here is Ndudi's actual commentary:

'The spirits (*ginaji*) exist. They build villages like we do. Like us, they possess horses, cows and sheep. Some days in the middle of the bush, when you approach a *bokki* tree (baobab), you hear village sounds: cows that low, sheep that bleat, children who cry. Those sounds come from a village of the spirits (*ginaji*). Another time at night, not far from those same trees, you see a big light. Being curious, you approach: the light goes out; you no longer see anything.

The *ginaji* have a body like ours, but they're invisible. They look like the *nassara* (the white people). Some of them are also black like the pagans. There are good spirits and bad spirits. It's the latter which cause insanity when they get into the heads of people. Others suck blood. They paralyse people from the waist to the feet. There are people who are capable of chasing away these *ginaji*: those who possess knowledge of "black medicines" or of the Koranic scriptures. Many people chase away the *ginaji* by using fumigations with stinky plants. The *mallams* use water from the Koranic scriptures. This is obtained by washing the tablets on which Koranic verses have been written. The water is used as a potion or a lotion. or both ways at the same time. Small leather pouches, which some call "*gri-gri*", are also used.

Certain *ginaji* are the object of invocations. They can be addressed to help one become an expert in a particular activity or art, for example a guitarist, an expert in Koranic knowledge, or even an excellent truck driver.

If you pray insistently, the spirits come to you. They ask you, "What do you want?"

"I want to accomplish a certain feat."

Someone who has direct recourse to the spirits without an intermediary can go insane. It's very risky. In my opinion, it's better to obtain the same result by going to the experts in Koranic knowledge. If they agree to intercede for someone with the *ginaji* they'll spend days and nights invoking them. Night and day they tell their Koranic beads. The *ginaji* finally make themselves visible. A dialogue will ensue between the two. And the prayer will always be answered in the end.'

Ndudi continues and ends this commentary by citing the example of a Hausa driver who, in this way, was able to do extraordinary miracles with his truck. When he wanted to, he could drive his truck from the outside, without sitting behind the steering wheel in the cab.

Figure 10.1: Herd boys

Figure 10.2: Young man playing the *garaya*

CHAPTER 11

Memories of Seasonal Migrations

The three years following our final departure from Wuro Ginaji were spent coming and going through the bush. It seemed to me we'd lost interest in the Yola area near the Cameroon border. Why? I cannot tell you. I was too young to take part in the councils of elders.

What I do know is that each year, in the harvested millet fields of the Borom farmers, our cows gained more weight and became more lively. It was a pleasure to see them devouring the stalks that had been left in the fields after the harvest. They benefited from this for three years in a row. We had to pay the proprietors for the right to the pastures, but we did that willingly. We were sure our cows would be in better condition to face the rigours of the dry season to come, which we spent at our encampment at Wuro Nagge,[1] several days further walk to the south.

Those three years were difficult for me. My illness grew worse. The medicines from Jembu had not been very effective. I went back to taking the medicines my father made for me. I have some very vivid memories of those three years. Here are some of them which I recall.

Handicapped People

One day my father had had to carry me on his back for a good part of the day. He stopped often to catch his breath. In spite of the rain of the preceding days, the sun was still scorching. All at once we were passed by a herd moving at a fast pace. The man walking at the head of the herd was a Danagu. He hardly noticed us. He ran more than he walked, with the first cows right on his heels. You could say they were pushing him with their horns. You could see that he was proud to walk so fast. My father was full of admiration. He could not stop telling me that if those animals were so lively, it was thanks to *karfa*.

We were sitting in the shade of a tree to rest when we saw their rear guard. It was less proud. In fact, it was pitiful. There was an old, emaciated horse with a man tied on it; he was insane. With his head bent over, he tried to spit on the horse's hoofs. Someone hung on to him from behind so he would not fall off. Another man, the one who held the bridle, pushed his head up from time to time.

Farther back was an old grandmother, all hunched over. She held a little boy by one hand; with her other hand, she leaned on a stick.

I've never seen so much misery among the Mbororo as I saw that year during the long weeks of moving from one place to another. Without a doubt, this was partly due to the deplorable state I was in. But later I saw many others who were miserable: those with injured feet who pitifully trailed behind, as well as sick people who were extremely thin and could hardly stand up. And this was not counting the people with shrivelled up hands, the blind and the dwarfs.

One day I met a little girl, a woman actually, who was all knotted up. She was always sitting. She couldn't stand on her legs; they were only useful for crawling. Besides that, she'd become blind. But she could eat by herself, manipulating the lumps of manioc porridge with her tiny baby hands. She took part in conversations. Sometimes she hummed and chattered. I never understood how she managed to sit on a horse.

There are also the insane, those people who – because they are under the control of the Spirits – say anything they want, insult people, walk around nude and take care of their needs anywhere, just where they are. Those people also follow the herd. The Mbororo prefer to keep such persons with them when they move. They usually do not want to leave them in the care of people in the villages because they're afraid they would suffer too much. So a horse is bought for an insane person, or at least a donkey. Sometimes someone must ride behind the person in order to keep him on the animal's back. When the Mbororo reach their evening camp, the person is often chained up so he won't run away and get lost.

Old Women and Old Men

All the old women and old men whom we bring along when we move cause us a lot of worry too. I want to speak especially about the old women who can hardly see anything and can just barely stand up. As soon as they're on a horse, they say they're tired. They ask to get off. They cannot ride any longer. They worry about everything. It doesn't matter if they're in the middle of the bush and cut off from the others who are already far ahead. We try to make them be patient. 'Look, Grandmother, be reasonable. We're far behind the others. There are many hyenas in this area. There are also bandits. Do you want to spend the night in the middle of the bush? What shall we do? All the food is ahead of us. Bear your discomfort patiently; we must go on!'

Nothing doing. The old woman insists on being taken off the horse. As for dying – she says – she would rather die on the ground than on the back of a horse! So she is taken down and given a little water to drink. We give her this and that … 'And now, can we leave?' we ask.

'Oh no! There's no question of putting me back on that horse!'

So everyone sits down. There's nothing else to do. We cannot insult her or strike her!

It's good if one of her grandchildren is in the group. It doesn't bother a grandson to speak to her in plain language. That is the rule between grandchildren and grandparents. 'Ah, Grandmother! If you were already dead, we'd finally breathe a sigh of relief! Really, this is too much. You wanted a horse, and here is one. It was bought just for you, and now you refuse to get on it. Don't you see the others are already far ahead of us? Do you really want to stay here? Oh, yes, it would be better if you were dead. At least there'd be peace!'

Only a grandson would allow himself to speak like that. Certainly not a son or a stranger to the family!

And the conversation may continue in that tone: 'Oh well, I wish I would die! And as fast as possible!'

'Go ahead then! If you feel that way, why didn't you stay on the horse where you felt like you were dying!'

This language is the kind used between 'joking relatives'. It must not be misinterpreted. It's a sign of great intimacy.

Hearing some people talk, you'd think the Mbororo would not hesitate, in one way or another, to get rid of all these old men and women, those who are useless and can no longer do anything. This is a pure lie, at least today. I do not know what happened in times past.

Nowadays the Mbororo have great regard for those who are feeble, old, sick, or handicapped. They do nothing to get rid of them. They let them live right to the end, that is, up to the end of their days, the end that God has determined for each one. It's a question of religion. I say 'of religion' because if you believe, you cannot throw away a life that's just like your own. Absolutely not. On the other hand, when it's a question of a cow that's sick and dying, you slaughter her and eat the meat with your friends, or you abandon her and let some pagan have her. But a son of Adam, no matter what condition he's in, you take care of him.

A Bewitched Child

One day, in a group of Mbororo who were walking ahead of us, a child fell under the grip of a sorcerer just as we were about to join their group. There were four children sitting on the same horse. All at once, the man accompanying them saw one child about to fall off. He had just enough time to catch the child. He took the child down off the horse. Everyone thought he was dead. Crowding around him they said, 'But what has happened to him?' The other children were taken down and set in the shade. Someone brought out his remedies.

You must understand that a Mbororo is never without his medicines: remedies for people and remedies for animals. He has powders wrapped in bits of cloth, potions carried in flasks hanging at his sides and leather pouches of medicine in his pockets. He's careful that his remedies are always within reach; a sorcerer can attack a person at any place, at any time.

The child who had been struck down was placed at the foot of a tree. A fire was lit. Powder was brought out. The powder was thrown on the embers and its smoke was fanned over the child. He was also given a few drops to drink from a gourd. The child got better quickly. Someone took the child on his back and we continued together on our trip, hurrying to arrive at our stopping place before night fell.

Those who had got there ahead of us told us how worried about us they were. 'What kept you so long?'

'One of the children, Kessiri, fell under the spell of a sorcerer. Luckily we had some remedies. We treated him by fumigation. The sorcerer released his hold on him.' They did not try to find out who the sorcerer was.

Wild Animals

The bush is also hostile to us. It's a refuge for wild animals. And between the animals and ourselves, there's open warfare.

There's the hyena, that animal which reappears so often in the stories we tell in the evening. It's voracious, jealous and cowardly. But it doesn't just exist in our stories. How often we hear it said when we wake up in the morning that a hyena came for a visit during the night! The hyena slips in, creeping between two sleepers without waking them. In the paddock it seizes a calf which begins to bellow. The cows are afraid; they moo and scatter in all directions. This disturbance arouses the Mbororo from their sleep. With one leap, they jump from their blankets. There are shouts everywhere: '*Kai! kai! kai!*' From everywhere you hear, 'The hyena, the hyena!' The children, who have been abruptly awakened and are scared, run anywhere, and they must be caught.

The next day the people inspect the hyena's tracks and try to discover the path it had followed. 'Look, it inched its way in here … It slipped between us two … It almost put its foot on the head of the baby!' It's well known that the hyena is very skilful in making its approach. It walks on velvet paws. No one hears it. It takes its time, fixing its eyes on its prey – a calf or sheep.

In some regions there are lions. Where lions are present, the cattle must be tied together in pairs, attached by their front legs. A herder must always be armed with his bow and a quiver of poisoned arrows when he's with his animals. It's true that some Mbororo only carry a bow to make an impression; they don't know how to shoot it. If they must use it, the arrow flies off in another direction from the one intended! And their awkward hand falls back on their chest.

Anyway, where there are lions, a herder stays constantly on the alert. At night he doesn't stop patrolling around his herd with a flashlight in his hand.

Sometimes a cow which is lagging behind escapes the herder's surveillance. The lion is lying in wait for this to happen. With infinite stealth, the lion approaches the imprudent cow. Then, with a leap, it's on top of the cow. The cow can be heard bellowing. Alerted by this, the rest of the herd moves toward the place of the drama, at least if the cattle have had a good treatment of *karfa*. The herder does the same thing.

Then something strange happens: the herder, without dropping his light, pulls the cow from one side while the lion pulls from the other. The herder holds out his bow and hits the lion with it. While pulling and hitting, he calls for help. People come running. The lion releases its prey, but it does not flee. It stays there! If a good archer arrives, he'll shoot a poisoned arrow. Then the lion lets out a cry and runs off. The next day the dead lion can be found by following its tracks, at least if the poison on the arrow wasn't stale. The hunter is congratulated. He's a hero!

Such strange scenes are not rare. When it's a question of pulling one of his animals out of the mouth of any wild animal, every Mbororo can manifest an extraordinary courage. However, sometimes it happens that the lion is the stronger. If the rest of the herd saw nothing or has fled, the lion drags the cow over and eats the intestines.

It wasn't every day during the three years of coming and going between Borom and the village of Wuro Nagge that our herds were attacked by hyenas or lions. But nearly every night such stories were recalled as we sat on our mats during the evenings. The men didn't recount tales; they reported stories, true or false! But you could never show you doubted them!

I've never seen any leopards, but I've often heard about a Mbororo killed by one of them. That herder, whose name I have forgotten, was watching his animals at pasture. It was night. A leopard was lurking nearby. The man's cows had gone down into a stream valley where they grazed peacefully. Their guardian watched them from up above, sitting on the trunk of a tree, with his bow on his knees. With one leap, the leopard was on him. It pinned him to the ground, pulled the skin off his head and killed him instantly. The cows must have heard the far-off echoes of the fight between the man and the leopard. They fled and returned to their paddock.

When the wife of the Mbororo heard the cows come back, she thought her husband had also returned and that he was lying down in his *buteru*. After a while, a leopard – no doubt the same one – came to eat a sheep. The people got up and called for help, 'A leopard, a leopard!'

It was then that the absence of the man was noticed. His wife said to the others, 'I heard him leave to go to the pasture with the animals earlier tonight, but I did not hear him come back with them.'

'And so?'

'Oh, he must not be far away.'

They went back to bed, but no one slept.

Early in the morning, the men set out in the direction the herd had followed. They had no trouble finding the tracks which led to the man. He was dead. The leopard had killed him. There was no doubt that it was the leopard: the skin torn from the man's head and hanging over his eyes was proof.

With regard to lions, I have told you Mbororo herders are valiant in saving their cattle from the teeth of ferocious animals. But cows also know how to defend themselves. When a cow at pasture is attacked by a hyena or a lion, it's not unusual to see all the other cows run to her aid. Dangerous bulls and some belligerent cows charge with their heads down. They gore the hyena in the stomach and toss it in the air. Once the hyena falls back on the ground, it takes to its heels! Then the cows circle around the cow that was attacked. If she has a bad injury which prevents her from getting up, the cows stay there, all of them, waiting for the arrival of their herder. If she is still standing and she has enough strength, the other cows mass around her. Some precede her and others follow; they return to the camp. Such events do happen.

If a cow has just given birth and a hyena attacks her new calf, the hyena won't be able to get the calf. Absolutely not. No matter how hard the hyena tries to grab the calf from one side and then the other, no matter how often it circles around and around again, until dawn – it's just lost effort! The mother guards her calf between her front legs. There's no way to take the calf!

This is the effect of *karfa*. You see why it's so important to us.

The Pagan 'Man-eaters'

There were nights when the men told stories that would make you tremble. Those who told the stories never failed to say they were true. Some added that they were living at the time those events happened. Others swore such things could still happen.

The stories were about the Wawa, very evil pagan people. You could say we were always at war with them. When they knew that Mbororo were going to cross their territory, they went on the warpath. So the Mbororo redoubled their vigilance; they increased the dosage of their 'medicines'; they added talisman after talisman; they activated a whole list of magic spells. In this way, they were seeking to protect themselves against attacks with iron weapons or the poisoned arrows of these awful pagans.

Indeed, those people were well-armed. Besides poisoned arrows, they had spears and their famous throwing knives made by their blacksmiths with many ear-like protrusions.

When Mbororo arrive in those inhospitable lands, they unite in groups of ten or twenty families. They surround their herds, forming an impressive group. At a certain place, they must take a narrow passage between the fields, with crops on each side for kilometres and kilometres. There's no other possible route. When the Mbororo start walking there, the farmers post themselves on each side. They're ready to intervene if, by chance, a cow touches the smallest millet leaf. You can even hear them call the animals so they will get excited and enter the fields. If that happens, there's a fight. The Mbororo do not hesitate to kill some of the pagans ...

The arrows of those pagans never strike the Mbororo. The Mbororo are protected. They only have to use their sticks. When one of those farmers who's had a good blow behind his ear falls down, the others immediately scatter. All those cowards run away, looking for safety. The pagans are always fearful.

In spite of all this, we dread the Wawa because among them there are the man-eating Firé people. If an isolated Mbororo falls into their hands, he will be eaten. They live in the rocks on mountain tops and only come down to the plains to cultivate their millet fields. Eating human flesh is a normal thing for them. They practise the custom of sharpening their teeth. I know them well.

The Cattle Thieves

We do not like crossing the territory of the Kitaku either. They have a well-established reputation for being cattle thieves. These people follow nearly all our traditions but they're one of the clans that refuse to be called Mbororo. It is the same, as I've told you, with the Kessu and the Kiri.

Light-complexioned, they can be confused with the Fulbe of the towns. They get drunk and when they have a few cattle, they're quick to gamble them away in games of chance. They steal from each other, but they steal Mbororo cattle even more. Each time we crossed their territory during the three years of seasonal migrations, which were so difficult for me, my father was very nervous. Every evening when I saw him in the middle of the paddock, he had a potsherd of embers in his hand for fumigating the herd. At night he would not let anyone watch the herd but himself.

These Kitaku are very enterprising. They know how to subtly entice an animal towards them, right from under the nose of the herdsman. Once within their reach and a little away from the herd, they put a long rope around her leg or neck – and our cow disappears in an unknown direction!

One of my uncles had a cow stolen that way. The thief, one of those Kitaku, hurried to sell the cow to one of his butcher friends in Numan and, that same day, the meat was sold.

My uncle who, like all the Mbororo, had an astonishing ability to recognise each one of his animals, wandered around the side of the slaughterhouse in hopes of finding some sign of his cow. He saw her horns. There was no doubt about it. He took them and went to find the butchers. 'Where did you get this cow?' he asked them.

'Why ask such a question?'

'These are the horns of one of my cows, which I did not sell to you. There's no doubt about it. But where's the skin?'

'We've already sold the skin,' they told him.

'Very well!' said my uncle as he left them.

He immediately went to the *lamido*, where he registered a complaint. The police quickly put their hands on the thief. Naturally, it was one of the Kitaku. He was taken to the butchers who were forced to admit that this was the man they'd bought the cow from. The *lamido* pointed out to them that they knew very well that this man was a notorious thief. And he concluded, 'Therefore you are accomplices.' The thief was sent to prison. But he'd already spent the money on liquor or lost it playing cards. So the butchers were ordered to reimburse my uncle. In addition they spent five days in prison!

My uncle was lucky. How many goats did those Kitaku steal from my grandfather Jumba when we traversed the Bandjiram region? Our only defence was to threaten them with all our magic powers which they know we possess.

Chapter 12

A Stay in Gire

We didn't spend a fourth rainy-season in the village of Wuro Nagge. The last rains had not stopped when we set off in the direction of Yola, just as we had done for the last three years, ever since leaving Wuro Ginaji.

The elders decided we would settle at Ngawa. It was near this little village that we built our permanent camp. There we found some Fulbe, Yanguru, Tambu and Bata. There were also some Hausa and Witi there.

The big market that was closest to us was in Gire. Going there was a good day's walk at a brisk pace. This was where the *lamido* resided. For questions concerning the *bariki* we had to go to Jimeta, the town of the *gomna*.

Soon after we built our camp, there was a small incident which had very great importance for me. One morning two horsemen stopped near our huts. They were the 'cattle counters', coming to make preparations for collecting taxes. Coming from Gire, they were stopping at all the Mbororo camps to count the cattle. For several days we'd known about their coming, and we'd taken our precautions.

On that particular day, my father was away on a trip. He'd left for several days to visit the far-away region of Selem. I was there just by chance, because a moment later I left, with a calabash on my head, to sell milk in the village. Since my sister Gogo had married, I was often asked to replace her as if I were a girl!

After greeting us, the horsemen were surprised to find neither the herdsman nor the herder nor the animals which they'd hoped to see. One of them noticed me. He asked if I was suffering from leprosy. He saw my face covered with sores. He no doubt pitied me because I could only look at him by lifting my head directly up toward the sky. 'What are you waiting for to send this poor little boy to be attended to in Gire? Don't you know there's a medicine in the clinic there that heals lepers? Are you waiting for him to die?' he said to the women who were busy doing their hair. But they did not pay much attention.

'We can't do anything about it,' they said. 'It will have to wait for his father to come back. He'll decide what he must do.'

Another Clinic

My father returned two days later. I ran toward him to announce the news. 'The "cattle counters" came; they said there's a new medicine in Gire which heals lepers. We must go right away!'

'Is it a medicine of the Whites?'

'Yes,' I answered, 'and I've learned it's stronger than the medicine in Jembu.'

'Very well. We'll go.'

The following Saturday I was with my father at the leprosy clinic. Many sick people were there: men and women, children and old people - nearly all of them were farmers from neighbouring villages. Like me, some of them had difficulty making themselves understood when they spoke. My father asked one of them if he'd been coming for treatments for a long time. With difficulty, he succeeded in telling us he'd been coming for three years. That was hardly encouraging!

I saw each patient pass from one window to another. At the first window, he received a pill that was no larger than a Nivaquine; at the second, he was given a glass of water by someone inside this round house.

When the distribution was finished, my father presented me to the doctor. He wrote my name in a big book and gave me half of a small pill. It was different from the ones I'd had in Jembu. These were better, the doctor told us, while explaining to my father it was necessary for me to come to take them regularly. 'With you Mbororo,' the doctor added, 'we never know!'

And so I began a difficult series of trips back and forth which lasted three years. We'd leave early Friday morning and walk to Bundanre where we'd spend the night. Saturday morning we were at the Gire clinic about ten o'clock. I'd take my pill, drink my glass of water and – without delay – we'd start our return journey, with a stop for the night at Bundanre again.

This treatment was not interrupted by the dry-season departure of the herds because my father boarded me with the chief of a little village, Demsare, which was near our camp; the chief's name was Zoro Ajiya. The first weeks my landlord went with me like my father had done. But he became tired of this and, in the end, he entrusted me to some donkey drivers who would pass by his door early on Friday mornings. When he'd hear them arrive, he'd wake me quickly and I'd follow them, having taken only a gulp of water. I'd leave them at Bundanre where I was accustomed to spending the night, and then the next day I walked the remaining kilometres which separated me from Gire by myself.

Later I was even able to do without the company of the donkey drivers.

I was very happy in this village of Demsare, at the home of my landlord Zoro Ajiya. He had a daughter my age, Adda Gire. I went with her to the groundnut fields at harvest time. Late in the afternoons, we would go together to water the donkeys, bring in the goats, collect wood and get water. After the evening meal, we shelled groundnuts together. The two of us would work together on a single pile; we shared the profits; five measures out of twenty were our share!

Inseparable during the day, we were also inseparable at night. We'd move our mats together and sleep one against the other. In the morning we were careful to move our mats apart.

We also made trouble together. Often, when night had fallen, we went to steal ears of maize from the field of Baba Lau, our closest neighbour. One time he caught us in the act. He tied up my wrists with straw and summoned a mean woman who took a burning ember and threatened to set it alight.

One day I took the risk of not returning on Sunday evening. I had decided to make the trip from Demsare to Gire and back to Demsare no longer. I wanted to stay in Gire and wait there until the following Saturday. My landlord, who was worried, made the trip to Gire to find out what had happened to me. It did not take him long to find and scold me, but he really understood my point of view. He decided from then on not to count on me. We would see what my father said when he returned to take up his rainy-season camp near Demsare. I reassured him, and he was calm when he left.

Welcoming Friends

At the clinic I had made friends with a number of the lepers. So it was only natural I'd spend my first nights at their homes. They were all very poor. Most of them did not have wives, and they lived off charity. There was one I really pitied. 'Come to my house,' he said to me. 'You'll never lack food. I don't even need to beg; people bring food to my house.' It was true. And so from the first day, I knew where to stay.

I went to his house with the idea of being of some service to him. He no longer had any hands. In order to eat, he used a spoon with a long handle that had a hole pierced in it for a piece of elastic. I'd attach the spoon to his arm, but he still had a lot of trouble getting the spoon up to his mouth. He was covered with sores. The sores on his feet were particularly deep. They smelled bad. You have to be a leper yourself to endure such a stink for the whole night. At least that is what I said to myself. I understood his misery better than a lot of others did. I was the one who had to tie up and untie his trousers. I helped him go to the toilet. I washed his sores and bandaged them. I washed his bandages so he'd always have clean ones.

Every Friday I went with him through the streets of Gire. On that day the streets were overrun with lepers and lines of blind people walking in single file preceded by a boy who guided them with a stick. I knew all those poor people, and when I compared myself to them, I could only be thankful. The people of Gire, who were really poor for the most part, were generous since – for a Muslim – giving alms is what must be done on Fridays. It's a habit.

The residents lived in four quarters of the town: the Hausa; the Jumo, who were related to them; the Fulbe; and finally the Lelewaji, who also had a link with the Fulbe. It was the Hausa who dominated everything. Next were the Jumo, who were almost as rich as the Hausa. Outside the town, along all the access roads and quite far into the bush, you'd see the huts of many pagan farmers.

At the hospital and at the clinic for lepers, there were only African doctors. From time to time, the clinic had a visit from an important white doctor. He looked at each leper and took a sample of blood. Normally there were three Blacks who took care of us: one recorded our names, another distributed a pill at the first window and the third gave us water to drink at the next window and satisfied himself that we'd really swallowed the pill.

I had noticed when I waited idly around the market that people would give me their purchases to carry home for them. 'Take this,' they'd say to me as they handed me meat wrapped in a large leaf. 'Carry it to my house; you'll have two pennies.' That gave me confidence; looking at me was not distasteful for people. At that time the swellings on my face had disappeared. There was just a little swelling left in other places, especially beside my ears. People did not notice right away that I was a leper.

There was a certain Dan Giwa who especially used my services. One day he offered to let me stay at his house for good. In return for doing some errands, small tasks like carrying water or collecting wood, he would feed and lodge me. I accepted, but I kept thinking about the distress this decision would cause my leper friend.

This Dan Giwa made his living as a transporter. He was neither the owner of a truck nor a driver; he simply rented a small bus month by month for an agreed-upon sum. At the end of the month when he had settled his debt with the owner, everything left was his own. He hired a 'chief of transport' who collected the money for passengers and baggage. Dan Giwa's business was successful and he was already rich. His *sare*[1] was well kept, and so were those of his wives. He was a Hausa.

When I began to work for him, he only had one wife, a Bata who had recently converted to Islam. He divorced her in order to marry a very young Hausa girl. Before long he gave that girl a co-wife, who was also Hausa. From that time on, everything went better around his house. When he would find things in order after several days of absence, he'd never fail to give me a gift. The wives were kind to me. I'd asked them to speak only Hausa with me. This enabled me to make progress in that language.

Once the morning errands were finished and after I'd done the marketing, I did whatever I wanted. I'd get together with my friends. There were five or six of us boys who got along well together. We'd go and gather wood, which we'd sell in small bundles. The coins we earned were used immediately to rent a bicycle!

I'd never refuse to do errands for the neighbouring families. They gave me a bit of money and invited me to share their porridge when I wanted to.

More than the others, Mala Buba, whose house was adjacent to Dan Giwa's, would use my services. He was a tailor by trade, and he also cultivated some fields of millet and manioc. He wandered through all the markets of the area selling the things he'd made. When he returned, he'd gather together his many children to teach them Koranic writing. From time to time I'd sit with them in their entry house. I'd always find one of his daughters there who I liked a lot; her name was Adda Kano. She helped me after class and encouraged me not to miss school.

Very soon I felt just as much at home at Mala Buba's as at Dan Giwa's. I worked as much for one as the other. No one had anything to complain about. One day Mala Buba offered to let me live at his house. 'You'll be able to follow school better if you live with me and my children.' I began timidly by spending one night, and then two, in Mala Buba's *sare*. More and more I ate my meals at his house. Little by little, I'd stop at his house first when I was off to do my errands.

Dan Giwa, who had been alerted by his wives, found out about my little game and about Mala Buba's behaviour. There was an argument between the two of them, with hot words exchanged about me. I also had my say. I put major emphasis on the issue of Koranic school. Dan Giwa, who was upset, concluded by saying, 'You must decide: either him or me. If you want to stay with him, I'll look for another boy to do errands in your place.'

I Become a Tailor

Tired of these discussions, I moved to Mala Buba's house for good. He had a sewing machine which interested me. I always took advantage of his absences by using it. At first I didn't make anything in particular, but soon I sewed little things from bits of cloth or old clothes.

One day when he had been called away in the midst of his work, I took his place. He was putting a hem on a wrapper-skirt. I finished the job. You can guess his surprise when he came back to his work. 'Who did this?' he asked.

'Me.'

'Liar! Oh well, since you say it's you, show me a little of what you can do! Take this cloth.'

Then he realised I had not lied. From that moment on, he'd cut skirts for me to hem on the days he went to sell his merchandise in the markets. Soon he put a pair of scissors in my hands, and it wasn't long before I was cutting out shorts and small shirts for children.

When it came to sewing, I never tired of it. I'd extend my day well into the night, sometimes until the sun came up. Some evenings I'd ask my boss for permission to sew all night. 'I don't feel like sleeping,' I'd say to him. It was true. But what he did not know was that I was drugging myself with pills called *anabarsi*.[2] It was the Whites who taught us to use them. They were sold secretly in all the markets. One pill was sufficient to keep me awake and able to work hard. I'd sing and sew all night without being tired. Sometimes I'd even use up all the kerosene in my lamp! At dawn I'd wake up my boss and proudly ask him to come count the shirts and shorts I'd cut out and sewn during the night.

It was not surprising that, with this schedule, I was often sick. Actually, my illness was due to a lack of sleep. I knew that very well; if I worked slowly and slept well for two to three days, I would feel strong again. Then, feeling better, I'd go back to working furiously.

I was proud when people would see me at work. My machine was usually near the entrance to the compound, under a tree which gave a little shade. What a pleasure it was for me during the day to see some of my family who had come to the market, sitting on the mats at my feet and not taking their eyes off me! 'Really! This Ndudi . . .' they'd say to each other while nodding.

Confident in my honesty and my business sense, my boss sent me in his place to sell the things we'd made. I went on his bicycle to the different markets in the area. Once I arrived, I'd lay out my merchandise on the ground like most merchants did. The Mororo were even more surprised when they saw me transformed into a merchant. 'Oh yes,' they said, 'This Ndudi! He never stops astonishing us!' Moreover, they proved to be good customers for me. Knowing their tastes, I cut clothes they would like. I earned a lot of money, which they noticed. My boss also noticed, which made him think all the more of me.

But many customers in Gire needed to be coaxed to pay for their purchases. Many of them never paid at all. Debts accumulated to the point that one day Mala Buba did not have enough money to buy pieces of cloth in advance. Soon he had nothing more to cut out or sew. We had to go back to farming.

So I Become a Farmer!

Due to the circumstances, I became a farmer – me, a Mororo! There was no hiding the fact that I considered this to be a step down.

If there's a crop I know well, it's manioc. I could describe for you all the steps of preparing it in detail. When it's mature, this is what you do: dig it up, peel it, soak it, drain it, dry it, sweep it up, put it in a sack, carry it on your head and sell it. Every day there's something to be done; I was treated more like a slave than a son of the family.

Mala Buba's daughter of my age, Adda Kano, brought food to the place where I was working early each afternoon. Often it was manioc porridge, with sauce in the Witi style: bland, made from powdered baobab fruit and the leaves of a tree called *kabihi*,[3] spiced a little with *daddawa*.[4] However, I must admit that from time to time a little bit of meat could be found in the sauce. Mala Buba, having become a town dweller, had to do what all people who live in the town do: buy a little meat!

Some days Adda Kano brought me a mixture of millet grains and cooked beans. Because I ate with my fingers, I had to swallow this runny mixture by lifting up my head and letting it fall into my mouth. I had the courage to complain about this to Mala Buba. 'Look,' I said to him, 'is this all you can find to give me for doing such hard work? The food of a farmer!'

My complaint deeply annoyed my boss. He was angry and insulted me. 'And your father, what does he eat?'

Insulting my father! My blood boiled. This was too much! I felt such an anger that I preferred not to reply and just left it there. I returned to the house and stretched out on my mat without responding to Adda Kano's requests for an explanation. When Mala Buba returned from the fields, he said to me, 'Excuse me, Ndudi. I know I got carried away. I want you to know I did not insult your father.'

'Whether you insulted him or not, that's your business. But what made me angry is that you would say the name of my father in that tone!'

He said nothing.

I added, 'After all, I'm not your slave. Didn't you encourage me to leave Dan Giwa? You assured me I'd have nothing to do but go to school. You lied to me!'

The affair finished like that, and I went back to my work.

However, in Gire I did have time to play, especially at certain times of the year; and I had time to be with my friends who, like me, always had an idea for making a little money. Although a true son of a Mbororo, I was probably the most ingenious among them! We had a thousand-and-one ways to earn a little pocket money.

On a piece of land that was nearly always wet and easy to water, we laid out a little field where we cultivated vegetables. 'We' – that is, my best friend Bala, Saliyu who's been an '*Alhaji*' since he made the pilgrimage to Mecca, Mustafa Aba who became an important university professor, and Musa Kessa. We would gather wood and carry bundles of firewood into town on our heads. As soon as we arrived, we'd pass through the various neighbourhoods. We were quickly called. 'Ah, little one! Is that wood for sale? Bring it here!' Often we had to bargain hard so the price would not be whittled down. Sometimes we were asked to bring sand. 'A penny per bucket!'

The Rascals' Stunts

Almost every evening of the dry season, we met on the shore of a little stream which ran between the town quarters of Gire. We danced the *dogoleya*, a very rhythmic dance accompanied by clapping hands, or the *yarindo*, which demands great agility.

We played pranks. One of them, a particularly stupid one, comes to mind, but I shouldn't be proud of it! When we found one of our friends sleeping on the sand, tired out from the heat, we tied a string to one of his toes. At the other end of the string, we made a slip knot. Then with infinite precautions, we slipped it over his penis as he was lying on his side with his legs tucked up. The string was short, just what was necessary. We stretched out around him; then suddenly we jumped up, waking him up with a fright. You can guess what happened . . . What a cry . . . ! We ran away, letting him work on the slip knot.

Such a joke often ended badly. The boy told his father, and the trouble always fell on me. 'Dirty leper! Son of a Mbororo! Son of filth! Aren't you ashamed of doing this?' I could only keep quiet.

But as soon as I had a chance, I dreamed up another trick. The parents would take up the matter again. I'd let them shout, having already decided to do whatever I felt like, all the while repeating, 'It wasn't me! It wasn't me!'

What I didn't do with my friend Bala! Here's another story. In Gire there was a woman of a certain age who must have been beautiful long ago. She had remarkably light skin. People gossiped about her a lot. Some claimed she received lovers; others said no, insisting she'd passed that age. Bala and I wanted to know the truth.

One night we went and loitered around her little house, which was somewhat isolated at the entrance of the village. In her doorway, there was a straw mat supported between two wooden posts by a solid bar which she could slide across in order to open it. We had a plan in our heads.

I approached, knocking discreetly and I called out in a loud voice (I've always been able to imitate any voice, man or woman, young or old), 'Datuwo! Datuwo!'

I heard her grumble before answering, 'Who's here at such an hour?'

'It's me!'

'Who's that, "me"?'

'Me, Abdullahi!'

'What brings you here at this hour?'

'I came for you, that's all.'

'Ah, I see what you want. To tell the truth, I'm not against it, but with people like you who are quick to talk . . . ! What shame if my children hear about it . . . At my age! And what will people say?'

'Look, do you believe I'm such a beast as to go and tell? Come on, open up!'

'Good, but make it fast before anyone sees us!'

Bala was on the other side of the door with a big stick in his hand. We heard Datuwo push the bar. Just at the moment she put her head out to see her visitor, Bala gave her a good tap on her head. Datuwo stepped back and fell backwards, shouting, 'A robber! A robber! He wants to kill me!' We ran away very quickly.

The neighbours came running. 'Someone has robbed Datuwo's house,' they said, spreading the news. Bala and I jumped into the grass so we could see what was going on. People were jabbering at a great rate. When calm had been somewhat restored, we left our hiding place to pass in front of Datuwo's house.

'What happened?' we asked the people, with an air of innocence.

'Don't you know? Robbers just attacked Datuwo!'

'You don't say! We had a narrow escape! If we'd passed just at that moment – we were coming from an evening in the Kanuri section of town – what would have happened to us?' And with that, we went off to bed.

Bala and I were always looking for a fight. Often enough, we found one. The Hausa children held us in contempt but we gave as good as we got. We called them 'pepper-eaters'! And they made fun of our unrefined food. We'd provoke them for the slightest reason. They were stronger than we were at fist fighting, but we'd try to force them to wrestle with us. We had the upper hand there.

We'd also get after the children of the pagans, those peasants who came to offer their services to do all the work the Fulbe and Hausa did not want to do. We'd insult them, calling them 'good-for-nothings' and 'sons of pagans'.

Some market days, we town boys would lay ambushes for those children. We'd fall upon them. 'Today you're going to see what town boys are worth, you farmers, bastards and sons of bastards! We eat meat, not just leaves like you do!' They'd put down their loads: vegetables, bunches of bananas, chickens, eggs, etc. The girls used their head-scarves to fasten their wrapper-skirts more tightly around their waists. The fight would begin. The blows fell all over the place. Often they were stronger than we were. Then we'd stop and flee. But, generally, before running away, we'd have time to break all their calabashes and reduce their eggs to an omelette! That was enough for us.

Their parents went to the *Lamido* of Gire to complain. He summoned the chiefs of the various neighbourhoods. If questioned, we'd planned to blame it all on the neighbouring quarter; that would confuse everything. We felt strong because we knew that not one of us would confess that day; no one would denounce a friend.

An Appealing Proposition

Once there was a certain man at Gire who passed himself off as a *Serip*.[5] He said fire could not burn him. I often went to visit him. He liked me a lot, and he also liked one of my good friends – not Bala – but a boy named Zoro. In return for a little money, we washed his clothes, which he always liked to have very clean and sparkling white.

One day he made us a proposition. 'Come with me to my far-away country. I'll teach you the Koran; I'll make you important marabouts (*mallams*).' That was all the two of us wanted: to study the Book. But Zoro had his parents. They lived in Gire. What would they say? As for me, it was simpler.

We deliberated. 'Shall we follow him, or shall we not follow him? It would be really good to go study in Sokoto!'

'OK! We'll follow him.'

One morning before the sun rose, the three of us set off. My only baggage was a blanket. The man gave me a package of sheep skins to carry on my head. Zoro carried nothing. As for the *Serip*, he followed us very solemnly with his head completely wrapped in an enormous turban that had a tiny slit for his eyes.

We came to Ngawa, where I was immediately recognised and congratulated on my good health. 'Really, Ndudi,' said my old friends, 'we hardly recognise you. You're completely healed! But where are you going now?'

'I'm going to Sokoto to study with the great marabout who's travelling with us, with me and my friend Zoro.'

We continued our journey. Before arriving in a village, the man would arrange for his visit to be announced to the chief. He insisted on a welcome worthy of his rank. Then once he'd arrived at the house of the chief, his dignity forbade him to leave that house during his entire stay. The people, informed of his arrival, would come to consult him. But note! He didn't receive just anyone. He selected his clients. They had to have a certain rank. Zoro and I sat on each side of the door, like those slaves you see at the entrance of the palace of the *lamido*. Each visitor had to pass by us if he wanted an audience.

When a visitor was introduced, he would have a hard time seeing the important person in the depths of the gloomy room. The *Serip* would be sitting aside a pile of sand. A strong perfume radiated from his clothes. 'Ah! Is it you?' He began by calling the visitor by name. 'Before you came here, didn't I already see you at such-and-such a place? Weren't you there? (A pure lie!) What do you want from me?'

'Oh!! Dear *mallam*, I want you to perform a divination for me. I'm under the spell of an evil curse; I can't have a child.'

Bowing his head, the *Serip* traced lines in the sand, marking points, erasing them and making more lines. Then after a long silence, he'd give his response: 'I see …' In Mbororo camps, he was content to respond to the requests with a simple prayer. Then he would make the person sell an animal at once in order to pay him. When he 'worked' in the villages, he received a lot of money.

I often rebelled against the way he did things. For example, he had the strange habit of making us gather wood far away from the village where we were headed.

We were tired out for no reason at all because of this load we carried on our heads for a good part of our trip!

Little by little, he encouraged me to quarrel with Zoro. He would not allow Zoro to sleep near me on the mat. He made us eat separately. Gradually I unmasked his hypocrisy. He always pretended that he could not feel fire or rain. On rainy days, he presented himself to us in dry clothes; he stayed behind us to keep under shelter! This could not last much longer.

We were at the village of Waltandi. The *Serip* gave me a jug and told me to bring water from the well. I went. The area was marshy, and there had been a lot of rain during the preceding days. The well was drowning under a large swamp, making the edges of the well invisible. Being a stranger to that area and not knowing exactly where to find the well, there was only one thing for me to do: follow the tracks left by others. But they knew where to stop; I didn't. Suddenly I felt the earth give way under my feet. At the same time I began to sink lower and lower until I was all the way to the bottom. There I gave a kick in order to get back up to the surface. I pulled myself out, but I no longer had the jug. It had gone right to the bottom with me where it was still lying, no doubt broken.

A chill seized me. I returned sheepishly, with my teeth clattering. 'So, Umaru,' said the *Serip* when he saw me in that state, 'where's the jug?'

I explained my misfortune to him. He was only worried about the jug. According to him, I'd broken it out of pure naughtiness.

'What do you mean, my dear *mallam*? I almost drowned, and you think only of scolding me for a measly jug?'

That response angered him. He began to shout louder than ever.

Alerted by the noise, our host approached us. He thought I'd done something really terrible. But when I explained to him what had happened, he began to excuse himself for not having given me any information about the edges of the well. 'What's a broken jug compared to the risk you took? Really, think first about the luck you had to escape in such good condition, and thank God.' The *Serip* kept quiet. He had nothing more to say.

I sat down next to the fire to dry my clothes and warm myself. I saw the two of them – the *Serip* and Zoro – mocking me. They thought I did not see them. They were both against me. At the next meal, the Serip watched all the more carefully to see that my plate was kept separate from Zoro's.

That was too much! I abandoned my reserve, and I spoke with the frankness I've always had in such circumstances. I told him to his face just what I thought of him: 'You pretend to be a *mallam*. You're nothing but a liar and a hypocrite! You told us you'd teach us the Koran. How many lessons have you given us since we've been with you? You've shown us your greed. Remember our trip to the Mororo camp? You "ate" them with your imitation prayers.'

I spoke those words in Hausa. He did not believe his ears. He could only respond, also in Hausa: 'Is this how you dare insult me, Umaru?'

'These aren't insults. They are simply the truth. Don't you remember the counterfeit money you made by magic which you asked us – Zoro and me – to exchange. I – everyone knows I'm the son of my father – I refused. I don't agree with such behaviour!' And I added, 'I've made my decision; I'm leaving. Just give me a few coins for my return journey.'

'Well go then! Anyway you aren't smart enough to study.'

'And you're nothing but a hypocrite!'

'What! You dare speak like that, Umaru?'

'I'm free to say what I think is the truth. I'm going!'

Zoro said nothing; however, I saw that my plans suited him. From now on, he would not have to share any money with me. He still believed that one day he'd become rich, thanks to the magic of the *Serip*.

I was in a sad state when I left: my clothes were all ragged and I was half dead from hunger. For a long time I was hungry because in the houses where I found a little corner to stay, I only nibbled at my food. I didn't dare say I was starving. Such is Fulani pride. The second night I was still obsessed with hunger. Within my reach, under my eyes, there were some women selling doughnuts. If I'd told them I was starving but had no money, they'd have been happy to give me some doughnuts. But I refrained from doing that, in spite of my desire, because of Fulani pride.

It took me several days to return. I walked one entire day without meeting anyone. After several nights, I finally arrived at Gire. Zoro came back several weeks later, tired and thin. When he saw me, he broke out laughing: 'You were the clever one! If you knew the things I saw after you left! I had to run away so I wouldn't end up in prison with him. You, you saw nothing!'

I learned a good lesson from that adventure. I had thought that I was unhappy at the home of Mala Buba and that he was exploiting me. I was always hoping I'd be happier somewhere else. I realised I was mistaken. I appreciated all the more the chance I'd had at Mala Buba's house to eat until I was full and to do more or less what I wanted.

My friendship with Zoro was strengthened by this experience. Now when we meet, as we did recently, we do not miss the chance to joke about our adventure with that hypocrite, the *Serip*.

CHAPTER 13

The *Soro* of the Adolescents

During my stay in Gire while I was boarding at Mala Buba's house, I made contact with my family and the Mbororo world each year. It was with deep sorrow that I saw them leave the Gire region for their long annual wanderings through the bush. But what joy when they came back to settle at the beginning of the rainy season! For three years, that was the way we'd lose sight of each other and then find each other again.

But I must admit that little by little we grew apart. Their Mbororo customs became a little strange to me. The life of the bush did not mean anything to me anymore. I had become accustomed to life in the village. I had learned to like it. The day even came when I would respond slowly to their invitations. I'd find excuses for not going. And when I did visit them, I planned to return the same day.

The First Confrontation

During the same season each year, Gire would be in turmoil. In every section of town, people would say, 'The Mbororo are returning! Soon there will be a *soro*!' With the announcement of that news, I would be full of joy. I was not the only one; the merchants would rub their hands. The butchers, the doughnut sellers, the petty merchants who sold kola nuts and cigarettes – everyone would profit, including those who offered to the many visitors the hospitality of a bed or a mat in their homes.

I waited impatiently for the day when the first sound of the drum would resound in the village square. As a Mbororo, I could enter into the dance, while the Hausa were ruthlessly chased away.

The *soro* is the affair of young adolescents who are called the *suka*. I was their age, but I did not give that impression because my body was not well developed. Because I was short, I was still taken for a child when I stood next to some of the *suka*. That is why they would not accept me in their game. But the main reason I was absolutely excluded from their circle was this: I had my hair cut in the Hausa style and my clothes were those of a town dweller. I no longer looked like a Mbororo. You cannot be a *suka* without braids! 'Really!' the girls said to me. 'Are you not ashamed to walk around with this head of a farmer?'

A young *suka* is completely preoccupied with his braids and with girls. He's never separated from his mirror and his bottles of perfume. He puts salves on his face. He drinks sour milk to which he has added certain powders which are supposed to make him attractive. From his magic belt, he hangs many flasks full of liquid ointments. And he certainly does not forget to obtain 'the medicine of courage' from his elders, the *kori*, who are his *soro* sponsors. They have already done the *soro* and they know what is effective against fear. The last days before the festival, they spend all their time making potions and pastes, ointments and brews, which they pour into small containers.

There is no fixed date for becoming a *suka*. It's a question of development. Some boys are more advanced than others. The change is noticed when a boy begins to take care of his hair and worry about looking handsome. Women are more interested in him. He joins with older youths to go running after girls, sometimes very far away. Sometimes he stays away several days without setting a foot at home. His parents no longer have any hold over him. They notice their boy has become a *suka*. From then on, he has left childhood behind. Some games no longer interest him, like running after the calves. He is indifferent to the herd.

The same must be said about the girls. When their breasts begin to point out, they no longer stay at home. A young girl of a certain age thinks only about her body, her clothes, her teeth, which she cleans with a tobacco flower, and her hands, which she colours with henna. All this in order to attract the attention of the boys, seduce them and make them love her. There's no public dance she does not go to. Who cares about her mother; she will have to do the work alone!

I will never forget the first *soro* I had the opportunity to attend in Gire. The Jafun were on one side; on the other side were the three clans of the Ba, Geroji and Didimanko. To simplify my story, I will just refer to the Didimanko. The Jafun president was Guda (known as Tumbadi), and the Didimanko president was Dogoyel (the son of Kurmajo). It was the Jafun who had challenged the Didimanko, so the Jafun were the 'hitters' in the first round, and the Didimanko would be the 'hit'.

One morning I heard the rolling of the Jafun drum on the square. That was the first announcement of the *soro*. It could be heard resounding all day long. The drummer wanted everyone to know the big festival of the Mbororo was beginning. He counted on the women who were selling milk to spread the news.

As planned, the first *suka* arrived two days later. They were from the Jafun clan. The next day others arrived, still the Jafun. They stayed in the Hausa section of town. Each day another group arrived. Soon they were the only people seen on the streets. I lived with them. They were my family. Mala Buba no longer saw me. I went to his house only once a day, just long enough to replenish the wood and water. I did that secretly. What shame if the Mbororo had seen me doing that labour, as though I were a common farmer!

The Jafun awaited the arrival of the Didimanko. One day late in the morning, the Fulbe arrived from the Jimeta market spreading the word that they had seen the Didimanko in two trucks waiting on the other side of the Jimeta ferry. The *kori* sounded the alert, and soon all the Jafun *suka* came, sticks in hand, to the road where the Didimanko would be arriving. The *kori* shouted in Hausa: *babaya ayifu*!

(the bottom has given birth), in other words, 'Watch your behinds!' This was only a false alarm, a joke.

The next afternoon we heard voices raised, coming from another section of town. These were the chants of provocation which the Didimanko *suka* shouted from far off to call the Jafun *suka*. All the Jafun *suka* were on alert: the Jetanko, the Wuaduganko, the Nyakanko, the Goranko and the Ringimaji.

An hour later the Didimanko arrived, all grouped together. They came through a little alley which led into the square where the Jafun were waiting. They were dressed resplendently, as tradition demanded. In their excitement, some of the Jafun pounced on the Didimanko. Their malicious attitude was immediately condemned by Tumbadi, the Jafun president. He brusquely called them to order. 'Your conduct is unworthy of a Fulani! You have elected me president of your assembly. I invited Dogoyel and his people. They're my guests. Let them come forward.' And it was agreed, according to tradition, that the competition would start only when Dogoyel, their chief, had touched his hand against the tree that was in the square.

A few minutes later the Didimanko regrouped and advanced, preceded by their president Dogoyel. Tumbadi went solemnly toward them. He turned toward Dogoyel and put his hand on Dogoyel's shoulder. Dogoyel did the same. And like that – joined one to the other – they took small steps toward the tree in the square. When they arrived at the foot of the tree, Dogoyel moved away from Tumbadi and put the palm of his hand flat against the tree trunk. Then turning toward Tumbadi, Dogoyel raised his arms and clasped his hands over his head. There was not a noise. Everyone held his breath. Someone offered Tumbadi a *soro* staff. He gathered his forces, shook his stick and, unleashing himself, hit Dogoyel's chest. He did that four times in a row.

That was the signal. Each Jafun *suka* chose a rival among the Didimanko and hit him. He hit this one; he hit that one. A violent strike here, a softer one there. Some moderated the strength of their blows because they knew the rival they hit today would return the favour on the day of revenge. Besides, all the hits were counted by the *kori*. Blows given haphazardly now would be returned by those who were hit and who would remember what had happened.

There were no accidents that evening, and each clan went back to its section of town in peace. But during the night, few in either camp succeeded in shutting an eye. From far off, they insulted each other. 'Tomorrow morning,' said a Jafun in the camp of the 'hitters', 'I will not need to buy doughnuts in order to break my fast. With you, Mr So-and-so, I will have more meat than I can put my teeth into! Slaughter, skin, grill and eat!' Those provocations were chanted in a singing tone.

Strangers, and particularly the Hausa who understood our language, were astonished to hear those chanted insults and responses. 'Ah,' they said, 'only the Mbororo are capable of this!'

Well before dawn in the camp of those who would be 'hit', the boys practised the stance they would hold while waiting for the blows. With their hands above their heads, they held mirrors against the sheaths of their decorative swords. The young Didimanko were nude to the waist. Their hair was finely braided. They were wearing necklaces around their necks and many bracelets on their forearms.

Cloths of many colours were rolled around their waists. From them hung gaudy-coloured aprons trimmed with cowry shells and metal pieces that jingled and sparkled.

In the morning the Jafun were the first to be at the village square. They waited for the Didimanko. And here is one Didimanko come to offer himself for the blows. A big circle formed around him. All eyes were directed toward his face. How would he behave? He was there, with his legs planted solidly, holding his sword at arm's length, his eyes raised toward his mirror. He smiled at his reflection. Close by, another *suka* was waiting to take his place.

Bent forward, his staff whirling in all directions, his Jafun opponent advanced, stepped back, came forward, moved away again, searching, searching for the place where he would strike. After all this feinting came the blow – brutal and hard – lacerating the chest of his rival, who did not move a muscle. Once. Twice. Then it was finished. On to the next one! The *suka* seated at the feet of the first stood up, stepped forward and said, 'Now, for me!' He lifted his mirror, fixed his eyes upon it, smiled and waited. A new *suka* was already sitting at his feet, ready to take his turn. And so on for the rest.

During this scene, shouts of encouragement rang out and the women ululated. The *kori* and the girls did everything they could to sustain the courage of their favourite *suka*.

An excited Didimanko found his turn to be hit had not come quickly enough. Tired of waiting, he pushed through the crowd, shoving them away and leaped into the midst of the Jafun. With arms raised, he said to them, 'Go on! Hit me! I'm the only one left!' The more moderate *suka* tried to calm him. But some excited Jafun jumped toward him and threatened him with their sticks. As many as ten of them were ready to hit him. Then the *kori* intervened and prevented something worse from happening.

About ten o'clock there was a break. The women had arrived to sell milk. The *sobal* merchants were there too. Those selling doughnuts were not the last to do business. When two *suka* of the opposite camps, a Jafun and a Didimanko, found themselves in front of the same merchant, they did not say a word to each other. They did not joke between themselves. In the square, each group gathered in separate places.

They only came together to dance. It was not unusual for a fight to break out during the dance. In general, this is what would happen. A Jafun *suka*, wanting to be noticed, would jump right in the middle of a group of Didimanko who were dancing. He would raise his stick to hit them. Instead of defending themselves, some Didimanko – in the blink of an eye – would unbutton their shirts to offer their bare chests for the blows. In both camps, some would interpret this gesture as a return to the *soro*. Then blows of staffs would fall like rain; but this time there was great disorder, as if war had erupted between the two groups. Everyone got involved. Blood ran. The girls, who were the most vicious, used their thick herding staves. They laid open the boys' scalps. The *kori* were overwhelmed. They would run in every direction, but sometimes they were the first to inflame the situation by throwing themselves into the melee.

The Hausa spectators did not hesitate to take sides with one camp or the other. In the mean time, other people had alerted the police. The single word 'police' made a good number of the Mbororo run away.

It was save-yourself-if-you-can! There is nothing in the world the Mbororo fear more than the police. So when the police arrived, they found no one! Everyone had gone back to his section of town.

Once the alert had passed, the *suka* came back to do the dance where, with all the clans together, the boys chose girls and the girls chose boys.

Each morning the contest was taken up again, followed by a break, and then the dance. The Didimanko who wanted to be hit presented their bare chests. Some came every day in spite of the marks from the cuts which had been made the previous day. They were proud of their injuries. For these *suka* it was really glorious to have bloody marks, which they did not hesitate to reopen by scratching. To make the blood run even more, some picked up bits of broken sticks from the ground and scraped their flesh with the splinters. When the *kori* or the young girls saw the *suka* doing that, they would jump on top of them to get the sticks out of their hands. But the *suka* continued scratching with their fingernails! Some would quit scratching themselves and go to beat their heads against a wall or a tree trunk, rebounding like balls. People would try to pin those *suka* down on the ground.

In the midst of all this disorderly activity, nothing escaped the attention of the *kori* who were counting the blows: the strikes given and the strikes received. They knew who hit who, how many times and with what intensity. They played the role of judges. Sometimes they encouraged a youngster who was scared; sometimes they calmed down a *suka* if he was too spirited, reminding him there would be a 'day of revenge'.

The girls constantly had insults on their lips, sometimes very crude ones. Our Jafun girls, far from admiring the courage of the Didimanko who were gallantly receiving the blows, made fun of them. 'Did you see his "thing" move when he was hit? My word, he did it in his pants!' And, leaning toward him, they'd say 'Ah, yes, he really went in his pants!'

To console their *suka* for the blows they had received, the Didimanko girls spoke to them about 'the day of revenge'. 'You will hit them until they die, whether you are on the ground or not, sick or not, bewitched or not!' Some girls' voices rose as they talked. Their sticks rose too, those herder sticks they had taken from their brothers and cousins. They would not hesitate to strike a rival girl on the head. Sometimes they would drop their sticks and tear each other's hair out. It was their false hair made with skeins of black wool which was pulled out. More than one felt her hairpiece hanging down her back. She would be laughed at by everyone and she would be furious.

Sometimes the dancing was interrupted by some Didimanko who, coming from far off, had not been able to arrive any earlier. From the time they were seen by the *kori* who were in charge of watching the entrance to the *soro*, the dancers were alerted by the traditional shout: *babaya ayifu!* Immediately the drummers threw down their drums, letting them roll on the ground. All the Jafun *suka* would run toward the new arrivals, their *soro* sticks in hand. The new arrivals had to have plenty of courage to keep calm when all those sticks were raised against them. It is true they had confidence in the effects of the sparkling liquid they had been careful to drink as they entered the village!

There was no dancing in the evening. From the end of the afternoon when the dance was in full swing, couples could be seen pairing off; boys and girls got together without hiding themselves from the crowd. A young *suka* often had one hand resting on the shoulder of his companion. If the girl agreed to the 'favour' the boy had asked for, they discretely eluded the others. He would take her to the room where he was staying. Then he would lock the door, very happy with his conquest.

But the manoeuvring of the *suka* would not escape the surveillance of his sponsor. His *kori* would follow the couple, standing out of sight, and would note the place of the rendez-vous. He would keep it in mind for the right moment. When he judged the time was right, he would go alone or with a friend and knock on the door of the two lovers. 'Who's there?' the boy inside would ask.

'It is me, your *kori*. Open for me. I've got the right to my share!'

The boy would open the door and beg his *kori* to leave 'her' alone. 'You know, this is my girlfriend. We've been seeing each other for a long time. Please leave us alone. If you want five hundred francs, I will give it to you.'

'To the devil with your money! It is the girl I want!' The *kori* would push him aside and send the *suka* off for a walk while he stayed inside, alone or with his accomplice.

When the young girl would meet her lover again, she would be furious and accuse him of betrayal. 'Yes, it is you who arranged for them to come and rape me!' No matter how much the young man would swear he had nothing to do with it, she would not believe him. It is a fact that when a *suka* succeeds in seducing a stranger, he hurries to boast about it and, in a certain way, offers the girl to his *kori*. But, I repeat, this only happens in the case of a stranger.

Anything was possible for the *suka* on the evenings of *soro*. A particular *suka* might be full of charm for the beautiful girls. He would obtain the 'favour' of one of them and lead her away. She would willingly permit him to hide her while they waited for nightfall. Then the boy would set out to look for another girl. He would succeed, lead her away and hide her too. And some boys would even find a third girl. Of course each girl was put in a different place. He would save one girl for himself. Then, being proud of his success, he would go and share his conquests with the *kori* of his clan. 'Come see. I'll point out the houses to you. Here, take the key. There, another key. Don't worry about it. I have my own!'

There is no question of money in these transactions. Prestige is the only recompense desired. Between the Mbororo, money is never exchanged in such circumstances. Any young girl who gives herself for money would be called a prostitute, and we would despise her very much.

But exactly what does the expression 'to ask for a favour' (or 'to obtain a favour') signify? Yes, what is this *kebal* (favour), this great preoccupation of the young people? It means spending a moment in romantic company. Nothing more! This private liaison does not necessarily include a sexual relationship. This is especially true when, as sometimes happens, a very young girl who has never known a man agrees to give a favour to an older boy. But the only thing that takes

place is romantic conversation and caressing. 'I love you . . . You love me . . .'
This is said ten thousand times and in ten thousand ways. That's all.

For us Mbororo, this self-control is part of our heritage. We were very conscientious about it. What shame for a boy if he allowed himself to get a young girl,
who had come to enjoy herself at the festival, into physical trouble! But certainly
when it is a question of a married woman, the rendez-vous is different. It is easy
to understand why!

You must realise that if there were no girls at the *soro*, there would be no interest in it. The custom would quickly disappear.

The Revenge

The first part of the *soro* was finished. Often it lasted more than a week. The *kori*
set the limits, but it was the president who had given the invitation (the president
of the Jafun) who decided when to call an end to the first part of the *soro*.

Tumbadi declared, 'Our competition has lasted long enough. For two days, no
new Didimanko has presented himself. Many of the youth have no more money in
their pockets. If you do not disagree, we will go on to the "revenge".'

'Agreed. Let's begin the revenge!'

With the announcement of that news, all the Jafun *suka* – who up to that point
had had the agreeable role of being the 'hitters' – rushed for their medicines, their
talismans, their amulets and their charms. They had something for every purpose:
to stop haemorrhages, both internal and external; to make the hand soft that was
going to hit them; to make the stick fall before it touched their bodies . . . They
went into the bush to look for roots, bark, leaves, fibres, creepers and parasitic
plants. Each boy had a formula which his 'sponsor' had taught him. Sometimes
the girls furnished them with things which they had found and had pounded for
them.

The *kori* approached their *suka* and placed a small bit of kola nut, held on the
end of a needle, into their proteges' mouths. They must not use their hands. The
suka also chewed the fibres of certain trees which their 'sponsors' had brought
them; these would diminish pain.

Those of the other camp, the Didimanko *suka*, left their village to look for *soro*
sticks. They brought back the sticks on their heads tied in bundles, and piled them
in the village square. Each Didimanko came to choose the stick that suited him
best. Some sticks were knotty with parts that pointed out like needles. Some *suka*
used knives to make their sticks even more pointed; usually those sticks came
from the tree we call *dingali*.[1] Long, flexible roots were also used. The *suka* came
to look at the sticks and discuss their size and suppleness, exchanging jokes.
'There,' someone said, 'exactly what's necessary to put so-and-so in his place, that
half-caste! That pagan lost among the Fulani! If only he could leave his skin
there!'

There was some trading of sticks among the *suka*, sticks that had been treated
with occult powers and magic. Certain rites could be used to render *soro* wounds
incurable. Other magic prevented wounds from healing over until many months

had passed. Other rites insured that the flesh would be so deeply cut it would require a white doctor to sew it up. How did they make their sticks so dangerous? I do not know. It was done by magic. Whether the sticks were poked into graves or covered with urine – the way of doing it is not important – what I do know is that these sticks, which were supposed to 'shatter courage', were successful. Indeed, boys who were very strong could be seen dropping their arms when they were hit with those sticks. Everyone wanted to know why!

Early in the morning of the new day, the drums could be heard. The Didimanko's festival was beginning. Their spirits were aroused. Facing them, the young Jafun *suka* were surrounded by their *kori* who spit on the bodies of the *suka* while uttering formulas in order to protect them. The young girls were there, silent and apprehensive. Each hoped nothing serious would happen to her beloved! What if he would fall? Or if he would collapse because of the curses put on him by an evil sorcerer? The girls were in anguish.

The hour approached. The Jafun *suka* were just waiting for the starting signal. They were bound around their waists, and they were protected by one or more magic belts. An apron decorated with cowries and pieces of sparkling glass hung from their belt. Here and there were bits of variously-coloured wool. Their torsos were bare. The *suka* had taken special care to fix their hair so it was finely braided and decorated and to make their faces shiny and coloured with make-up. Rattles were attached to their ankles.

In the middle of the village square under the tree, the Didimanko awaited their future victims. At the place of honour, a group of young men were seated. They had passed the age of being *kori* but they were not yet really adults. At this intermediary stage, they were part of the group called the *sabon-gemu*,[2] 'those whose beards have started to become pointed at the chin'. Seated on cloths, which had been spread out for them, they had an air of self-importance.

All eyes were fixed on the other end of the square where the first Jafun would emerge. They were finishing their final preparations under the tense eyes of the Hausa women who had been housing them. The women gave the *suka* their best wishes and encouragement. 'May God protect you! May He give you luck!'

'Amen!' responded the young men to those invocations. Then they broke into their traditional song. They advanced without hurrying, their eyes fixed on their mirrors. They sang, they praised themselves, they laughed. Each adolescent was preceded by his 'sponsor'. The young girls followed. Everyone sang and boasted about the merits of these courageous *suka*.

The Jafun arrived at the appointed place. The drums were now in the hands of the Jafun *kori* – the rhythm was wild. The excitement touched everyone. Some *suka* were so overcome by violent shaking that they had to be made to sit down. It was then that Tumbadi, conscious of his role as president, moved away from his peers and gallantly stood in front of the audience. In his hands he held his sword at arm's length, smiling and fixing his eyes on his mirror. He was humming to himself.

Dogoyel, the president of the opposing clan – the Didimanko who are having their 'day of revenge' – stepped forward in turn. He went toward the sticks laid out before him and chose one. While the whole audience watched, he made a show of looking for the thinnest one. Our *pulaku* code requires this. Then, without violence, rather softly but a real blow nevertheless, he hit Tumbadi four times in a row on his chest. Dogeyel was immediately followed by his assistant who also hit Tumbadi four times. The 'hitters' continued without stopping, some giving one hit, some two, some three.

The principle is as follows: each Jafun received from those he had hit on the preceding days as many blows as he himself had given and, if possible, blows of the same force. Before beginning, the first 'hitter' had to make sure everyone was following him. There could not be any interruption in the distribution of blows.

Sometimes a strange thing was seen: a *suka* would crouch and wave his stick in all directions. He made it whistle through the air. The stick seemed evil. He was searching for the place he would hit. But at the last moment, he would throw his stick on the ground and be content to touch his rival's stomach softly. This noble gesture was nearly always misinterpreted by the Jafun girls. 'This *suka* wants to make us believe he has renounced his vengeance for the love of God. Not true! He is simply afraid; he is already thinking about the next *soro* where he really hopes this boy he just spared will do the same for him!' The girls would say this very loudly.

Then the girls from the other clan, the Didimanko, would respond, 'That is false! Our *suka* wants yours to avoid the shame of falling down. Our *suka* knows very well that yours would have rolled on the ground with the first blow of the stick.' Ah! those Mbororo girls who always found a means of complaining about someone who had spared their own brother! They would even insult someone who had made this dignified gesture of a true Fulani. That is the deceitfulness of women!

That day Tumbadi was courageous: he received twenty-five blows without showing the slightest weakness. He never stopped smiling. The spectators congratulated him, and a circle formed around him: his friends wanted to lift him up and carry him back to his house. He pushed them away. 'Let me alone!' he told them. 'Do I not have the right to see how the others behave?'

'Look,' insisted his friends. 'Do you not see all the blood you are losing? Do you not see all these cuts and swellings? You must go quickly to drink the water of *gabay*.'[3] And they dragged him away almost by force to his compound. The water of *gabay*, which must be very hot when it is drunk, had the ability to help blood circulation. Big pots of this bitter water were always ready for those who came back from the competition with their bodies striped from the blows.

Tumbadi had not yet left when his assistant took his place. All the Didimanko – all those this Jafun had hit on the previous days – were there, standing in line. The Didimanko passed by rapidly, one after the other. Then another young Jafun stepped forward for his turn. All went well.

The fourth Jafun *suka* began by checking that all those who were going to hit him were really there. He said he would not allow any stragglers to come an hour later to reopen his cuts and revive the pain. 'I refuse to let you begin if everyone is not here!' The voices of the Didimanko were then heard calling so-and-so and another one. They were accused of sabotaging the *soro* by the lack of interest they were showing in it. It is a fact that on the side of the 'hitters', some are quickly tired of striking the blows. They do not present themselves for the revenge and prefer to wander around town. The *kori* must look for them and remind them of the *soro* rules so the competition will progress well, in the interest of all.

While the 'victims' passed in succession, the songs continued without stop, enlivened by young girls who did not want any part of the entertainment to be lost. Coins kept raining down on the courageous *suka*. The *kori* collected the money. The young girls gave the boys pieces cloth, which they had torn from their wrapper-skirts. Maternal uncles, proud of their nephews' behaviour, announced they were giving their nephews a sheep, a calf or even a heifer. A courageous boy from a prosperous family could receive up to five head of cattle. The coward received nothing except jeers and insults!

I remember a certain Babayo Katakore, a handsome coward who knew how to put on an act like no one else! At the first blow of the stick, he fell, his eyes rolling. The girls from his clan quickly encircled him and cried. 'The sorcerer! The sorcerer!' We knew the sorcerer had nothing to do with it. We knew Babayo very well. At each *soro*, he put on the same act.

'No! You cannot do this again!' And everyone hit him. Although he was on the ground, the Didimanko *suka* were pitiless. Once they had given him a real thrashing, they dragged him like a sack to the foot of a wall.

There were, however, cases that could not be explained except by the influence of a sorcerer. It is said a sorcerer 'eats' his victim. That is really difficult to explain. One day I will try to do that. Incomprehensible or not, there are deeds of sorcery which are certainly real. Here are some examples. A young Jetanko from the Jafun clan was hit by four boys, one after the other. With his arms lifted up high, he seemed full of courage. Everything was going well for him. And then all at once, as he would explain later, he saw a big hole open up in front of him which he fell into; he felt like his legs were being lifted up in the air. In fact, he really did fall.

The girls of the opposing clan, the Didimanko, mocked him. 'Did you see that coward?'

And one of the girls bent over him and shouted, 'Ah! Did you think you could hit our boys without them taking revenge? You were wrong! Now see what this costs you!' But those imbecile girls did not see that someone had put an evil curse on him. In the end, however, they figured out what had happened. It really had been the act of a sorcerer. But the girls found nothing better to do than blame the poor *suka*'s own clan. They said the clan was 'well known' for being a breed of dangerous sorcerers.

The spectators picked up the boy who had fallen to the ground and carried him to the house of the Hausa where he had been staying. They summoned some Mbororo who had experience in such matters and who never went to a *soro* without taking along their traditional medicine. They always foresaw work for themselves. So they began by taking out their fragrant powders and enveloping the patient in a thick smoke. Under the effect of the smoke, it wasn't long before the young Jetanko 'named' the sorcerer or sorceress who was responsible: 'It is so-

and-so; it is so-and-so that took me and "ate" me!' Instead of going to look for that person, which they did not do that day, they continued to apply their 'medicine'.

Then the boy stood up. He was very surprised and asked, 'But what happened? Why am I here and not at the "revenge"?' Without waiting for an explanation, he left, running back to take his place at the *soro*. Naturally those who had seen him fall refused to accept him back into the competition. 'No,' they told him, 'not after what happened.'

Let's look now at the case of the little brother of Tumbadi, that courageous Tumbadi responsible for organising the *soro* we are talking about. His younger brother was named Arnega. He was really a handsome boy, and as brave as he was handsome. He was afraid of nothing. He presented himself in the square without showing even the slightest sign of nervousness. He stood in the midst of the other boys his age, including my older brother. Tumbadi had loaned him a belt to knot around his waist and the apron which was attached to it. Then something surprising happened. When his turn came, right after my brother, he refused to allow himself to be hit. 'Do not touch me. I am certain I will die with the first blow of the stick!'

Tumbadi heard that and he quickly responded, 'It is your choice but it is better that you should die!'

The *kori* tried to reason with him. 'Look, Arnega, you know very well it is the rule. Those you hit have the right to hit you back.'

'It is not true,' he replied. 'I did not hit anyone.'

How could Arnega make such a statement? The *kori* in the opposite camp knew why and they understood the problem. They were the first to ask that he be allowed to leave which he did. He never again set foot in another *soro*. You can understand Tumbadi's anger and bitterness. He told anyone who would listen that he would commit suicide. And Tumbadi did make an attempt. But there was just enough time to take the knife out of his hands. 'Look, Tumbadi,' his friends said to him, 'it is nothing!'

'For me,' he responded, 'it is not nothing!'

Arnega's attitude was the result of a curse put on him by a sorcerer. Everyone was in agreement.

We Mbororo also know that sometimes there are reasons other than sorcery for such cases. I remember a young man who was sick when he arrived at the *soro*. In spite of the advice of his friends, he presented himself at the final round of the revenge. He died that same night. People were unanimous in saying, 'It is a sorcerer who killed him!' That was their first reaction. But a little later it was learned that he had just spent a month and a half in the hospital at Jimeta where he had gone because he had been extremely sick. He had left the hospital when he was barely well, and he was in that state when he absolutely insisted on participating in the *soro*. When the people heard that, they changed their minds. They attributed his death to his illness, which the *soro* had only made worse. But that did not prevent all the Mbororo from scattering as soon as they knew about his death. They emptied their camps and fled in all directions, fearing the police would come in a hurry! Certainly the police would have held the *soro* participants responsible for the death!

Many people go to a *soro*. There are problems of lodgings and of food in the village where the *soro* is held. That is why the *soro* can only take place in fairly large villages.

For the people of those villages, we used to be only 'savages' who hit each other with sticks. Gradually they accepted the idea that our *soro* is a game. Today this spectacle attracts the Whites who only think about one thing: taking photos. At first we let them do it. We were happy to beg medicines and candy from them. But it is not the same now. We start by talking about money, even for a very ordinary dance. All the Mbororo know that the Whites earn a lot of money in their country for the photos they take of us!

The *soro* now takes place under the authorisation of the *gomna* and the *lamido*. In northern Nigeria, this authorisation is nearly always granted; but across the Cameroon border, it is constantly refused. In the Central African Republic, the *soro* is also forbidden, to the point that the people there do not even know what it consists of. But the Mbororo are clever enough to know what to do so they will finally be given permission to do what is forbidden!

In spite of all these restrictions, I have the impression that the *soro* will never end among the Mbororo. If it is true that it has disappeared in certain clans, particularly among the Jafun of Adamawa (it is said they are under the influence of a certain Idje who has been dead for a long time, but whose memory is still very much alive), it is also true that there are still fanatics who do not hesitate to cross two borders to take part in a *soro*. But it must be acknowledged that each time a Koranic school is opened, a little of the *soro* disappears. In fact, it is not proper for a Koranic student to indulge in this game which, more than any other, is forbidden by the Holy Book. The *suka* with their braids are not admitted to those schools.

I said that in spite of everything, it seems to me the Mbororo will always have their *soro*. Listen to what follows and you will understand. The Prophet Usman dan Fodio[4] spread his banners of Islam in what was to become the great empire of Sokoto. His emissaries had wandered throughout the country, but the Jafun nomads – the Mbororo – had been forgotten. Then one day their women, as they were making their rounds to sell milk, learned that the Prophet was soon going to make up for that omission. By choice or by force, he wanted those forgotten people to be part of the holy war. They were Fulani. When the women heard that news, they were afraid. They spilled the milk they had not sold out on the ground and fled as fast as they could to tell their husbands what they thought would soon happen. They found their husbands gathered under a tree, braiding ropes and conversing. Of course they would have been talking about their herds.

When the men saw their wives arriving at that unusual hour, they understood at once that the women had something important to tell them. 'And so, what is it?' they hurried to ask their wives.

'We just learned,' the women answered, all out of breath, 'that tomorrow we will have a visit from an important person. His name is Shehu Usumanu. They say he is more important than a *lamido*. Surely he is coming to "eat" us! If you are men, let him come; and when he is at a good spot, attack him and make him go away.'

'OK,' the men said. And they prepared for battle.

The same day Shehu Usumanu sent an emissary to them, charged with telling them to stay in their camps because he intended to visit them. 'Very well,' they responded to the messenger. 'Tell your master we will not go away. When he comes, we will be here to welcome him!'

The next day they waited for him where they had prepared an ambush. Far off they saw the dust raised by horses' hooves so they made their final preparations. At the same time, Shehu Usumanu realised there was a plot against him, thanks to the gift of second sight he possessed. However, he continued to advance as if all were well. But at the right moment, just when the Jafun at the ambush were going to jump him as he entered a narrow pass, he shouted this command to the Jafun: 'Fight among yourselves! Hit each other!' The effect was immediate. Each one, leaving his hiding pace, jumped on his partner. The second man turned around, and the two of them clashed with their staves.

This is the origin of the *soro*. We are quick to say it began as a result of the prayer of a holy person and that no-one will ever be able to stop it.

As for the women, the ones who had given bad advice to their husbands, we say that Shehu Usumanu put a curse on them. Since that time all domestic labour falls upon the women: feeding their husbands, constructing their houses, drawing water, gathering wood. He has also burdened them with having to walk long distances to sell their milk in villages, which are so far away they can only return home at nightfall. They do all this while their husbands rest.

It is said this is the effect of the prayer of the Prophet Shehu Usumanu, the founder of the Sokoto Empire.

Figure 13.1: *Suka* and their braids

Figure 13.2: Young man prepared to receive blows in the *soro*

Figure 13.3: Young man with armpit drum in town

CHAPTER 14

From Village to Village

The Tarbiya Sect

One day my father sent word that a dispensary for lepers had just been opened in Ngawa, near the place where he was spending the rainy season. That was an invitation for me to move closer to him. I decided to take up this invitation; I was hoping to find a large Mbororo clientele there. I spoke about this to Mala Buba, my landlord. He had no objections. His business was not going well and he himself intended to leave Gire.

I left and went to settle in Ngawa, at the home of Zoro Babayo. I did not know then that nearly all the people of that village were part of a Muslim sect called the Tarbiya. Followers of this sect were very strict. They forbade public smoking; they opposed the drinking of alcohol; they chased away women who led bad lives and they severely condemned adultery.

A lot of strange stories were told about them. It was said they met each Friday late in the afternoon. They formed a circle around a white cloth that had been placed in the middle of their mosque. With their prayer beads in their hands, they repeated a phrase in Arabic as an incantation. They accompanied that chant with a very rhythmic movement of their heads and bodies. Sometimes crying could be heard. Their session lasted more than two-and-a-half hours, until night fell, until it was time to say the *mangariba* prayer.[1]

Entry to this brotherhood was like joining any religion: I mean like the pagans enter the Catholic, Protestant or Muslim religion. In order to become a member of the Tarbiya, you had to receive the prayer beads of the brotherhood from the hands of their great *modibo*, after assuring him that you were capable of keeping the faith. In my opinion, anyone who really adhered to this sect would exhaust himself in a hurry and become an abnormal person.

Consider this: at any moment the idea came into his head, a person would look to the sky, open his mouth and shout *'La Illa Illa'llah!'*,[2] no matter where he was or what time of day. Those who refused to enter this brotherhood said all sorts of things about the members. For example, if a young girl were taken to the *modibo*, he took her and did what he wanted with her. Contrary to genuine Muslim practice, women could enter their mosques. When the Tarbiya were in the midst of their incantations, they would say they were entering another world. And when they awoke from their pretended sleep, they would say they had seen God. 'There He is! There He is!' they would say. And they would fall down, to the point of losing consciousness. They would shit beneath themselves and then say it was God who had told them to do it in front of everyone.

Some were seen walking straight ahead with their eyes shut, saying God had told them to go to a certain place. Then they would return, alleging that God had spoken to them. Someone else, in the morning when he woke up, told this story: 'What joy I had last night! I saw the best of all creatures (the Prophet Mohammed)!' I was part of the group that had nothing but contempt for such idiotic and evil practices that could lead people astray. The following story shows the justice of my opinion.

This event happened in a village along the road, between Borom and Yenda. The *modibo* gathered all the people so he could communicate a message to them: God had told him that on this day he would fly in the air so he could find God. The *modibo* dressed up in his best clothes, placed his most beautiful turban on his head, and climbed to the top of the tallest tree. All his followers – men and women – were at his feet. Some were crying. Nearly all of them said they too wanted to join God. At a certain moment, he ordered silence. He told the crowd the Spirits had told him, 'Fly, go to God.' Then he stretched out his hands and threw himself into space. He crashed to the ground, right on his stomach. His insides spilled out on the ground. Seeing him bathed in his own defecation, his followers were still able to say, 'Ah! It's God that wanted this!' They became even more the object of derision by those – like me – who refused to become part of their group.

The Tarbiya were against me because I smoked. Besides that, they knew I had an illegitimate wife. But on one point, I was irreproachable in their eyes: I did not drink alcohol. That was true. But how could I take them seriously? I saw their men, those who condemned adultery, run after all the women around. They knew very well how to hide what they were doing! The men met the women in the fields or in the bush. And despite that, it was enough for one woman – even from far off – to smell tobacco, and then everyone would shout 'scandal' at me. All day long I heard their reproaches: 'He smokes. The young people also tell us he has a strange woman at his house. We really don't like that.'

Once more my father called me to account for myself. And once more I lied shamelessly, saying that all the young people were jealous of me because I was the one preferred by all the girls in the area. And I insisted, 'Yes, jealously is at the root of all their stories.'

Wanderings and Mishaps

I hurried to leave that village where I had the impression that every movement I made was watched and every word I spoke was reported. I decided to go back to Gire so I would be near my family again. But when I arrived there all I did was put my sewing machine at Mala Buba's house. His business was not very good. He had a lot of debts and few new customers. I preferred not to impose on him.

I left without knowing exactly where my travels would take me. I knew my first stop would be the village of one of my uncles who pastured his herds near Goro, beyond Borom. In fact I had no trouble finding him. My visit made him happy. I felt right at home with his family.

One morning everyone had left for various tasks and I was alone at my uncle's house when I saw some policemen arrive. They were looking for robbers who were passing through Mbororo camps where, it was said, refuge and accomplices were available.

When the policemen saw me, with my bushy hair and my appearance that was so different from that of the Mbororo, they grabbed me. 'You,' they said, 'if you are not one of the robbers we are looking for, you are one of those Nyamiri from the south who has been hiding.' No matter how often I said I was a Mbororo and that I was at my own home, they did not want to accept that. I do not know what would have happened if my uncle had not returned at that very moment. He quickly reassured them, and I was released.

Each day I told my uncle I had the intention of leaving the next day. 'Ah good!' he replied. 'So you want to leave?' But he did not talk about giving me anything. The next morning I stayed, and I told him again that my departure would be the following day. He made the same response and again gave me nothing. Each time he had good excuses. 'You see, Ndudi, I would really like to give you some money, but it has been a long time since we have sold any animals. Greet your family for us.'

I left at last and soon reached the banks of the Gongola River, at a spot where the river was very wide. Like everyone else, I had to take a ferry to cross the river. Passengers paid for their tickets after the ferry set off from the bank. When I saw the owner approaching me, I began to feel in the bottom of my pockets, saying aloud, 'My money fell out of my pocket where I slept last night!' A good smack was the only response from the man who held out his hand for my money. I rolled on the floor. He continued to kick me in the ribs. I lost my breath. People came and tried to calm him down. 'Thief!' he shouted at the top of his lungs. 'You knew you did not have any money and you got on my ferry! I am throwing you overboard! You will pay one way or another!' Because I did not even have a blanket with me – all I had were my clothes, which were in rags – he was furious that he could not even take something from me as compensation.

When I left the ferry, I walked in the same direction as everyone else. It had rained a lot during the previous days. We were walking in big puddles. Some people had donkeys with them. There was a big market nearby. I was hungry, but I did not even have a penny on me. What to do? I went toward a small group of market women. There were some women selling millet balls (sobal); others sold milk. Many customers were buying sobal and then breaking up the balls into the milk. As soon as someone finished eating, I ran to the calabash which he had put down in front of the women so I could lick up the little bit that was still on the edges. Some customers were kind enough to give me what they had left. I succeeded in this way in satisfying my hunger.

I took the Numan road and joined a Mbororo who was walking in the same direction. We knew each other, but we did not know where or when we had met.

I stayed with him, hoping to get something from him. I congratulated myself because he invited me to his house, which was a little off the road. I had plenty of milk to drink and plenty to eat – but money, none! But he did give me a big white, poorly washed tunic; I put it over my rags. Dressed like that, I had more confidence when I went back to the road, which led to the big town of Numan.

Numan – where should I go? What should I do with no money in my pocket? The same day I arrived, I made friends with a tailor who was sitting outside in front of his machine. He left to go to the market for a moment. As soon as he turned his back I took his place and made what he had planned to make. When he came back, he was surprised by the quality of my work, which he thought was superior to his own. He loaned me his old machine and invited me to work beside him. I helped him satisfy all his customers who had been complaining about his slowness.

Our collaboration was perfect. I even went to the small markets around Numan for him. I faithfully brought back the money from the sales to him, until one day I got nostalgic for Gire, Mala Buba and the friends I had left behind. I kept the money from several shirts I had just sold and took off in the direction of Gire without saying goodbye to him. I did not know that he put the police on my trail.

I was at Demsare, at the square where the buses park. I was squatting down, drinking my millet porridge, when I heard two men behind me speaking Hausa. They said, 'That is him. It certainly is him; no doubt about it.' I turned around and, just as I put the spoon to my mouth, I received a resounding smack from one of them. 'This way!' The direction: their car.

That is how I came back to Numan, where I was immediately confronted by the tailor. He gave his explanation, grossly exaggerating the wrong I had done to him. He talked about seven Nigerian pounds! He concluded by saying, 'This is a thief!' I did not open my mouth. I was taken to the police station. The tailor went with me. The discussion was rapid; so was the conclusion. 'Six months in prison. Do not whip him.' I did not have a word to say about it.

The Numan prison was crammed full. There were men, women, many Nyamiri from the south, murderers, thieves, highway robbers and also political prisoners. It was said that some were waiting from one minute to the next to be shot. Others seemed to be very much at ease, even playing cards and betting. Some never stopped fighting. There was a big strong man who had fist fights constantly; he had been there for twelve years and he thought he was the law. In the prison there was an unbearable odour of urine and human waste. The women had their own quarters.

I was locked in a very small cell called a *kurkuku*.[3] It was so narrow I could not stretch out. I was alone. The heat was unbearable that afternoon. Around six o'clock, a guard took me out. I was given something to eat that was the equivalent to two mouthfuls of porridge. But I had nothing to complain about compared to the Biafran prisoners that I saw with heavy chains on their feet and with their hands tied behind their backs or attached to their feet. Other prisoners were locked in iron cages about the size of a man. Anyone inside such a cage could not move. He had to stay perfectly immobile so he did not touch the iron spikes. The guards kept saying to the prisoner, 'If you move, you are dead! If you do not move, you will make it out of here alive.'

Many prisoners – the least dangerous ones – were made to carry sacks of groundnuts to the big barges on the Benue. Others transported bails of cotton. That is what I did. All along the path we took for this task, there was a hedge of fairly thick bushes. The first day I found a place which I would be able to get through, in spite of the uniform I was wearing. A week later I succeeded in escaping.

During all my wanderings, I found friends who gave me hospitality: in Ngawa, where I spent four days at the home of Zoro Babayo; at Demsare, where I was welcomed for three days at the home of Zoro Ajiya; and at Gire, where I naturally presented myself to my old landlord, Mala Buba.

I found him making preparations to move. This time he was serious. His bundles were packed. I offered to help him transport them to the road where he hoped to find a passing truck. His three wives accompanied him. I stayed with them until we reached their destination: Gongossi.

At Gongossi with the Witi

Most of the people in Gongossi were Witi. They hired the local people (whose name I have forgotten) to do many tasks for them. Those farmers cultivated a little millet, but it is not an exaggeration to say that all their millet was used for making alcohol. They sold only enough so they could buy clothes for *Kirsimet* (Christmas). They preferred being hungry to being without alcoholic beverages. When they were too hungry, they went to hire themselves out to the Witi.

Fights were frequent among those people. When they were drunk, their knives came out quickly. They were always in court in front of the village chief. In order to pay their fines, they lost the few goats they had. When they were drunk, they were careful not to walk around the village of the Witi, who detested alcohol.

The Witi did not have that fault, but they had others, particularly jealousy. Profound rivalry reigned among the Witi: everyone wanted to have the most beautiful millet field. This led them to shameful practices in order to make the field of their rival totally unproductive when the millet ears began to open. They cast evil spells. They made their rival sick so he would not be able to work in the fields. At least that is what I heard when I was living there.

At harvest time, you should have seen how proudly they counted the number of baskets they heaped up in their granaries. It was not unusual for one family to have five granaries. They sold some to wholesalers, that is, they sold a whole granary at a time. But, as I told you, if the harvest did not produce all they had counted on, they looked upon each neighbour as someone who had put curses on them.

Besides working in the family field, each adolescent had his own field. Actually it was by selling his own millet that a young Witi was assured of being able to buy clothes, blankets, etc. It is true that they were not hard to please; they slept anywhere and they never washed themselves, even when they returned from their fields covered with dust. Their children were as dirty as little Mbororo children. The shirts they wore were never washed; they were filthy dirty! Their parents gave them a hard life. Parents took their children along with them even before dawn to do the weeding, and they did not return home until night fell.

Nearly all the Witi had 'slaves', but not exactly in the sense we have heard about from times past; their slaves were a little more free, except for some old ones who did not want to change their habits. Those old servants still considered themselves part of the inheritance of the house which was passed on from father to son, but the young ones did not want to be called 'slaves'. When they were asked who they were, they answered proudly, 'We're Witi.' But you could tell by looking at them they were lying! The Witi settled their conflicts among themselves. They did not accept arbitration from any stranger. They also used the technique of snubbing someone. In that way, they were a lot like us Mbororo, even sharing our language and many of our customs. For us, they were real brothers even though they did not accept the name Mbororo.

They were more religious than most. When they came back from their fields, they hurried to their Koranic writing tablets. They sat reading long into the night. Many even carried their slates along with their hoes, in order to learn a text from the Koran in between two furrows. When they were tired of weeding, they rested while they read; when they were tired of reading, they relaxed by weeding.

Among the young people my age, I had friends whose behaviour surprised me a lot. They were so anxious to have money that they would hire themselves out to anyone who would pay them immediately, neglecting the work in the family field and even in their own field. They needed money so they could spend it right away for their romantic evenings. But when they hired themselves out, they did it secretly, fearing that the young girls they wanted as their friends would see them and call them 'slaves'.

I saw something strange among those farmers. For many years there had been a magician in their village who had been very effective. When he died, four walls were put around his grave. But over the years, the rain washed the mud enclosure away until eventually there was nothing left of it. That man had been known for the power of his *ronga*, a curse which could make someone invulnerable or, on the other hand, strike one's enemy on the head with lightning. Knowing him to be dead, no one thought the magician had any more power. But then it was noticed that any goat which walked on his grave died right away. I myself was a witness. Fearing for the lives of their children, people had to rebuild the walls which had fallen down.

Nearly every day I learned of new magic practices which the Witi used to harm others; one such practice was a certain *karfa*[4] which would unfailingly produce a quarrel between two lovers or between a husband and his wife.

It was said these people had many methods for attacking the virility of an adversary and for making him totally impotent. How many times did I hear about young married people being forced to go find someone who could take away the evil curse which was weighing on the husband!

Among the farmers who lived around us in Gongossi, there were some who were influenced by the mission. But for us, all those farming peoples – pagans, Christians or even Muslims – were *Kado* that is, 'non-Fulani'. We made no distinction among them. We knew that some met to pray and sing, but we never heard the name of Allah on their lips. They never once spoke about Allah. And since I never asked them questions on this subject, I did not know what their religion consisted of. Anyway, I was not interested in it.

But I had a good friend among them who was my own age. I often discussed this with him, and I invited him to become a Muslim. 'Look,' I said to him, 'why do you not come pray with us? You have everything necessary to become a Muslim. You speak our Fulfulde well, you are light-skinned, your nose is straight. You are not like a pagan farmer. You know everyone likes you. Please, come to our religion! Anyway, is this a religion you follow? You never speak the name of Allah!'

'But we do!' he replied. 'Those of us who follow the religion of the Nassara (the Whites) call on the name of God.'

'Do you know Mohammed? Do you follow him? If not, who do you follow?'

'We follow Issa (Jesus).'

'If you do not follow Mohammed, how can you pretend you have a religion? The Nassara are only bringing you damnation. You will burn in the fire of hell.' I teased him in that way.

When we were together, we would talk among ourselves: 'Have you heard those pagans who are shouting? Do they even know what they are saying?' They would meet on Sundays. They always came to their meetings well dressed. Often I myself had cut out and sewn their best clothes. They were some of Mala Buba's good customers. They often paid for their clothes with measures of millet. I had good friendships with many of them. They knew me well.

The big festival of those farmers, which is called *Kirsimet*, was drawing near. That year it coincided with one of our Muslim feasts, the 'feast of the lamb'. I was bold enough to say to my boss, 'Mala Buba, it is festival time, the big feast for everyone. Could you not give me a piece of cloth so I could make myself a robe?'

'What?' he answered curtly. 'Are the clothes you are wearing not good enough? Are all your friends not dressed just like you?'

I wanted to tell him everyone was dressed up for the feast. Nearly everyone had new clothes except me, everyone in the whole village of Gongossi. But I did not say a word, and I did not go out all day long, refusing to mix with either the pagans or the Muslims. The next day in a moment of rage, I went to the village nearby, to Asira Maba, and took up work with a farmer so I could make a little money.

Very soon I had a visit from my father. It was Mala Buba who had sent him. Mala Buba regretted not being generous with me and asked me to come back. I refused. The next day I thought about it again. I returned to Gongossi. But it was only so I could bid Mala Buba my final farewell. He refused to let me leave. He followed me right to the Ngurire market, near Yenka. When I got on the truck, he asked the driver to make me get down. I shouted louder than he, and the truck started off.

I did not want any more of Mala Buba. Proof of that is that when I learned about the death of his old father and I hurried to give him my condolences, he tried again to make me change my mind, but I remained firm.

CHAPTER 15

Memorable Events

It was only natural I should return to Gire where I could count on the hospitality of Dan Giwa. I had no thought of going back to my old job of gathering his wood and carrying his water. I rented a sewing machine, a *singa* (Singer), and I quickly found my old customers, particularly among the Mbororo who were once again together around Gire for the rainy season.

My *Kori Soro*

But several weeks after my return, I quickly abandoned my *singa* and my customers: a *soro* had just begun. Nothing else counted with me any longer! Dan Giwa knew this very well, and he let me have a lot of freedom. I heard what the Hausa were saying. 'Look,' they said among themselves, 'it has overpowered him. As soon as he comes back to our village, Ndudi picks up Mbororo customs again as if he had never left them. At the first roll of the drum, he cannot sit still any longer. The Mbororo side of him takes over!'

For this new *soro* my place was among the older young men, the *kori*. I was a *kori* like the others; at least I thought so. But you will see that they did not consider me to be exactly like themselves. Nonetheless I no longer needed to eat at Dan Giwa's house. I took all my meals here and there with the *kori*. I should say our food did not cost much; we felt everything was owed to us! A *kori* came with his pockets empty; he did not have a penny to spend.

Before starting our competition, we were careful to go as a group to present ourselves to the *lamido* and ask him to permit us *kori* to do as we pleased, according to our Mbororo customs. We asked him to speak to the merchants in the following terms: 'If these young people ask you merchants now and then to give them something free, accept that with a good heart. If you do not, watch out for yourselves and your merchandise! It will be useless to complain to the *lamido*!' The *kori* had carte blanche.

The little Hausa girls who were selling things knew all that very well. Before beginning their rounds they were careful to run over to us and offer us some of the doughnuts which they were supposed to sell. The other women – those who sold *sobal*, sugar cane, manioc tubers – did the same thing. The goat-skin sack which each *kori* carried on his shoulder did not stay empty very long.

All the merchants were, you could say, 'taxed'. We were even quite choosy, refusing what we did not like. In general, they served us with a good heart. At least outwardly!' Because they feared nothing more than seeing us get angry and leave. They knew the punishment they were asking for: nothing other than being ostracised! We would order a boycott of their shops, and our orders were always followed.

Everyone knew this because we had been careful to make a proclamation when we arrived: 'If we Mbororo order a boycott against a merchant, anyone who breaches the order will expose himself to the worst misfortune for the rest of his days!' I heard the Hausa say among themselves in hushed voices: 'It is in our best interest to take what the Mbororo say seriously. No people in the world can put curses on others like they can!' So each merchant took every pain to serve us.

A *kori* would be considered dishonoured if he bought even one kola nut. On the other hand, the *suka* each had to sell a cow in order to come to the *soro* with his pockets full. This gave them about twenty thousand francs which they spent right to the last centime. As for us, once more we filled our pockets with the money we received and which we took care to share among ourselves.

Any method was used for squeezing money out of people. For example, in groups of ten, we blocked all the roads and paths which gave access to the marketplace. We traced a line in the dirt with our sticks. To cross it, every young girl and every *suka* had to pay. There were no exceptions! Anyone without money had to borrow some. And any merchant who came to this 'border' with his goods on his head had to pay a tax. Then we would get together to count the money and replenish our nest egg. There were certainly some who tried to trick us, but we watched carefully so no one took that too far.

We also blackmailed people. We would say, for example, to a girl, 'Were you not "taken" last night by the *kori*: True? Not true? It is in your interest to pay us so we do not spread this around and so all the *suka* will not be against you.'

'I have no money!'

'Go borrow some,' we would advise her.

All caprices were possible for the *kori*, as I know myself! The *kori* could carry out the most ludicrous idea, either in the middle of the day or under cover of night. For example, one morning a farmer arrived at the *soro* locale; it was obvious he knew nothing about our Mbororo customs. He was carrying a sack of guavas on his head. The *kori* naturally asked him to give them some. He refused. 'Did I carry them here for you? I came to sell them!' he said angrily. And he struck a *kori*. When the *kori* pulled himself together, he hit the farmer on the head with his stick. The farmer rolled in the dust.

The Hausa witnesses at the scene pleaded on behalf of the farmer. 'This time you Mbororo have gone beyond the limit. Really, you have gone too far. We are going to complain to the *lamido* and ask him to put an end to your *soro* immediately. We have seen enough of you in our village!' And they did make a complaint.

The *lamido* summoned our leader. We were gathered all around him. That great *lamido* threatened to expel us. All in unison, we addressed him, saying, 'O Lamido, all respect to you! May God give you a long life! We "fart" before you![1] Yes, we "fart", we "fart"!' We should have said we 'apologise', but by mispronouncing the word, we actually said, 'We fart, we fart!'

'What did you say?' asked the *lamido*. We repeated what we had said, bowing deeply and throwing dust on our heads. All the onlookers started to laugh, including the old man with the guavas.

The *lamido* also took this joke in good humour. 'Ah, these Mbororo!' he said. 'They are not like other people. They're nuts! They are all half crazy!' And addressing himself to the plaintiff, he said, 'You see what they are like. What can we do? Did you see how they spoke in my presence? Nothing good can come from this!'

He turned toward our president. 'Go,' he said. 'Go back to your insanity. But do not start any more!'

'We will not start any more. That is a promise. We swear!' We went back to our dances, after giving the sack back to that brave man who did not know anything about Mbororo.

I myself was a victim of the caprices of those *kori*. They did not want me to be just like them. They particularly disliked my hair which they thought was too bushy. They would not stop pulling my hair. 'If you do not decide to cut your hair,' they said, 'we will shave it off with our fingernails.' So I was obliged to have my head shaved, keeping only a tuft. All the young girls were invited to come and braid it for me. They took turns; one of the girls braided my hair, the next one took it apart and so on. How many girls took part? More than fifty. This session took place in the middle of the square, after the *kori* had quieted their drums, stopped their dance and gathered the spectators around.

When I was freed, I began to have terrible headaches. There was no doubt about it, my illness had come back. I had to lie down. I was panting, my chest was heavy, as if I were going to die.

My father was called; he did not waste any time getting out his medicines. He enveloped me with smoke. I quickly uttered the name of a young Bodi girl who already had a well-established reputation for being a sorceress. As soon as I pronounced her name, I was able to sit up. The first thing I asked for was someone to cut off the tuft of hair which was left. 'In the name of heaven, cut it quickly if you do not want me to die!' It was cut off right away.

After I had rested three days, I went back to the *kori*. They made fun of me. 'Oh, you wanted to be on our side?! You joined us but you also took up with witches.'

They did not say a word to the young girl who was said to be a sorceress. But no one doubted she was responsible.

So I took my place again among the *kori* and participated once more in all their effronteries. The festival was not over.

The next day the president stopped the beating of the drums and addressed the gathering: 'Silence! As you know, Ndudi has not been able to participate in our games for several days. We have decided to give him some compensation, particularly since he has become an authentic *kori*. We are offering to let him touch the breasts of all the young girls who are here; their warmth will finish curing him.'

While some *kori* barred the exits, other *kori* put all the young girls in lines, including the Hausa girls from the village. I had to pass them all in review. An exception was made for my older sister and the daughters of my father's brothers. None of the girls were hesitant. Any girl who might have been tempted to sneak away knew very well what would happen!

A *kori* in front of me uncovered each girl's breasts. I touched them and had to make some remarks about each one. I had to say something, even if it was the worst sort of remark. I did not do so badly, judging from the laughs I got.

The ceremony of the *soro* is, as you have just seen, an important event for the area where it takes place. Besides the Mbororo, it attracts a crowd of people: merchants (as we know) and also performers. Many praise singers circulate through the audience to earn a little money for their merriment. Shows are put on by women who contact the *bori* spirits. Specialists in *boka* and *burda*[2] are there, and so are conjurers.

Nigeria at War[3]

The year of my unforgettable *soro* in Gire was the year that a *kudata* (coup d'état) took place in Nigeria. The *Sardauna*[4] had been killed. The Nyamiri, people of the South who lived in the North, showed their great joy. The Nyamiri are also called the Ibo. Among them were government workers, as well as rich merchants and skilful artisans. None were Muslim. They had all adopted the customs of the Whites. Many were Christians and they had a deep contempt for those who were not of their own people. It was sufficient to wear a robe like the Hausa or the Fulani to be considered worthless by the Nyamiri. They insisted on eating luxury foods like the Whites, refusing local food. They put on superior airs.

At the announcement of the death of the Sardauna, there was a great explosion of joy in the Nyamiri neighbourhoods. People said they had records and cassettes which allowed them to hear the groaning and the death rattle of the Sardauna's last moments. Some added they had listened to these sounds as they laughed, clapped and danced. That was too much for the Hausa. Fighting broke out between the Hausa and the Nyamiri, especially in Jimeta, but also in Gire.

The police were under great pressure. They searched every passer-by. They feared a traffic in bullets and bombs. Nyamiri trucks were inspected from top to bottom, especially when they had come from the South where they were re-supplied. It was said that the relatives of the Nyamiri were cannibals and that, when they had killed someone, they skinned his head in order to make a mask and kept his teeth in order to decorate their homes.

At this time there was a strange event which aroused all of Jimeta. In that town there was a young girl of remarkable beauty. Everyone knew her. One day she disappeared. Actually, one of the Nyamiri had killed her. He had cut her into pieces, which he had wrapped up in paper and placed in a trunk. A chemical prevented the flesh from decomposing. On top of the packets, he had put a pile of things in order to trick whatever authorities came along.

He locked the trunk and gave it to some boys so it could be carried to the place where trucks were parked. The Nyamiri followed the boys.

As soon as the trunk was set on the ground, it was spotted by the police. They asked the owner to open it for inspection. 'What?' said the Nyamiri. 'Am I not from this town? Am I not a merchant whom everyone knows, including you? I am not going to open my trunk for you. It only contains merchandise for my shop!' The police insisted. The merchant refused to give the key to the police. But in Jimeta there was a White who was able to open all the locks in Nigeria. He was sent for. He had no difficulty opening the trunk.

At first the police saw nothing abnormal. Then they dug a little deeper while the Nyamiri was arguing like the devil to prevent their search. All at once, while opening a packet which seemed suspect to them, they found a bit of human flesh. The Nyamiri held his head in his hands.

A whistle brought other policemen. Soon there was a mob of people around the open trunk. The Nyamiri merchant was taken to Yola where he was executed along with some of his 'brothers' who had been found with him near the trunk. At the announcement of this news, all the Southern merchants – the Nyamiri – indignant about the executions, revolted. They fell on the Hausa but the Hausa, who were more numerous, killed the Nyamiri. That was the beginning of the Nigerian war in our area.

The water carriers, armed with the solid cross-bars they used for carrying buckets, ran into the Ibo shops to vandalise them. All the Nyamiri who fell into their hands had their skulls smashed by those bars, which the water carriers handled like big clubs.

I was at the market when I heard the first shots. Before long, smoke was rising everywhere. The market emptied as if by magic. Some people abandoned their donkeys and their goods in order to run faster toward the Benue River. The ferryboat owners, not knowing what had happened, let the people pile on with their merchandise, bicycles and other things. Soon the ferry was so full that the people who were at the sides had a hard time withstanding the pressure. Several fell into the water. When the ferry had crossed the river and unloaded its passengers, the owner refused to return to pick up other customers – more and more of them who were waiting on the opposite bank.

The Ibo who were chased by the Hausa were to be seen jumping into the water. One of them was shot at many times. Each time he disappeared, only to reappear. Finally he raised his hands, begging not to be killed in the water, but rather on land. The Hausa let him swim back. Then, as soon as he put his feet on the ground, they killed him. Many people watched that scene.

During that time, all the Ibo in town were being chased down. Those who fell into the hands of their pursuers were thrown onto trucks. Their hands were tied, and they were taken to Yola. Others were imprisoned in Jimeta. That prison was soon too full.

Little by little, by telephone or by radio, people learned that the Ibo had revolted in Jimeta and that the Hausa were capturing the Ibo they knew in their towns and villages. That was the case in Gire, and later in Kompani and Wuro Bokki. In this last village, the Ibo were chained together two by two. They were put on a barge which was taken to the middle of the Benue and then sunk. Several Yola residents saw the cadavers pass by them, carried away by the current.

Then an order came by telephone from Lagos: 'Stop killing the Ibo. Do not touch any more of them. Let them return to their country.'

As soon as the Ibo shops had been abandoned, the Hausa hurried to pilfer the merchandise. They filled sacks with radios, watches and clothes. As soon as someone had put aside his full sack, it was stolen from him while he was filling a second one. Those who were more interested in money went to the banks. Armed with iron bars, hammers, or even rocks, they smashed in the walls and took the bills and coins. They also filled sacks which they stole from each other.

What confusion! Some ran toward the shops in order to steal; others fled from the same shops to escape death. At that time the Ibo no longer were attacking anyone. They themselves were being killed by the police or by the Hausa.

Later I learned the violence had been much worse in the towns of Jos and Bauchi. It was said that blood ran in the streams there. The Ibo were taken by the dozen. They were doused with gasoline and burned alive. The 'wart hogs'[5] were brought to make big holes where the cadavers could be buried. The Ibo who escaped that massacre ran to the bush where several died of hunger. According to what I know, the war then exploded in the South. Ojukwu wanted to rule all of Nigeria. Ironsi[6] revolted against him and claimed the presidency was his. I think Ironsi was killed. Anyway, Ojukwu took command and led the war operations.[7]

There was a mobilisation in the North. All the young Hausa presented themselves at the barracks. Among them were a certain number of Mbororo, especially those from the Danagu clan. They had no idea what war was, but they found it a good occasion to show their courage. It is even said that one of them became a colonel. Now it is said that all those soldiers have nothing to do except spend money ... I still have a photo of one of those Mbororo soldiers; he was a commander. He had not had any training, but he succeeded in distinguishing himself. And now he is a very contented man.

One day one of my friends by the name of Assar told me he intended to join the army. 'Me too!' I responded. We presented ourselves at the barracks. We were told to come back the next day. The following morning they began by weighing us. We had to take off our clothes. They quickly saw I was sick, so they could not take me. I cried in rage because I saw my friend leave, dressed in a beautiful, brand new military uniform.

A little later, Assar sent me his picture in uniform. He was wearing rainy-season clothes; he had a bush helmet on his head and a gun in his hand. With one knee on the ground, he held his gun as if he were shooting something. 'And just to think,' I said to myself while admiring the picture, 'that I could have been like Assar if I had not been sick!'

It was at Borom that my friend Assar and I had tried to join the army. I went back to Gire all alone to become a tailor again. I kept up with what our soldiers were doing. I could do that easily because of the daily radio announcements: so many Ibo killed, a certain village captured, our armies entered a certain town.

I always had news about my friend Assar. I even knew where his *bataliya*, number twenty-five, was. There were other *guroup* with numbers too. And so we knew, for example, which group was taking its turn to go to war.

I heard it said that when the hour came for Muslim prayer, some of the soldiers gave their guns to another group who kept watch. Then they traded places; the first group stood guard while the second group prayed. Then they all went back to the war. There was a lot of talk about the exploits of one or another of the soldiers.

A lot of Frenchmen, during the period when they came by plane to bomb the soldiers of the North, joined Ojukwu's army in order to earn money. One day one of those Frenchmen went alone into the bush, well armed and alert. He found himself face to face with a Muslim soldier who was also alone. The mercenary sent a burst of bullets in the direction of the Hausa soldier. But the shots never touched him. A second blast did not have any effect either. The Frenchman used up all his bullets on the Hausa who just watched him, standing with his arms crossed. Having no more ammunition for his gun, the mercenary took a *gernet* off his belt and threw it at the Hausa. It exploded with a great din. There was thick smoke, which took a lot of time to disperse. When it had disappeared, the Hausa was still there in the same place with his arms crossed. The *gernet* had had no effect.

The two men then began to fight hand to hand. Each man drew his big war knife. The White, who was very athletic, dodged all the attacks of the Hausa. Soon they were grappling with each other. The White wanted to stick his knife between the ribs of the Hausa, but he could not make it penetrate. He tried several times with no luck. For a moment the Hausa had the upper hand, but he was not successful either in stabbing his knife into the stomach of the White.

There was nothing left to do but fight with bare hands. The Hausa, who was stronger than the White, pinned the mercenary on the ground and strangled him until the Frenchman's breath was cut off and death came. Then the Hausa took everything the White had on him: his gun, his war knife and the number he was carrying.

The news of that man-to-man battle quickly spread the great glory of that Hausa, whose name I have forgotten. He had his hour of fame.

But I still have not forgotten the name of another hero who was also famous. He was a Kanuri by the name of Bukara Mandara. He alone attacked an entire village. For a weapon, he only had a *galiyare* (a throwing knife). He threw it in the direction of the enemy and, while he stood there, he saw it pass from one head to another, cutting them off right at the base of the neck. His knife never fell to the ground, but it came back into his hand when he wanted it to. After killing all the villagers, he burned the whole village. This is what people who had 'knowledge'[8] could do during the war.

Afterwards this powerful Bukara Mandara was demobilised. He would have killed everyone! Ordinary soldiers were preferred, like those in other armies of the world.

Among the army of the North, there were also pagan soldiers, the Bata, who formed their own companies. In the midst of a battle, one of those Bata companies took fright. It disbanded and tried to flee to the rear. Seeing that, the Hausa shot at the Bata, hitting them in the legs. Among the Bata was a Hausa soldier who had followed their example and was fleeing too. Another Hausa found him in the midst of the Bata, his legs broken by the blast. The other Hausa did not hesitate to finish off the man, saying to himself that that man would never again be good for anything anyway. Many escaped, and today they have wooden legs.

These were the stories we told each other in Gire and in the area around Jimeta at the time of the war with the Ibo.

When the Mbororo came home on leave, they talked forever about their protection from bullets. They attributed it all to their many charms. They said when the enemy started shooting them, either the bullets did not leave the gun or the gun exploded when they pulled the trigger. If necessary, in order to get out of a bad situation, the Mbororo could transform themselves into tree leaves or simply disappear from sight without anyone knowing where they'd gone. This was called 'entering the *bushin*'!

The Mbororo did not forget to use this magic when they felt surrounded by superior Ibo forces. Thus they never suffered the dishonour of fleeing from the enemy, nor all the consequences of such behaviour.

This was a prosperous time for the *mallams*. There was not a soldier – not a Muslim, Christian or pagan – who would agree to go to the front without being protected by the magic of the *mallams* or by their prayers. The most sought-after were the Mbororo *mallams*, reputed for their knowledge and their 'bush medicines'. The Nigerian war was the source of fortunes for many of them.

There were also a certain number of Mbororo who abused the belief people had in them by offering so-called magic protection, which was only *'perlimpinpin'* powder! On the other hand, it cannot be denied that some prayers of real *mallams*, especially the *modibos* of Sokoto, were genuinely beneficial. All those people prayed night and day so their country would not be 'eaten' (conquered). In the Sokoto region, the country of Shehu Usumanu, public prayers were said each Friday in the mosques, like they were in all of Nigeria.[9]

In Anassa one Friday afternoon, the mosque was full of the faithful who had gathered for the great prayer. That was the moment the Ibo chose to bomb the mosque. All those present were killed by the bombs or burned to death. That event certainly provoked another outburst of violence on the part of the Hausa against the Ibo who were still there. It ended in a blood bath.

I personally saw some of the events of the Nigerian war which I have just told you about. Some other events I have only heard about. For as you must know, the war did not come to Jimeta and Gire. It took place in the west and the south. But there was a general coming-and-going of soldiers returning from the front and departing again. The government made many proclamations. Every day the radio gave us the news.

The Massacre of our Herds

The Mbororo suffered from this war more than other people; let me tell you why. Some of them had the good idea of moving with their herds toward the Cameroon border. They crossed the border easily. But others decided to have patience and wait for better days. They stayed where they were. It should be said that the Gire area was renowned for its good grazing. More herds were there than anywhere else. They were spread out in every direction. My father was in the south.

But toward the west, the first signs of a terrible cattle disease appeared, pleuropneumonia. Cases broke out here and there. It is a contagious disease which Mbororo fear, attacking the lungs and the liver. The stomach bloats. The animal bellows and foams at the mouth. As it grazes, the animal can leave this foam on the grass. Another animal passes, grazes on the foam and is contaminated.

It was sufficient for a veterinary inspector to declare an animal infected – rightly or wrongly – for the herd to be threatened with destruction. What a terrible possibility for a Mbororo! Everyone did whatever he could to keep absolutely secret any case within his own herd. He would go as far as possible into the bush. But betrayals were frequent. A Mbororo who had been the object of a severe inspection and had lost a large part of his herd did not hesitate to betray his neighbour. 'I'm not the only one who has sick cattle. Go to so-and-so and see if his cows are not the same as mine.'

The accused Mbororo would receive an order to present his herd to the veterinarian. But before he went, he was careful to take suspected animals further out into the bush. He tried hard to show only those animals that were well. The veterinarian often judged them to be well. Then the Mbororo might hear, 'OK, your animals are not infected yet, but the disease will come. We know your animals have been in contact with your neighbours' and they had to be slaughtered last week. Yours are certainly contaminated. It will be necessary to kill them too.' No matter how much the Mbororo begged, it was a waste of time! To console him, he was told, 'The total number of animals slaughtered will be written on this paper. Later when you present it, you will be fully reimbursed.' But we knew very well that was nothing but a joke. Actually the animals which were slaughtered were not put in a hole and covered with gasoline, as ought to have been done in such a case and as had been done until then; that meat was carried away!

The Mbororo were intelligent enough to know what to do in case of an epidemic and to take the necessary measures themselves. When they had an infected animal, they killed it immediately, buried it and then went far away into the bush with their herd. Then they treated the rest of the cows with their 'bush medicines', which were as effective as the medicines of the Whites. Thus they managed to do something and, by themselves, to save part of their herds. However, during this war, the Mbororo who fell into the hands of the veterinary inspectors saw their cows slaughtered one after another. Sometimes up to five *mallams* were doing this work and slaughtering the cattle according to the rules, working all day long. All the slaughtered cattle were thrown, without being skinned, into trucks which were guarded by the military.

One day I passed one of those trucks on the road to Jimeta, near the place where you take the ferry. It was full of slaughtered animals. Feet were sticking through the sides of the truck. When some of our women selling milk saw that sight, they could not stop themselves putting down their calabashes and sobbing. In the villages where the *mallams* were slaughtering, you could only hear the crying of children and the wailing of the Mbororo women. It was pitiful!

Some Mbororo went crazy. Without their cows – and knowing nothing about commerce or agriculture – what could they do with their lives? Others got hold of themselves and swore no-one would come again to take away their wealth. They armed themselves with bows and arrows. A real revolt! But what could they do against soldiers who arrived in trucks, well armed and very much determined to have their way?

This was how they killed the animals of Babayo from the Goranko clan; the animals of Gobi, who was one of Babayo's relatives; those of my uncle Haroji; and those of another relative named Suley. One Mbororo in my family lay across one of his big steers when they were going to slaughter it. 'Kill me at the same time!' he shouted. The soldiers forcefully took him away while the *mallam* did his work. On the other hand, Suley made no move of revolt. Even today when someone reminds him of that painful time, he always repeats, 'What could we have done? Did God not send this?'

We learned later that those trucks full of slaughtered animals were taken to a factory where there was a machine which took off the hides. Then all the quarters were sent by plane to combat areas.

Very few received their money. Some animals here and there were given as compensation. Mostly it was in vain that the Mbororo presented their papers attesting to what they should have been reimbursed. They were not told 'no', but pleasure was taken in making them wait many days in front of banks with their papers in their hands. And because they did not know how to read and they understood nothing about financial dealings, many took the path back to the bush without obtaining any money at all.

Do not go and talk about this today to the Mbororo in the Gire region, where it was rare to find any Hausa who showed sympathy or felt sorry about our enduring such a great loss! And do not talk to them about the *mallams* who were told to come slaughter the animals and who, for the most part, seemed to take pleasure in that work which they were paid to do! And finally, do not talk to them about the *lamido* who did not lift his little finger to defend them! Actually he did not say a word, offered no help and did nothing to prevent what could be called a massacre.

And during that time not one animal of the town Fulbe was touched! Furious over that injustice, the Mbororo left the inhospitable land of Gire, vowing never to set foot there again. Many of them went to the area around Malabu, some to Jabi Lamba and others to Ngawa. Our only consolation was learning that the three principal *mallams* who had collaborated in this operation of destruction went crazy. One of them often walked in the town streets with a knife in his hand, shouting at the top of his lungs that he was going to cut off his male organ. These punishments did not surprise us; to the contrary, we were waiting for them. We have always known that cows slaughtered for pure pleasure or out of malice revenge themselves on those who killed them. To be precise, we say their Spirits seek revenge.

Gire gained nothing from this massive departure of the Mbororo. It had been a big town, thanks to the Mbororo. Now, it became a place of no importance. Many shops closed because there were no customers.

I should have left Gire with all the Mbororo. However, I stayed out of fidelity to my inseparable friend Bala. People always saw us together. We shared everything. When there was a prank to pull, we were both there! One day he was not with me. He had gone for the day to get some sugar cane at the home of a relative ten kilometres from Gire. When he arrived there, he became very sick with stomach pains. That night he died. When this news came to me, I did not want to believe it. By the time I heard the news, he had already been buried.

I felt very alone. Not being able to endure Bala's death and my isolation, I left Gire for the village of Wuro Bokki (the Village of the Baobab) where members of my family often visited. They had their rainy-season camp several kilometres away.

CHAPTER 16

The Dance and the Wodabe

I bid my goodbyes to Gire the day after Bala's death.

For some time, I'd had nothing: no rented sewing machine, no customers, no work. With my friend Bala, I had lived by my wits. In order to have a little money, we spent our days watching for the arrival and departure of buses. We would offer our services to the merchants to transport their bundles. We had to be content with the little money we earned that way. So on the road to Wuro Bokki, I carried nothing with me. I had old, ragged clothes and not a penny in my pocket. I arrived on Thursday, which was market day.

Knowing no one, what could I do except go back to living the life of a Mbororo? My father's camp was not far away. He was living on the banks of the Benue. I went back to herding the cows. Anyone who would have seen me in the midst of my animals with a staff across my shoulders would never have imagined I had been a town dweller. But the young people my age knew I had lived in town, and they never stopped reminding me about that and laughing at me!

This village was also called Kompani because of a commercial company which stacked mountains of groundnuts there. Workers carried the groundnuts onto big barges to be transported to Lagos and made into oil. Kompani was a very animated village, especially in the groundnut season.

Soon I knew all the tailors in the village. When I would arrive at the market, I would always go over to the place where they were sitting. They saw I was burning with desire to show them what I could do. Musa was the first to invite me: 'Take my place!' After several minutes, he could not believe his eyes. 'It is the first time,' he said, 'that I have seen a Mbororo sitting behind a sewing machine!' From that moment on, he would call for me to help him when he had a lot of orders. While he would cut, I would sew.

Among the people of Kompani, the one I got along with best was not a tailor; he was a petty trader. His name was Ado, the son of Mal Guru. We were the same age. His father, who was also a merchant, had just bought him a shop on the banks of the Benue, a shop which had belonged to an Ibo who had been killed behind his counter. We got along so well together that he offered me a room in his house. And he encouraged me to go back to my sewing. I did not say 'no', but I did not have a sewing machine. I hesitated to ask my father for permission to sell one of my cows. But a friend of my father, a Mbororo, intervened for me. He told my father that since I was not exactly like the others, the day would probably come when I would abandon the life of the bush for good. 'Because he knows how to sew, it is better that he buy a sewing machine.' My father went along with that advice; I got my sewing machine.

So I set myself up in the room which Ado had offered me. Our house was well situated: along the main access road to Kompani and on the banks of the Benue.

The bulk of the local population was made up of Bata, the farmer-fishermen. They were not poor. They'd send whole barrels of dried fish to the towns of Jimeta and Garoua.

The *Gerewol* Dance

I had good customers among the Wodabe who were particularly numerous in this region. I knew their tastes and I was always good at making their trousers and tunics, sewn in the special way they liked them. A Wodabe I was sewing for said to me one day, 'Soon we will have our big *gerewol* gathering. I will let you know about it. Do not miss it!' This Wodabe was named Adamu. He had been my first customer. He had encouraged many of his friends to order clothes from me. After several weeks I had taken all the Wodabe customers from the other tailors. There was nothing surprising about that: I was a Mbororo; I knew the kind of clothes they wanted and made the prices as low as possible.

One Sunday morning, Adamu said to me, 'The *gerewol* is going to be on Wednesday. I am inviting you. Do not forget to bring merchandise to sell. You will find customers right away! I will wait for you. Come see me when you arrive.' The following Wednesday, I went there. I did not try to see my friend Adamu because I knew he was very busy. On the ground, I spread the bundle of merchandise I had carried on my head: tunics and wide, baggy trousers that the Wodabe liked. I had customers immediately.

Soon Adamu arrived, excusing himself because he had not been there to greet me. He invited me to save all my merchandise for his friends. 'Do not worry. They will buy everything from you!' And that is what happened. Two hours after my arrival, I had already sold everything and – with money in my pocket – there was nothing left for me to do but watch the *gerewol*.

What an astonishing spectacle! The dancers were completely transformed by their costumes and make up. I looked at one, I looked at another - their faces were tattooed in vivid colours. It was impossible to recognise a face! They danced, each one as beautiful as the next! The audience – that is, their relatives, the Hausa merchants, the farmers and some Jafun who were there (including my oldest brother) – admired them.

Here is what happens at the *gerewol*. When night falls, a big fire is lit - an immense fire, the size of a big truck. Its flames are fed by throwing on very dry twigs. The light of the blaze reflects on everything the dancers are wearing – especially the metal and glass spangles around their necks and on their chests. The costumes of the dancers are quite varied: there are rattles on their ankles and ostrich

plumes, both white and coloured, on their heads, plus bracelets, pendants, trim-
mings and many other ornaments. Around their waists, the dancers wear magic
belts with aprons decorated with cowries and thousands of sparkling things.

Before lighting the fire, two young girls are summoned and told, '*Pe'ine,
pe'ine!*' – that is, 'Choose, choose!' So one girl, covered with a veil which she discretely lifts, advances with small steps toward the dancers. She passes along the
line of *suka* who are humming and shaking while they wait. All eyes are on the
girl's right hand. She holds it at her side. When she uses that hand to touch the
right hand of one of the dancers - all of them have their arms dangling – she is
pointing out the one her heart has chosen. By that gesture, the boy is chosen for the
day. Then the young girl disappears, passing between two boys who move aside.

The next day the elders – assembled at the foot of a tree on a thick cushion of
barkehi leaves covered with mats and facing east in the direction of the dance
music - make a proclamation. Moments later all the young Wodabe can be seen,
with *barkehi* leaves in their hands, squatting before the elders and looking up at
them. A *kori* stands and acts as the elders' spokesman, saying, 'We are gathered
under the sign of *pulaku*; please remain thus until the end of our assembly. Anyone who is jealous should pick up his things and go back where he came from.
Jealous women can do likewise. Boys who know too many tricks had better be
careful. There will be no fighting over women. A curse on anyone who infringes
our *pulaku*! Evil will fall on him. He will not see or be seen! He will farm, but he
will not have any harvest! He will raise cows, but they will be sterile. In place of
cows, he will have vultures to watch over!'

I paid close attention to what was going on. I saw a boy leave the line of dancers
and go toward the elders. He knelt and greeted them and then got up again, dancing all the time. He went back to his place in the line. His 'sponsor' accompanied
him, tapping the ground with his feet and striking it with his stick. The sponsor
encouraged his 'protégé' and praised him while dancing, saying, 'You, so-and-so,
son of so-and-so, there is no one like you among all the dancers. If you do not win
first prize, no one will be declared the winner. You, so-and-so, the son of so-and-
so, no one is your equal!'

'The *kori*,' Adamu explained to me, 'closely examines all the details of his protégé's costume. If one of the necklaces or bracelets falls off, the *kori* picks it up
and returns it to him. He watches to make sure the ostrich plume is always straight
on his protégé's head. Each day, even several times a day, he sprinkles a whole
bottle of perfume on his protégé. The ground is strewn with dozens of bottles.'

Everything Adamu told me was exactly right ... I saw it happen. Once it even
happened that, enchanted by a certain dancer, I made a sign to his *kori* to come
over to me. I gave him a bottle of perfume so he could pour it on his protégé's
clothes. 'This *suka* pleases me very much,' I said to him as I gave him the bottle.
I also offered the *suka* some kola nuts, but always through his *kori*.

Because Adamu was very happy to answer my questions, I asked him more. 'I
suppose your Wodabe *suka* do what our Jafun *suka* do: before participating in your
contest, do you protect yourselves against the evil your rival could inflict on you?'

'Yes we do. From the moment that the date is chosen for the next *gerewol*,
this festival becomes our only preoccupation. We use our usual methods to take

precautions against sorcerers. We exchange formulas among ourselves. Some formulas make us handsome, others are evil charms, which we put on rivals we are particularly afraid of. We all use charms to attract the love of young girls. If you come and visit us in the midst of our preparations, you will see some who wash themselves, others who smoke themselves with scented plants, some who prepare or have made ointments for one part of their body or another. No *suka* forgets to make cuts on the top of his shoulders; he rubs a little *kerma* into the cuts to make his shoulders tremble during the dance.'

'I have heard talk about the charms you bury around the dance area. Can you tell me what that means?'

'Those packets are prepared at home before leaving. They contain different things which I will not tell you about. But let me tell you that the person who makes the packets must say while he ties knots on the top of them, "This is against so-and-so, the son of so-and-so, who I want to attack by burying this cloth. May his feet swell and may he die before my eyes!" The man must say those words in a loud voice. Another may say, "May his eyes weep and prevent him from appearing in the midst of the dancers! May his eyes get red!" These curses are especially directed toward the eyes because, for us, the eyes are the part of the face which we give the most care to. We want them to be big and bright. We have what is needed to make them huge and what is needed to make them smaller again. Our curses can also make wrinkles suddenly appear on someone's face and make him look old all of a sudden. But after the festival, his face will be normal again.'

I could not help asking him, 'Is everything you have told me really true?'

'Of course,' he answered. 'Anyway, you saw for yourself that someone buried one of those packets. You remember!'

'Yes,' I replied. 'I saw someone bury something, but I did not know what he was doing.'

'Well, he had one of the charms I just told you about. They are called *irde*, and they are buried so they can work evil against someone.'

'Did you notice,' continued Adamu, 'the men buried the packets without being secretive about it? They did it openly, right under the eyes of the elders? Indeed, there were several people burying those packets. It is even possible to have a long line of people burying packets. The person whom a charm is aimed against knows what he must do. At least he will know what to do if he is forewarned by one of our magic processes, which allows him alone to see a little smoke rise over the hole. He will know then what he must do. And he is not secretive when he digs the packet up. In front of everyone, he will get rid of this evil which has been directed toward him.'

I asked Adamu some more questions. 'I told you I had not got a close look at the packets that were buried, but yesterday I saw some chicken's eggs buried. What does that mean?'

'Those eggs will be dug up the day after everyone leaves, and they will be found to be cooked.' Adamu saw my great surprise, my incredulity, so he continued: 'It is as I tell you. It proves the place where we dance belongs to Satan. The *mallams* and the *modibos* are always saying our *gerewol* dance is an abomination before

God. It is Satan who leads this dance. That is the explanation for finding the cooked eggs.'

'In that case, is it still possible for you to do the five prayers of our religion?'

Without hesitation he answered, 'We do not do anything about religion during the days of *gerewol*. That is the last of our worries. This is not a place for praying. Anyone who comes here leaves that worry behind him; but he can take it up again, if he wants to, when he goes back to his everyday life.'

I pointed out to Adamu that everyone did not reason the way he did. I had seen some dancers take off their costumes and dress up like good Muslims to say their prayers. I had already asked about it and I knew this was the case for the people of the Wojabe clan,[1] real Mbororo and also genuine Muslims, whose men follow Muslim rules when they take a wife. However, this did not prevent them from being among the best singers and dancers. They considered it an insult to be called a Wodabe. They did not miss any of the five prayers.

Adamu did not contradict me. 'I know that,' he said to me, 'but among us, it is different. No dancer prays. In fact, many men don't pray at all.'

'In that case,' I told him, 'aren't there many animosities and jealousies during your gatherings?'

'If you only knew,' he replied, 'all the evil we can do! Here is an example. Some of us go to the blacksmiths to have small pieces of iron made for us. They are as big as hammer heads. They are attached to the dancers' belts, in the back, at the end of a strong cord. They are placed so that during the dance, when the dancers are spinning and twirling very fast, the mass of iron will hit the private parts of the boy they want to eliminate. They are happy when they make him fall over.'

'And your elders do not say anything? They let them do that?'

'No, they do not,' he told me. 'When the elders hear the excited *kori* encouraging their protégés to use those hammers, they stop the competition. All the dancers come quickly with *barkehi* leaves in their hands. They squat down and listen to the following warning: "May every Fulani who knows how to use a long cord for tying bundles on the backs of his cows, every Fulani who respects what is 'demanded of him by the *barkehi* fibres', every son of *barkehi*, every Fulani who understands *pulaku* – everyone must immediately get rid of the hammer that may be hanging from his belt!" At that point, it is not unusual to hear enormous pieces of iron fall on the ground!'

'And do you know what evil we can do with the ostrich plumes we wear on our heads?' Adamu asked me.

'I have no idea,' I replied.

'Listen. Some dip their feathers into wet powder made from hot pepper. Then, during the dance, they spin in front of their rival's face and, with a quick shake of the head, they sprinkle pepper in his eyes. It will take until the next day before he can clear his eyes. And for that day, the dance is finished for him.'

Adamu continued. 'Everyone does everything he can to be recognised as the best dancer. He must attract the elders' attention. The judgement of the girls counts only a little. Every few minutes a *suka* moves away from the group of dancers and goes toward the elders, who are always sitting together on their mats placed over *barkehi* leaves. In his left hand, the dancer holds an instrument which looks like a little axe. He spins at a dizzying speed, twirling the wool pom-poms of many colours, which are attached to his shoulders; then, while continuing to shake, he takes his place back in the group.'

While I listened to this, I was watching exactly what he was so vividly describing. Near me, I saw a little old man so enraptured by the spectacle that, without realising it, he contorted himself to the point of falling over. One dancer really showed his worth. We applauded him more than the others. Continuing to turn around, he bent to the ground. Around me, nearly everyone – even the old people – did the same thing! Everyone thought this Dakuna was the best dancer; but he was not the most handsome. It's unusual for one boy to have all the best qualities. One has a handsome face, but his body is out of proportion. Another is noticed for the unusual way he shakes his shoulders. A third one has beautiful eyes. Another has a fine neck or sparkling teeth. Some are distinguished by the elegance of their costumes, which are immaculately clean. The spectators discuss and compare the merits of one dancer versus another. They never forget to mention the qualities of the magical formulas which the dancers know in order to obtain such effects.

These dances are very exhausting. Some could not get over their fatigue: especially a desire to sleep, which could come on anywhere or at any time. That is why many carried a medicine which they had secretly bought. This medicine is called *anabarsi*[2] and can be found in pharmacies in all Nigerian towns. It chases away sleepiness, but is dangerous when misused: it makes you drunk and can make you go crazy.

People saw evil charms everywhere. Did someone feel a sudden fatigue which forced him to lie down? That was because he was under the evil influence of someone. Pain in the knees, pain in the 'parts', a constant desire to go off in the bush – that was the act of a jealous rival ready to do anything to eliminate someone who threatened him for first place! Everything, in their opinion, is subject to sorcery.

You can imagine the feverishness with which each man woke up at dawn on the last day!

I will say nothing about the way the first hours of that morning passed. We experience the same atmosphere when we wait for the 'revenge' at our *soro*.

What was especially noticeable was the excitement of the *kori* as the hour for choosing the best *suka* approached. While putting the last touches on his protégé's costume, each *kori* vied with the others, shouting, 'It is you, so-and-so, son of so-and-so, who is the strongest. You are the most handsome. Next to you, the others do not exist. It is you who will "put the bundles of reeds on your back"!'

Another shouted, 'If you are not chosen, do not count on me to return home with you. You will go in one direction; I will go in the other. Be the conqueror, you, son of so-and-so!' Everyone got worked up without interrupting the dance.

All the young girls were there, adorned and made-up. They stood in a tight group. Some *kori* approached the girls and, after a discussion, two of the girls were designated for the task of choosing the conqueror.

The solemn moment had arrived. The dance had stopped. All the *suka* were placed in a line, facing the elders. The ostrich plumes, which adorned the tops of their heads, had been adjusted; they were pushed back so they did not touch the eyes of the young girls who were approaching. One behind the other, the girls walked with measured steps toward the contestants who were in a line. The girls' heads were covered with veils that had been slightly lifted.

One girl always behind the other, they passed in review and stared into the face of each *suka*. When the girls reached the end of the line, they came back again. They stopped sometimes. It seemed that the first girl had made her choice. It was only a bluff. The girls continued. Each *kori* shouted to the girls when they reached his protégé. 'Stop there! Don't go any further! Stop!' The girls played deaf and walked on.

Then all of a sudden, at the moment least expected, the girl in front rushed between two boys. In passing, her right hand took hold of the right hand of one dancer. That was the one she had chosen. He was the conqueror. Then the two young girls disappeared toward the east. The *kori* of the chosen one and all those who had put their hopes on that boy exploded with joy. They threw their sticks into the air and then adroitly caught them. They beat their sticks on the earth at the winner's feet. Some twirled in front of him. On the women's side, there were piercing yodels. His body shaking, with his shoulders jerking frantically, the happy victor presented himself before the group of elders who congratulated him. His dancing then surpassed everything before.

Among the spectators, people were heard talking about who he was. 'Did you say this is so-and-so, son of so-and-so? That does not surprise me! I know his father very well.'

Another said, 'I would never have thought he would be chosen!'

And another added, 'Me neither. I would have picked out someone else.'

And this remark was also heard: 'It is true. He is not the most handsome but he certainly has the best "charms".' That was a point everyone agreed on.

The selection of the winner marked the end of the *gerewol* but not the dispersal of the guests, who would not leave until the next day. That evening the dance continued and the singing went on very late into the night, exalting the beauty of the victor and thanking the people of the village for their generous hospitality.

The next morning the guests, the *kori*, the *suka* and the young girls lined up one behind the other. The women carried calabashes on their heads, and the men had bundles tied on sticks across their shoulders. All the young people walked in a line toward the place where the cows were kept. They surrounded the area, making a circle. They all chanted in unison. For them, it was like a prayer to call for the benediction of God on the herd of that village: 'May your cows be as numerous as the grains of sand in the Benue River!' Then the procession, always in the same order, passed between the huts of Adamu's village and the temporary shelters which the guests themselves had built for their stay. They headed toward the east. As they faded into the distance, their songs could be heard from far away. The *gerewol* was finished.

On the return path, there are often arguments between the young people, who may fight with sticks among themselves. When they were in front of the elders – and so as not to bring curses on themselves – they had controlled their anger. But from that point on, they could let their feelings out. It was often during this return trip that a young man who had the intention of stealing someone else's wife tried to do it. The shamed husband would not let him get away with it, and soon the clashing of sticks would be heard.

The Wodabe

If the *soro* is characteristic of us Jafun, it's the *gerewol* dance which is the mark of the Wodabe.

The Wodabe are a major group of the Mororo. They are particularly numerous in Niger, but they can be found in many other countries like Cameroon, the Central African Republic, Nigeria and Chad. Our relations with them are anything but cordial. Our contacts are not very frequent. In fact, we have a reciprocal mistrust of each other.

The Wodabe make fun of our herds, which have thin coats compared to theirs. Our animals have smaller horns than theirs and have coats of many colours. The Wodabe are well aware of the tradition, which we do not discuss, according to which they were the first herders to be given the Cow. They are more than just a little proud of that. They constantly boast of the quality of their big, red cattle with their long, thick horns.

They make fun of our dances which they think hardy merit the name 'dance'. What a difference from their own dance, so spectacular, the famous *gerewol*! They make fun of our men. They see us as 'slaves' to our wives because we milk the cows. They also reproach us for doing the major part of the work when we build the houses we settle in for the months of the rainy season.

But when we talk about them, we never stop criticising them either.

The first thing we do not like about them is the way they eat. When their wives have finished selling milk, they pass by the homes of the villagers – Fulbe or others – and collect food left over from the evening before. Often there is extra millet or manioc porridge, which has been broken up and put outside to dry on a mat. Here and there they find bits of black crust that have been scraped from the pots. Chickens have been pecking through it. When the women arrive home, they wash the scraps, pound them and make a kind of couscous which they cover with milk. That is their daily diet.

Those Wodabe women are dirty. They put rancid butter in their hair. None of our boys are attracted to them. You have to have real desire and not be hard to please if you want to sleep with one of them. (Our women are not especially clean, but they still have what is needed to attract the attention of the young Wodabe.) Their sons and daughters often have tattoos which disfigure them. They put tattoos all over their arms and feet. Even around their necks! However, not all of them; there are people among the Wodabe who do not have tattoos. Some of their women have very beautiful faces.

For us, the Wodabe are the most bush of the bush-men. Their appearance cannot be mistaken. They are recognisable from far off. They sleep anywhere. During the rainy season, they do not bother to put their beds up on four stakes like we do. They add no decoration to their shelves, while our women always hang up a square of basketry decorated with shells and multicoloured wool.

Let's not talk about their milk. It is bad, and their butter is not washed well. The women take milk to their customers in deformed calabashes which have edges that are black with dirt. One only needs to notice what happens: our milk is quickly sold, long before theirs! Obviously the Fulbe avoid buying Wodabe milk. I have heard some Fulbe say that when they travel, they would rather break up their millet balls in pond water than in Wodabe milk.

The designs which the women carve on their calabashes are badly cut and are not pleasing to us either. The designs are etched with a large needle. Then, into those grooves, the women rub a mixture of crushed charcoal and butter, which makes an indelible black pattern.

When it is time for the Wodabe to marry, it is a matter of an 'abduction', not a contract. A Wodabe does not worry about whether or not the woman he has 'kidnapped' is already married. He takes her home for the night. Before sleeping with her, he slaughters an animal in the midst of his herd in order to show his determination. The marriage is completed. The next day the guests come. The couple begins to have children; but it is only when the fertility of the wife is certain that some Wodabe consent to contract a marriage according to Islamic law.

We really fear the Wodabe because of their knowledge of the occult. They have the skill to use evil curses. And we especially scorn them for their incestuous origin. Is it not said their clan is the offspring of the marriage between a brother and sister? An abominable thing! In our eyes, their race is therefore marked from its birth and will always be marked by that shameful sin.

You see we have many reasons for not liking the Wodabe. Can it be said we despise them? Let's say we are totally indifferent to them. And when we learn that one of our women has let herself be seduced by one of the Wodabe, we are very deeply disturbed. 'What got into that woman? Are there no more men among us?'

However, when the Wodabe and the Jafun are neighbours, they often invite each other to their camps. Not many Wodabe respond to the invitations. They never actually refuse but rather they will say, 'Of course, we will come.' However, we feel they come against their will. At the most, perhaps one woman comes, or two. They keep to themselves and do not pitch in like other women who want to be useful in one way or another. They are content to bring a little milk and, as soon as their calabashes are returned to them, they get up, take leave and go as they came – trying not be to noticed. At the markets, the Jafun and Wodabe women are never seen together. They avoid each other.

However we are obliged to say there is one thing the Wodabe have which is superior. That is the dance called *gerewol* which I have just described for you as I saw it.[3]

Figure 16.1: Henri Bocquené and Wodabe couple, dressed for *gerewol*

CHAPTER 17

The Spectacle at the Market Place

After the *gerewol* festival of the Wodabe, I went back to my tailor's scissors and my seat behind the sewing machine. Almost every day I took my machine to the market, but little by little I gained enough customers so I could stay in my shop. I knew lots of people at the market. When I had time, I loved to linger and watch some of the spectacles offered by snake charmers, hyena trainers, scorpion handlers and other performers. Like all Mbororo, I had a certain contempt for those sorts of people.

The Praise-Singers

I had less contempt for the praise-singers and guitarists. I was attracted more to those two professions than I'd have thought possible. The praise-singer Sabaldu, a Witi from Gombe, had asked me to accompany him on his tours. I really liked his songs. I'd perform them myself and imitate him, and he knew it. Even though I would not have accepted his offer for anything in the world, I asked him if he'd tell me how to become a praise-singer. 'The most natural way in the world,' he responded. 'You become a praise-singer when you realise you have a good voice which people like. One day they'll give you some money to show they like your singing. That will encourage you, and then you can apprentice yourself to another praise-singer. He'll teach you how to flatter people and extract money from them, even against their wishes. He'll give you a formula for making some powders. After the powders have been transformed into smoke, you can use them to perfume your mouth.'

'I'm told a praise-singer gets rich very fast but that this money runs even faster through his fingers.'

'You're right, especially if the praise-singer is well-known like I am. There's no name-giving ceremony, no marriage, no feast at the end of Koranic studies, no visit from the President, no occasion of any importance which I'm not invited to. People know I love my profession and I'm always looking for something new. A customer is always more generous when a praise-singer sings the tune he prefers. If I prepare myself well by using my usual medicines on the days of big feasts, I can sing a long time without showing any fatigue. My voice will be just as clear in the evening as it was in the morning.'

The life of a praise-singer attracted me. I thought that profession would allow me to lead an easy life. No hard work - the normal lot of anyone who wants to earn a living - no fields to cultivate. I had the impression people liked me and that I had a good voice. There was a tune I really liked to sing when I practised. It was saucy; but when I got to the shocking part, I hummed or mumbled, depending on my audience!

I was most relaxed when playing the guitar[1] and I did not have to worry about flattering people, as does the praise-singer. We call this guitar the *garaya*. From the time the Mbororo are little children, they are familiar with that type of guitar and the armpit drum. When I was very young, I entertained myself by getting other children to dance to the sound of that instrument. I did not stop playing it when I moved to the world of the villagers. I spent hours playing it for myself. Certain tunes went along with the verses I'd made up.

Making a *garaya* was no secret to me. Half of a small calabash is covered with sheep or goat skin, a nylon string is stretched over a piece of wood, some small pieces of metal are used as rattles and some shells become the decorations. That's all. I've made lots of them. In order to earn a little money, I've even sold them to the Whites.

Everyone who heard me kept telling me I had everything it took to become an excellent musician and to make that my profession. I thought about that for a time, as I've already told you. But I would have had to go far away from my family so my father would not be ashamed when he saw one of his sons adopt such a despicable profession!

I really admired a player who could bring all the sounds he wanted from his guitar. Once I was brave enough to ask, 'In order to play as well as you do, isn't it necessary to use magic?'

'Of course,' he told me. 'And if you're interested, some day I'll tell you the secret.'

And this is what he told me a week later. 'Get some fresh meat and cut it lengthwise. Make it into a strip and wrap it around your left wrist. You must spend the night in an abandoned hut, like the Mbororo leave behind when they travel around. Lie down. Then thrust your left arm – the one with the bracelet of meat wrapped around the wrist – through the straw wall of the hut. It must be the east wall. Stay like that, with your hand outside, until dawn if necessary. Anyway, sooner or later, you'll hear the Spirits arriving. They'll argue about what to do with you. "Cut off his hand!" "No, breaking his arm is enough!" "Let's go home and eat it instead!".'

'When you hear this hubbub, don't be afraid,' the praise-singer continued. 'If you're able to control yourself, you'll keep your bracelet of meat. Then all you'll have to do is grill the meat and eat it. If everything goes as I've said, you'll be able to play anything you can think of on your guitar. You'll be able to express all beauty, even the beauty of a single eyelash of a handsome boy or of a charming young girl.' And he continued his explanations which were too long to repeat here.

I had a hard time believing what he told me. Seeing my hesitation, he anticipated the question I was going to ask him. 'I did exactly what I just explained to you. I followed precisely the instructions given me by the praise-singer who initiated me, a certain Sarkin Mbaka. Oh, I remember the arguments between the Spirits! "Kill him!" "No, make him go crazy!" I kept perfectly calm. It was about ten minutes before silence fell. Then I ate the meat, and ... you can see the results! But there's one thing you must keep firmly in mind: anyone who panics will go crazy.'

And the guitar player continued, 'Here's another test I had to do. One night I had to put a piece of meat on a *bambahi*[2] leaf. When I woke up, I found the meat moving, twitching: it was alive! I had orders to take the meat and burn it. I did that and my hands didn't tremble. I knew if I ran away in fear, I'd go crazy. On the other hand, if I could control myself, I'd be assured of possessing the art of music and song for the rest of my days. That's what I did. Why don't you do it yourself?' And he carefully explained some other things to me: how to keep from being possessed by the Spirits; how to call up those same Spirits, to see them, to talk to them, to obtain what one desires from them.

When he left me, I was really perplexed. One day I said to myself that, after all, what he did was not so difficult. He did it; why not me? The next day I'd changed my mind. What if I were afraid and went crazy? One morning I thought: I'll do it tonight. When night came, I retreated and gave up my plan. Actually I never did it. So that's why I did not become a famous guitarist. My friend is a virtuoso who can play all the tunes that pass through his head. I can only play those I make up myself, nothing more.

In the big markets of Nigeria, praise-singers are seen everywhere. Some walk around and insult anyone who doesn't give them something. Many of those insults are aimed at imperfections of the body: the stomach, the ears. All parts of the body are included, with comparisons that are not very flattering but which amuse people. When praise-singers are seen coming, it's best to make the first move by giving them a little money. Those praise-singers always carry a wooden sword so they can threaten people who are not generous. Other praise-singers walk around the market with round, closed calabashes under their arms. Those calabashes contain human excrement. The praise-singers open the covers under the noses of people they consider to be misers, who are only fit to eat what they have been given to smell!

The Tattooists

Tattooists are also classified as praise-singers. You can ask many things from them: to shave your face or head, to make tattoos on your skin, to cut your uvula, to apply cupping horns and to do certain operations.

When I lived at Wuro Bokki, it was still popular among the Hausa and the Mbororo to have their faces tattooed. Here's the process. When a young girl goes to a tattooist, this always takes place in the market place, in the midst of a crowd and with the sound of a drum. She's immediately encircled by some friends and other young people. With the first incision, they clap and throw her money. That encourages the young girl so she can control her pain. The noise of the blade can be heard as it cuts the skin. Blood drips on the ground. Powder made from finely sifted charcoal is applied to the face. Care is taken so that the powder penetrates deep into the cuts. Soon her whole face disappears under this mixture of black powder and blood. Marked like that, the young girl gets up and moves away so another girl can take her place. The change of customers is done without stopping the drums.

The designs that are made have different names. You have to be a woman to know them precisely! Each girl who comes explains, in general, what she wants. 'I want everything at once!' Soon her face is nothing but blood. She leans forward and gathers her wrapper-skirt so it won't be soiled by the big drops which are clotting. Sometimes during these sessions, a voice shouts that anyone who spoils her face in this way is an imbecile. Some people do not react well to the incisions. Pus forms on the sores and after several weeks scars appear instead of tattoos. There are people with tattoos who look like they've been burned.

A lot of imagination goes into the designs. One customer wants a snake around her neck. Another wants a bracelet on her wrist. The names of young girls appear on the chests of some men: pretty nicknames like Grace and Moonlight. Tattoo specialists are ready to design anything they're asked for, providing they're paid.

Among the tattooists, there are some who apply cupping horns in order draw water or blood out of the body. There is no bleeding with the first type. Those cupping horns only produce blisters on the skin, as a burn would do. Then the blisters are cut with a piece of straw, and the water comes out.

This is how we proceed. We use what we call an *ampul*. This is a short antelope horn that has a hole at the end. We put a little bit of fresh, pliable wax around the hole. The base of the horn is put on the body of the patient. The tattooist inhales through the little hole which is the size of the piece of straw. When he feels the cupping horn is holding and is really stuck to the skin, he just has to close the opening by quickly moving the wax with his teeth and lips. Anyone who does not have teeth certainly cannot put an *ampul* in place.

When blood-letting must be done, an incision is first made on the bruised part, right where the blood has accumulated. When the tattooist inhales, the blood flows into the horn, which gets heavier minute by minute and often, because of the weight, falls away from the skin by itself. It's full of thick, black blood. Simply seeing those big clots gives the patient the assurance his illness has been taken away!

Many Mbororo use this remedy, especially the Jafun, the people of the *soro*. When they are young they often ram their heads against trees while participating in the *soro*. They do not feel a thing. But as they get older, they feel pain at the back of their necks, in the middle of their backs and around their kidneys. This is the only remedy they know: the *ampul*. Some internal haemorrhages due to the blows from *soro* sticks cause an accumulation of blood. The only cure is blood-letting. Often one session is not enough, and it is necessary to go back to the barber many times.

One of my uncles had a child who vomited a lot. He already had a tendency to throw up the milk his mother gave him when he was very young. My uncle, whose name was Zatao, asked me to go with him to the most skilful barber in town. I took him to Siroma. He opened the child's mouth really wide, inspected the back of his throat and concluded, 'It's just what I thought: his uvula is too long. Look for yourself,' he said to me. 'And besides, it's white. It's time to take it out.'

The barber worked nimbly. For instruments, he had a long stick, the end of which was forked and slightly open and a really sharp knife, like all barbers have, but bent at the end. When he operated, he held the uvula at the end of his forked stick and sliced it with one cut. He took out the part he'd cut with the end of his wooden instrument. The child bled. He cried. He had to swallow warm water and then the bleeding stopped. The child was cured.

Barbers always lay out many razors within their reach. There are razors for hairs in the nose and on the ears! If, by their clumsiness, they make the smallest scratch which bleeds, the customer is exempted from paying.

While the barber was busy with my nephew's uvula, I was watching a 'tooth-breaker'. Equipped with a special hammer, he tapped lightly on the middle tooth on the upper jaw of a Kiri. By extracting a tooth in this way, the 'tooth-breaker' made it possible for his patient to spit accurately and powerfully through the gap. In those days, this had become nearly an art, very much appreciated in some areas. But not among the Mbororo!

Some pedicurists also circulate in the markets and offer their services, right there where they find their customers. While talking away, the man hardly notices that someone is busy with his toenails!

And also at the markets are the big shows which are put on by performers of every type. Among them, the animal trainers arouse the most interest.

Animal Trainers

Some praise-singers are also animal trainers. In order to make this profession profitable, it's necessary to have an unusual knowledge of the occult and of magic.

When I was in Wuro Bokki, a praise-singer surprised the spectators by working with scorpions. He walked around with a big calabash, as round as a ball, which had an opening just wide enough for a hand to pass through. The calabash was full of scorpions which he fed on crushed groundnuts. I remember the name of the praise-singer: Adamu Waga-Waga. We trembled for him when we saw him take out one of the scorpions and lick its tail before putting it back with the others.

One day two praise-singers, who were snake charmers, came to that same market. They mixed in with the spectators, who were watching this scorpion-licker. One of the two, to test his skill, had an idea. He put a curse on the scorpion trainer which was supposed to break any alleged magical power that was not fully authentic. That's just what it did. At the moment Adamu Waga-Waga put a scorpion into his mouth, the scorpion jabbed out its stinger. The scorpion trainer grimaced in pain and then spat out blood. Angry, but not saying anything, he closed his calabash full of scorpions and threw it in the Benue. He came back with his cheeks swollen like a balloon.

In the evening, the snake charmers invited the people to their show. They began by watering the ground. Snakes feel more relaxed on cool ground. Then the snake charmers took the snakes out one by one so they could start their show. Our

Adamu Waga-Waga appeared. When our two snake-charmer accomplices saw
Adamu silent and sad, they exchanged smiles which said a lot. So Adamu realised
it was one of those two who had 'broken' his occult power. People like me who
were witnesses to that scene, and who knew what evil tricks those 'people of
knowledge' play on each other, were also aware of what had happened.

I could cite many other such cases for you.

I remember another story about snakes and occult power. This took place in
Gire at the time I lived there. One day one of our mutual friends – a friend of Bala
and me – offered us the chance to earn some money by putting ourselves at the disposition of a snake charmer who had just arrived in the village square. We went
along.

The praise-singer began by rubbing our backs with a 'medicine'. Then he put
leather charms in our mouths. He took out a snake which he wrapped around my
neck and then a second snake which he slid into my shorts. (I wore very short ones
at that time.) People clapped for me. All of a sudden, I caught sight of my father
who was in the midst of the crowd. Ah! If I'd only known he was there . . . ! When
I met him the next day, I expected to be scolded. He was brief. He simply said,
'You're the shame of the family. You have betrayed *pulaku*.'

The friend who had asked Bala and me to help offered to work for the snake
charmer. The snake charmer accepted the offer and took him home to Gombe. My
friend's work was to feed and take care of the many snakes which were kept in the
snake charmer's large house. When people living round about would see a snake
that was a little different, they came to tell the snake charmer and my friend.
They'd go and, by using secret methods, they were nearly always successful in
luring the snake into a sack and capturing it. Without any real training from his
boss, the apprentice tried to discover for himself some of his secrets.

One day some people came to tell the snake charmer they'd seen a rare species
called a *dakel*[3] at Damare, near Jimeta. The snake had a white neck and the top of
its head was red. They knew the exact place where it could be found, near a termite hill. The snake charmer went there. He took his young apprentice with him.
That day all their efforts were in vain. They returned the next day. Two assistants
accompanied them. They beat their drums in a special way by loosening the skins
of the drums and playing with thin sticks. The snake responded to the call. But
when the snake was ordered to crawl into the trunk, it refused and returned to its
hole. The snake charmer tried a third time, but again without success. After this
failure, he gave up his plan to capture the snake for good and did not think any
more about it.

Some months later, our friend, who now knew all the secrets of this profession,
thought he'd begin to work on his own. He had even hired two young men to help
him. Remembering the stubborn *dakel*, he said to himself that he would now succeed where his old master had failed. So he went to that termite hill near the place
where – as the people said – the snake with the white neck and red head was still
living. He knew the tune he had to hum. He knew which scented plant he had to
find in order to fumigate the hole. He was sure he could capture the snake. And,
in fact, the flattery he used in his song attracted the snake. He had no trouble getting it into the trunk.

Proud of his acquisition, my friend left the next day with his two assistants to give his first show at the Jimeta market. While the assistants sang, accompanied by a drum, he played with the snakes. He took one of them, put a lit cigarette in its mouth and ordered it either to inhale the smoke or blow it out. He took another snake and aroused it by giving it his hat. The snake ended up by striking, leaving a small black mark on the white fabric. 'Look at the venom!' my friend said.

Finally it was time for my friend to impress the people with his special act. 'Attention, good people, you're going to see a rare species of snake, a *dakel*. Anyone bitten by this snake won't have time to say "oof". Here's the *dakel* that resisted the charms of my master. But I – the one you see before you – I succeeded in capturing it. You'll admire it. Here it is!'

The people moved back. My friend opened his trunk and, thinking he held the snake under his charm, he imprudently put his hand inside the trunk. Then he drew his hand back quicker than he'd put it in: the snake was hanging from his hand. He shook his hand vigorously and the snake fell into the trunk, which my friend shut with a bang. 'The snake bit me! It bit me!' The people laughed and applauded, thinking my friend was putting on an act. But all that stopped when they saw blood flow where he'd been bitten. Many ran away because they were very afraid.

The snake charmer had the presence of mind to tell his assistants, 'Quick, take me to the hospital,' and then he collapsed. The people picked him up and transported him to the hospital. The white doctor had just gone away. By the time he came back, the apprentice charmer was dead. Black blood ran from his mouth, oozed from his eyes and everywhere he had hair.

The news of his death circulated quickly among the people at the market. Everyone looked with awe at the trunk, which – thank goodness – was closed. Next to it, the two assistants were drumming. The drumming stopped. Their first reaction was to think about the money. All the receipts were closed inside the trunk, in the midst of the snakes!

And now what should they do with the trunk? A big truck with a crane was brought. The trunk was caught by the hook, swung into the air and then disposed of in a big hole that had been dug for that purpose. Fagots covered with gasoline were thrown on the trunk and a fire was started. Returning to the market place, the people joked with the two assistants. 'So, you haven't inherited your boss's trunk? Didn't he leave you anything?' The assistants disappeared with their drums on their shoulders, thinking about all the money they'd collected in the last ten days, which was lost forever in the trunk.

For the people, this event confirmed the idea that all trainers of dangerous animals – snakes, scorpions, hyenas – come to a bad end sooner or later.

This makes me think about the misfortune of a certain Adamu Mai Kura.[4] I knew him very well. He was a Mbororo from the Bodi clan, who are reputed for their 'knowledge'. Mai Kura had lost all his cattle in an epidemic. He decided to use the knowledge of the occult he'd acquired as a hunter in order to earn his living. He knew how to use magical practices in order to preserve himself from the teeth and claws of wild animals.

Even before he lost his herd, Mai Kura had raised a hyena which he'd watched grow up and which had become very tame. So Mai Kura decided to become a praise-singer – a trainer of hyenas. He could be seen arriving at market places, riding his hyena. Two assistants stood near him playing drums while he danced with the hyena. This was a big scandal for the Mbororo, who could not admit that one of their own people would shame himself like that in public by having such a great friendship with an animal like a hyena that is so dirty and causes so much damage!

One day when Mai Kura was walking with his hyena near the butchers, the hyena succeeded in undoing a link from its muzzle. The hyena was free! There were shouts everywhere: 'The hyena! The hyena! The hyena is loose!' Respectable people in turbans were climbing trees and losing their headpieces in their haste. Old women ran in every direction, pulling up their wrapper-skirts. Soon there was no one left at the market place except Mai Kura, who didn't have much trouble catching his hyena. He chained it up again and took it to its kennel.

From that day on, he lost his confidence. Little by little he became convinced he'd lost his power over the hyena. He became afraid. One day when he took it to a market, the hyena was especially stubborn and so he decided to kill it. He found a branch at the foot of a tree which was shaped like a club. He quickly used it to smash the hyena's head. He took off the muzzle and chain, and then dragged the animal to the edge of the road where he abandoned it.

A little while later a salt merchant who was coming back from the market saw his donkey that was walking in front of him swerve out of the way and then quickly step backwards. When he saw it was a hyena that had made the donkey afraid, he too was afraid, he and all the donkeys with him. Then there was a Kanuri man, then some people from Yola on bicycles, then some Mbororo women … All were scared and turned back. They alerted a hunter who came, armed with a gun. He shot. The animal did not make the slightest move. He shot a second time and then a third … It was only after the fourth shot that they all understood their mistake!

As for Adamu Mai Kura, no one knows what became of him. Deprived of his means of bread-winning, he took his wife and moved away with no fanfare.

The Great Hunters

It was while he was a member of the Society of Hunters that Adamu Mai Kura became a hyena trainer. The same must be said for Adamu Waga-Waga, the snake charmer, and for all the others. Actually, every hunter must first learn how to protect himself from the bites, teeth and claws of wild animals. He must also know the secret of how to become invisible in case of danger; how to put evil curses on rival hunters or how to prevent them from coming into an area full of game; how to have sharp eyesight in order to see game far away or to follow the tracks of an animal; how to protect himself from attacks of the bush Spirits. He must also know how to make poisons and counter-poisons and how to set traps.

Those 'great initiated hunters', who are called *Maké* must not be confused with minor hunters like the Gbaya farmers, who wander in the bush with dogs and who think all meat is good: monkeys, rats, lizards. A great hunter is only interested in noble animals: all sorts of antelope and buffalo.

We can say that every Mbororo child is born with a bow and arrow in his hands. When he's very young, he practises with his bow on sparrows and squirrels. No herder is ever seen without his quiver. However, there are some Mbororo clans which, by tradition, hunt more than others – the Goranko clan, for example, and the Jetanko. In contrast, our Diganko clan has no real initiated hunters. We know very few secrets. When we need to use a certain spell, we go and ask for the formula from the Goranko or the Jetanko.

The great hunters have their own praise-singers. Like the praise-singers I've told you about, they circulate from village to village. Some young people who play drums and guitars accompany them. Under the spell of the music, the initiated hunter is quickly seized by the bush Spirits. He moans, twists and somersaults. Suddenly he throws his hat on the ground. The hat is transformed into an antelope. He turns tree bark into bloody meat that has been cut into strips . . . Sometimes great hunters agree to offer exhibitions. Here's a hunter who displays his bow dripping with blood. Another bends down, kneels and begins to skin a bush goat which appears from nowhere. A third says to a boy, 'Take this animal alive. I give it to you!' There's always a very lively competition among the hunters. The gathering ends by designating the best of the great hunters.

I'd never finish describing the exhibitions I've seen in small villages, presented by real professional hunters, such as those found among the Hausa in the Gombe region, the Kambari of Yola or certain Fulbe slaves who have become Muslims. Among the Mbororo there are also true hunters here and there, but they do not have time to do exhibitions because they're too busy with their herds. Anyway, they do not have their own praise-singers.

Great hunters have big competitions among themselves. If two clans are inhabiting the same terrain, there'll always be disputes over the curses they put on each other. Each clan will try to harm the other. They can 'tie up the bush', as they say, so their rivals cannot find any game. I do not know the method they use. But I do know this: when they feel misfortune weighing on them, they quickly suspect they're under the effect of a magic spell. Very naturally they suspect the neighbouring clan of hunters who have killed an abundance of game. They look for a way to exact vengeance, and they know how to do it. It depends who – from these two clans who watch each other and are jealous of each other – has the greater 'knowledge' and the more effective antidote. If the two are equally strong, they're each able to hunt what they want, thanks to this game of curses and counter-curses. If not, the weaker group gives way and chooses a new hunting ground away from the evil influence of the other clan.

Each of these hunting stories is as astounding as the next. I was quick to learn as I walked around the Wuro Bokki market and talked with people, that anyone wanting to be a 'big hunter', a 'great initiate', had to go to a school. I knew the initiation took place in a mountain village two days' walk away. The first person who told me about it described that village where the houses blend in with the rocks. Its inhabitants have resisted all attacks. Thanks to the secrets they hold, no one can ever come near, not even the Whites. They even prevent airplanes from flying over their territory!

'What surprised me,' added my friend when he was telling me about this village, 'is that the people are bent over the Koran from morning to night. They sit on their mats; next to them are pots of beer that are never empty. Their eyes only leave the Scriptures when they take the pots up to their mouths. They tell anyone who wants to listen that their drink isn't strong, that it's non-alcoholic. They say it's simply a light porridge made from millet, which they call *mbordam*. But I don't believe it.

If you go to their village, you'll see bulbed plants everywhere. They have whole fields of them. They're found around their houses and even inside them.'

'You must go there too,' he added. 'You don't have to want to become a hunter to meet those people. They know everything, and anyone who goes there finds out what he wants to know. I encourage you to make the trip.'

I spent two weeks deciding. Then I returned to see my friend and asked for directions. Here's the advice he gave me, telling me to follow it to the letter: 'When you arrive in their village, introduce yourself as someone who's looking for work. Tell them you're ready to do anything because you have no more money to continue your trip. Do not try to be clever. Do not give them the impression your pockets are full of money. Offer to do small tasks for them: carry water, collect wood, weed a field.'

I left, having decided to follow his advice. I was well received. After a week, my boss paid me his compliments. 'You're very reserved. Since you've been here, I haven't learned anything about you. Do you intend to leave as you came, or is there something you're looking for?'

I replied, 'I'm travelling with no particular purpose, but I don't refuse opportunities that come my way.'

'Very well, my child. What would you like to have before you leave?'

I responded, 'If I could learn how to attract the love of a woman, I wouldn't refuse it.'

'Very well,' he said. 'I have what you need. It'll cost you two hundred francs. It comes from the bulb you see here. Take it. But be careful to use it only on unmarried women. It has a very strong effect so the woman will not be interested in anyone but you. But beware if she has a husband! Take it, and do as I've told you . . .'

I scrupulously followed his instructions. But several days later when I wanted to use it, I could no longer find the packet I'd put my powder in. I'd lost it.

Every true initiate – which was not my case – never leaves this village without being given a red copper ring. He wears it from then on as a visible sign of his acquisition of 'knowledge'. But anyone who usurps that title will be sorry! If he's confronted by a true initiate, he risks losing his life. Anyone who's acquired this 'knowledge' inspires great respect and fear. No one dares to put a magic spell on him! That magic will always return to exert its effect on its maker.

This is the case of the curse called 'needles'. Made locally, the needles are put in a horn and nourished with the fat of a human cadaver. When they're directed toward someone who has better protection, the needles can come back and re-enter the horn they went out of. This is a sign that the rival the needles were thrown at is stronger than the one who threw them.

These great teachers and initiates fear nothing. They make use of the eyes of dead people and hair taken from a child who died before he could talk. All this is done – for a price – for the satisfaction of a customer who wants to be able to steal with impunity, even in front of witnesses whose tongues will be tied.

One day one of my uncles watched the return of one of those great initiates, who are also called *Gardi*. His 'skill' was still very new. I often heard my uncle tell this story in the evenings. As soon as the *Gardi* arrived at his house, he took his bow and hung it up . . . on nothing! In open space! It didn't fall down. You can imagine his joy and pride! He said to his wife and children, 'Light the fire so we can grill the meat.'

'But, Papa,' one of his sons asked him, 'where's the meat? You didn't go hunting!'

'Don't ask questions,' insisted his father. 'Do as I say. Put a long pole between two forked sticks in front of a good fire. I'll take care of the rest.'

And then an antelope appeared before them. 'Slaughter her, skin her and cut the meat into strips.' That's what they did.

Another of my uncles said he'd heard one of these great initiates, on the day he returned from his training, say to his wife, 'Wife, here's a second wife that I've just taken, this girl with big breasts.'

'What?' said his wife when she saw her. 'You did this without my consent? You didn't even tell me about it!' And she got very angry.

'Calm down,' the husband told her. 'Look closely. Is this a young girl or something else?' Actually the only thing there was a tree stump, not a young girl!

This subject often came up when we talked in the evenings. This is how I learned when I was very young that hunters, even the most experienced hunters, are constantly haunted by the fear that one day they'll fall under the spell of the animals they're hunting. This possession always manifests itself in shouting, crying and moaning, which sounds like the beast that's being hunted. The animal avenges itself against the hunter in this way. That nearly always happens to those who begin hunting big game without being sufficiently protected. They fall on the ground, flop around and groan like a mortally injured animal. They foam at the mouth. They're lucky if they're discovered in time and if one of the great *Gardi*, whose 'knowledge' cannot be questioned, is brought to them.

Without having such a crisis, some hunters come back from the bush with black eyes like those of a kob antelope or with red sores all over their bodies. Everyone believes this means they did not know how to take the precautions needed to face the Spirits of the game they were following.

I myself have not seen all these things I've just told you about concerning the knowledge of the *Gardi*. Most of these stories I've heard during the evenings I've spent with the Mbororo and when I've travelled here and there.

CHAPTER 18

Marriage and Weddings

My friend Adamu, the Wodabe, liked to come and visit me. He spent hours sitting on a mat at the foot of my sewing machine. He was a talker! It was through him that I learned many things about the Wodabe, those Mbororo who are so different from us. One day I had a long conversation with him about the way young Wodabe men take their wives. In fact, I did not learn much. I already knew that among the Wodabe (except for the Wojabe), marriage takes place without going before a *mallam* – at least to begin with.

A man makes an agreement with a woman. He takes her to his house without even talking to her father or mother. One morning at sunrise, people simply notice there's one more woman at their camp. For us, such a way of behaving is wrong.

An Abduction

However, it would be false to say that such marriages, which we call marriage by abduction, do not exist among us Jafun. I'm going to tell you about the first such marriage I witnessed. In my village there was a certain Mala who had lots of success with women. He had natural charm. His parents were therefore not in any hurry for him to get married. Any day he wanted to get married, he could quickly have a wife.

At one *soro* festival on the day of the 'revenge', Mala received about forty blows at one stretch without showing the slightest emotion. His courageous attitude aroused all the young girls and all the women who witnessed it. Among them was a certain Beldo, who was especially pleasing to him. Mala proposed to Beldo that he 'take' her at the end of the game. She was married to a man named Adulahi. Her husband was there, but that was only an unimportant detail for Mala. Beldo accepted.

So Mala abducted Beldo. Some days later, the concerned families heard that the two of them had taken refuge at the home of Mala's paternal uncle. The families quickly learned that Mala, in order to stifle protest, had sent out invitations for the celebration of this marriage. People were even talking about two steers being slaughtered for the occasion.

The young woman's father made frequent visits to Mala's father. He begged Mala's father, in the name of *pulaku*, to ask his son to come back. 'What can I do?' Mala's father responded. 'You know very well that ever since he was a child, Mala's always done whatever he wished. What can I say? What can I do with such a boy? Don't you know I've already chased him away from my house twice?'

In view of what he considered to be great weakness on the part of his parents, Mala thought he'd won the round. He became more and more self-confident and even had the audacity to come back to his father's house with this new wife. His return did not pass unnoticed; it was even an event for us children. I still remember what we had to say. 'Did you see Mala? They say he took a wife without having a wedding. How is that possible?' At that time in my life, I had no idea what a marriage by abduction was. I did not even know the Fulfulde word *deetawal* which is used for such a marriage. From time to time the word appeared in our grandmothers' tales and we would ask, 'Grandmother, what's a *deetawal*?'

Everyone among us extolled Mala, especially the young men who admired him, saying, 'Ah, this Mala. He really has charm! He goes alone to a *soro* and he comes back with a wife. There's no one like him!'

Some days later, he pushed his insolence even further: he slaughtered another steer and again sent out invitations. Many people came to celebrate this feast, without showing the slightest astonishment or asking any questions. It was really like a wedding. For the next two years no one talked about Mala and Beldo. Then one day the two of them went to a *soro*. Adulahi, Beldo's first husband, was there too. Beldo, who was no longer entranced by the charm of her 'abductor', gave Adulahi to understand that she was ready to go back to their life together. Adulahi, who had never renounced Beldo, quickly carried out his plan: they crept away and were not seen any longer at the *soro*. When Adulahi returned home, he slaughtered his most beautiful steer in order to show his joy, and he invited all the neighbours to join him in celebrating what some people called a 'remarriage'!

It did not take Mala long to learn that Beldo had been taken back by her first husband. Mala decided to seek revenge. He went to the edge of Adulahi's village. He scouted out the paths Adulahi's cows used to go to pasture. He lay in wait and when Adulahi passed by, he jumped on top of him. 'I've got you. I won't let go of you until you promise to give Beldo back to me!'

'Beldo,' said Adulahi, 'is my wife. You didn't have the right to "steal" her. Why did you do that?'

'She loved me,' responded Mala. 'She didn't love you any more so I took her.'

'Perhaps,' replied Adulahi, 'But she has changed her mind again. Now it's me she loves and that's it!' Mala had brought ropes with him. He used them to tie up his rival. Mala tied the ropes securely and left Adulahi in the middle of the bush with his hands and feet bound. Before leaving, Mala took time to chase Adulahi's herd and disperse the cattle.

With that done, Mala – happy with himself and proud of his superior strength – sat down at the edge of the path which the women took each day when they went to the spring. Beldo appeared. Mala grabbed her and dragged her into the bush, leaving her companions to go back to the village without her. She let him do it.

Mala went back past the place where he'd left his prisoner. 'You see,' he said to Beldo 'there are different kinds of men. They aren't all alike, are they?' He took the ropes off Adulahi and said to him, 'Go back to your house! I have my wife back. That's enough for me.'

Each man went in the direction of his village – Adulahi alone and sad; Mala, with his head held high, in the company of Beldo.

This situation lasted two more years. But during that time, Beldo never had a child. So Mala's father said to him one day, 'Now this is enough. From this day on, I declare your union with this woman illegal. Separate yourself from her. Send her back to her first husband!' So Mala told Beldo he was divorcing her. She returned to Adulahi, who took her back again and contracted a second marriage with her. Later I learned that she'd given him many children.

Stubborn Young Girls

Among the young girls, some are self-assured enough to say, 'For me, there's only a certain One who counts. I'll marry him and no other. No matter what my parents say or do, I'll never accept a marriage they impose on me. I don't want to marry one of my cousins. No one can tell me who to marry!'

Sometimes they declare, 'If I marry a stranger, I may regret it someday; but I'm certainly not going to complain to my family. When they learn about it, they can say what they want. It doesn't matter to me. But I'm the only one who will make the choice.'

Among the Mbororo you find young girls like that. The first case that comes to mind is that of my cousin Fatu. Here's her story. On the day of her 'name-giving ceremony', she was 'taken' for one of her paternal cousins who was then three years old. His name was Aliyu. We called them 'husband' and 'wife'. It was the same for her sisters. Their traditional marriage was celebrated without them being able to show their disapproval. On the other hand, when Fatu reached puberty, she obstinately refused the husband who had been given to her when she was born. Her mother, in place of her father who was dead, tried in vain to get her to agree.

As soon as the wishes of Fatu were known, many suitors came to court her – all handsome young men with nicely braided hair and brilliant white robes. They all gathered under a tree. From time to time one of them sent a messenger to ask Fatu to have a private conversation with him. 'How,' she answered, looking up, 'can such a One ask me to go with him? How dare he ask me to move! What would I have to say to him?' And she refused to receive the suitor.

Days and months passed. Fatu continued to be obstinate. Her attitude, however, did not discourage the suitors. They came from far off. Respectable Mbororo made long trips for the purpose of asking for her on behalf of their sons. They began by speaking to her mother. 'Where are things with your daughter? Would it be possible to unite Fatu in marriage with my son?'

The mother could only respond, 'What can I say or do about this? Nothing! Fatu has a strong personality. She has even more character than I. We've tried everything. Imagine this: the son of so-and-so came, but she didn't want him. Then the son of another one came, but she pushed him away; and still another, but she would not stoop to receive him. She even refused the son of my own brother. She sent away the son of her uncle, the brother of my husband. Now we've decided to leave her alone with her bad character. She'll do what she wants!'

This is what happened later. There was a young man named Bakari. He was very short but with a very nice face. All the girls had eyes only for him. Naturally, Fatu did too. Because of Fatu's stubborn refusals, one day – in the intimacy of her house – Fatu's mother asked, 'My daughter, tell me who you like. Which young man would you like to marry?'

Fatu was silent for a long time and then said, 'I'll only accept so-and-so' – making a very clear allusion to Bakari. And she added, 'If he is not the one, I'll spend my life as I see fit, no matter what happens.'

But this Bakari that Fatu liked so much was of another clan. He was a Jetanko. And besides, his parents were not very wealthy. He had almost nothing. And everyone knows the Mbororo look down on those who have little. Someone who has not been successful is not well thought of in our society. Friends of Fatu's mother tried to reason with her. 'Look, Fatu. Have you thought about Bakari's lineage? They aren't rich. And do you know that among those people, the men send their wives away for any little reason?'

'I know all that,' said Fatu. 'It's not important. Whatever happens, happens. But he's the only one I want.'

Bakari knew all this. Bakari and Fatu often met in secret. They were, you could say, promised to each other. But Bakari's father did not dare ask for Fatu in marriage. He was afraid Fatu's mother would refuse him. Many times he told his son they were too poor. 'Fatu has refused people who are rich and respected. She's said she didn't want them, and you think she would marry you? It isn't possible! No, I will not do it. I don't want to leave myself open to a refusal.'

In spite of everything, in the end Bakari's father decided to make the request. I happened to be there when he heard the response, 'Very good. Fatu, you'll be given to Bakari.' Soon afterwards, the 'household money' was paid to Fatu's mother and the marriage was finalised.

Fatu's parents-in-law moved to the Central African Republic. Of course, Fatu followed her husband. But she came back at the end of Ramadan that year to celebrate the feast with her mother. Bakari came with her. He left her with her mother and returned to Paoua, where they had come from.

Several days later the news came to Fatu: 'Bakari's dead!' Fatu took up widowhood and was forced to follow the custom of spending four months and ten days in seclusion. The day after the lifting of this mourning period, the visits of suitors started again. And Fatu was again difficult and slow to say whom she wanted for her new husband. She sulked and even refused to get up when someone came to see her. Her mother kept saying to her, 'Even so, you could stand up just to be polite when someone comes to see you, especially if he's a respectable man! You must at least respond to his greetings. Go see him. Say what you want to him, but be polite. It is not forbidden for someone to talk to you.'

'I won't do it for someone I don't like. What would I have to talk to him about?' And she stayed there, free of all engagements. Many of her old suitors were not married, but they were afraid to visit her because they were thinking about the death of her husband …

I forgot to give you Fatu's and Bakari's ages. When they were married, he was seventeen and she was fifteen. He died one year after their marriage.

The Chastened Lover

During my stay in Wuro Bokki, I attended numerous weddings. Invited or not, I went just the same. My leprosy was still there, but my general health was good.

I remember the wedding of Sadau, where my friend Bunjum – he is dead, may God pardon his sins! – and I did something scandalous. During the dance, we had eyes only for a certain Ida, the wife of Haroji. She was the only one we chose in the dance of partners. Bunjum was especially in love with her. This could easily be seen and Ida's husband, Haroji, noticed too. He could not take our intrigues any longer. He had a flashlight which allowed him to see what others could not see. He went up to Bunjum and, right in the middle of the dance, hit him behind his ears with a stick. Then Haroji came for me. I succeeded in ducking the blow.

But all that did not go unnoticed. The father of the young married man learned what was going on. He soon arrived and scolded us for what had just happened. 'Dance,' he told us. 'Dance night and day. The longer you stay at my home, the happier I'll be. But please, respect our *pulaku*!' He stopped there and decided it was not necessary to make a 'proclamation'.

But several weeks later such an announcement was made, and very much according to our customs. It was at the marriage of Sandawa. There was an incident caused by a certain Bayu-Nyunyule. He was one of those 'pagans' who have become integrated with the Mbororo by living with them. There is a special name for these people. Born as slaves, they remain so no matter what.

Bayu-Nyunyule had come with his wife. She impressed us with her unusual strength. Anytime a man made a little sign to her or touched the hem of her wrapper-skirt, she followed him. She considered those secret meetings during the dance to be a sign of friendship, and of this she was very proud. She even accepted one man's coming right after another. 'Wait a little,' we'd say to her. 'I'll signal one of my friends to come keep you company.' And she'd wait. And then friends of the friends followed one after another.

Bayu-Nyunyule noticed the disappearance of his wife. He looked for her and found her just when a certain Sarara had taken his place next to her. Bayu-Nyunyule jumped on Sarara. There were lively words and then we heard the blows of staves. Sarara succeeded in running away, followed by the husband he'd made a fool of. His wife ran off in another direction.

The rhythm of the dance was disturbed by these wild shouts. 'What's happening?' everyone asked.

'It's Bayu-Nyunyule!' shouted someone. 'It's Bayu-Nyunyule!'

The elders got up and shouted, 'What! It's Bayu-Nyunyule, that dirty-assed farmer, that frightful pagan, that slave!' They made him come before them and called him all sorts of names. 'Don't you know any better than that? Don't you know how to behave like a Fulani? But what does a pagan like you know about our code of honour, our *pulaku*? Because of this, we banish you. We forbid you to have any contact with our clan forever!'

On that very day both Bayu-Nyunyule and his wife were forced to leave. Bayu-Nyunyule's master was obliged to chase him away. The banished man had to seek refuge in a village of farmers, where he was miserable.

Several weeks later, unable to endure the banishment any longer, Bayu-Nyunyule decided to sell his last steer, which he had earned by working as a herder for five months.[1] With that money he was able to buy ten calabashes[2] of kola nuts. He had heard the announcement of Jingulo's wedding for the following week. He carried his big sack of kola nuts to my uncle Kadiri's house and asked my uncle to be his representative. 'Please,' Bayu-Nyunyule said, 'accept these kola nuts. Keep them until Jingulo's wedding. You can pass them out and tell the *ardos* I beg them in the name of *pulaku* and "by the *barkehi* cord" to let me return from banishment as soon as possible.' Having said that, Bayu-Nyunyule broke off a *barkehi* leaf which he placed on top of the kola nuts.

He continued to insist, 'Tell them in the name of *pulaku* and of "the *barkehi* rope" that I'm sorry for what I did. May they lift this disgrace from me! May they let me come back to this clan which has always been mine! I promise I'll behave like a real Fulani.' My uncle accepted the kola nuts. He promised Bayu-Nyunyule he'd be his spokesman and advocate.

When all the guests at Jingulo's wedding feast had eaten their fill, my uncle asked to speak. 'You see these kola nuts! It's Bayu-Nyunyule who is offering them to us. He begs you to release him from the isolation which you imposed. He promises to respect *pulaku*. He asked me to represent him. I accepted. Please, "by the *barkehi* leaf", remove the ban which weighs on him. Let him come back to his clan.' That's how my uncle spoke.

An important man stood up. He asked a young man to shout the traditional cry of *ye kwa*. This 'summons' was heard, and soon all the guests were assembled in front of the elders. When there was perfect silence, a voice was heard. 'Today we lift Bayu-Nyunyule from his misery of isolation. Anyone who meets him should exchange our usual greetings with him and shake his hand. Talk with him and accept him as you did before. Yes, today Bayu-Nyunyule has been reintegrated into his clan. As a sign of reconciliation, let each one of you accept a kola nut which he's sent. May this news reach the most remote Mbororo villages and camps!'

Bayu-Nyunyule's master went to announce the good news to him. 'It's done. Your stay in isolation is over. You may come back and resume your place.'

Polygamy

Polygamy is not forbidden among the Mbororo. It's not unusual to see a Mbororo married to two wives, but rarely three and never four that I know of. The celebrations which mark the marriage with a second wife are not as lively as with the first wife. But invitations are sent, praise-singers liven up the gathering and dances last long into the night – often until dawn.

As with all Muslim marriages, the families' representatives first exchange their mutual consent before a *mallam*. All then proceeds as usual, just as it did for the first marriage.

The arrival of the bride is less solemn. She comes with all her belongings, and sometimes she's carrying a child on her back. The bride is received by the first wife, who is busy serving everyone. She's pleasant with the guests, even if her smile is a little forced. She accepts her cousins' jokes. They do not fail to remind her that the good times are over for her. 'To the contrary,' she says, 'I'll have less to do. With two, the work will be easier. I'm tired of doing everything: meals, children, selling milk and other tasks. Now I can rest a little. I can even go spend several weeks with my old mother. I will leave with peace of mind. My husband and children will be in good hands; they will not starve to death.'

The children don't know exactly what is going on. They're happy to know there will be another person in the house. They always like having visits and welcoming passers-by. They don't ask questions about whether this new person will be nice or mean to them.

A man is very pleased to marry a woman who comes with a baby that's still nursing or who's left one or more children with her first husband. That's a guarantee for the future. Children, isn't that what a man expects from a wife? On the other hand, a man will only reluctantly marry a woman who, after several years of marriage, has not given birth to a child. It's very difficult for such a woman to find a husband. A sterile woman must have a lot of strength and good health in order to find a new husband. A Mbororo views the woman he loves, first and foremost, as the mother of his children.

From the time the second woman comes into the household, the husband feels he has the obligation to have some special regard for the first wife. So on the day when the marriage is 'tied', he offers her a pretty wrapper-skirt which is called the cloth of the '*dada sare*',[3] that is, the cloth of the 'mother of the house'. From then on, that is the title she's given. She accepts it with a certain pride, but with mixed emotions.

During the first days of life together, the children of the first wife are with the new wife from morning to night. They do not leave her house. Actually, according to custom, the new wife must take special care of her husband during the first ten days. And the children find an abundance of everything they like at her house. They can stuff themselves with rice and good couscous!

When the two wives have good characters and good hearts, the children can be seen passing from one to the other as if they had only one mother. The younger wife hurries to offer her services to the 'mother of the house'. She takes the older wife's place at the market selling milk and buying supplies. The wives gain the admiration of their neighbours who are quick to heap praises on them. 'My word! We've never seen women be so pleasant and live so happily with the same husband!'

All the wives must be treated equally. However, there's always a 'mother of the house'. She's not necessarily the one preferred by the husband since that title goes to the first wife. Her only privileges are not very important ones, like distributing the gifts which the husband offers to his wives. She's the one who assigns cooking days to each wife. But since the cooking is assigned to the wife who will receive the husband that night – and not to the wife who received him the night before – the 'mother of the house' actually has the last word in deciding if the husband's conjugal visit will take place two nights in a row in the same house or each night in a different house. Islam has taught us this, but it was not like that in our own customs. People still talk about a time not very long ago when the wives disputed over the 'blanket'. The husband would put his blanket on the bed of the wife he wanted to visit that night, but during the day the blanket was sometimes taken away by the other wife!

Sometimes a boy begins his married life with two wives. Such a boy would always have a father with the reputation of being very rich, with two or three herds. His mother would have 'taken' the first wife for him from close relatives eight days after the girl's birth, in accordance with our custom of *nangaru*.[4] But in order for the father to demonstrate his importance and to maintain his reputation, he thinks he's obliged to offer his son a second wife. He has no trouble finding a wife about his son's age.

A third wife may also be offered to the father by a friend who sees that union as an honour to himself. And so he insists, 'I give my daughter to your son. I promise you I'll refuse anyone who asks for her.' The future father-in-law will never think about refusing the girl because his son already has two fiancées. Prestige comes first!

I've never seen a marriage with three wives. In the course of the stages which precede marriage, one or another of the girls always refuses to go ahead with the marriage. But a marriage with two wives who arrive the same day, yes. Sometimes that makes a problem for knowing who will be the 'mother of the house'.

I'm thinking of my cousin Njarori who saw the families of his two fiancées arrive in the same truck with the two trousseaus all mixed together. Everyone laughed as they put the baggage on the ground. It was all right that the trousseaus arrived at the same time, but several days later when the fiancées would arrive, who would be the 'mother of the house'? It was decided that although both of them would come on the same day, notice would be taken of who came first so the title could be given to one woman. The order of arrival could not be foreseen. One woman had to come from Bassama, the other from Jangay. Actually it was the one from Bassama who arrived first at the threshold of the house. So she was declared the 'mother of the house'.

During the first year of marriage, the two co-wives make an effort to control their jealousy and to avoid quarrelling in public, in the name of *pulaku*. Why? So they do not feel shame. They know very well what people would think if they heard wives arguing. People always mock such wives, saying, 'They're still disputing over the "blanket"! They're not fighting about the cooking; they don't do any. They're not fighting about the children; they don't have any. It can only be about the bed. They should be ashamed!' But after some years of marriage, the wives don't hesitate to pull out each other's hair in front of other people.

But if the wives get along too well together, the husband isn't really satisfied because he always has them on his back. They act like two accomplices who promise to shut their eyes on each other's bad behaviour and adulterous affairs! The husband knows that, so he arranges to plant trouble between them. To do this, he takes one aside and tells her about the alleged slanderous remarks made about her by the other wife. And vice versa.

But he must watch out not to arouse too much jealousy. Life in the future could become unbearable. When that happens, he's sneaky enough to profit from it. He sends away the wife he likes the least, charging her with all the vices while he attributes all the virtues to the other. One day he says to the wife he likes least, 'Leave! I renounce you.' He states his repudiation in that tone, and it is final. He can also make his statement in front of two or three witnesses.

Most often bad feelings arise because of children. Take the case in which one wife is a mother and the other is not. The wife without children will never be consoled about not having children because she lives in fear that she'll be divorced or, even worse, that her husband will die. With no child to inherit anything, she'll find herself completely impoverished. The family inheritance will go to the children of the other bed and to her co-wife, who therefore is only a rival to be extremely jealous of. For this reason, each wife – when both of them have children – prefers boys. In fact the largest part of the inheritance goes to the sons, to the detriment of the daughters who are largely left out.

Because of this, the behaviour of the co-wives toward the wealth of the husband is very different. A wife who has sons jealously guards the inheritance and stops the husband from spending money. On the other hand, the wife who has no children or who has only daughters will push her husband to spend money. It's not important to her if he gets richer or not! She has only one wish: to profit immediately because she knows she will not inherit anything.

The calf rope is often a source of disputes. The calves are divided between the two wives, and that also divides the milk-cows. When the husband has finished milking, each wife should receive the same amount of milk. But that's not always the case. The wife who gets less never stops complaining

At the height of the dry season, the sale of milk is not sufficient for buying daily food at the market. The husband digs into his purse. One wife always thinks the husband is giving the other wife more money! Another occasion for quarrels: children. When the children fight amongst themselves, each wife defends her own children. Voices rise. The wives exchange insults, then blows, and finally a real fight on their doorstep. The next day and in the days following, the wives will be seen sitting with grim faces in their doorways, watching each other and resolved not to talk to each other. This is often what happens in polygamous households. They insult each other, they fight, they wound each other, and they take each other to court. The husband spends his time trying to mediate.

However, there are households where the co-wives live in peace. This is especially true when the first wife has desired a second wife, as for example, when the first wife is growing old. She knows she will not have any more children, but her husband is still well and strong. Sometimes she encourages him. 'If the occasion presents itself, don't hesitate to take another wife!' So she's not surprised to see a second wife come to the house one day, a young and robust wife. This is for the benefit of all. I know many such households where life is good.

CHAPTER 19

Mbororo Marriage

Before telling you about marriages where a second wife arrives, I should have described the kind of marriage our parents desire for their children: a marriage between relatives. This was the kind of marriage Yidikau, the son of one of my father's brothers, had. We were the same age. For him everything went according to our customs, the customs of my clan, the Jafun from north of the Benue.

The Stages of Marriage

For us, every marriage passes through the six following stages: the *nangaru*, the *gettile*, the *kobgal*, the *tegal*, the *bangal* and the *bangtal*.

The *Nangaru*

This is the moment when a little girl is 'taken into possession' for marriage. Eight days after her birth, on the day of her *inderi*, every girl is 'taken' by a mother for one of her young sons. In general, the girl who's 'taken' is the cousin of the boy who is the 'taker'. The boy is about three years old.

As soon as Yidikau's mother learned of the birth of a daughter in the home of her brother-in-law, she had only one idea: to 'take' the girl for her son who was nearly four years old.[1] She'd had this plan in her head for a long time. Her determination and her haste were repaid because she was the first to 'put the beaded necklace' around the neck of the little girl who was named Sippi. I've forgotten her 'big name', the one given her by the *mallam*. The members of our kin group soon learned about the event: Sippi had been 'taken'! She'd been 'taken' for Yidikau! Some were disappointed and regretted they'd let Yidikau's mother get ahead of them. 'This Sippi would have been perfect for my son! I should have been the first to put the necklace on her!'

The grandmothers joked about it, as is their custom. They pretended to disapprove: 'What! How dare they take our sweet little Sippi and give her to that awful Yidikau, to that runt who doesn't have two pennies worth of breath! This must be stopped . . . !' The conversation went on like that in good humour. And finally everyone agreed to the union.

The *Gettile*

Years passed. Each child grew up in its own home. Yidikau was eight years old and Sippi five. They were already called 'husband' and 'wife'. But were they still? The agreement had to be reaffirmed. So one day Yidikau's father delegated one of his friends to ask Sippi's father the question, 'Does the *nangaru* between our two children still hold?'

'Of course! What would stop it?'

'Very well! In that case, Yidikau's father asks you to set the date for the *gettile*.'

'If he doesn't find it inconvenient, tell him it will be next Saturday.'

The following Saturday an old woman left Yidikau's village and headed toward the village of Sippi's parents. She carried a large calabash of fresh milk on her head, with a colourful and finely woven basketry cover. On this round cover had been placed small cotton balls, dum-palm fibres, *barkehi* leaves and some coins. A little boy preceded the messenger.

The calabash was put down in front of the doorway of the future mother-in-law. The intermediary who was bringing the good news squatted in front of the door and greeted the family. 'We were sent to carry the *gettile* milk to you, as well as the *gettile* money. Those who sent us thank you and pray that God will bless you.'

The response was, 'Thank those who sent you. May God bless them too!'

The milk was then divided into small calabashes which the children carried to the neighbours without needing to explain why. The coins were given to the relatives. The children themselves received some of the small coins. By accepting the coins, the adults were agreeing to help with the costs of the marriage, in one way or another, when the time came. This is an obligation of our *pulaku*.

I must add that Sippi was there, in the midst of the people of her village, because – at her age – she did not think about running away. But she was not given any of that milk to drink. It was arranged so she did not drink any. The distribution to the various people was done very quickly so she would not think about drinking the milk. If, by accident, she had touched it, there would not have been any fuss. This would simply have been a small breach of *pulaku*.

When the milk had all been passed out, the old woman messenger left, still preceded by the little boy. She hurried to give her report: 'They greet you. They thank you. They're particularly happy that you're taking the agreement between their daughter and your son seriously. They're pleased to know this gesture was not just a joke for you.'

The *Kobgal*

Four years later, the parents of the two families conferred: 'Let's agree a day to hold the *kobgal* for our two children.' They chose the tenth day of the following month. The parents hurried to send invitations and to start accumulating food. For meat, they'd agreed that each family would give a four-year-old steer.

When that day arrived, the steers were brought early in the morning. Each family prepared its own animal at its own fire. But when it came time to eat, all the meat was mixed together before it was served to the guests so there would not be any question about the source of the meat they were eating.

During the long preparations, people kept arriving from all directions. The Fulbe and Hausa merchants hurried to spread out plastic sheets on the ground so they could display their merchandise: kola nuts, packages of sugar, boxes of matches, candy, soap, radio batteries … while the neighbouring farming people offered their services.

Yidikau was not there. He would not be coming. As for Sippi, if she'd been a little older, she'd have been told, 'Go spend the day in the village of so-and-so.' 'Chased away' in this way, the young girl would quickly have understood what was happening and have done as she was told. When she came home, she would not touch the meat, the porridge or the *sobal*, which may have been left over from the feast. She'd be given other food that had been specially prepared for her.

The feast took place as usual: the women sitting on their side, the men on the other, seated two-by-two, each one facing another in three double rows, one next to the other. This was reminiscent of the calf rope. It was like a prayer to assure the prosperity of the herd.

The *Tegal*

Years passed. Sippi reached the age of puberty and Yidikau was seventeen. The time had come to 'tie' their marriage. It was agreed that this would be done on the next market day at Fada, at the compound of the village *mallam*. The *mallam* arranged for the meeting to be held after the noon prayer. On the appointed day and hour, a group of men in robes in which the colour white predominated could be seen gathering in front of the *mallam* of Fada, whose name was Mal Abo.

The *mallam* was seated on an old sheepskin in the left corner of the mud-walled room. Well-used mats were spread all around him, the full length of the room. When there was silence, he asked if the representatives of the two future spouses were present. Then he asked the question: 'Where is the *rubu* money (the bride-price)?'

'It's here,' said someone, spreading out before him a beautiful, brand new five-thousand-franc note.[2]

'And what about the *sadaki* cow to be offered to the bride?'

My father answered, 'We've agreed on a two-year-old heifer. Her name is Ole and she's fawn-coloured.'

'Has this heifer already been sent to the woman or is she still in the father-in-law's herd?' asked the *mallam*.

'The heifer hasn't yet left the herd. But do not worry; she'll be delivered at the proper time.'

The *mallam* asked more questions: 'And the entry-house money (the *jauleru* money)?'

One of the men waved a five-hundred-franc bill,[3] which he placed on the ground.

'And money for the *mallam*?'

Three one-hundred-franc coins were each placed on the note near the calabash full of kola nuts which had already been placed under the *mallam*'s eyes.

On invitation from Mal Abo, my father, who was Yidikau's sponsor, turned toward Sippi's sponsor and addressed him this way, 'Do you agree to give me Sippi?'

'I give her to you.'

'Do you give her to me?'

'I give her to you.'

Three times the same question was asked; three times my father responded, 'I accept.'

Then the *mallam* turned toward those present and asked them three times in a row, 'Are you witnesses?'

'We are witnesses.'

And so the *mallam* could 'tie' the marriage. Someone reminded him of the names of the future couple. Then he consulted his books and began to read the Arabic texts, beginning with this phrase: 'I intend to "tie" the marriage of Sippi and Yidikau. May God give them a happy life. May he give them children and wealth!'

He invited the witnesses to join him in a long prayer. All the people present lifted their hands to the level of their faces. The *mallam* moved his own hands slightly as if he was reading a text. When he'd pronounced the final phrase, all the people present passed the palms of their hands over their faces and down their chests and expressed their approval, saying in one strong voice the *Alfatiya*.[4]

The *mallam* then said one last prayer: 'May God give them fidelity to one another! May the wife be faithful to her husband and the husband to his wife!' And then the marriage was 'tied'. This is what had befallen Sippi and Yidikau. Then the *mallam* took the *rubu* money and put it in the hand of the wife's representative, charging him to give it to the bride's mother. That money belonged to Sippi. Her mother would have no right to touch it without her daughter's consent. The daughter was free to do what she wanted with it.

The *sadaki* heifer also became the property of the bride, even though the cow stayed under Yidikau's control. If she needed money, he would not prevent her from selling the cow. But if she suddenly had an impulse to leave the marriage home, her husband might legitimately refuse to let her take the heifer. When the woman dies, this cow and her offspring become the property of the woman's children: it's the cow of their mother.

The *jauleru* money is paid to the village chief. The *mallam* gives it to him at the same time he notifies the chief of this new marriage. As for the *mallam*'s money, there is no need to beg him to put it in his pocket.

Mal Abo, who was a town Fulbe, was only interested in the *rubu* money, the *jauleru* money, the *mallam*'s money and especially the *sadaki* cow. If he'd been a Mbororo, he'd have known about another payment we make among ourselves: this is the money of the house (*sudu*). But even if the *mallam* had known about it, he would not have had anything to do with it. This custom does not come from Islam. It originates with our *pulaku*.

I want you to take note once again of the absence of Sippi and Yidikau. Even if the meeting had taken place in Yidikau's own village, he'd have gone somewhere else. Often it's when a young man sees people coming back from the *mallam*'s house that he knows his *tegal* has been 'tied'. He learns the news simply by hearsay.

The *Bangal*

The *bangal* took place the following Saturday. The evening before, a group of boys and girls, as well as some young women, left Yidikau's village and went toward Sippi's village. As they approached, Sippi ran off, taking refuge with friends away from her village. Her mother, knowing the intentions of those who arrived, welcomed them with kindness. She prepared a special dish for them, called *njabordi* (the food of welcome): couscous bathed in butter. That Friday evening passed calmly and everyone found a place to sleep wherever they could.

The next day, the morning and early afternoon period passed as usual in Sippi's village. Since the two villages were close to each other, there was plenty of time. There wasn't any hurry because it was the custom to arrive at the husband's village as the sun was setting. It was only when the heat diminished that people became more active. The trousseau, which everyone had been admiring the last few days, was taken out and divided into loads: the men took the heavier sacks and the women the lighter things. Everyone arranged themselves in a line: the men first, headed by the man carrying the heaviest load. That man was nicknamed 'the pack ox'.

At that moment Doya arrived, the praise-singer friend of the Mbororo who was always on the lookout for what was happening in the bush. Some young apprentice praise-singers accompanied him. This time Doya hadn't come on his own accord; he had been invited by Yidikau's father who wanted to give more excitement to the occasion. Doya immediately went to the head of the parade so he could set the pace. Drawing sharp notes from his instrument, which he blew with bulging cheeks, he set off with his companions, one of whom kept time on a drum.

The parade soon arrived at the edge of the husband's village. A light fog covered the straw roofs. Instead of going toward the entrance of the village, Doya turned off toward the bush, with the parade following him. Everyone acted as if they didn't see the roofs. Wandering from right to left, they seemed like people who were lost.

The joke continued until someone from the village went to bar their path. Convincing them to go in the right direction took lots of effort and was a test of patience.

They were welcomed. But when the porters were invited to unload their baggage they refused, especially the women, who walked around in circles. The invitation to put the baggage down was spoken more and more emphatically. 'Get rid of your baggage! Please!'

'No, we'll go back now!'

'For the love of God, stop being stubborn!'

The old woman who'd taken the lead of the parade when they came to the village said, 'OK! But where's the "anger money"?' The villagers had to pay up. The old woman took the money and put it in her pocket.

Everything was placed at the entrance of the house. A brand new straw house had been prepared for Sippi. Then everything was brought inside. The porters found food prepared for them by Yidikau's mother: rice, couscous with butter and even mutton. They ate and danced very late into the night.

The next day the praise-singer Doya spread out all the things in Sippi's trousseau, displaying them slowly one after the other and holding them up. He was pleased to make this session last a long time so he would get more money. When he had what he wanted, he finally decided to put everything on the ground. However, the people were impatient. 'Look! Hurry up!' But he did just what he wanted. For himself, he received three pieces of cloth and one mat, without counting the money.

Finally the time came that everyone was waiting for, especially the young people. Everything that was spread out on the ground – or nearly so – was 'taken away', as if it were stolen by the cross-cousins[5] and the grandparents. This was done as a joke.

You should have seen these people dart in like birds of prey and run off with everything. One had a mat and another a piece of cloth! Even little children who could hardly walk were taking things. Often their mothers urged them on: 'Go! Take something!' The little child would take what he wanted or what his mother gave him and then run as fast as he could.

One could see grandmothers running away with pieces of cloth. The young people would shout, 'Hey! You can't do that!'

'Why not! Aren't I Sippi's *dendirawo* cousin?' Sometimes one of them was caught by another who wanted the thing that was being carried away.

Everyone wanted to have a wrapper-cloth. A close relative could also take a mat, but it was not right to take two pieces of cloth. First one would take something, then another, never both at the same time. Anyone who 'took' something quickly put it in whatever safe place he could find; then he came back and stood to watch the others play the same game. Of course, the girls participated too.

During that time, other people were making the bed in Sippi's hut. The young men went to look for big forked logs. They carried back a dozen of them and placed them solidly like posts in the six holes they'd dug. Two cross-pieces were set in the forks of the logs. Then the *gaude* were placed perpendicularly to span the cross-pieces. These big, solid – though lightweight – reeds, which are as long as an arm, were part of the trousseau. So that the reeds would look as pretty as possible when they were set up at Sippi's house, they'd been rubbed with butter. We always carry the *gaude* with us, even during the seasonal migration.

On this grid, two reed beds (bed rolls) were unrolled and set end to end. A good thickness of mats was piled on top of the beds, perhaps a dozen or so. All of this was covered with a blanket, or perhaps two. The bed was made.

This work was carried out with good humour and joking. The grandmothers managed to uproot the posts, throwing everything on the ground. They ran off with the posts and would not give them back except in exchange for some coins.

An old woman could be seen covering the blanket with cow dung, saying, 'Ah, that! It's too pretty for Yidikau! His wife can wash it!'

As they must be, these festivities took place in the absence not only of Sippi but also of Yidikau. He'd 'fled' to spend the day somewhere else and only came back when everything was finished. He knew that his house had been neatly arranged and his bed had been made. But when he returned, he would not enter that house. That was absolutely out of the question.

The Arrival of the Bride

Only a week later, often on a Saturday, the groom's family comes to collect the bride. Sippi's family was waiting for this event. The messengers introduced themselves to her mother. 'We've come to get your daughter.'

'That's good. Go ahead and take her.' In some clans, the family refuses to give the daughter, on the pretext that the brideprice is not high enough or the young girl does not want to leave. This comedy can go on for weeks.

Sippi was ready, dressed in a pretty wrapper-skirt. Her hair was neater than usual, but without any ornaments. She wore no necklace or bracelet either. Her little brothers and sisters began to cry: they did not want their big sister to go away. Her mother was sad too: she'd have to do all the chores alone from then on. She sat there, in a pensive mood.

The messengers had arrived early. They took Sippi back in the evening, as night fell, carrying her little bag and her personal belongings. A veil was put on her head to hide her face. But Sippi refused to go, crying softly. She had to be pushed. She stopped many times to sit down and then walked very slowly, as if she were counting her steps. This is the custom. The people walking in front of her had to keep begging, 'Let's go! Don't act like this!' She sulked and moaned and had to be begged and then sat down again. They pulled her to her feet and then it started all over again.

Night fell. At last they came to the village, but Sippi did not go in. She sat all alone a certain distance away, behind a bush.

A little later, Yidikau's mother sent her children to get Sippi and Sippi followed them without saying a word. When she arrived at the house, Sippi refused to enter and she sat outside in the dark – a little distance away. She had to be begged again. Once she was inside, she sat on the ground next to the bed. A very small fire had been lit to chase away the darkness. It was left to die out. No one spoke. When someone brought her food, Sippi hardly ate any, even though she was begged by her little sisters-in-law who were spending the night with her. This is the custom of *pulaku*. Sippi stretched out on a mat on the ground and refused the bed that had been prepared.

Very early the next morning, well before dawn, the people heard a pestle pounding millet in order to prepare the flour needed for the family gruel. Three days in a row Sippi performed this task and then she returned to her mother, all alone. The next day, after endless begging, she went back.

During that time, Yidikau had styled his hair. He ate with everyone and spent the evening with the men in the *dado*. When the men went to bed, Yidikau did too. But he only pretended to sleep. In the middle of the night, he arose with the greatest of care and, after making sure that everyone was sleeping very soundly, he entered Sippi's house and spent the rest of the night there. At first light, he took his place again among the men. Everybody knew what had happened during the night between Sippi and Yidikau. But no one talked about it. This is according to *pulaku*.

Three weeks later Sippi returned once again to her mother in order to make herself beautiful. She put on all the finery which she'd been forbidden to wear. The hairdressers fixed her long braids, which they thickened with black wool. Her hair nearly disappeared under copper spangles and rings which shone like gold. Her whole forehead was decorated with shiny golden wires almost like a crown! Her necklaces were piled one on another and she wore many bracelets.

Plenty of time was taken over these preparations – five or six days in all. No one was in a hurry. People who saw the young bride could not help making comments and flattering her. 'How beautiful she is, the wife of Yidikau!'

Sippi's return 'in her beauty' to her parents-in-law's home was done without any particular ceremony. She moved in very naturally with her new family, ready to do whatever she was asked by her mother-in-law, whom she treated with the greatest discretion.

Soon Sippi was pregnant. Her parents-in-law chose the day she'd go back to her mother's house, a Saturday, according to tradition. There's an expression we use in such circumstances: 'Sippi must go back for *pulaku*.' After her departure, we say, 'she's gone for *pulaku*' or 'she's gone home to nest'.

The next Saturday she saw several old women arriving. She understood right away they were coming to 'mess up her hair'. In spite of her refusals and her shouts, they led her a little ways into the bush. There they took off her pretty wrapper-skirts by force. The women pinned her to the ground so they could dress her in a piece of white cloth which would be her only clothing until she had her baby. Then they attacked her hair: they replaced her pretty adolescent braids with two big tufts of hair on each side of her head. Sippi struggled, she tried to bite them and to run away. But it was in vain. She went back to her house all dishevelled.

From then on, Sippi was not allowed to go to the markets, to get dressed up, to put on make-up or to use perfumed ointments. No adornments were allowed. She could no longer talk to anyone outside her close family: her father, mother, brothers and sisters. If a stranger approached her, she would not respond even if he asked her for directions.

The First Birth

When there were signs that the birth was near, Sippi's mother avoided going to the market for fear the event would happen in her absence. She even had an experienced grandmother come to help her.

When the baby arrived, Sippi did not ask about its sex. With perfect indifference, she did not even respond to the greetings of her neighbours who hurried to congratulate her. Her face remained impassive as is the custom, and it was only by accident she learned that it was a boy. 'Bravo, Sippi! You have regained your feet. Congratulations on this beautiful boy! *Barka! Barka!*' All the women who came to see her had small *barkehi* branches in their hands, which they placed in the thatch above her doorway before entering. Gifts came pouring in for the celebration of little Jam-Jam's birth: milk, butter, millet flour.

As I've told you Sippi seemed to pay no notice, hiding her face under a veil. Sometimes, so as to avoid stares more easily, she put her head under her blanket. She stubbornly refused to give her breast to the baby. When the baby had been given enough sugar-water, he was placed on his mother's breast while her hands were held behind her back. The grandmother took care of the new baby.

Sippi ate by herself: millet gruel which had been well spiced and peppered. Every day she did ablutions behind a straw fence which protected her from indiscreet stares. She splashed very hot water on her body with a *barkehi* branch. We see nothing religious in this. It is simply an *alfalu*, a magic rite which brings well-being that originates from our *pulaku*. This practice ends the fortieth day after the birth.

It's also in the name of *pulaku* that a mother is obliged to maintain the greatest reserve toward her baby. Is he crying? She doesn't do anything to calm him. Is he exposed to the sun? Is he moving toward a fire? She does nothing, at least not if the grandmother is present. She lets him eat whatever he wants and put the dirtiest things in his mouth.

Should he get sick, his mother simply watches. If she's asked about her baby, she'll act like she did not hear. The father is not sent for, no matter what happens. Is the baby dead? The parents do not shed a tear – neither one nor the other. Both of them suffer inside, but this cannot be seen.

What happens when the parents are alone? Perhaps they permit themselves to cry? Maybe … But I don't know. All I can say is that I've never seen a mother cry when she is in this 'nesting' period. And yet I've seen many of these babies die. But I've never noticed that mothers go off and hide so they can weep. The family takes care of the burial. The mother does not intervene.

A mother's extreme reserve (*semtende*) toward her first child is no small thing. In my opinion, it's very difficult and it's bad. I know some mothers who maintain the same reserve after each birth, all during their lives.

Even when the mother is alone with her baby, she refrains from playing with him. She does not even smile the slightest bit. If anyone should happen to arrive unexpectedly she'd be so ashamed … ! And a habit is quickly formed. This attitude does not cause our mothers any problems. It's the custom, that's all. When someone asks them the reason, they're content to say, '*Pulaku* is *semtende*, and *semtende* is *pulaku*.'

It does not occur to our young girls that this custom could be bad. I'm speaking here of young girls of my clan, the Jafun from north of the Benue. Today, in Adamawa, more and more families are starting to free themselves of this constraint.

Those families even acknowledge illegitimate children. But the rest of us have nothing but contempt for such people, even though they're Mbororo like us.

I have to add this: a first-born can always be recognised when he and his brothers are with their father by the way the father speaks to him and the way the son responds. The first-born son is always treated like a liar. In conversation between the father and his son there's always an argumentative tone. The youngest son, even if he lies shamelessly, is always judged to be telling the truth, whereas the oldest son is always wrong.

This double standard is really brought out in our tales; many of them are about the first-born. All his life, he'll be marked by his early experiences. His spirit is less lively. I've often heard it said when talking about someone who is not very intelligent that he is 'stupid like a first-born (*afel*)'. This has even become one of our proverbs.

How could it be otherwise? His mother never has the right to pronounce her son's name, not even to refer to another boy who has the same name. She calls her son without naming him and, in conversation, speaks about him as 'him' (*kanko*). She lets him do what he wants. Not even the slightest spanking. Never any advice. Absolutely no explanations. Only the grandmothers take care of this child, without telling him what he should or should not do. If you meet a first-born who is particularly clever, it's because he has developed the gifts God gave him, either alone or with the help of his little cousins or neighbours.

But let's go back to Sippi. She has only one occupation: basketry. She throws herself into accumulating as many calabash covers as possible. This work is time consuming. It's hard on the back and fatiguing for the eyes, especially if the pieces of basketry are decorated with designs made of coloured fibres. Sippi, whose friends encourage her by noting her efforts and congratulating her on her ability to use a needle, devotes herself to making holes through which the ends of the fibres are threaded. The designs have pretty names: orphan's tears, pigeon feet, sun rays …

Jam-Jam was already walking on his own and babbling when, one morning, Sippi's mother gave her a calabash full of milk. 'Go to the market. Sell the milk for me. It's time you got out!' For a long time Sippi had been impatient for the arrival of this great day. At the market, all the women selling milk noticed her and showed how happy they were to see her with them again. With the money she got from selling milk, Sippi bought some small pieces of candy which she gave to the women around her. She bought some adornments for her clothes and hair and she was allowed to go to evening gatherings. She was said to have an 'open mind'. One evening at the *soro*, she even spoke a few words to her husband. Yidikau had taken the initiative for this brief encounter, profiting from a moment of noise – a fight between two young men. He approached her and whispered several words into her ear, slipping a little money into her hand. He was careful no one was watching them. What shame if they'd been seen next to each other! Both of them understood very well that extreme prudence was required. What would happen if Sippi became pregnant during this period of separation? What disgrace for them and for their families! What a calamity for the child! Gossip would brand him as an illegitimate child, and he'd carry that disgrace to the end to his days!

Yidikau occasionally went to visit his parents-in-law. When he entered their village, he always avoided passing near his wife's house. In front of his mother-in-law's house, several steps from the doorway, he'd squat down. From outside, he'd greet her most respectfully, using the greetings which are common in this case and keeping his voice low.

Another event in Sippi's life during this semi-seclusion was the weaning of little Jam-Jam. One morning, as soon as he woke up, Jam-Jam came to his mother to take her breast. He found her chest coated with cow dung. To make it worse, Sippi told him it was the excrement of his little cousin. Jam-Jam cried, stamped his feet and turned in circles. His mother did not give in. The next day she disappeared from his sight and did not return for three days. So Jam-Jam – willingly or not – had to eat what his grandmother offered him: rice with butter which she had carefully spiced. Jam-Jam pouted, but finally he started to like it. His aunts came to offer him some candy.

The *Bangtal*

Once Jam-Jam was weaned and could walk well, Sippi could go back to her married life. Until now the only things that kept her busy were her clothes and her make-up. Now she would have a household to keep.

More than two years had passed. Yidikau had had to be content with news he heard here or there about his baby and his wife. He had not yet seen them, neither one nor the other. He was absolutely forbidden to visit them. Do not imagine he tried to cheat by asking a friend to arrange a secret meeting in the bush. Ah! certainly not! That is not done! Personally, I've never heard anyone tell about such a thing happening in my clan. Not even in our tales. Such a secret meeting is unthinkable for us. It's too serious. The shame! The abomination!

For the return of his wife, everything – or nearly everything – took place as it had for the 'first' marriage. There was 'house money' sent by the father-in-law. Sippi hurried to buy things: mortar, pestle, sieve, clay pots, calabashes, aluminium plates, enamel plates and big enamel bowls. The 'house money' was not enough. Her parents had to add some. As with the *bangal*, the trousseau was spread out for visitors to look at. No one came with empty hands. Moving the baggage from one village to the other was accomplished this time on the backs of pack-oxen. During the trip, a certain Alima led the singing. Actually, there was only one song: a Hausa song entitled 'Victory'. Alima lengthened the couplets as she wanted, but the refrain was sung tirelessly by her companions: 'Victory! Victory!'

As with her first departure, Sippi play-acted: she walked slowly, sometimes not advancing except when someone shoved her, stopping often to sit down on an upside-down calabash which served as her stool. When the people accompanying her arrived at a small stream, they pretended to stop and acted like they were going to spend the night there, as they would do at the end of a day during their seasonal migration. The baggage was taken off the pack-oxen, which were led to the watering place and a fire lit.

But then they had to move off again. And the comedy of the 'lost path' was repeated. The procession did not find the village, which was right there in front of them. At last they consented to enter the village, but the people waiting for them had all the trouble in the world getting them to put their baggage on the ground. They demanded money. When the trousseau was finally spread out, the cousins once more played their trick. They tried to see who had the most nimble hand.

When the guests left, Sippi got busy preparing her first meal: couscous, with a sauce that was generously peppered. To serve it, she chose her best *leal*, an ebony-black bowl carved from the heart of a tree. A large piece of multi-coloured basketry covered it. All around the cover hung colourful pompoms and coins that had holes in them. A piece of glass, which came from a broken mirror, was placed in the middle, on top of the cover.

The men sitting on mats fell silent as Sippi approached their circle. At a respectful distance, she bowed with her knees on the ground, putting down the bowl carefully so it sat steadily. When she had left, the youngest guest got up and ceremoniously put the bowl of couscous and the sauce which had been prepared separately in the midst of the guests. Yidikau had the honour of taking the first mouthful. That meal marked the resumption of their married life. It has a name which only those insolent *kori* love to remember: 'the one that unties the pants'. From that time on, Sippi was another person. She took turns with her mother-in-law doing the cooking. She was a real woman, a wife and a mother.

Some weeks later, Sippi received what she'd still been missing: her own calf rope. This rope was given to her in the natural course of events when her father-in-law gave Yidikau the cattle which were his own, separating them from the family herd in the presence of some of the elders.

My father, as the paternal uncle, congratulated Yidikau's father for watching over Yidikau's wealth and giving him his cattle in good condition. Then my father gave a beautiful heifer as a gift. My other uncles did the same.

'Thank you!' said an old man. 'Thank you! May God bless Yidikau! May God give him as many cows as there are grains of sand in the Benue.' All the elders who had made a point of being there for the occasion joined together in the invocation with a loud *Amina*!

Yidikau could be happy. He had everything a true Fulani needs: a wife, a child and a herd.

CHAPTER 20

Divorce and Widowhood

Seclusion

Unlike the sedentary Fulbe women, our Mbororo women are not confined. We know that a good Muslim must take care that his wife's face is not seen by a stranger, but it's not possible for us to keep our women in seclusion. Our huts are not surrounded by fences. And how could our wives go from door to door selling milk and butter with veils on their faces?

When our women see the Fulbe women who are forced to stay behind a fence, they feel sorry for them. Our women would not accept being enclosed like that. They even reproach these women, particularly for not being ashamed to use the same leaves as their husbands for their personal needs. A single hole for everyone behind the house: an abomination!

Our wives have no illusions about those women who are separated from the outside world. 'They're worse than other women!' our wives say. In fact, nothing can prevent a married woman from doing wrong; she quickly spies any weak point in the fence that she can slip through to join her lover! That kind of woman will always find some pretext to go out: 'My mother's sick.' 'My father has to go on a long trip.' Family fetes, which are sometimes celebrated a long way off, are occasions many women profit from to be free of the constraints of confinement.

Only a woman who believes in God and fears him can give her husband the assurance that he does not have to worry about her fidelity. Being enclosed or not has no value in itself. A licentious wife would stay that way no matter how she lived. She's ready to climb to the top of a tree to meet the one she loves!

That's how our women think, and I do too.

Divorce

The Mbororo are much less likely to divorce than the Fulbe.

The Fulbe are almost proud of the number of divorces they have. They even brag about it. It's not unusual to see a man with four wives send one away from time to time so he can take another. He takes care always to keep the same number. But the wives change; divorce and remarriage take place in succession. The man simply has to be rich. And usually, the older he gets, the younger the wife he chooses! Acting like that is considered by the Fulbe to be a sign of prosperity.

As for we Mbororo, we divorce almost with regret. A wife is ready to do anything so she will not be repudiated because she knows very well she will have a lot of trouble finding a new husband. People will say she carries 'bad luck'. If she doesn't have a child right away, she will be considered to be sterile forever.

Many divorces are the result of traditional marriages arranged by the parents when a girl is born. As the boy and girl grow up, they very frequently find there's no attraction between them. But the young girl, respectful of her parents and of tradition, does not dare admit that. The stages of marriage follow along until the day when, overcome by her aversion for her husband, she refuses him and runs off. She is brought back. She escapes again. She says to anyone who will listen that she does not like the man who was given to her as a husband when she was eight days old.

In the face of this persistence, the relatives get together, and there's every reason to believe they will be sensible enough to conclude, 'It's true. When she was a baby, we gave her a husband without consulting her. Because she absolutely refuses to have anything to do with this boy today, let her leave him. If not, she'll continue to run away. Who knows – maybe one day she'll meet someone who will kill her? Who knows if her husband, in a fit of anger, won't beat her to death? Both of them are young. It's better we break off their marriage.' And that is what takes place, all very naturally.

There's never a question of their going in front of a judge. The affair is straightened out between the Mbororo with reference to *pulaku*, that is, our code of honour. The boy's father goes along with this point of view, saying, 'We allow your daughter to leave. She's free to go where she wants. May she marry whomever she wants!' That's why there are many divorces among the very young women.

But when a young man has lived with a young woman who has given him children, divorce is rather rare. Both the husband and wife know very well the children would suffer. The mother must give up her children to her husband. How would they be looked after by their stepmother? The father himself thinks about all the miseries his own children would have to suffer with a new wife who might not like them. For this reason, the couple often prefer to continue living together.

When there is a divorce, the children – both boys and girls – always go to the husband. The mother only takes a baby that is still nursing. And she must give the baby back to his father when he is weaned. When this man is alone and doesn't remarry right away, his children are certainly a big worry for him. Sometimes, overcome by remorse, he tries to go back to living with the wife he has just sent away. He makes many approaches to his parents-in-law, pressuring them, insisting, swearing he'll change his behaviour. And since both husband and wife find it's to their advantage, there's a remarriage.

Among we Mbororo, it's never the wife who divorces the husband. It's always the husband who repudiates his wife. The wife can only run away. She does not hesitate to do that if she finds her husband is too hard on her. For example, if he doesn't give her enough money for food, if he refuses to clothe her, or if he beats her.

A Case in Point: Titi and Bango

This leads me to tell you about the role I played in obtaining a divorce for my 'older sister' Titi, the daughter of a paternal uncle. It would be better to say 'my cousin Titi', nicknamed Titiyel, 'Little Titi'. It was the third and final year of my stay in Gire. Titi had married one of her cousins on her mother's side. His name was Bango. This marriage, according to custom, had been arranged for her one week after her birth, on the day of her *inderi* (name-giving). Each of them grew up in their own families. She never agreed with her parents about this arranged marriage. However, she went along with it, not refusing the principal step of marriage, which we call *bangal*.

She became pregnant after a few months, and she returned to have her baby near her mother, following our custom. She lived with her mother for three years, separated from her husband. This is normal among the Mbororo. At the moment when she should have gone back to her married life in her husband's village, she absolutely refused to go. She preferred to stay at her mother's house with her son who was a little more than two years old. The reason she was determined not to return was that she'd learned that, during her absence, her husband had bought a house in the town of Numan where he entertained prostitutes.

He liked to pass his time with the townspeople and tried to imitate them, acting as if he was a White man. I personally remember being astonished when I saw, for the first time in my life, a package of sugar in his house. 'How is it possible,' I asked myself, 'to have enough money to buy such a large quantity of sugar?' When I knew he was gone, I peeked inside his house. I was amazed by everything I saw – a chair, several blankets, a package of sugar!

Bango lived in this house with his brother Kirijo. Both brothers had the same foibles. One behaved as badly as the other. When their father died, they had inherited a beautiful herd. But they agreed to waste their wealth on low-life women whom they entertained generously.

The Hausa merchants knew the brothers were rich. The merchants flattered the brothers and invited them to their houses. The praise-singers ran after the brothers, who gave them bank notes in exchange for false praises. The brothers bragged about having too many animals to count – so numerous, they said, that they'd never see the end of their animals, even if one were sold every day! The brothers seemed to forget that, aside from God, everything has an end here on earth and that the day would come when, having sold all their cattle, there would be nothing left.

The worst of the two, at least in the beginning, was Kirijo. All you had to do was to see him sitting on a fine rattan chair that was covered with beautiful, coloured cloth. Each evening when he was home, he put his chair outside his door. He sat there majestically watching his animals being brought back by his hired herder.

Before long Kirijo did not have a single animal left. His mother thought it would be good to help him rebuild his herd. She gave him fifteen head of cattle. She made this gesture of pity out of love for her daughter-in-law who was threatening to leave him. They had two young children. Kirijo's mother did everything she could to help him out, but he never changed. He sold one cow, then another and another … His mother decided it was best to take back the cows that were left. She was determined that from then on she would not give him anything, not even the tail of a calf!

Having lost everything, Kirijo fell into a black mood. He went crazy. He could be seen begging from the same merchants who, a short time before, had sold him merchandise at three or four times its price. He wore rags. None of the tailors would repair his clothes. Covered with shame, he fled to the Adamawa Plateau. He found one of his uncles who at first was very kind to him. But the uncle could not do anything with him and so he finally said, 'Work as a herder wherever you can. I do not want to see you any more.' And his uncle chased him away.

Bango followed in the footsteps of his older brother. Soon Bango had nothing either. His mother, who lived near him, was really counting on the return of her daughter-in-law to bring him back on the right path. But he kept telling his friends he would not take his wife back when she returned from her mother's house. He would not even hesitate to kill her. Under those conditions, you can understand why his wife, my cousin Titi, who knew about those menacing words, refused to return to his house and wanted to leave him forever.

But among the Mbororo, a wife can never ask for a divorce. Divorce is done by repudiation, that is, by the husband's sending the wife away. So that Titi could regain her complete freedom, her mother went to meet Bango. She begged him to separate from his wife with a legal divorce. Bango absolutely refused. He even threatened to put an arrow through his mother-in-law if she dared come to him again for the same reason. So it was absolutely necessary to 'break' this marriage. But how could this be done without the husband's consent? It was for this reason my family thought of me.

One market day at Gire, some of my family came to see me at Mala Buba's home. 'We want you to return home with us tonight. We need you for something important.' I asked myself what this could be about because at that time I was still quite young. I went with them. As soon as we arrived, one of my uncles said, 'Ndudi, we need you. We want you to accompany your older sister Titi to Yola. She wants to make a formal complaint against her husband Bango. You must help her obtain a divorce. Can we count on you? You know town people. You know how things work and you aren't afraid.'

'Me, afraid of such a little thing? Nothing's easier than getting what you've asked for! Just give me some money.'

I understood right away they would not refuse me anything.

'How much do you need?'

Seeing they were willing, I thought I could exaggerate: 'Forty Nigerian pounds!'[1]

'No more?' said one of my uncles.

I regretted not having asked for more. Too bad!

'Here!' And as he counted out the money for me, he felt it necessary to give me all sorts of advice.

My father cut him short: 'Don't worry about Ndudi. He's more clever than you or I. He understands about money!'

And so we left, my cousin Titi and I. The first stop: Gire, where we spent the night. The next day we took a truck which brought us to Yola.

I did not succeed in having an interview right away with the Judge. But we found a place to stay at the home of one of his assistants, a dignitary in the *lamido*'s court. 'Is this your wife?' he asked me when I introduced myself to him.

'No, she's my older sister.'

'What brought you here?'

'We've come to the court concerning a marriage that we want to see broken.'

'Nothing's easier,' he answered. 'I'm on the council. Do you have any idea how this is done?'

'A little, but in fact, I don't know very much.'

'What do you know?'

'I think I must get in the good graces of someone in the *lamido*'s court '

'How?' he asked.

'By offering him a gift.'

'That response proves you're a Mbororo – aren't you?'

'That's right.'

'But where did you learn these things?'

'I went to school.'

'Where?'

'In Gombe.'

'Now I understand why you're so smart! Good, then since you've come to my house, I consider you like my son ... , especially if you give me ten Nigerian pounds.'

I hurried to take the money out of my pocket and give it to him.

That evening he introduced me to some people who were close to the *lamido*. I gave two pounds to one, one pound to another. I didn't have a set amount. Our rounds finished with a visit to the Judge himself. I gave him ten pounds. And I didn't forget to give some coins to the police of the court. Thank goodness my uncle had not been stingy with the money! I still had enough.

The next day, on the recommendation of my host who had had a word with the Judge, I was first to be summoned. I waited at the door. I heard my name announced inside the house. A policeman came out and shouted in a loud voice, 'Umaru Ndudi!' I answered and entered. I left my older sister outside, trembling all over. I took off my hat and sat down on the hard ground. I bowed deeply. 'May God protect you, *Lamido*!'

'Thank you, thank you' '

All the assistants were seated, their backs leaning against the wall. One of them had a pile of papers in front of him. 'What's this about?' asked someone.

'I have come with my older sister who wants to have her marriage broken.'

'Why should her marriage be broken, just because she wants it done? Does she have some reasons to bring before the court? Since she has come with you, ask her to tell us the reasons herself. Then we'll say what we think.'

I signalled Titi to come in. She entered, very nervous, and she stammered as she spoke the conventional greetings.

'So,' someone said to her, 'you want your marriage broken. Is this simply a whim?'

'May God bless you,' she answered in a voice that was more confident. 'it's not without reason that I make this request. My husband has said he'll kill me when I return to his house. That's why I do not want to live with him any longer.'

'What's this story? Weren't you married so you could live together?'

'Maybe, but now he doesn't love me any more. Since he's taken two other wives, he only has contempt for me. To justify himself, he says I run after all the men. That is absolutely false. You yourselves know that Mbororo women do not act that way. There's no prostitution among us. Since he threatened to kill me, I'm afraid; and that's why I've come,'

'Very good. We register your complaint. But where is this Bango? Do you live in the same village?'

'No. He lives in a camp quite far from here, to the west of Jimeta.'

'We'd like to see him and hear from him too.'

I intervened. 'May God bless you, O *Lamido*! If you write a letter summoning him, I'll carry it to him.'

'Very good. But first go tell him we want to see him. If he refuses, we'll write him a summons.'

So the next day I took a bus, still accompanied by Titi. We knew we'd find Bango in the company of his cousin Alaji, a man who feared no one. People even said Alaji had chased away a well known robber, the famous Hitila.[2] He'd been well protected by his talisman; no metal arms could harm him.

We arrived in the evening. Bango was there, sitting in the place reserved for men. It was Alaji who received us. He gave us something to eat. Without delay, Titi went by herself to her husband who was sitting next to his brother Kirijo. She greeted them respectfully. Then she explained the object of her visit. 'I came concerning our divorce.'

With the word 'divorce', Bango got up abruptly; he was very angry and threatening. 'May the plague take you! If you come closer, I'll kill you! And don't send your mother in your place. I would kill her too!'

From where we were, Alaji and I could follow what was happening and could hear everything. Speaking the name of Titi's mother was an insult. For Alaji as for me, it made our blood rush. Alaji could not resist. He insulted Bango's father in return. Bango jumped up and so did his brother Kirijo, and the insults continued. The whole village got into the act. I did too. 'My God! My God!' shouted the women. 'They'll kill each other! Please stop!' It sounded like the women were wailing for the dead.

Alerted by the shouting, the neighbours came running. When they arrived, they thought someone had just died. In fact, it was only a fight, but a serious one. All the women on Bango's side advanced toward us, brandishing their pestles. Alaji grabbed his bow. Someone jumped on top of him to overpower him; but with a slap of his hand, Alaji sent anyone who came too close rolling to the ground. He threw off his tunic and, an arrow on his bowstring, he threatened, 'I'll shoot this arrow at the first one who moves!' Turning toward us, he added, 'I'll stretch out on the ground the first one who touches me. Let me settle this affair with this evil

Bango, who isn't even ashamed to insult his own aunt, who's also his mother-in-law.' Finally he calmed down.

Everyone went to bed. The night was tranquil. The next day Titi and I went back to Yola. We made our report to the court. 'It went badly. There's no explanation for Bango being so stubborn and agitated. There was even a fight; and if the neighbours hadn't intervened, there'd have been people hurt and perhaps even killed.'

The Judge was silent for a long time. Then he asked, 'Could you go back there again, this time with a summons? Are you afraid to confront him again?'

I said I was not afraid. On my own, I again took the Yola road with the letter in my pocket.

I found Kirijo. He was sprawled out on his bed with, as usual, a package of sugar within reach . . . , even though he'd lost all his animals by that time. Bango was not with him. 'He's not here,' was all Kirijo would say. There was no explanation.

I gave Kirijo the letter for his brother. 'This is a summons for Bango to go to the court in Yola. His wife Titi has registered a complaint against him.'

The word 'court' frightened Kirijo. All Mbororo react like that. 'Take the letter to him yourself,' Kirijo said to me. 'I refuse to be responsible for it. Or wait until he comes back.'

'Very well!' I said, putting the paper on his kilo of sugar. 'Do what you like. I've accomplished my commission. But I'm warning you that if you don't pay attention to this, you can expect to receive a visit from the police before long.' And I left Kirijo still sprawled on his bed.

Back in Yola, I made my report. The next day the court was not yet in session when Bango arrived. He seemed lost, not knowing where to go. I signalled him to join me. He made no trouble.

We were called; I was first, then 'he who has been summoned by letter'. Bango got up to follow me. Like all Mbororo from the bush at that time, he was wearing a light blanket thrown over his left shoulder. A knife hung from his belt. As soon as he crossed the threshold, a policeman grabbed him by the neck and spun him around. 'What's this knife?' he said, taking it away from him. 'And that cloth thrown over your shoulder?' The policeman also threw that on the ground. 'And that hat?' The policeman knocked his hat off with a slap of his hand. Then he bundled up everything and threw it outside.

Once Bango was inside, he sat on the hard ground in a way that showed a certain lack of respect. He forgot he was before the judges. His head was raised and he was looking right and left. The policeman put his hands on Bango's head and made him lower his eyes.

The judge said to him, 'Bango, your wife Titi has registered a complaint against you. To begin with, do you acknowledge that this really is your wife here?'

With a little nod of his head, Bango agreed.

'You know what she has accused you of. What do you have to say? But first, give us your summons letter. Titi, do you want to repeat the complaint you have registered against your husband who is now present?'

Titi repeated what she'd already said.

'And you, Bango, what do you have to say in response to this accusation?'

'May God bless you!' he said. 'I don't agree with what she just said. I've never made such threats. I didn't say I wanted to kill her.'

I could not stop myself from interrupting. 'That's not true. You said it. Besides, you repeated it the other day in front of me when you were angry. You'd even have gone through with it if your neighbours hadn't intervened.'

'What else could I do?' he replied, 'with a personality like mine!'

'If you have any real character,' said the Judge, 'show it by taking back your wife here. That will show your courage!'

'Oh, no! I can't do that!'

Turning toward Titi, the Judge asked her, 'What do you have to add?'

'For me,' she responded, 'my marriage no longer exists. I don't want anything more to do with this man who threatens to kill me. I only want one thing: a divorce.'

Then the Judge asked Bango, 'Do you agree to repudiate your wife, Bango?'

'No, I don't want a divorce!'

'Agreed or not,' continued the Judge, 'we're going to order the divorce. We've decided to break your marriage with Titi. We only ask her to repay the "refusal money" because she's the one who's renouncing your life together.'

I found the decision quite fair and very favourable. I hurried to give them the five pounds I still had remaining so the decision would not be reversed.

Three days later, the judgement was pronounced. Before that, I'd had time to get the 'refusal money' from my family. That amounted to thirty pounds. Bango received half of it for compensation. The other fifteen pounds went to the court.

I was congratulated on how well I'd taken care of this affair. The success was attributed to my long stay among townspeople. My mind was 'open' to them. But if I gained friends on one side, I attracted deep hatred on the other. The people in Bango's family had it in for me. Later when they saw me in the Gire market, they avoided me and refused to speak to me. Needless to say, they no longer patronised my tailoring business!

Widowhood

When I spoke about the marriage of Fatu (the vain girl) to poor Bakari – he is dead; may God forgive him! – I told you about widowhood, about the competition between suitors and about remarriage.

If a woman has seen two husbands die, one after the other, she will be treated as a 'career widow' or a 'professionally veiled woman'. She will find it difficult to remarry. Men think about the third hearthstone on which a pot is placed: all three are burned by the same fire! And nearly all women refuse to have one of these 'deadly women' as a co-wife.

What happens when a young woman loses her husband? As soon as he's dead, she takes off all finery and has the simplest hair-do. She covers her head with a veil. She does not wear any particular clothes but during the whole mourning period, she wears what she had on the day her husband died. This period of seclusion lasts four months and ten days. During that time, she's obliged to remain retiring and quiet.

She must pray a lot, even if she's never done that before. Old Fulbe women come to teach her the prayers if need be. She does not go to the market and does not participate in any fete. She must not accept any invitation – to a name-giving ceremony, marriage, etc. She cannot receive a suitor who comes to make her a marriage proposal.

On the prescribed day, she makes millet doughnuts, called 'alms doughnuts', which she distributes in the surrounding villages, beginning with the children. She also makes small *sobal* balls with finely sifted flour from a particular kind of millet called *yadiri*. Why this custom? I do not know the reason. I only know that this gesture is not supposed to help the dead man enter paradise. Absolutely not. Some people are afraid to eat this food, which has been made because of a death. When it's offered, they take it, saying, 'May God look favourably on these alms.' But once they are alone, they quickly throw the food away. The children are just about the only ones who eat the doughnuts. Certainly not the *suka* or the *kori*!

On the night of the tenth day which follows the four months, the men gather and pass the night praying. Seated in a circle, they endlessly repeat the same phrase; it's the *jikiri*.[3] Women are also there, busily preparing doughnuts. The widow puts on the clothes she wears to feasts. She fills a calabash with millet and puts her widow's clothes on its cover. She adds some coins and a lump of butter and takes all those things to an old woman as alms.

The next day the widow 'comes out of the water'. This is the expression we use to signify the end of her period of mourning.

That same day the suitors go into action. More than one would like to be the first to arrive to make his request, but he does not dare appear too soon before the others. Actually he's afraid people will come to the conclusion that he had wanted the first husband to die … Often this man would have arranged to see the widow by accident, for example, when he happened to pass through the village of his future parents-in-law.

Once the first suitor has taken the first step, the others come in a hurry. One after another they visit the young widow who, from this time on, is a candidate for marriage. Some are bachelors, but there are also married men with two or even three wives. They come from everywhere. Each one does what he can so he'll be noticed: some offer kola nuts, others thousand-franc notes. Each one is given the same response: 'My dear, if luck is with you, be assured you'll be my husband!' The widow does not hide; she even goes where the men are gathered to offer them a big calabash of *sobal* well bathed in milk. She speaks with some individually. Like many women, she may use her skill and cunning in order to get money from each visitor, letting him believe he's the one her heart has chosen. 'I never accept a gift offered by anyone I don't like!' And she continues this little game as long as possible when she knows very well from the beginning whom she'll marry.

For a widow looking for a new husband, the ideal suitor – among the Mbororo – is the brother of her dead husband. Not an older brother, but a brother born after him. This is our custom.[4] We have inherited it from our ancestors, and it also conforms to the Muslim religion.

There was a big scandal last year when a widow agreed to marry the elder brother of her dead husband. When the elders heard about that, they said unanimously, 'That's impossible!'

And the father said to his son, 'I declare that your union with this woman would be illegal. If you sleep with her, it would be like sleeping with your own daughter.' Those words had their effect: the marriage did not take place.

When there's no younger brother, or in the case where he or the young woman refuses, a cousin is always welcome. When the cousin appears, sometimes coming from far away, everyone puts pressure on the widow. 'Accept him. It's your paternal cousin. Your children will always be with you. And as a relative on your husband's side, he can only treat them well.'

Inheritance

In all these discussions about the remarriage of a widow, there's one overriding issue: the children's inheritance. The wealth reverts to them; that is, they'll inherit the animals which their father owned. When a brother of the dead husband claims the guardianship of one or several of his nephews, he's also thinking about the cows and steers which the orphans will bring to his herd. The intentions of the uncle are sometimes contested by other paternal uncles. The maternal uncles stay away. Through the elders, the family is always careful to warn those uncles who dispute among themselves. 'These animals remain the property of the orphans. Don't take advantage of them by "eating" them. You'll have to account for the cattle and, if necessary, pay for them. Their mother is here. When these children grow up, they must find themselves to be the owner of a good herd.'

As I've told you, when the inheritance is being distributed, girls are not well treated. They hardly count. They may receive practically nothing. This actually was the case in times past, before the religion of Mohammed appeared among us. That's why – as I've already explained to you – a mother has such a great preference for boys: her husband's inheritance passes through them.

Is this the reason why we boys feel so superior to our sisters? Maybe. But there's also the idea that girls are raised for others. Even when we're very young, we realise that. It's not unusual to hear boys saying amongst themselves, 'Look at those girls. Just when they are old enough to be good workers, other people – the family of their husbands – get the benefit!' Indeed, once girls are married, they leave their parents and spend the rest of their lives working for their husband's family. 'So we have to take advantage of them quickly!' That's what we think. That's what we do.

That's why we boys, even the least lazy among us, give our sisters lots of work. If a boy has three days of work watching the cattle, a girl will have five or six. We say: 'One week for us, one month for them. That's a good proportion!'

When we're a little older, we're likely to start calculating all our family will have to pay out for a daughter – for her marriage, for example. The house money given by her father-in-law is not enough. Our father must also sell a steer. As for the invitations for the name-giving ceremony of her baby, our expenses are higher than those of the in-laws. When it comes to completing the girl's trousseau, who's responsible for that? Her father, not her father-in-law.

Our sisters cost us a lot of money. We know that, and we do not hesitate to insult them and hit them if they rebel. 'What! You dare refuse work you've been asked to do!' And we add, using the words we hear from our parents' mouths, 'Good for nothing! Profiteer! Pagan! When we need to rebuild our house, will you come to help us? If we're hungry one day, will you come to give us food?' Even the youngest brothers think they can talk in this tone. They're allowed to hit their sisters right under their parents' eyes.

An elder sister accepts, without too much protest, being treated in this way and to live in a degree of submission to her younger brother. She's very aware that when the day comes that her parents are gone, she'll be able to turn to her brothers. She'll come to them for refuge, after a divorce, for example. It will not matter if the brother is older or younger than she is.

We boys think about all that. If we're older than our sisters, we look down on them. If we're younger, we treat them the same way. They all must obey us.

Illegitimate Children

Among the Mbororo, illegitimate children – even males – are less acceptable than legitimate girls. We are absolutely opposed to such births, not for religious reasons but to avoid the shame of not fulfilling our *pulaku*. In order to avoid such disgrace, we know what must be done. When a mother detects certain signs in her daughter, she tries to get her to confide in her. If there's no longer any doubt, the mother begins to look for certain roots. She'll try to cause an abortion before the people around her suspect anything. I've never heard of a death after using one of these remedies, which only women know about.

The Mbororo are well aware that causing an abortion is something evil in God's eyes. But giving birth to an illegitimate child is also bad. When the Mbororo have to choose, they prefer to sin against religion rather than against *pulaku*. They're really afraid of being dishonoured by the arrival of an illegitimate child in their family! What shame for a mother to learn by public rumour that her unmarried daughter has gotten pregnant! The girl becomes the laughing stock of the whole world. She's mocked in songs. Those lurid remarks rebound on the whole family. Neither the mother nor the daughter dares to go to the market any longer. They're no longer seen in public.

Sometimes an old woman gives abortive plants to a young girl. Then the parents never know anything about it.

Who does not know such a child whom people take pleasure in humiliating, calling him a 'dirty bastard'? It's better to be a leper! People fight with him and hit him. He'll keep this defect his whole life. Even when he's married, people will speak about him with a certain contempt. His wife and children will also be treated disrespectfully.

I've heard that in past times fathers did not hesitate to slit the throats of their own daughters in order to avoid such disgrace. Today, fathers are content to banish the daughter from the family. But in the Country of the Mountain, Adamawa, I know a young girl who had an illegitimate baby at home and who, after two years of seclusion, reappeared in the markets of the area. I heard her old grandfather say about that child, one of his great-grandsons, 'After all, wasn't it God who gave him to us?'

CHAPTER 21

Religion[1]

Life was easy in Wuro Bokki. I had my own sewing machine and many customers. I could have put money aside, but I never had any desire to.

Ah! Those Kessu women who did everything they could so they'd be noticed by young men! They had a way of rolling their hips which they alone could do. Under their wrapper-skirts, you could just imagine the beaded belts they wore around their waists to arouse men's desires. They were known for their loose morals. When they made their rounds, everyone knew they were selling something besides milk – that delicious unwhipped sour milk they sold by the ladle-full. They called it *kindirmo*.

So it wasn't difficult to find all the women I wanted in this Kessu milieu. When one of them came to sell milk, I paid her well; I even gave her back the milk I didn't drink. Because of the women, money just ran through my fingers!

My Approach to Islam

Ado, my friend and neighbour, led the same life I did. We were often visited by his father. He knew what was happening, and he came to preach to us.

At that time in Gire, there was a famous Islamic preacher. The whole village gathered around him each evening. Ado's father never stopped scolding us because we did not go listen to the preacher. It was true. Young people my age were not interested in him. Some evenings our lively band would pass by not far from the preacher's gathering, pretending not to know what was happening there. But you should not conclude that we were unbelievers or ungodly. That was not true. Our behaviour, not very acceptable in the eyes of a pious Muslim like Ado's father, should be attributed to our youth. We had a little money in our pockets, beautiful girls around us – why should we think about death? We could think about serious matters later. For the moment, we were enjoying our youth! Anyway, people who saw us playing around and neglecting our prayers said to themselves, 'That's youth; that age has its seductions. With time, they'll change.' Anyway, that's what every Mbororo thinks and says, without exception.

'They'll change ... ' In fact, that's what happened to me later, not at Wuro Bokki, but several years after I'd left that village, during my travels here and there. Little by little I was led to reflect on the benefits of religion. In the end, what benefits would I get from such loose living? Progressively I understood I had to put religion above everything else; the rest would come later.

I also began to consult those who knew about religion, the *modibos*. I asked them questions about the way to do the five ritual prayers. I asked them what you had to do to purify yourself after sex, how serious was the sin of adultery, why it was so serious not to show respect for your mother and father, how I could be pardoned for my sins, how a sinner would be judged. To be pardoned for sins, you have to do this and then do that. After the ritual prayer, you have to recite the beads, saying for each bead: *Istijin Faru!*[2] a hundred times, a thousand times. You have to be persistent if you want to ask God to pardon your sins. God does pardon someone who repents; he pardons a sinner again and again. But one day God will no longer give his pardon. Think a little about incorrigible drunkards: today they say they will not drink another drop of alcohol, and the next day they're drunk again. They promise to stop; they stop for one day and then they start again. What would happen to that man if he died the day he fell back into his bad habits? Who knows which day he'll leave the world?

The *modibo* explained to me that everyone who touches wine in any way, to whatever extent, brings the curse of God down on himself; certainly anyone who drinks, but also the wine merchant, the wine merchant's supplier and – our Book says – anyone who passes a glass to someone else! The *modibo* insisted: strong drinks are the root of all crimes. He drew an analogy to a calf rope. All other vices are attached to that bad habit. A drunk person is capable of anything: robbery, rape, murder, adultery.

The *modibo* also told me that the greatest sin is killing someone. Anyone who kills – not by accident or in a war, but voluntarily – is guilty of an unpardonable sin. He put me on guard against gossip which makes people say bad things about others. He told me it's also a sin to drive your cows into a farmer's millet field. Doing nothing to help a blind man on a difficult path is a sin. Allowing someone who's hungry to remain in his distress without giving him anything is a sin.

He also told me a poor man should not blame God for his sorry state. He must not say this is proof that God does not love him. Certainly not! To the contrary, in every circumstance, we must thank God. If he created us, it was because he loves us. There's something more important than riches or poverty; life – which God gives us – is more important. It's enough to think about the skin covering our flesh to know that God loves us and that we should thank him. We should also remember the limbs of our body which allow us to move about, the organs which permit us to see, hear, speak … All this is marvellous! There's nothing better in the world.

We see people in our country who live like us, but they no longer have hands or their fingers are cut off. Some have eyes that do not see or a mouth which does not speak. That also comes from God. You do not have to look anywhere else for the reason. It's God who created everything; everything comes from him. We do not have the right to say those people are like that because God does not love them. And no one should boast of being healthy. No one has the right to despise a leper or to mock a blind man who, with a stick in his hand, bumps into obstacles.

I went to see another *modibo* to discuss adultery with him. 'Adultery? My child… you know that every married man must regularly, each time he has intercourse with his legitimate wife, purify himself. We call this *janaba*. This purification takes away all stain. Then the man can be clean when he prays. But it does no good for someone who has committed adultery to use this rite of purification.' This is because, the *modibo* explained, at the moment the sinner takes off his clothes to commit this sin, his skin turns inside out. That means the side of his skin which is usually in contact with the flesh comes outside while the side of the skin which is usually outside, in contact with the air, turns to the inside. But once the adultery is committed, the skin goes back as it was before. So it's easy to understand that the water of purification has no effect on the pollution he's received. The side of the skin which the water touches isn't the side that has sinned. What applies to the man is true for the woman too.

With regard to the sin of adultery, the *modibo* also told me, 'Look, my child. When a man is tempted to let himself do such a reprehensible act, the angels intervene to restrain him. They say to him, 'We beg you, so-and-so, don't do that. Abstain!' Every man hears these exhortations. It is the angels responsible for guarding us who are speaking. These same angels write down everything we do, the good and the bad. The angel on the right, the good things; the angel on the left, the bad things. Didn't I already say,' the *modibo* added, 'the angel on the left waits until someone has committed ten faults before he writes one in his book while the angel on the right writes down ten good things for each good action? All this must be attributed to the love God has for all his creations, and particularly for man, God's creature.'

Another *modibo* explained the following to me. 'To get rid of a bad habit, it is useless to try magic formulas. You simply need willpower. And you must have courage in what we can call a fight against Satan. No charm can make someone give up drinking or smoking. You have to want to give up the habit. But you can turn to the Scriptures to help you in this fight. It's recommended you write the Koranic texts on a slate. Then rinse the slate and drink the water in which the ink is dissolved so all your thoughts will be about God. This is called *imanaku*[3] or "drinking the Scriptures".'[4]

Still concerned about adultery, I asked that *modibo* whom I'd got to know, 'What happens to someone who dies while committing the sin of adultery?'

'Oh! my child,' he said, 'someone who dies like that has terrible torments awaiting him. First, his feet are bound in fiery red chains. Then he's grabbed by his testicles, which are pulled until his insides are torn out. Then his genitals are cut off as if they were the tumour that was the cause of his impulses. His head is suspended over the fire. His arms don't hang down; they're pulled upwards. His chest and hands are pierced by an iron bar. God sees to it that the life of this torture victim is preserved. It would be too good for him to end up dying: a dead man does not suffer any more. God does not let the agonies of hell threaten his life itself.' When I heard that, I was really frightened!

I didn't learn in Koranic schools what I've been telling you here about religion, and what I still have to tell you, because I hardly ever attended them. I'm not a *mallam*, and certainly not a *modibo*. But I learned what I know and what I'm telling you by talking with *modibos*, those experts of the Science of the Book, either at their homes or in mosques. During Ramadan, mosques are open all day so people can hear commentary on the Koran. This is done in the language of the people, Hausa or Fulfulde. A passage from the Koran – which is written in Arabic – is chosen; it's translated and commented on. Those explanations are called *tafsiru*. Then anyone can ask any questions that pass through his head. Here's an example.

A person asks, 'Imagine I am in a place where there's no water. It's time to pray. What should I do?'

The *modibo* will explain that in such a case, water is replaced with clean sand. The gestures are the same as if the sand were water. Later, when some water is found, the same prayer is repeated.

These long sessions of readings, followed by commentary and explanations with questions and responses, took place after the *jura* prayer at the beginning of the afternoon. Sometimes I'd ask questions and I'd hear the response. 'Very well, my child. That's a good question. It proves you want to be a good Muslim!' I was new in the area, and I began to be noticed in this way. My questions made people sympathetic to me. I quickly figured out that a *modibo*'s greatest pleasure is being asked questions. In that way I gained his favour, but I did it unintentionally because, at that time in my life, I feared committing sin. I had pity for the poor, for those who were suffering, such as prisoners. Sometimes I pitied myself: I felt useless, without a reason for living. It was often the idea of death that inspired such thoughts.

I would not have done all this thinking, I would not have had all those feelings, if I had not left the world of the Mbororo. I would not go so far as to say I was lucky to have leprosy, but I realise that without that illness I'd have stayed an ignorant Mbororo. Because I was a leper, I was able to see other things and meet real Muslims who taught me the proper way to pray. By asking questions, I was able to make a list of sins in the order of their seriousness, while the Mbororo in the bush often consider real sins to be just trifles. For all this, I can only thank God.

The Mbororo and Islam

Concerning what I've said about my Mbororo brothers, don't think it isn't their fault they are the way they are. No! They're largely responsible for their ignorance. Nothing prevents them from learning about the ways of religion, certainly not their occupation as herders. They hardly pass a day without going to the markets. Instead of idling in the shade of a tree or a house, why don't they go and learn from a *mallam*?

They could even do more than that: they could invite a Koranic teacher to come and spend the whole rainy season in their camp so he could teach the Koran to their children. They're wealthy enough. Why won't they sacrifice a little of their wealth to pay a teacher-*mallam*? They do not do it, and the idea does not even occur to them.

To be fair, I must admit that every year more and more Mbororo children are learning to read and write the Koran, at least in Adamawa, but what good will that do? Most of them, when they've obtained the title '*mallam*', put their slates away in a corner. They abandon all further practice, believing they've accomplished all their responsibilities toward God. They're convinced that God has already wiped away all their sins and those of their relatives! There are even some people who say, when they see these young people, that it would be better if they had not gone to Koranic school. The young people would not know anything, but they would be less responsible so their sins would be smaller!

What I've said is true for the Mbororo of Adamawa. It's not the same for those of us who live north of the Benue. The Mbororo who live around Garoua do not send their children to Koranic school. There the Mbororo only think about their braids and their *soro*. They're too afraid that when they go to learn from a *mallam*, they'll have to renounce their fine clothes and their competition. And how can a man get married if he has not proven his virility?

Concerning our religion, there are Mbororo and there are Mbororo. There's practically nothing in common between the religion of the Mbororo of Adamawa (the Jafun in particular) and the religion of the Mbororo of Niger (the Wodabe). I'll speak about the Mbororo I know the best, my own people, the Jafun from north of the Benue, around Garoua.

First, it must be emphasised that no Mbororo, without exception, ever bows down before a piece of wood or a stone. Pagans do that, and they make a cult out of those objects. They believe their idols serve them. They expect their idols to give them good harvests. They bring their seeds before these idols and they beg them to help them in their farming. They ask their idols to give them long lives and good luck more generally.

We Mbororo have always known the name of Allah. We did not have to wait for Shehu Usumanu[5] to tell us about him! The name of Allah was on our lips, but we didn't know who he was. However, we swore oaths by Allah! If someone really tried to know God, he'd lift up his hands to the sky, point to the clouds and say, 'There He is and He sees me!'

Some people refuse to listen to God when He invites them through the Prophet to convert to Islam. If they're told their refusal will lead them to the fire of hell, they respond, 'But who's gone to see that fire and has returned to tell us about it?' When they think of the very end, they have only one opinion: when a man dies, everything's finished for him.

As for their way of behaving in the past when faced with a death, I have no idea. I don't know how they buried people. Did they abandon the dead like a dead cow? Or did they put the dead in the ground without ceremony?

I've heard it said – at least this is what the Fulbe say in order to make fun of us – that in past times the Mbororo liked to bury their dead in the sand. The Mbororo thought that being buried in lightweight earth, earth that could be dug up easily, was a sign that the dead man had been pardoned. Still today some Mbororo consider it lucky when a sick man lives long enough to arrive during the seasonal migration at one of the camping places where we live on sand near a river, so he can die there. The finer and moister the sand is, the more confident they are in the salvation of the one they're burying. It's a real consolation in the midst of their grief if a spring starts gushing while they're digging a grave. They drink the water and they wash their faces with it. They consider the water to be miraculous, a water of paradise which God had prepared for that dead man.

The idea of being near a fresh-water lake after death is enough to give the Mbororo an idea of paradise. The heavenly dwelling places reserved for the chosen which, according to our Book, resemble dwellings on earth, have no appeal for them. Paradise for them is a temperate place where the grass is always tender, where inexhaustible pastures stretch as far as the eye can see, where friends meet by chance during the seasonal migrations. That's the idea they have of happiness for the Future.

Today the Mbororo who have become Muslims look with a jaundiced eye upon those who want to bury their dead in the sand as they used to do.

Regarding our dead, you must not believe the stories which the Fulbe peddle in order to make fun of us. They allege that when one of us dies, we hurry to place the cadaver near a tree where we also tie a heifer. We choose a place which people often pass by, as if we were saying, 'When you pass by, bury our dead and the heifer is yours!' Those same Fulbe say that when our old men and women live too long, we abandon them with a little food. There's nothing like that in our traditions.

The Return from Mecca

Among the Mbororo who are won over to Islam, more and more are going to Mecca. When the pilgrim returns, he's feverishly awaited at the encampment: he's congratulated; he's embraced. The old women caress his face in order to receive the blessings he's carrying. From then on, he'll carry the name of 'Alhaji so-and-so'. For a Muslim, that is the most wonderful title there is. For a Mbororo, there's no title more prestigious. He's proud of it. A great deal of comradeship exists among the *alhaji*. This brotherhood is as strong as if the *alhaji* all had the same mother. They're called 'brothers of milk'.

During the evenings, each man tells his own story. Some go on forever. They're happy to talk about the marvels they've seen. Others prefer to say nothing, convinced that anything they could say would be inferior to what they saw. One says he saw this; another hurries to add he saw that. Enthusiasm prevents some from saying what they mean. Their sentences are punctuated by *kai*! *kai*!

'*Kai*! Anyone who's seen Mecca has seen everything! There's nothing else to be seen anywhere.'

'*Kai*! If you saw those cars! From Jedda to Mecca, you can't even see the road. When people want to cross, the cars have to stop. And the airplanes! They're as numerous as bees. As soon as one lands, another takes off. It makes you think of vultures.'

'When you look at the houses, you can count the number of generations that live there; each generation builds on top of the preceding one; the grandfather on top of the great-grandfather, the father on top of the grandfather, the son on top of the father. And so on way up high until you get to the present generation. If you want to see the tops of those houses, you have to bend your head all the way back. Then your hat falls off. And even then you still don't see where the house ends in the sky. That's how tall it is!'

'Those who live there don't come down once they've finished their pilgrimage. They only put their feet on the ground when they do their next pilgrimage. Anyway, they don't need to come down; they find everything they need where they are: water for washing their clothes, which you can see drying like flags; fire for cooking; everything. The people are never seen!'

Everyone who returns from Mecca says the food there doesn't agree with them. The rice is like porridge. It's hard to live during the pilgrimage. The stay is very fatiguing. That explains why the people are nervous. They can be trampled by the crowd. Disputes arise over nothing. From words, they pass quickly to blows. Fighting starts in spite of bystanders trying to intervene. 'Look here! Aren't you ashamed to be fighting in such a place!'

There are belligerent characters who become mean over nothing. This is true with the Hausa, who are always ready to make fun of the Mbororo. They call them imbeciles and idiots. 'You Mbororo,' they say, 'what in the world are you going to do in Mecca? . . . Look for cows, no doubt! That's all you're interested in.'

'And you,' the Mbororo retort, 'aside from money, what do you come to Mecca to ask for? Aren't you ashamed to bring prostitutes with you?'

Who has not heard talk about the plane full of Nigerian pilgrims, all Hausa, which crashed when landing in Kano? Among the passengers was a notorious prostitute.

It's a fact that in the Holy Place where you go to be pardoned from your sins, some show off their bad behaviour. This is especially true of the Arabs. It's not unusual to see one or other of them leaning against the wall of the mosque smoking cigarettes. It's said that many people there never do their five prayers.

What surprises pilgrims is that they don't always turn the same direction for prayer as we do here in Cameroon where we turn toward the east. There, those in the south turn toward the north, and those in the north turn toward the south.

Everyone wants to return with that miraculous water, called *biri jam-jam*. But to get some, you have to wrangle. People insult each other and hit each other. People are killed. It's scandalous when you think about what happens in the Muslim Holy City, the place of prayer and peace.

One man marvels at the lights of all colours which he saw here and there. Another says what really struck him was when he was shown the place where Mohammed made his last ablutions. 'That happened thousands of years ago and the place is still wet!' Everyone talks for a long time about the place where they threw rocks at the great idols. They are the idols which the enemies of the Prophet bowed down before, the idolatrous Nassara. The pilgrims throw rocks there as if they wanted to stone Satan. If they do not have rocks, some throw their shoes. Everyone must throw something. This is done in good humour.

You must listen to the pilgrims' stories, but you also have to see what they bring back in their baggage. For some, to say 'pilgrimage' is to say 'business'. This is especially true of the Hausa who only think about money. They bring back everything: watches, radios, tape recorders, rugs. Their intention is to sell those things for a good profit. Others are content to bring back gifts, which they distribute to their relatives, neighbours and friends. It's a tradition. No one who comes to greet them when they return must leave with empty hands. You often hear it said, 'Look at these prayer beads. They were given to me by so-and-so the year he came back from Mecca.' But these gifts are not at all the same as the shameful commerce of the others.

If I personally ever have the chance to make a pilgrimage to Mecca, I will not let myself go there with my eye on business. If I go there, it will be first of all to ask God to wipe away my sins. I'll also pray that he give me enough wealth to live on and to help those who have less than I do and that I'll continue to follow the right path. And I'll ask him to give me children. But not just any children: children who will be my joy and my consolation.

Religion and the Wodabe

When someone speaks about religion among the Mbororo, he must speak separately about the Wodabe. You'll understand right away what this means when I've told you the following anecdote. A *modibo* had reminded the people in the mosque about the great truths. He had spoken about God, death, sin, prayer and other subjects. Then everyone was invited to ask questions to enlighten themselves about any particular point. Well, there was a Wodabe at the mosque – no one knows how or why. He thought he was obliged to ask questions too. But the *modibo* knew those people well. He knew the Wodabe never prayed and never contracted a religious marriage, and – in general – knew nothing about the Koran. So he thought it was useless to explain something in detail to a Wodabe. What good would it do? Their ignorance was so great! So when the Wodabe said to the *modibo*, 'And we Wodabe?' the *modibo* responded that all such questions and all such problems were of no concern to his people.

That man returned to his home and was quick to say, 'We Wodabe are really lucky. There's a great *modibo* who said we do not need to be concerned about religious questions. We won't have to account for our sins!'

One can therefore say about the Wodabe of Niger, who for us are the real Mbororo, that they have no religion, at least not up to now. Or if you wish, you can say it's their *pulaku*, their faithfulness to their Fulani traditions, which constitutes their whole religion.

To behave like a real Fulani, that's their ambition. For them, being a Fulani is simply being a man. Does that mean they don't know Allah? No, they simply have no concern about his teachings. They consider themselves neither unbelievers, sceptics nor pagans; they're simply Fulani. For them, the good and the bad are simply a question of observing or not observing the code of Fulani honour. Shame, that's what sin is. To refrain from doing what would make us ashamed if other people saw us doing it, that's living right. That assures salvation.

Even aside from the Wodabe, some Mbororo can still be found who think Islam was just made up. The fire of hell is a pure lie. Such threats have only one purpose:

to make people afraid! It is hoped that, because of those threats, people won't harm each other.

In past times, some went as far as to say, 'It's useless to pray like the Muslims do. It's even harmful to your good fortune.' They scolded their children who had fun imitating the way Muslim believers pray. 'What!' they said. 'Don't you know that when you act like that, you're bringing bad luck on yourself, on your father and on your mother, and that you could even die from doing that?' Actually they all believed that if they became Muslims, they would soon die. But in spite of it all, the name of Allah is on the tongues of all Wodabe. They pay attention to what they hear from the mouths of others. They do not know what they're saying when they pronounce that name, but they say it anyway.

However, since the name of Allah is on their lips – even the lips of those who do not believe – and they pray that their evil magic will be successful, Allah answers them. Allah always answers someone's prayers, even for something bad, on the condition that the man praying accepts the responsibility of the sin – and all the unfortunate consequences which it brings in the other world.

Yes, even if a prayer goes up from an impious heart, even if it's expressed in the form of a curse, from the moment it's made in the name of Allah, it is effective. God gives the man what he asks for on earth while waiting for him to burn in the other world. The impious know this very well, but they do not believe in punishment in the other world since there isn't any such place! When some of them are asked what becomes of a man after death, they say, 'And what becomes of our cows?'

The Jafun and their Beliefs

We Jafun from north of the Benue are not like the Wodabe, those people who believe themselves to have a 'special' status with regard to religion. It's commonly said about them, *vodaabe vodiibe diina*,[6] which means, 'Those who are set apart by others set themselves apart from religion.'

However, we are not exemplary Muslims. For as long as I can remember, I've seen my aunts and all the young women rub tobacco flowers on their teeth to make them red, even during Ramadan. I've seen the women, during the time of fasting, eat doughnuts in the middle of the marketplace. I've heard the Fulbe merchants of Garoua insult them publicly. To make the women feel ashamed, the merchants would not hesitate to call them carrion eaters!

When I'd go back to be with my family during the Ramadan period, I felt vivid emotions of indignation, which made me unashamed to say, 'Oh really, you make me ashamed, seeing you live like pagans!'

When I'd say to my grandmothers, 'Don't you know you'll burn in the fire of hell for not fasting!' they'd respond, 'Look, my dear. Don't I have a pure heart? What can happen to someone who has a pure heart? What can happen to someone who gives alms and shares her food with others? Giving alms, that's enough!' And with those words, right in the midst of Ramadan, my grandmothers would take a bite of millet porridge. This is still what they say and do today.

Sometimes their granddaughters ask this question: 'Grandmother, tell us what you have to do to go to Paradise.'

'Look, my children, to go to Paradise . . . to go to Paradise, all you have to do is give alms!'

You never hear, 'To go to heaven, you must do the five prayers.' Absolutely not. This is the occasion for our grandmothers to repeat once more the tale about the old woman and the marketplace in the other world. That's the tale of the old woman who never gave anything away during her life, except one bone to a dog. I told you that tale when I told you about how the children would spend their evenings.

To be fair, it must be said that for the last fifteen years the Mbororo around Garoua have made progress in the practice of religion. More and more heads of families are inviting a *mallam* to come so they can 'drink the Scriptures'. But this change has not yet been sufficient to make the Fulbe change their opinion of us. Probably for a long time to come, the Garoua butchers will refuse to buy our meat when it comes from an animal that had an accident and was slaughtered by us. For them, an animal killed by those 'Mbororo pagans' can only be carrion. There are more and more learned and pious Muslims among us, but the Fulbe do not want to know that.

That makes me think about one of my uncles, Mala Jimau. When he was very young, his parents sent him to a Koranic schoolteacher. When he grew up and became a *mallam*, he taught the Koran to his whole family. So there were many *mallams* among his children and his grandchildren. One day Mala Jimau had to kill a sheep that had had an accident. Obviously, he cut the throat like all Muslims do in such cases. He went to offer that meat to a Fulbe butcher. The butcher said, 'I don't want that meat! Is a Mbororo capable of slaughtering an animal properly?' Those words were spoken to my uncle, considered by us to be the most learned member of the family!

Another time this same Mala Jimau had the intention of giving alms on a Muslim feast day. He wanted to give the head, feet and skin of a sheep to the first old Fulbe he met on the path. I went with him. I myself carried those pieces on my head. A lively old man came along, walking back from his field where he'd been working. 'Here!' my uncle said when he caught up to the man, 'I want to give you all this for the Feast of the Sheep.' The man absolutely refused, with an air of disdain. I was a witness.

My uncle had to suffer that shame before my eyes. He said to me, 'Even before I opened my mouth to offer him this gift, I was almost sure he'd refuse it. But be aware, my nephew, that all this is the fault of some Mbororo whose bad behaviour reflects on us all. Because of those people, we're all looked down upon. But let's be quiet and let God judge us. God knows. What good would it do to proclaim that I, Mala Jimau, am not like other Mbororo, that I say my prayers regularly?' God distinguishes between true believers and those who are not.

Yes, around Garoua our reputation as men who use sorcery and charms is so strong that we absolutely cannot persuade a real *mallam* or *modibo* to come pray over a dead Mbororo. They have too much scorn for us. They would not touch one of our dead for anything in the world: they would be defiled.

In such a situation, we have only one solution: to fall back upon one of the mallams who's more or less a charlatan, those we disdainfully call the *bitiri mallams*. They are the ones who travel around the cattle herding areas, selling their Scriptural texts and their magic formulas to Mbororo who are too willing to believe in such things. With enough money, you can arrange anything with them, even the burial of a *suka* who died from a blow from a *soro* staff, a *suka* buried with his braids.

Only the Fulbe in Nigeria, those we call the Witi, are sympathetic to us in such a circumstance and will agree to bury our dead. They've known us for a long time. We feel they're close to us. They understand us and know we're not as bad or as despicable as the Fulbe of Garoua say we are. Those Fulbe of Nigeria sometimes express surprise when we come to them when someone dies. 'What!' they say. 'Can't you find one man among you who knows his prayers well enough to bury the dead? You should be ashamed to know so little about your religion!' There's nothing we can say because we cannot deny we have no confidence in ourselves when it comes to praying.

However, the time is long past when no one in my family would fast during Ramadan. I was always ashamed then when I went to spend some time with them. I could just barely bring myself to eat meat from an animal they'd killed! I never stopped saying to them, 'The way you live is bad. Your lack of religion is the reason the Fulbe despise us. Make an effort! Fasting never killed anyone. Look at me: am I less healthy because I abstain from eating from morning until evening for thirty days? And do not try to tell me it's your work as herders or the kind of life you lead that prevents you from fasting and from saying the five prayers! Why do you never pray?' And I continued to talk to them in that way. That was twenty years ago. They've really changed.

Now it's not unusual to see a woman fasting seriously on days when she stays at home, but not keeping the fast when she goes to sell milk in villages two or three hours away. 'It's too tiring, and it's too hot!' But this is certainly better!

Nevertheless, on one of my last visits, I argued with my older brother about this. We were travelling together. Night had fallen, and it was time to go to bed. My brother unrolled his mat and spread it out for sleeping while I was doing my prayers. I told him it was not good to go to bed without saying his prayers. 'You're neglecting the most important thing. How do you expect God to protect you if you don't turn to him? How do you expect him to take care of your possessions? You aren't protected against Satan's power! Everything is easier for someone who prays. Anyone who does not pray struggles in vain.'

After all I've said, you'll understand that when I hear people around me saying, 'Ah, those Mbororo, they're real pagans!' I let them talk. They can think and speak as they like! But I know that, if some among us do not pray, others do.

People who do not know me – me, the Mbororo – place me among those who are 'ignorant and pagan'. I let them say it. I will be judged by God who knows if I really pray to him, why I pray and how I pray.

Figure 21.1: Slaughtering a ram at a Muslim festival

Figure 21.2: Young men eating

CHAPTER 22

Pulaku

I've told you that when I was a child I never heard anyone speak about God or the fear he ought to have inspired in me. No one around me prayed. Religion had no part in our lives as children. But I've also emphasised that from the time we were very young, we felt the burden of what we call *pulaku* weigh upon us.

A Mbororo can do without religion, but he cannot live outside the rules which make a Fulani what he is. We have a way of behaving which belongs only to us, the people of the world of cows and the bush. It doesn't belong to the town Fulbe. They've abandoned its rules. This code of life is our heritage. We knew it long before we knew the religion of Mohammed. But today in Mbororo families which practise Islam, it's sometimes difficult to divide things up and to distinguish what comes from *pulaku* and what comes from religion.

The Tree

We Mbororo, who aren't people of the Book, have always had the habit of saying, '*Pulaku*, that's the *barkehi* fibre.' In place of 'fibre', you could also say 'leaf'. That's why, when someone asks me who I am, I respond, 'I'm Ndudi Umaru, the son of Koyne. I'm an authentic Mbororo, a son of the *barkehi*.' And I add, 'I was shaven with milk.' After that, there are no other questions to ask. I've said all there is to say about what makes a Mbororo: the bush and the cow. Certainly we know we're not the only ones to have herds of cows, but we're conscious of having been the first to raise cattle. It would be nonsense to talk about a Mbororo who does not have at least a few cows.

If we've chosen the *barkehi* tree as our emblem, it's because we find in it everything a herder in the bush needs, especially fibres which are fresh and supple in all seasons. Without fibres, there would be no ropes and no herding! The leaves, bark and roots of this tree are also useful to us. We make them into powder which we use to ensure the fertility of our herds. This tree deserves its name: 'the tree of blessing', the tree that brings happiness.

Anyone who knows the Mbororo well knows they never do anything important without having a leaf from this tree of good fortune in their hands. As I've already mentioned, a woman who goes to visit the mother of a newborn carries a *barkehi* leaf in her hand. She puts it in the thatch over the doorway of the house before she crosses the threshold.

We also find it in the hands of spectators who gather when the title '*mallam*' is conferred on someone who's finished his course of Koranic studies! Is this a way of showing the union of religion and *pulaku*?

Simply evoking the name of this leaf lightens people's mood and calms their tempers. If two Mbororo are on the verge of fighting, it's enough to beg them, 'Please, in the name of the *barkehi* fibre, stop arguing!'

All calls for help, all prayers expressed with reference to this leaf or to this fibre are always successful. For example, you may hear someone say to his relative or neighbour, 'I know you're ready to break camp tomorrow morning, but not me. Please, wait for me! I ask this in the name of the *barkehi* fibre!'

The word *pulaku* has the same resonance as *barkehi*. One doesn't go without the other. One can replace the other. Frequently one hears, 'I beg you in the name of *pulaku*!' When a young girl insists she'll never accept the husband who has been imposed on her, the elders ask that she be given her freedom in the name of *pulaku*. It's also in the name of *pulaku* that some parents believe they are obliged to give their daughter in marriage, even against their wishes, to a young man who their daughter is not the least bit interested in.

This *pulaku* permeates all aspects of our everyday life. Because of *pulaku*, nothing in the world could make us share the same leaves. How can men, women and children go to the same latrine, like those town Fulbe who only dig one hole behind their houses?

Leading a Proper Life

Besides the *barkehi* – its leaves or its fibres – every Mbororo also knows what he's speaking about when he invokes *pulaku*. It's a style of life; it's what is proper, appropriate, polite. And if someone insists on knowing what the qualities are that make a Fulani, he invariably hears the response: *pulaku woni hakkilo, munyal, semtende*, that is: good sense, self-control and reserve.

Our manners require that everyone should be in his place when there are gatherings. When groups form during a family reunion, the young people keep to themselves, according to their age groups, and the older people do too. Among the adults, further distinctions are made: men who simply are of a mature age do not sit near the respected old men. Each group finds its place on different mats which are separated.

During a meal when the young people bring food to those who could be their fathers, courtesy requires that the youths take off their shoes out of respect. Simply forgetting this will be immediately remarked upon. 'Look,' someone will say. 'This *suka* (or this *kori*) has trampled on our *pulaku* with his dirty old shoes!' No matter how the young man tries to say he simply forgot, such an excuse will never be accepted.

His friends will say to him, 'If your thoughtlessness is not severely punished today, you'll do it again tomorrow.' The delinquent will not argue. He will agree with them.

He will not balk when he sees himself condemned by the council of elders to pay a fine of two or three calabashes of kola nuts.[1] 'These kola nuts,' the elders will say when they pass them out, 'are offered to you by so-and-so who forgot our rules and trampled on *pulaku* with his sandals. He asks for forgiveness and offers you these nuts as recompense.'

It's because of *pulaku* that young people must not join up with a group of men going to the market in the morning. A man who has younger men around him will be embarrassed if he has to go out into the bush to take care of his needs. He would be ashamed to be noticed by someone younger. When a group of adolescents who are walking rapidly catches up to a group of men on the path, the adolescents must hurry to pass the older men so the men will be at ease among themselves.

Pulaku teaches us what kind of respect we must show our relatives according to the closeness of the relationship. We single out relatives on our father's side, giving special regard to his brother (*bappanyo*) and his sister (*gogo*). We have different names for a maternal uncle (*kao*) and an aunt who is our mother's sister (*yapendo*). There are nuances in the ways we must behave toward each of them. And our behaviour is different with regard to our parallel cousins and our cross cousins.[2] We learn all this naturally from the time we're babies, as I've already told you.

Our traditions also tell us how to do business amongst ourselves. It's not forbidden for a Mbororo to buy a sheep, for example, in order to resell it for his own profit, but there's a way to do it. Suppose someone bought a sheep for four thousand francs. If he offers it to an interested relative, he must tell the relative straightaway the exact price he paid for it. 'I bought it for four thousand francs. If you want it for that price, you can have it.' The buyer will show his sense of *pulaku* by paying more so the seller will make some profit. This is done very simply.

It's the same when two Mbororo are discussing the purchase of a heifer, for example. Everything is done in a sidelong manner. The seller never wants to fix the price. The buyer also demurs. They carry on a dialogue of subtleties, with questions but no answers: 'It's your cow,' says the buyer. 'You must set the price.'

'No,' says the other, 'because you're the one who wants to buy it, tell me what price you want to pay.'

Finally a third person, secretly consulted, will close the discussion, remarking that it does not matter a great deal because the property is not leaving the clan.

You can never talk about commerce between a father and his son. If the father wants to sell an animal which belongs to his son, he can do it. The son cannot say anything about it. But *pulaku* will push the father to compensate his son, giving a heifer to replace a bull, for example.

There are also rules about propriety between a healer and his client. There's never any question about selling 'medicine'. When someone comes to have his eyes healed or to ask for a remedy for a sick child, we do not talk about money or about a deposit to be paid. And you'll never see a Mbororo run after clients. Only the Wodabe do that. A Mbororo healer never worries about being well known. He simply makes use of his skill to help those who know about his abilities. 'Take this,' he says. 'Try this. Come back to see me and tell me what happened. But I'm confident because this remedy has already been successful in many cases like yours.'

If the medicine works, the client never fails to come back to see his healer and to offer him 'kola money'. *Pulaku* requires that the first offer be refused. 'Oh no, please, keep your money. I just did what I should have done, with a good heart.'

The other will always insist, 'Look, it's not a question of 'paying'. I know very well you would not accept that. I only want you to accept what I'm offering with a good heart, without thinking about it.' The healer accepts the money. The dialogue always finishes that way.

Sometimes a Mbororo, profiting from the natural fertiliser which he gets from his herd, makes some furrows for cultivation. Then he runs the risk of seeing his field damaged by his neighbour's cows, if it is not done by his own animals. In that case, there are obviously reactions, but they're very different from those seen between farming peoples and Mbororo herders. The Mbororo whose field has been damaged will not get excited and chase away the animals: no shouts, no complaints! He will be content to ask the owner of the herd kindly to watch his children, who are not very attentive when they're guarding the cattle. And he'll make that observation indirectly! For example, he'll say, 'Our children are all too negligent!' And he'll minimise the damage, 'It's really not a big thing! And God saw to it that I was close by so I could move the animals away quickly!' No bitterness, no anger – on the contrary, an extreme effort not to hurt the feelings of his neighbour.

What a difference from those pagan farmers who, for the least ear of corn or millet that is damaged, come shouting and threatening, 'I'm going to start a legal case; I demand you pay such-and-such an amount for the damages!'

These rules about how we live follow us everywhere.

When we leave very early in the morning with empty stomachs and we arrive at someone's house late in the evening without having eaten anything, we must show great self-control. We must show neither our fatigue nor our hunger. We can only touch what is brought to us with the tips of our fingers, taking only two or three mouthfuls. We must energetically refuse invitations which people feel they're obliged to give us. 'Thank you, I'm satisfied. Everything's fine. Thank you!'

These rules concerning food and drink are most carefully adhered to by a son-in-law who comes to the home of his parents-in-law to get his wife. It's practically an obligation for him to fast during his stay!

Mbororo mannerliness also forbids any father from entering his married son's hut, even if his daughter-in-law is sick. The daughter-in-law's entry into the house of her mother-in-law is strictly limited to extreme necessity. A young man would be considered to have been badly brought up if he entered the house of a woman, especially if she has daughters.

When approaching a house you wish to visit, you must stop a long distance away, signal your presence by clearing your throat, for example, and wait for someone to come welcome you. We're not really astonished by the way the

Whites so lightly break our rules of courtesy: they do not know the rules. When they come to see us, they enter everywhere, being curious and eager to discover things they've never seen before.

When travelling, a man and wife must keep as much distance as possible between themselves. The man always goes first. When he stops, the woman does the same and, if necessary, backs up a little. She watches her husband closely, waiting to see when he gets up to leave; then she does too. In general, you never see one next to the other, ear to ear. If a woman follows her husband closely, we'd say she's immodest. Even in a bus, when possible, the man sits in front, the woman behind him and they act as if they do not know each other. When they get to the end of their journey, to the home of their relatives or friends, the husband and the wife are each received separately, the husband by the men and the wife by the women. They only communicate through an intermediary.

This attitude of great reserve, of self-control, which we call *pulaku* is part of our heritage. I know when it is lacking, I know how it is passed on, but I do not know its origin. If I asked the elders about this, I'd only get this response: 'We woke up to this life and we've always had it.'

When is *pulaku* missing? I could go on forever giving more examples. They always reflect a lack of judgement, reserve or self-control.

Self-Control

To be self-controlled (*munyal*), this is what makes a Fulani. Anyone who controls himself will never seriously misbehave. Everything works out in the end for such a man. Always inclined to credit others with good intentions, he considers the wrongs done him to be only inadvertent. But an impulsive person risks committing an irreparable error before he's thought about the seriousness of his act. He lets himself be guided immediately by ideas about instant vengeance. He shouts, he hits out and he inflames the situation.

Yes, a Fulani is asked to control his heart. Emotions always have a tendency to 'bubble up', like milk on a fire. Cold water is added to milk so it doesn't boil over; the heart must be pressed down so it doesn't rise up. To be self-controlled is to hold your tongue, to avoid passing on news carelessly. Take the case of a messenger who has been sent to announce the death of a father to his son who lives far away. If the messenger arrives late in the day, he should wait until the next day to talk about it. In the meantime, he'll take part in the evening conversation in good humour. When he's asked for news about the father, he'll answer that the father is well, even though he's seen the father dead! Often it's at the last minute, even at the moment when he's leaving his host who's walked with him to the end of the camp, that he decides to speak. He will have shown in this way his great self-control. He'll also have had the pleasure of spending an enjoyable evening and night without being disturbed by the family's crying and weeping! Anyway, it is better not to witness the pain felt by a family you do not know very well.

Shame and Modesty

More than anything else, a Fulani is sensitive to shame. He must do everything possible to avoid a shameful situation. There's nothing more serious for him than hearing, '*A semtii*! You've forgotten Fulani honour! You should be ashamed!'

I could tell you dozens and dozens of our tales which would make you understand – more than all my words – what we Mbororo feel when talking about this emotion of shame which we call *semtende*. Here's one story about a husband, covered with shame, who thought he had to get a divorce.

A young married man went to get his wife who was finishing her stay with her own family. The husband had never gone there and had never met his parents-in-law. Late in the morning, he came to a market where he asked for directions. By chance, the woman he talked to was his mother-in-law. But of course he did not know that. 'Could you tell me, my good woman, what is the direction of the village of so-and-so? I want to go there.'

The woman had no difficulty realising this was her daughter's husband, her nephew; there were family resemblances which were unmistakable. But she did not let any of her emotions show and simply responded, 'Oh, this is a bit of luck! So-and-so's village is located just by my own. I advise you to wait until I've finished at the market; then you can follow me.'

'Very good,' he said.

To pass the time, he walked around the marketplace, buying peanut sticks here, doughnuts there and farther off some manioc tubers. He took them all to the woman and said, 'Keep all this for me, little mother. I'll take them when we leave. You have to be careful, right? Who knows how I'll find things at my parents-in-law. Maybe food is scarce for them!'

'Yes, my son,' she answered him. 'You're right. You can never be too careful!'

Encouraged by her words, he continued to buy provisions, which the woman carefully guarded for him.

When the market was finished, they left together. The young man walked ahead. He turned around from time to time. 'Little mother, can you give me a doughnut? I'm hungry!' She stopped and gave him something each time he asked. He was insatiable and was not very worried about the impression he was giving her of his gluttony and crudeness.

When they arrived near the village, the woman said to him, 'This is my village. Come into the entry house and rest a little. After everything you've eaten, you must be very thirsty. I'll have some water brought to you. Then I'll send my children with you to your parents-in-law's house.'

The woman left him to go inside the *sare*. She hurried to tell her daughter, 'Go take something to drink to your big imbecile of a husband who's made me so ashamed! Go look! He's there, in the entry house.' And in a couple of words, she explained his complete lack of manners. When the wife saw her husband, she was so surprised she dropped the calabash of water she had in her hands. He fled! They never saw each other again!

Among the Mbororo there are many things which are shameful to do, which for non-Fulani are very natural.

That's why a young father seen playing with his first-born would feel very ashamed. The onlooker would always say, 'Ah, he has no shame! Playing with his child like that!' A son-in-law would show great disrespect for his father-in-law if he publicly pronounced his father-in-law's name, or that of a person of the same name. If he does it unintentionally, the moment he notices what he's done, he says, 'Oh really, that makes me ashamed!'

If a young unmarried girl gives birth to an illegitimate child, it's said she has dishonoured her parents. She must flee. For a Fulani, shame is sin. To be ashamed is to commit a sin.

All day we must be vigilant so we do not leave the path of our Fulani morals, of *pulaku*. It's so easy to break the code! Simply the word *pulaku* has a power over us which is unimaginable for those who are not Fulani.

Good Sense

Lack of reserve, judgement or courtesy are faults which a real Fulani must avoid. In all circumstances, he must show his intelligence.

Children are taught by watching how their parents live and by listening to them. Their parents often tell stories which provoke big outbursts of laughter. Slaves – both men and women – are the butt of ridicule. Our tales describe their stupidity, jealousy over women, all sorts of tactlessness, funny situations due to ignorance or an infringement of our *pulaku*. Here are some examples.

A slave goes on a hunt. One of his neighbours profits from his absence by going to woo his wife. The hunter returns unexpectedly. Where can the admirer hide in a straw hut? He gets the idea of hanging onto the rafters in the straw roof, just above the entrance. He curls himself up, making himself as small as possible. He hopes he won't be seen in the darkness (it being nearly night). The husband enters. Sitting on his bed, he notices a big black thing above the entrance. He asks his wife, 'What's hanging up there?'

'Ah!' she says. 'A stranger passed by. He had a drum which he forgot. I hung it there!'

Hearing the woman compare him to a drum, the slave begins to hit himself. Gong! gong! gong!

'Ah!' the man says. 'What a funny drum that plays all by itself! Let's see what sound I can get from it if I hit it myself.' He takes his herder's stick with its iron tip and violently hits the sides of the 'drum'. The slave falls to the ground where he rolls around, making the sound of a drum: *kiring*! *kiring*! Is there a story more stupid than that one?

Another example of stupidity. Three slaves get together to slaughter a cow. The vultures arrive at once and soar above the animal. One of the three slaves raises his head and, pointing at one of the vultures with the tip of his knife turned toward himself, says, 'Come a little closer! I'll show you what'll happen to you!' Then pantomiming what he's talking about, the slave effortlessly cuts his own throat. He falls down and dies.

People passing by ask the other slaves, 'What happened? It seems that your friend committed suicide by cutting his throat …'

'I'll explain to you,' one of them says. 'He saw a vulture approaching him. He took his knife and said to the bird, 'Come a little closer so you can see what I'll do to you.' And he cut his own throat … like this!' And combining gestures with words, that slave does the same thing. And now there are two of them on the ground.

Some other passers-by ask the third slave about this. 'Did they commit suicide?'

'No!' the last one says. 'I'll explain to you what happened. The first one saw a vulture. He threatened it by putting his knife to his throat. The second one did the same thing in order to explain to the people that came by what had happened. I'll tell you how it happened. They passed their knives under their throats like … this!' And the third slave is on the ground with his throat cut open!

The Mbororo know that many of them, once they leave the bush, are completely 'lost' and ready to believe anything. They make fun of themselves. Old people especially love to tell such stories. They even make these stories up.

But I've always heard it said that in past times no one told stories about slaves. The idiots that were talked about were the Mbororo; they were mocking themselves. But today we spend more time around the Fulbe – who do not hesitate to make fun of us – so we've stopped making fun of ourselves. In our tales, the word Mbororo has been replaced by the word *maccudo*, that is, 'slave'.

Punishments

Some infringements of *pulaku* can be very severely punished. Suppose there was a young girl, Fatu, who was spoken to by a *kori* to ask for her favour. Let's say she refused his demand and even showed him a certain disdain, as some pretentious girls are capable of doing who believe they possess irresistible charm. In such a case, she must expect an immediate reaction. 'Good! Very good! We'll teach you Fulani manners!'

Some days later when there is a gathering, the young men hatch a plan. When the festival is at its peak, they stop the drums and shout their usual proclamation: *Ye kwa!* Immediately a great silence falls over the crowd. The spokesman for the *kori* continues, 'All of you, whoever you are, *suka*, *kori* and young girls – *pulaku* calls you. *Pulaku* invites you to sit on the ground. We have a proclamation to make. Today we are putting Fatu on trial. It's our *pulaku* which condemns her. From now on, anyone who shows her the least sympathy will no longer have the right to the title "son of the *barkehi*, shaven with milk"! And moreover he'll fall under the power of this curse: 'He didn't see, he hasn't been seen. He farmed; he's harvested nothing. He raised animals; he's had no profit!'"

Such unpleasant words about the delinquent girl were spoken everywhere. '*Wu, wu, wu*! That girl! May God never put her in our path!'

The young girl who was so severely rejected holds her head in her hands. Sobbing, she leaves the place all in tears and goes back to her house. 'What happened?' ask her parents, surprised to see her returning so early all alone.

'The *kori* just put me in isolation!' Her father understands, nods his head and says nothing. *Pulaku* prevents him – even her father – from making any comments. Not a word! And from that time on, no one speaks to Fatu, not even the people in her house. The unhappy girl loses her appetite and is no longer to be seen in public.

One day Fatu´s father will go to find the head of the clan. He will explain the situation to him and ask him to intervene. He will beg the chief in the name of *pulaku* to call all the young *kori* together soon so they can state the grievances they have against his daughter and restore her privileges without delay. The *ardo* will take advantage of the first public occasion in his group to respond to the father's request. He'll make a proclamation which no one can ignore.

'*Pulaku* calls you!' A few minutes later, all the young men are before him, squatting down, with *barkehi* leaves in their hands, showing the greatest respect. 'It's our *pulaku* which calls you!' All the youth remain silent. 'I have a request for you. I've learned that you've isolated so-and-so, the daughter of so-and-so. Certainly you have your reasons. For my part I do not need to know about them because I know you've done this in the name of our *pulaku*, which is part of our heritage. We ourselves have taught you about *pulaku*. But her father insists on knowing the reasons you excluded her. Was it a lack of judgement? Or contempt for our traditions? Or a refusal to accept our discipline?'

'Yes, that's what it was: a refusal to obey. We *kori* must keep the *suka* and the young girls in hand. We cannot let a refusal to obey go without punishment.'

'But,' continued the *ardo*, 'can we know more precisely what she did?'

'It was this: at the last gathering we indicated to her that she should come. She certainly saw and heard that we had called her. But she was haughty. She wouldn't even respond to us and she left with a gesture of contempt. It's this arrogance which we wanted to punish. She must not forget she's only a girl. She can think of herself as she wants, but she must know she comes after the men. That's why we put her in isolation. She understood. She brought it on herself; we promise you that.'

At the following gathering, Fatu was present as the accused. 'First, you must understand,' said the President of the *kori*, speaking publicly, 'that we do not hold any animosity toward you. We just wanted to emphasise your lack of judgement. We would not have acted differently with one of our sisters. Do not think we had it in for you especially, out of all the other young girls your age. Let's not talk about it any longer. Just accept to pay the fine which we're giving you: five calabashes of kola nuts. We're waiting for you to bring them to us.'

Some of her friends stood up to argue on her behalf. 'Please, do not give her such a heavy fine. When it comes down to it, she'll have to depend on us! She is not capable of meeting that expense alone. We want to help her, but you have to be kind!' The *kori* changed the fine to three calabashes.

All was arranged with the briefest possible delay. Some young girls ran quickly to the closest village to buy three calabashes of kola nuts, which were distributed immediately: a few here, several there.

The gathering was then invited to sit down. One last proclamation was made: 'Today *pulaku* has reintegrated so-and-so, the daughter of so-and-so, into our ranks. She's offering you these kola nuts. Accept them in the name of reconciliation.' From that moment on, all her rights were restored. People would talk to her, joke with her and the boys would court her.

It should be noted there was never a question of punishment being imposed by force. We Mbororo do not understand force. You'll never hear someone say, 'Whether you like it or not, we know best so we must force you to do this or that!' There's no need to shout. It's with his full volition, almost with a smile, that the condemned does as he's ordered and offers the kola nuts to pay his fine.

But our submission is not that of a slave. Already when he's still small, a Mbororo knows how to assert himself by letting a certain time lapse between the calling of his name and his response.

CHAPTER 23

Magic and Sorcery

Everything was going well in Wuro Bokki. My work as a tailor allowed me to earn a living. Ado let me live at his house free. We shared the expenses for food: meat and fish.

We ate more fish than anything else. Every day the daughters of the Bata fishermen came to sell us fish. It was cheap and very good. Once the fish was gutted and trimmed, we put it on a piece of basketry about the size of the pot and then cooked it in a broth with salt, pepper and spices. When the water had evaporated, we put in some butter. The basketry, which was shaped like a grid, prevented the fish from sticking to the bottom of the pot. The white meat stayed firm and the backbone came out all by itself.

Sometimes the girls sold us pieces of fish which their mothers had prepared. They added pinches of salt and spices.

I was spoiled with regard to food; I was also spoiled with regard to women. Neither Ado nor I was married. After the Kessu women, we'd taken up with the young Bata girls. The Bata lived on the other side of the Kilangue River. A ferryboatman brought the girls to us in the evening; we took them back to him the next day. I earned plenty of money but because of the girls, I never had enough. Sometimes I even had to borrow!

Magic and Talismans

The Fulbe tailors in the village were out to get me because I'd taken away their customers. They said among themselves, 'Look at that Mbororo! Since he came here, we've lost all our Mbororo customers.'

'It's not surprising,' said another. 'Those people are unbeatable when it comes to preparing potions to attract the sympathy of people!'

Actually I did not use any magic; the Mbororo came to me because I was one of them and I knew their taste in clothing.

One day I had a lot of pain in my arm; I also had a gland in my groin which I could roll around with my fingers. My hand became swollen. It became impossible for me to work. I suffered so much that I lost sleep. When Sarki Mbaka, one of my relatives, saw me in that condition, he understood right away what was happening. 'You're under the effect of an evil charm. Someone has attacked you with the "needle charm"!' From his big pocket, he took out a flask; he drank from it and rinsed his mouth. Then he made an incision on my swollen arm with the end of a razor blade. He placed his lips on the part that had been cut and sucked in forcefully. Right away he spit into a dish that had some water in it. He spit out a piece of broken glass, some human hair and a needle without an eye that had been made by a local blacksmith. When he spit everything out, I clearly heard the sound of metal.

I called the people of my family who were standing at the door so they could see for themselves what had happened. I was the first to admit I'd been imprudent to face the world with no protection against human evil. From that time on, I knew I must protect myself, and I also swore revenge. If some people were capable of acquiring magical knowledge, I would be one of those people.

Sarki Mbaka gave me a leather talisman and said, 'Never take this leather pouch apart, for any reason!' I decided to follow his advice, so I put this charm in my belt. I never knew what it contained. I had confidence in my relative.

Some days later I went to visit my father. I told him about the battle with the 'needle' and how Sarki Mbaka had taken it out of me. 'It's your fault,' he said to me. 'How do you dare venture into the outside world with no protection? Sooner or later you'll be killed! Wait, I'll give you something.' Then he prepared a mixture of different powders which he wrapped up in a piece of cloth. Suspecting that the evil charm which had been directed at me had come from a jealous tailor, he told me to bury his small packet where the tailors usually put their sewing machines in the marketplace. 'On that day you'll see who tried to kill you.'

The next night I went in secret to bury my packet. When I put it in the ground, I spoke an evil curse against the one who'd wanted to get me and I added, 'Whoever you are, you will sew nothing today! Nothing! Absolutely nothing!'

I knew that in the morning all the tailors would take out their sewing machines and put them in a long line at the edge of the market square. At that time the tailors were more numerous than today because there was no license fee to pay. I went there early to watch what was going to happen. I saw a tailor take out a needle and put it in his machine. The needle broke with the first turn of the handle. He took another one. That one broke too. He took apart the head of his machine, cleaned some parts and then put it back together again; but nothing had changed! He added some oil. With the first move of the pedal, the new needle broke. Soon he only had one needle left in his package. People were waiting all around him with their fabric in their hands. They were getting impatient. Soon they spoke to the tailor next to him. In the end, the unlucky tailor quit. He put his machine on his head and went home.

I can only agree that the talisman prepared by my father was effective. I waited for the following night to go recover it; I wanted to put it aside for the next occasion. But it had disappeared from its hiding place. Certainly a rat had taken it away. I never found it.

Another time I was the victim of a sorcerer. I was alone at my house, next to my sewing machine, when all of a sudden I fell down. Disturbed by my groaning, the neighbours came to find out what was happening. Some Mbororo in my family were sitting under a tree a few steps away. They were called. As soon as they arrived, they concluded this must have been the work of a sorcerer.

Someone took out a powder which he had on him. He poured it in a glass of water and gave it to me to drink. He also made me drink water which he'd used for rinsing his mouth. I quickly pronounced a name, the name of the person who'd seized me. I was heard to say very distinctly: 'Adamu Wanjam'. 'Wanjam' means 'barber'. Therefore it was the barber with that name who had 'possessed' me; he was the sorcerer. I was frightened and cried out, 'I see him; he's holding a calabash in one hand and a knife in the other! I hear him; he says he's going to eat me!'

Under the effect of the potion, I soon sat up, and then I stood up. The first thing I asked for was sorrel, which I ate without cooking. No one pursued the barber.

Here is something else that happened to me during my stay in Wuro Bokki. Near the time of a great feast, I had to work especially hard to satisfy my customers. At that time I'd taken up the habit of swallowing pills so I could work longer at my sewing machine. The pills could be bought discretely in all the Nigerian markets. I'd take some in the evening, and I could work all night in the light of a feeble kerosene lamp. At dawn I'd take another pill, and I was ready to work all day. That went on for five days and five nights.

By the end of the week, I was feeling very funny. It was as though I'd been drinking. When I'd go out to take a walk, I'd pass from one group to another, speaking inanities. People took me for a drunkard. Others knew very well what was happening; they knew I'd drugged myself with *anabarsi*.[1]

I went staggering back to my house. As soon as I arrived, I fell down. Ado was there. He ran to call other people, 'Ndudi's collapsed! Ndudi's collapsed!' They came running. My eyes were closed. Someone opened them and noticed they were yellow. My body looked like a cadaver. My blood seemed like it had turned to water. 'This is the effect of *anabarsi*. He took too much. Give him some sour milk.' They went to get some. I drank several swallows and felt better. I got up. From that day on, I've never taken another *anabarsi* pill. When that happened, no one dreamed of saying I was under the effect of sorcery; I had none of the signs.

Another incident: sometimes I'd go to help Ado's father weed the field he cultivated on the other side of the Benue. We'd cross the river in a canoe. One day when I was working in that field with Ado and his little brother Maiduguri, my hoe struck a toad. I saw the toad swell up; its feet spread apart, and it exploded. I called Ado to see the toad which had burst because I hit it. There was every reason to believe its spirits would seek revenge.

That did not take long. I collapsed on the path going home. I had to be carried to the house. 'How could this happen?' asked the neighbours who saw me in that condition. Ado explained that I'd killed a toad. Everyone agreed its genies were avenging its death.

The healers worked busily around me. My father, who was told about me immediately, came at once. I stayed in bed for five days. They say I didn't recognise anyone and that I didn't even know where I was. I had visions. I talked about snakes with two heads that were menacing me. I sat up suddenly. I thrashed about and yelled. People had to throw themselves on me to keep me on the bed. Once they wanted to tie me down, but at the last minute someone intervened. 'Don't do that! That would only excite the genies and make them more active.' I described many things that I alone saw. On the fifth day I regained consciousness and began to eat. Then I learned all the things I've just told you about. 'Do you remember all the smelly drinks you had to swallow? Do you remember having said this? Or done that?' I remembered nothing!

All these events which concerned me took place in Wuro Bokki. During my stay there, there were many similar cases. I was not personally involved, but I knew about them because I heard people around me talking about them. These subjects would often come up in our conversations.

Sorcery and Magic[2]

One day a young Mbororo from the Bodi clan, whose name was Yukel, came and told me what he'd seen the night before. The young *suka* had wrapped up a stick in a big piece of white fabric which they pretended was a shroud. That stick, on which they each had urinated, was solemnly carried by them in absolute silence, like people do when they're accompanying a body to the cemetery. They pushed it into the fresh earth where someone had just been buried. The director of the ceremony said, 'If I hit so-and-so with this stick, may the prayer for the dead have to be said for him!' I did not need to ask Yukel any questions because I knew what was happening. Every evening they would go – motivated by their hatred – to repeat this same curse over the buried stick, which would be dug up on the day of a *soro*.

If the *yafi* was effective, you could be sure there would be a death that very day among the *suka*. It's probable that *yafi* would explain the death of a young *suka* I witnessed near Garoua some years later.

The magic practices called *yafi* are not all as bad as that one; but there are some that are worse, you might say. I'm thinking of the *kirankasko*. The sorcerer puts a pot with a wide mouth on the fire. He invokes the name of a person he'd like to attack. The image of that person soon appears on the surface of the water. The sorcerer sees that person where he is at that very minute, going about his business. The sorcerer can make him suffer in any way he wants. He can work on the person's organs and make him impotent. The victim suffers but who would be clever enough to say that he's under someone's spell?

For a Muslim, employing the services of someone who makes *yafi* so as to harm someone is a sin; handling things that are impure or dirty – like excrement or urine - is a sin; trying to acquire powers which belong only to God – even if the methods are not impure – is also a sin; trying to bring about one's own marriage, even by means that a Muslim would not hide, is evil. Why? Only God gives life. Only God makes people meet so they can be married. A man marries a certain woman and not another because of what God has planned for him. No 'medicine' can do anything. Doing something magic in order to change the course of events is to work against God's design. It's wasted effort. So, refuse to believe anyone who says to you, 'Give me a certain sum and I'll make the woman you like marry you. If my "method" does not work, I'll give back your money.' Pure lies! Since those fellows are often just vagabonds, you can say goodbye to your money!

Sorcery is sometimes very severely punished. Here's a case I witnessed in part. Hawa was a Hausa girl. Beautiful, in full bloom, she'd often been approached by a barber, a certain Adamu, whose advances she'd always refused. One market day she was sitting behind a big basin of *sobal* balls which she was selling. Suddenly the young girls who were nearby saw her fall backwards, as though she'd been roughly pushed. The girls panicked and fled. Some hurried to tell Hawa's parents, who came right away. They found Hawa thrashing on the ground, foaming at the mouth. All around people were saying, 'She's under the influence of a sorcerer!' Everyone agreed unanimously about that. They called a Mbororo from the village who was known for his skill in such cases. 'Go get me some water,' he said as he came near the young girl. Someone brought it to him. He drank it, rinsed his mouth several times and spat that water into a saucer which he placed at the young girl's lips. She did not need any coaxing. When she'd swallowed it all, she got up by herself and, in great agitation, shouted the name of Adamu. She added, 'Yes, it's Adamu who ate my heart. He took it. I saw him. I even know where he buried it.' With a leap, before anyone thought of holding her back, she left the circle of people and ran to throw herself flat on the ground near the place where Adamu, the barber, was shaving people. She dug up the ground, which was wet in that place, and ate fistfuls of earth in order to retrieve her heart.

Adamu, sitting on his mat, became frightened. He trembled all over as he stood up. Hawa's father, who'd followed his daughter, jumped on top of Adamu with a knife in his hand. Someone succeeded in stopping his murderous attempt. Adamu stayed there, flat on the ground, not knowing what to do. The Mbororo healer gave him a cup of water. 'Rinse your mouth and spit the water here. Hawa will drink some and recover her spirits. If you refuse, you'll surely die – immediately!'

This young girl had three brothers. Each of them did business in the market. When they heard what was happening, they came in a hurry. They were furious. They grabbed the barber and hit him violently. They threw all the razors which Adamu had spread out in front of him into a dry well which was nearby. They cut his mat into pieces. They tore his clothes, leaving only his shorts. They grabbed a fence post so they could hit him with it. They tied his hands behind his back, painted his face blue with the dye used for cloth, and dragged him like that through the village, walking here and there with him. In the end, they took him to the *lamido*.

'*Lamido*, may God bless you! We bring you a certain Adamu who's a barber in your village. He's a dangerous sorcerer. He works in the dark and "eats" people. Not long ago, he "ate"[3] a Mbororo from the Kiri clan. And just recently he made a young Bata girl die. The proof is that she never stopped saying his name while she was dying. We must be finished with this man!'

'Did you say "Adamu"? But would this be the same Adamu whose name my own daughter never stopped repeating when she was rolling on the ground after someone had given her a smoke treatment?'

'Yes, he's the one! It's him! It can't be anyone else!' shouted the people.

'Police, hit him!' ordered the *lamido*. The police threw him on the ground and beat him with thick, short sticks. Then they tied his feet and hung him upside-down from the branch of a tree. The police returned to their places near the *lamido*, who was already dealing with another incident.

The sorcerer's mother arrived, her shouts piercing the air. But instead of having pity for her, the police grabbed her. 'She too is a sorceress,' shouted the people. 'She's worse than her son!' She suffered the same lot as her son. And the wife of the sorcerer, who had been brought by force, was treated in the same way. How long did they hang there? A long time! And when they were taken down, all three of them were forced to sit in the hot sun.

In the afternoon the judgement was given. Adamu was condemned to pay six thousand francs. But everyone knew he had nothing. So the police were put to work, under the *lamido*'s order, taking out everything in those sorcerers' house and burning it. They only left a few filthy cloths which the three wrapped around themselves.

When the *lamido* learned, after looking further into the matter, that the three of them were originally from Selem, several days' walk away, he commanded the police to take the three to the Selem road and ordered them not to return to the village. The police led them away, held by a rope which had been well knotted.

When a sorcerer succeeds in saving his life, the affair nearly always ends like that – by his being expelled. That puts an end to the matter. But he must be watched to ensure that he goes far off and does not return to avenge himself and continue his evil deeds.

Actually it is very difficult to prevent a sorcerer from working. It's said that he uses invisible threads so he can catch his victims. He stretches the threads on the path where he knows the victim must pass. The threads resemble a guinea-fowl trap. When he sets this evil trap, the sorcerer must say exactly what his intentions are. 'It's so-and-so I want to catch. Only him!' What is 'taken' like that is not actually the person himself. It's his 'double', his image. This is somewhat like the Whites do when they take photographs. We believe a person leaves his shadow everywhere he spends some time during the day. When night comes, this shadow tries to rejoin the person who left it behind. The shadow walks in the dark and that's what the sorcerer wants to 'catch'.

The trap functions by catching the victim's big toe in one of many slipknots which hang all along this thread. The sorcerer is immediately alerted. He only has to untie the double and take it away for 'eating'.

If the sorcerer moderates his appetite and does not devour certain organs like a glutton would do, his victim – at that very moment – only feels some pains here or there in his body. He suffers from various pains which are difficult to explain. It's only when the sorcerer attacks the heart or the intestines that the person falls on the ground and the people around him see the signs of his being under the spell of sorcery. In this case, people know what they must do: they envelope the patient in smoke made from special herbs, which only certain experts know the secret of. Without a doubt, a name will come to the victim's lips. 'It's so-and-so. I see him. He has a knife in his hand. He has a pot. He's eating my insides. Help!'

Among the onlookers, someone will quickly describe the person corresponding to that name. Some people run to his house. They bring him near the sick man and make him do certain actions in order to release the victim. If the sorcerer is not at his house but is far away from the village, he's alerted by a mysterious voice telling him he's been discovered. So he releases his prey. In such a case, the distance does not make any difference; it's like the *telefon*.

I must say that for several years, in some regions at least – like Adamawa – there's been a tendency to abandon these methods of discovering a sorcerer. The effectiveness of the methods is doubted more and more. On the other hand, in cases of sorcery, witnesses will still be asked to swear on the Book.

When someone is accused of acts of sorcery, there are always people in his family or in his neighbourhood who intervene on his behalf. In order to rehabilitate the sorcerer, people often institute proceedings against his accusers. The judge may ask the witnesses to 'hit the Book' in order to assure himself they're telling the truth. 'Are you ready to swear on the Book you're really telling the truth when you say that so-and-so is not a sorcerer?'

'Yes, I'm ready!'

Then the judge says, 'Bring the Book!' He asks the witness to go out and make his ablutions, reminding him to do them with the precise intention of 'hitting the Book'.

The Book is brought. It's presented to the witness who bends over it. He listens to the judge make a solemn admonition. 'If you touch the Book knowing your witness is false, you're cursed by God. May God strike you dead immediately if he wishes! Or if he prefers, may he make you a leper or a blind man! May the worst evils fall on you!' And the witness touches the Book.

Several days later, it can happen that a witness has his house burned by lightning. Or it is learned that he drowned, or died in a fire, or was killed in a car accident. People quickly make a connection between the solemn oath he spoke and the evil which has befallen him.

Yes, it is no small thing to swear on the Book. This gesture will bring out truth or falsehood. There are Muslims, even pious ones, who would never agree to take such an oath. It is said that anyone who swears, even if he is certain he is telling the truth, loses seven veins in his body: they break the moment he touches the Book. And that's even if he is telling the truth ... , all the more reason not to lie!

CHAPTER 24

New Horizons

Toward the end of my stay in Wuro Bokki, I began to try to save money. I was living with a Hausa woman who insisted I marry her with a legal marriage in front of the *mallam*. I agreed, but my father did not. So I could not count on his helping me find the money. He'd just divorced and was preparing to remarry. To marry this Hausa girl, I needed fifteen Nigerian pounds.

Mala Buba agreed to advance me the money, and five days later we were married. I'd saved ten pounds which I'd used for the other expenses: kola nuts, toiletries . . .

It was my friend Ado who had gone to represent me before the *mallam* in order to 'tie' the marriage. Obviously, I was not there. When Ado came back, I learned from him that I was married and that I only had to pay seven more pounds.

Actually we'd settled on that sum, she and I. I'd also promised her a sheep for the *sadaka*. But those expenses which I still had left to pay did not worry me because she knew as well as I did that I had nothing. A few days later she arrived with her belongings. Everything was in one calabash which she carried on her head. We lived together in a very small room. She got pregnant. In the fourth month, she returned to her mother's house to have the baby; I never saw her again.

In order to straighten out my debt with Mala Buba, I borrowed money from some other people, and then I borrowed from someone else to pay back the second person and so on! I had work, but I spent more than I earned. I never managed to pay back my creditors. In place of one creditor, I now had many.

What should I do? It was out of the question to return to my father and ask him to sell an animal. He'd agreed to that once, but he would not do it a second time. There was only one solution: to run away.

Departure from Nigeria

I'd always heard about my father's brothers who had gone away many years ago to pasture their herds in the 'Country of the Mountain', as it's called. People also spoke of living in the 'South' or in 'Adamawa'. It was said they had found good pastures. They had wealth; they were rich. I'd join them! Why not? But I'd have to conceal what I was doing.

I learned there was to be a big Wodabe festival on the border between Nigeria and Cameroon. I let everyone know I intended to go there to try to sell some tunics which I'd made. So one morning I left all alone in the direction of Cameroon with a pile of eight robes on my head. I had no trouble finding the Wodabe gathering. Although I arrived on the eve of their departure, I succeeded in selling three robes. When they were leaving, I joined the first group I saw going toward the Cameroon border. They were going to Kolere. They walked in front of me, in single file, with *barkehi* leaves in their hands. They sang. Late that evening we arrived in that big village.

The next morning there was a market. I knew I'd meet several of my relatives who were living in the vicinity. While waiting for them, I spread out on the ground the five robes I had left to sell. It was Cameroonian money which was circulating because we were in the Province of Garoua. I sold each robe I still had left for a thousand francs.

My sister came to the market late in the morning. Right away I tried to get five thousand more francs from her. I knew her parents-in-law had it easy. I made up a story: I absolutely had to buy some pieces of fabric before returning to Wuro Bokki. I was careful to avoid explaining my project to her! But she had no confidence in me and gave me nothing. The next day I set out in the direction of Garoua, in North Cameroon.

It really was a flight. I left everything behind me: my sewing machine, my bedding and other little things – plus that woman I never again heard about. And all that to escape three creditors; I owed them five pounds, three pounds and two pounds respectively – everything for ten pounds total!

My Arrival in Cameroon

I spent the night in Garoua. The next evening a bus let me off six hundred kilometres further south, in the little town of Garoua Boulai. If I'd known better, I'd have stopped in Meiganga, well before Garoua Boulai. I had to go back to Meiganga, this time on foot through the bush. I almost got lost for good. I can still see myself surrounded by grass taller than my head, like you find when you leave the path on the high Adamawa Plateau. I had the impression I was confronted by a braided straw fence. Suddenly as I was trampling through the grass, I felt myself disappear into a deep trench. I hurt my legs falling on a big stump. How would I get out of there? The hole was deep and the sides were smooth like those of a well. I was happy to see a bush climbing toward the sky. It was strong enough to support me. I climbed up and in the process, succeeded in recovering my blanket which had caught on a clump of foliage. When I got out of that bad spot, I continued to walk as well as I could.

On the road which is called the 'road of the Germans',[1] I passed a man who was walking after his herd with a rope in his hand. We greeted each other briefly. When I arrived at his village, I stopped at the first house. That happened to be the house of the man I'd just met. He returned quickly. We recognised each other. 'Is this where you live?' I asked him.

'Yes. And so?' he answered curtly.

'Could you give me a place to stay for the night?'

'No. I don't have any room!'

'I'd be happy with a little corner in the entry house.'

'It's out of the question! Anyway, when a stranger comes here, the village chief must first be notified. If you want to sleep here, start by visiting him.'

I told him I was neither a praise-singer nor a government official so I had no reason to introduce myself to the chief.

'In that case, go find somewhere else to sleep!' he said as he turned his back on me. I went further on.

On the edge of the road, there was a group of men squatting in a circle, eating their evening meal. I greeted them. They answered me and invited me to join them. I approached them. 'Thank you,' I said. 'You're very kind, but I can't eat with other people; I'm a leper.'

They were surprised. I heard someone say, 'Ah! Really, this is the first time I've heard a leper introduce himself so frankly. He must be an honest boy.' They finished their meal and then, seeing that I did not intend to go on further, the master of the house called one of his daughters and asked her to take care of me. She warmed water so I could wash and brought me sweet potatoes, gruel and tea.

The master of the house came toward me. 'I'm still very moved by what you just told us. It takes a lot of courage to introduce yourself like that! I know more than one person who wouldn't have hesitated to come eat with us.'

I showed him by holding up my hands that the condition of my fingers would not repulse people. 'But despite that,' I added, 'I prefer to eat by myself so I don't repel those who are frightened by the presence of a leper.'

My words touched him even more. He asked me where I was going. I told him about my uncle Ardo Gauja. 'I know him well,' he told me. 'And also his brother Ori and his older son Mal Daneji. No doubt you want to find them as soon as possible, but – if you want – you can stay here with me. I understand medicine. It's true your uncle Ori is also a well-known healer. However, I know he's not interested in leprosy, but I am.'

Sitting alone on my mat near the fire, I could not help thinking that in this world you can find people who are really opposites: the one who refused to welcome me and shut the door in my face, the other who received me and honoured me as if I were his own son. There's everything here on earth, the good and the bad!

Continuing my journey, I arrived at Bafoum. I was tired so I rested in the midst of a group of men who were sitting in the shade. Among them were some Mbororo. One of them looked at me persistently. When I asked the men if they knew Ardo Gauja, that man said to me, 'And you, do you know him?'

'Of course,' I answered. 'Isn't he my father's brother?'

'He's your uncle? Do you come from Nigeria? Does the name Kadiri mean anything to you?'

When I responded affirmatively, he said to me, 'The more I looked at you, the more I saw a resemblance between you and this Kadiri who is one of your relatives. So we're relatives too. You've reached the end of your journey; come to my house. The day after tomorrow we'll go together to the Fada market where you'll surely find your uncle Ardo Gauja.'

Two days later I was at Fada. My uncle was there in front of me. He looked at me carefully. His two grown sons, Mal Daneji and Guda, followed him. They were driving several animals which were meant to be sold at the market. When he introduced me to them, they hardly looked at me. I thought they were in a hurry and would come back to me once they had delivered their cows to the cattle market. I waited in vain for them near a kola nut merchant.

When the market ended, my uncle suggested that I join a group of his wives who were returning to the village. When we arrived at the camp, they hurried to take me to the hut where my old grandmother Jebu was. This was the sister of my paternal grandfather. 'Grandmother,' they said from outside, 'there's a visitor for you. Someone you know well. He comes from north of the Benue.'

I heard the voice of Jebu and recognised her in the darkness of the house, squinting her eyes as she looked toward the doorway. 'Who is it?'

'It's me, Ndudi!'

Jebu broke into tears. She made me come near so she could touch me, caress me. 'Ah, it's you, Ndudi, my little Ndudi! . . .' And she cried. Then, she asked me many questions about the people of our family who were up there, north of the big river.

The men arrived from the market. Obviously they were not interested in me. No doubt they were ashamed to see one of their relatives in such a state of poverty, misery and filth. When the maize porridge was served, they were careful to put my food aside. They had decided I would not eat from the common plate.

A few days later, feeling sorry for me, they gave me some of their old clothes, which they wouldn't wear anymore. I was quick to notice how disappointed they were that I would not be of much use to them. I had no strength and my shortened fingers would not permit me to take ticks off the animals. There was no question of my being able to handle the ropes, which every herder must constantly be attaching and loosening, pulling, knotting and unknotting! If I tried that, my hands would be nothing but sores after several days. But because they were feeding me, I never refused to do whatever I could.

One day Ardo Gauja's brother, my uncle Alhaji Ori, whose reputation as a healer was well established, offered to care for me. He said he'd just received some plants from another Mbororo of the Bodi clan. I accepted. However, I had to follow a very strict diet: no fats, therefore no butter or fatty meat. I could only eat a sauce made from baobab leaves. No matter how much *daddawa* and how many bitter tomatoes I added, the sauce was never very appetising. I prepared it myself over three hearthstones in my grandmother's hut.

The more weeks that passed, the more I realised I'd been kidding myself about the members of my family. I had thought they'd give me a bull; and when I sold it, I'd have enough money so I could return to the North with my head held high . . . Alas! What was I to them? Nothing! I dreamed of leaving. I was going to leave when I fell sick. I hurt everywhere, and my leprosy seemed to flare up: my fingers had pus coming from them.

At just that time, God willed it that I met one of my father's old wives, Halitu. After her divorce, she had remarried another Mbororo. They were not lucky. An epidemic had killed all the animals in their herd. They'd left the North and come to work for a rich Fulbe herder who did business in a village between Fada and Djohong.

She took me into her house and treated me like her son. I stayed in bed five days, but she kept me for another month so I could go each day to the Sister's dispensary in Djohong, at least an hour's walk away. Once more, I made a friend among the tailors in Djohong: a certain Bindowo. He let me use his machine so I could earn a little money, but there were not many customers. I really lived on the charity of people who felt sorry for me. My friend the tailor clothed me from head to foot.

Once I'd got rid of my rags, I regained my self-confidence and decided to go try my luck in the Central African Republic. The road was there in front of me, leading to the Cameroon/Central African Republic border, about a hundred kilometres away. I told Musa Maroua about my intention. He was a merchant who had advanced me kola nuts worth three hundred francs. I told him I could not repay my debt right then. Not only did he forgive the debt, but he gave me a gift of one hundred francs and wished me good luck!

I had many adventures in the Central African Republic, the country of Bokassa, the country of diamonds. I stopped first in Bocaranga where I began to sell kola nuts in order to earn some money. But in that region, most of the young men at some time in their lives try their luck 'with the diamonds'. I went with a small group of Wodabe friends. Our venture ended in prison. As soon as I was out of the Bouar prison, I returned there again because of the dishonesty of a petrol station attendant who I was working for. He fled; I paid for him! Then the police who were wandering through the bush in pursuit of diamond traffickers thought I was a trafficker and took me back to prison again. I escaped and returned to Bocaranga. I began selling kola nuts again. As usual, I borrowed money. And once again, not being able to repay the money, I had to sneak away from Bocaranga.

Back at Djohong, a Return to Pastoral Life

I went back to my uncles' village in Djohong, living the life of a Mbororo with my cousins. Our village was situated on a little hill which had a stream flowing at its foot. At that place the stream could be crossed on big rocks. The women came there every day to get water. And it was where we washed our clothes and watered our herds of cows and sheep.

This had been the camp of my uncles' family for the last three rainy seasons. There were about ten huts with conical straw roofs. The huts had been positioned in the way we Mbororo usually build our encampments. The huts had only one opening, serving as both door and window, which faced the setting sun.

I noticed the herds were managed and discussed in the same way here as at home.[2] Like us, my uncles inspected each new calf to see if there was anything strange about its body, especially its coat. A black head on a white body was the sign of bad luck. The calf would be done away with quickly. It was the same with a calf that had white bracelets on all four legs or a calf whose body was speckled with different colours.

Like us, my uncles had a certain way of naming their cows according the shape of their horns, the colour of their coats, the placement of their spots, etc. They also passed on the mother cow's names to her descendants. I found the same words designating a cow given as a gift to a boy, a cow brought as a dowry for a woman, or the animals which young people exchange among themselves as a sign of friendship. They attached the same importance to the legend of the 'Black Bull' that we did.

Each household – that of my uncle Ardo Gauja, of his son Mal Daneji and of my uncle Alhaji Ori – had its own herd, its own milk cows and its own calves. Each wife had her own calf rope. Just like us, it was the men who milked the cows.

But if each husband was the master of his house, you could easily feel that the final decision rested with Ardo Gauja.

I'd noticed that the most beautiful cow wore a big leather pouch hanging on her forehead between her horns. This was a talisman meant to protect her from 'praise'. In fact, it will harm a cow if too much is said about her good qualities. There was also the cattle skull hanging on a stake of the calf-rope. It was the skull of a bull that had been sacrificed on the day of the name-giving ceremony of a child whose four grandparents were still living.

In the North as in the South, people believe in the existence of sorcerers who come to take milk from the udders of milk-cows. They replace the milk with blood in order to cause the death of the calf. This is the same kind of sorcery as when a woman succeeds in attracting into her mortar the grain which the woman next to her is pounding.

So I was completely at ease during the long evenings when the subject of conversation was nearly always herding. I remember an evening which extended well into the night, in the company of my uncle and a guest passing through, Ardo Nuhu. He was said to be a great expert, at least he pretended he was. My uncle never stopped asking him questions, especially about the hair on the coats of cows. 'What does it mean when, at a certain moment, hair of a certain colour appears?'

In response, the specialist asked questions. 'Exactly where is the hair?'

'On the flanks.'

'On which side?'

'On the left.'

'On the left side, you say? That's too bad! If you'd said on the right side, in a short while you'd have become the richest herder in the region. But because it's on the left side, get rid of her as quickly as possible. She would bring you bad luck! In particular, pay attention so she does not calve in your camp. It would be a disaster if you mixed her milk with that of the other milk-cows.'

But the healer my uncle consulted most often was Ardo Simba. I remember one day my uncle sent Guda to ask Ardo Simba to come. One of his heifers was limping. When the expert arrived, he sniffed the lame leg. 'It's a snake,' he said when he stood up. 'There's no doubt about it. Here's what to do . . .'

No one was equal to Ardo Simba for diagnosing and healing those illnesses which we attribute to the genies of the bush. We believe those genies shoot arrows. When the arrows penetrate the body of their victim, they have the same effect as poisoned arrows. The proof is that when an animal with that illness is killed, masses of thick, hard, black blood are found in its body. This strange illness, when discovered in time, was easily cured with a powder Ardo Simba knew how to prepare.

It was also Ardo Simba who was consulted in order to know why a cow delivered a still-born calf, or a premature calf, or a kind of embryo like a little rabbit. He knew how to prevent certain sores from enlarging on the back or flanks of an animal. With a sickle blade heated until it was white, he traced a circle around the injured part.

As for the sores made by ticks which negligent herders let become embedded under the skin, all Mbororo know what to do. In past times, a mixture of car oil and DDT powder was used. Today we use penicillin which itinerant merchants offer to all herders. Most of those merchants come from Nigeria and do their trafficking in secret. I don't need to tell you how quickly they make a fortune! At that time, Ardo Gauja, who watched very attentively each morning to make sure the ticks were removed from his animals, had few worries about such sores. But I knew he had a syringe with a needle at his house.

Concerning the castration of steers, my uncle had remained faithful to the old method. Several men help each other to pull a bull down on the ground. In fact, a single person could not do it. Then the bull's legs are fettered, with the back legs tied to the front. The testicles are placed on the wooden bottom of a mortar. Using an axe handle, the castrater taps the testicles and does not stop until there's nothing more to feel. Then he slits them open and extracts the deadened part and blows milk which he has held in his mouth on the testicles. The steer is then brought to his feet. He spends the rest of the day attached to the foot of a tree.

In general there's only one stud bull: the bull who is dominant because of his strength and size. In Adamawa the herds consist of about forty to seventy head.

Simply saying the name of certain diseases makes us afraid: these are the contagious illnesses. We talk about them in the evenings. When the subject is discussed, stories are always told which make the Mbororo look bad, but that's the way it is. Someone tells that so-and-so, whose clan he is happy to name, did everything he could to pass on the illness which hit his herd. Isn't it easier to accept a misfortune which no one is able to escape? Everyone has stories about that. 'Some years ago,' said one man, 'behind our camp one morning, we found a herd which shouldn't have been so close to ours. Later we learned that several of those animals were contagious. It was for purely evil reasons that their owner had brought them close to our animals. By the time we realised what was happening, two of our cows had already been infected.'

'Yes,' adds another, 'some people feel real pleasure in walking here and there with dubious animals, especially around watering holes.' A third one says, 'I heard about a Mbororo who went crazy when he lost his cattle. He took out the insides of one of his dead cows and went in the night to spread them in the herd enclosure of another Mbororo.'

Doing things like that is obviously contrary to our *pulaku*. A real Fulani must, in such a case, isolate himself deep in the bush, as far as possible from any other herder. All by himself he must courageously withstand the difficulties which such a situation brings.

I'd already heard similar conversations exchanged between my father and my uncles. The same facts were recounted with the same words. I concluded we were not too different! We had inherited an identical patrimony: cattle. This was the heritage my uncle Ardo Gauja guarded jealously. To give his children healthy cows, full of life, always more beautiful and more numerous, that was the meaning of his life. That is life for every Mbororo.

The Fertility Cult

When I heard talk about practices relating to the fertility of the herd, I knew well what was being discussed. Hadn't I worked with a 'crown maker'? A long time ago . . . when my father had lived around Gire.

It is also said of this man that he is a 'maker of cattle magic'. He is a member of that group of people who understand the language of animals and who are just what's needed in order to be successful with fertility magic. At the heart of this practice, there's always a crown of *kelli*[3] branches, which is where the name 'crown maker' comes from.

This man came from Sokoto, a large town in northern Nigeria. He'd travelled through the regions of Gombe, Bambam, Numan, Selem and Borom, where he'd built a great reputation. I was there when he introduced himself to my father just before the animals were leaving for the pasture. After greeting my father, he set to work right away.

He spoke to the herd with his traditional calls, chanted in the singing tone that every herder knows. All the animals lifted up their heads and turned toward him. Right away he became their spokesman. With his hand on his ear, forming a cone, his head tilted, he listened and reflected. 'These cows,' he finally said, 'are complaining about their owner. They just told me they're all going to lie down and die if he continues to deprive them of natron.[4] That cow over there is complaining that the cattle are hit too much.'

My father stood there, thinking. He could not say it wasn't true. Whenever the cows were stubborn, he hit them. Some days his stick never stopped falling on them. And recently he'd tied up a cow so he could hit her more easily!

At that moment the 'crown maker' noticed me, me in particular. I felt him stare at me. It was no doubt my leprosy which attracted his attention. He continued, 'This cow is one that belongs to your children. (Actually the cow was mine.) That cow over there has been given to you by a friend in order to maintain your good relations.[5] Do you see that bull over there? That one there – you absolutely must not sell him. As long as he's with you, the number of your animals will only increase. Do not sell him. He cannot be slaughtered at your camp as *sadaka*.'[6]

Everything he'd said was exactly right. People were completely dumbfounded. 'Not only can I see into the future,' he said, 'but I can also carry out the cult of fertility for you, the "*kelli* crown".' He exchanged glances with my father. They moved away from the group and began a discussion in hushed voices. They were certainly talking about money. They quickly reached an agreement. Then he asked me to help him. 'Go get me some *barkehi* branches. I saw some nearby.' I soon brought him what he wanted. He shaped the branches into a crown. To maintain the shape, he wrapped them with *barkehi* fibres which my father had quickly found.

During my absence, he had someone bring a bowl containing water in which he was soaking pieces of the millet porridge he'd taken out of his pouch. He made it into a soft paste and coated the crown with it. Then he gave the crown to me, saying, 'Go put it in *dundehi* milk.[7] The sap of the tree will be fine.'

Carrying a hoe, I went off in the direction of a wild fig tree I knew well. One of my cousins, Zae, carried the crown. I had no trouble making the white liquid flow all down the trunk of the tree. I took the crown and turned it over and over again in the sticky sap. After covering the crown with big *barkehi* leaves that stuck easily to it, I carefully carried the crown back to the crown maker, holding it on the end of a stick.

The man put the crown on his head and, crowned like that, with his hands toward the sky, he began a long prayer. 'I intend to give this *kelli* crown to Koyne, the son of Gursa. The *kelli* is the most excellent tree. I pray for his cows. May they be fertile! May they fill the Benue River! May they be as numerous as the *barkehi* leaves! May they give milk like the *dundehi* and the *kelli* … !' He prayed a long time with his head bowed.

Finally he lifted the crown from the top of his head and put it on the end of the stick which I still had in my hand. He asked me to give the crown to my father who was asked to attach it to the thatch of his house, above the entrance.

His work was not finished. He made a woman bring a big basin of water. He threw a white powder into the bowl and asked me to stir it with my stick. The water became white and soon there was foam on the surface, a thick foam which was sparkling white. I heard the women getting excited. The whole family surrounded us and watched, marvelling. 'How can this be done? Really, today we've witnessed something extraordinary! It's milk! You cannot tell this from milk! When people are that powerful, how could we go wrong asking them to perform the fertility ritual for us?'

Everyone took some foam in their hands. People put it on their faces, on their hands, on their feet, all over their bodies. A mother said, 'Quickly bring me little Musa so he'll get some too,' and she washed his whole body with this white liquid. When there was not a single drop left, the people wiped the sides of the bowl with their fingers. In the end, some of them put their noses in the bowl so not even the odour would be lost! They all said, 'May God grant our prayers! May God give us cattle! May God give us milk as abundant as this liquid we have before our eyes.'

Before leaving, the magician gave my father a big packet of powder. He gave him the following instructions. 'Take this powder. Listen well as I tell you how it should be used. When you learn there will an *inderi* of a newborn who still has his four grandparents, hurry and go there. When they offer you *sobal* balls, put one ball aside. Break it up and mix it with the powder I just gave you. Shape it like a ball again. Then wrap it in a piece of skin. But be careful! It can't be just any kind of skin. It must come from the top of the thigh of the slaughtered animal, at the joint between the thigh and the stomach.' There's a place where – after the animal's dead, even when it's been cut into pieces – the muscle continues to move; that's where this skin must come from. Quickly wrapped like that, this charm must be plunged into the belly of the slaughtered steer. Then the charm must go to a cobbler so the sewing can be finished. The crown and the talisman are tied together by a thread of *barkehi* fibres. One must never be seen without the other. These objects must occupy the place of honour on the shelf.

From that moment on, my father was on the lookout for any feast in a Mbororo family that had two living grandfathers and two living grandmothers.

Before leaving, the 'crown maker' reminded us of the usual prohibitions. To break these rules would render his prayer ineffective. Leaves for making sauces must never be pounded at night. A flaming branch must never be held up in the air during the night.

The paddock must never be crossed with a bowl of water on your head. Someone with hands tinted with henna must never be received inside the house . . . And I won't go on!

We took these prohibitions seriously, knowing that some had immediate implications for our wealth.

Figure 24.1: Mbororo elder

Figure 24.2: Ardo Gauja, Ndudi's uncle, at his calf rope

CHAPTER 25

My Uncle and His Herds

Life as a Herdsman

Not long after I returned from the Central African Republic, the season arrived for taking the herds from Adamawa toward the South. As in previous years, it had been decided that only the able-bodied people in my uncle's family would go along and that Alhaji Ori would stay near his old mother, Jebu. Peta, who was pregnant, would also stay in the village with some children. I was tired and had the intention of not going along, but at the last minute Mal Daneji decided I'd go with the others. He wanted me to be responsible for a half-wild donkey which he needed for transporting some supplies. I agreed to be of service to him, but realised I'd suffer a lot on the long walk. I was consoled by the idea that once we arrived in the South, I'd find life easy for several months.

When we stopped in the afternoon, it was my responsibility to make contact with the local farmers so we could replenish our manioc supply. In the meantime, Mal Daneji and Guda watered the animals and arranged a small, clean spot at the foot of a tree. The women, machete in hand, cut some branches, which they leaned against a tree, forming a shelter. When I returned, everything was ready. The hearth fire had been lit, and the fire for the animals too. The fire was fed with green branches which gave off a thick smoke to chase away the flies.

The evening meal did not last long. I stretched out on my straw bed near Guda. We were talking. I was smoking a cigarette. All at once, behind my ears, I felt a breeze accompanied by whistling. I thought it was a calf. I wanted to push it away with my hand. As I did that, I turned around. What did I see? A snake! 'A snake!' I shouted.

'Liar!' Guda responded.

Without answering him, I got up and grabbed the flashlight he had in his hand. It was definitely a snake, the kind that doesn't give you time to say 'Oof!' after it's bitten you. I kept it in the beam of the flashlight. Guda hit it several times with a stick and killed it.

I slept badly that night. I had nightmares. In the morning when we woke up, I told my companions what I'd thought about all night long. 'Yesterday was very tiring for me. I thought I could stand up to the journey, but it will be difficult. It's better if I go back near Jebu.' No one said anything; I bid my farewells, wishing them good luck.

I let them continue their migration toward the South. It was not a problem for them. Their itinerary was always the same; they'd known the route for many years. When they left in the morning, they knew what was going to happen during the day. Here was a river the herd would swim across and the people would cross by canoe. The next day there would be an area where the fields of manioc were close together. Another day they'd find a big market with a dispensary.

The Mbororo of Adamawa do not spend more than a month getting to their dry-season camp. And there, sometimes at the edge of the big forest, the conditions of the climate and pastures are such that everything is easy. Many young men take the opportunity of being near big towns to discover a world which they do not yet know anything about and which fascinates them. They even go to Yaounde and Douala. The Mbororo from the South are no longer real nomads. Their fathers were. Their grandfathers love to remember the time when they moved about daily, when they lived only on milk.

My return brought great joy to the heart of my grandmother Jebu. Alhaji Ori was happy to know he could count on me from then on to watch the cows, which his brother had left behind. Those animals, called *sureji*, were all either very old or sick or crippled. They would not have been able to make the long walk with the others to the South.

But often those animals cause a lot of worry for those who stay behind. There is nothing to eat nearby; everything has been burned by the sun or by bush fires. The animals are tempted to go further and further away, always looking for a little fresh grass. They are especially attracted to the edges of marshy places. Venturing nearer and nearer, they approach the water until they sink into the mud and get stuck. The harder they try to get themselves out, the deeper they sink. A lone herder can only shout for help, hoping that others will hear him. He's lucky if he sees someone coming, his shoulders loaded with ropes which every herder carries in this season. Once I tried to pull out a cow by myself. What else can you do when no one responds to your call for help? I began by wrapping the animal's tail around my hand. I pulled – so much the worse for my hands! Today I'm sorry I did that. Because of a such a situation, the sores on some of my fingers reappeared. I still suffer the effects of that.

There are also holes which no one suspects. Even if they are not very deep, a poorly nourished cow that falls into one often does not have the strength to get out. What happens then? Probably just what happened to one of my cows that disappeared forever. It might have taken place like this.

A Gbaya villager is walking in the bush looking for wild honey or going hunting. He discovers a cow lying in a strange position in the bushes. He knows he's the first one to see the cow. What an opportunity! He's careful to avoid alerting the Mbororo owner whom he knows perfectly well.

Out of the corner of his eye, he watches the animal as he moves away. He runs to get his son. He is going to ask him to hide near the cow in order to chase off the vultures. It's absolutely necessary to avoid a flock of vultures circling overhead. They'd attract other Gbaya who would be curious to know what the vultures were preying on, and certainly the vultures would help the Mbororo look for his animal. When night falls, the Gbaya comes – accompanied by his wife and maybe another son – to finish off the poor cow, butcher it right there and cut the meat into strips. Then he smokes the meat over an improvised rack, under which he maintains a fire.

If another farmer happens upon him, he'll say with the greatest aplomb that this animal had an accident and he bought it from a Mbororo.

Some time later the farmer, his son and his wife will be seen going back to their house with joy in their hearts. Each is carrying a load of meat on his head. The father will hide the meat but let it get around that people can come and buy smoked meat from him.

All this does not prevent that farmer from continuing to maintain the best of neighbourly terms with the cow's owner. He tells the owner he feels badly about the loss he's suffered and assures him of his complete devotion in looking for the lost animal!

Not all Mbororo are dupes. Some Mbororo lose their tempers when a farmer comes with a sad look to say he's found a dead animal in the bush, at the bottom of a hole. They accuse the messenger of having waited until the animal was really dead before coming to alert them. For a Muslim, as you know, an animal that dies without having its throat cut is only carrion that can bring in no profit, not even a thank-you from the person it's given to.

When my old cow Ole disappeared without leaving a trace, my farmer-neighbours helped me search for her in the bush. But I've always suspected they played a trick on me!

My Uncle, the Healer

When I was not guarding the cows at Djohong, I helped my uncle Alhaji Ori care for his patients. This uncle, the fourth son of my grandfather Gursa, had been chosen by my grandfather to inherit his 'knowledge'. His knowledge was profound and had given him a great reputation as a healer. People came from everywhere to consult him about illnesses of both people and animals. He also took care of people who were possessed by the Spirits.

Alhaji Ori was learned. He was a *mallam*; he taught his own children to read and write the Koran. He was intelligent, always benevolent, always worried about doing anything that would compromise his heavenly reward. He also graciously opened his door to strangers and paid attention to unimportant people.

Above everything else he loved his mother, old Jebu. Nothing in the world would make him want to leave her during the months when able-bodied people went to live in the South. In the absence of the children, he was the one who collected wood and carried water for her.

His reputation as a healer was well established. He was especially known for the power he exercised over the Spirits that possessed madmen. I saw those people coming from long distances. Often they were in chains.

Nearly every morning, we went together to gather supplies of medicinal plants for the day. 'Pick that parasitic plant for me while I dig up the root of this tree.' We also took the bark off certain tree trunks. He often gave me the responsibility of treating a particular patient. 'Go to the madman who's chained up, the one who never stops insulting his mother. Take some embers on this pottery shard. When you're near him, throw this powder on the coals. Surround him with smoke. But be sure you do not forget to give him three good slaps first. Continue as long as you need to, until he asks you for mercy.' After the fumigation, I'd douse several splashes of stinky water on the madman's body. The water came from a jug in which a mixture made from the dirtiest things you can find had been stagnating for a long time.

But there was one operation which I could not do in my uncle's place: the spitting session. I knew neither the phrases nor the verses to recite between the jets of saliva that were projected onto the patient's body. It only took a few days to get the upper hand over the Spirits that possessed that madman. My uncle lost no time in taking off his chains. The same day that man was freed, he offered to do some work.

During my stay with Alhaji Ori, I saw nine people troubled by the Spirits. The first was a woman who was not at all evil. She spent her time washing her hands, making herself beautiful, sweeping and smoking. Then there was a man who'd been brought from the Central African Republic. He spoke loudly and had only one topic of conversation: cattle. He was not chained up. It only took a few days until his conversation became like everyone else's. A Gbaya woman was brought to my uncle. She thrashed about and said incomprehensible things. My uncle healed her.

But he failed once. The patient cackled like a chicken. He saw frightening beasts all around him that were chasing him. The treatment was not successful. He died in Alhaji Ori's *bukaru*. That's the only madman I saw die at my uncle's house.

My uncle was very pious. He regularly performed his five prayers. At the entrance to his hut, he had marked off a place for his prayers. That area was covered with beautiful sand and was always clean.

My Aunt, the Magician

In my family the gifts of 'knowledge' were not only on the paternal side. I had the opportunity several years ago to spend some weeks with my aunt, Yakumbo. She was my mother's older sister. She was nicknamed Bebe. I've kept the memory of this woman like few others. She was a magician.

Bebe had also been a leper from the time she'd been a small child, I've been told. From the time she was very young, it seemed to people around her that she was possessed by the Spirits, those Spirits called *Bori* in Hausa. Her leprosy got worse. But that did not prevent the *Bori* Spirits from teaching her and from communicating an abundance of knowledge to her. It was said she could compete with the *Boka* and – people added – with the most famous of the *Gardi*. She could identify all illnesses. When someone arrived at her house, she told him why he was there even before he could open his mouth.

Her gifts manifested themselves very early: as soon as she could walk, she already would enter into trances when the *garaya* was played. She'd take leaves from a tree and put them in her mouth; when she spat them out, they were bank notes. Out of old cloth, she made brand new wrapper-cloths.

When someone was brought to her who could not walk or who could not talk because he was under the influence of the Spirits, she could find out right away what was causing the problem. She could say where the Spirit came from, why and how. Once I heard her say that a certain child had been possessed the day his mother, when she was pregnant with him, had stepped on a Spirit when crossing her threshold. My aunt always had an explanation.

People came from far off to ask her to perform a divination session. They wanted to know if their professions were the best ones for them. 'It's in your interest,' she sometimes told them, 'to change your profession, and also where you live. I see . . . you're a tailor. There's plenty of work, but you cannot manage to make ends meet. Change your work! Become a farmer! In two years, come tell me if I was right to give you this advice.'

She had the gift of reading the most secret thoughts in the hearts of people. Even hidden faults did not escape her, but she took care not to reveal them. She knew everything about those who came to see her. Everything, probably even the dates of their deaths!

When Spirits were brought to her for exorcising, she always kept very calm, assured that her own Spirit was stronger than the others. Without hurrying, she filled a small calabash with special water. Then she took the calabash into her hands and, facing the patient, raised it to the sky. She stared at the sky for a long time before putting the calabash to the lips of the possessed person. She was assured of success. The Spirit left and never returned. One simple session was enough.

She spoke to herself in a strange language, unknown to anyone around her. Anyway, it was not Fulfulde or Hausa. Besides, she understood all the languages people spoke to her, even if she was not able to respond in the same language.

She often used perfumes during her sessions. She voluntarily gave gifts to those who had need of her generosity. 'You want money,' she said. 'Nothing is easier! Wait.' She'd go into her house and come out with a handful of notes, real bills which the Spirits gave her. Where did they come from? A bank or somewhere else? That's a mystery! I learned from people in her family what I've said about the money.

She really loved to joke. She laughed at the slightest thing. Everyone respected her. Although her hands were eaten away by leprosy, she always had them tinted with henna. She was coquettish and loved beautiful clothes and adornments. She was always worried about cleanliness. She ate only good food. When radios made their appearance among the Mbororo, she was the first to buy one.

That did not prevent the people in her family from living modestly. Her brothers and sisters had no herds; but because of her, they never lacked anything. They ate meat every day: beef, sheep, chicken. To thank her, visitors knew how to be generous. They also gave her money.

The last time I saw her, she still had her mother with her, my grandmother. Her name was Yoyram, from the Diganko clan. In the past, her mother had been possessed too. It's said it was through Yoyram's contact that her daughter Yakumbo had become possessed by the same Spirit. Hadn't Yakumbo sucked her mother's breast when her mother was possessed? Hadn't she slept near her mother? It was said the Spirit of the grandmother was divided in two and that the daughter had just as much of the Spirit as her mother! And so, the mother and the daughter entered into a trance at the same moment when their Spirit was invoked.

One day Yakumbo took pity on her old mother, who was fatigued by these dance sessions. She used a 'process' to deliver her mother from that slavery. Yakumbo left the Spirit in her mother, but prevented it from leading her mother into dance. On the other hand, Yakumbo herself continued to dance all through the night without feeling the least bit tired. In her daily life, you saw Yakumbo dragging her feet which were covered with sores; but at the first sound of the *garaya*, she threw herself into the dance, stopping only to perform her magic.

That was my aunt Yakumbo, called Bebe, the leper who controlled all the Spirits that possessed her.

Yakumbo also came to visit us. I remember during one of her stays in Ngawa I saw something I've never seen since. I was squatting beside the fire where the men were sitting. It was cold. We were at the end of the rainy season, a few days before the big dispersal and before my return to the home of Zoro Ajiya in Demsare.

A woman came from the neighbouring camp. I heard her say to my stepmother, 'Today we would like to do the special rite that you know so Barkewa can get married. We need Guitel for this. He's the right age. We want Barkewa to marry Ali; she's two years younger.'

My stepmother objected, saying Guitel was already too old.

My father intervened. 'No,' he said, 'that's exactly the right boy. Wasn't his cousin the same age when he was used for this same ceremony? Get Guitel!' But Guitel would not agree to do it. He had to be caught and forced to come.

I followed them. When we arrived, I saw a large mat had been placed in front of the door of Barkewa's house. Ali was already stretched out on it. Guitel was put near Ali; they had to lie next to each other, with their feet toward the south, their heads to the north, in the position of a married couple, with the woman to the right of the man.

An old woman arrived with a black cloth. She spread it over the two of them. Another woman shook a round calabash in which she had placed twelve wooden spoons. It was a churn. She hit it rhythmically with a big spoon and sang our traditional marriage song, with all the women joining in the chorus: *Inna jomba! Inna jomba!*

Then all the spectators entered into the dance, including the children! Only one person was absent: Barkewa, for whom this ceremony was being done. He'd fled and was hiding like young men do on the day of their wedding. The dance around the black cloth lasted a long time.

A woman brought some fresh milk. With a *barkehi* branch, she sprinkled the children who were hidden under the cloth. Then she made them get up and she gave them some of this milk to drink. The milk that was left was divided between the other children. Then another woman took the mat and the cloth and threw them in a stream. We saw the mat and cloth depart, carried away by the current. Their disappearance was interpreted by us to be a good sign: the fateful obstacle which had opposed Barkewa's marriage had been taken away.

We were convinced that Barkewa was under the spell of an evil charm which prevented him from taking a wife. Why were his friends, the boys his age, all married and not him? He was neither a leper nor a cripple nor a one-armed man! To the contrary, he was perfectly healthy in body and mind. Why hadn't he succeeded in starting a family? He'd played around with young girls like all the boys his age. Why hadn't his parents been successful with the steps they never ceased taking on his behalf?

We know this rite, like some others, removes a magical curse, but we also know very well it only succeeds if God wants it to.

The Return from the Seasonal Migration

Time passed. And the first rains appeared. The people in the South would not delay their return. However, it would be several weeks before the grass here was high enough to provide pasture.

We'd had news from them. We knew they'd started to move and had already crossed the big road running from Ngaoundere to Yaounde. Nearly every day we heard about their progress. We learned they were suffering because of the rain and that they'd had a lot of trouble crossing the Lom River. There was even talk about a pack-ox having been carried away by the current.

At last they arrived. It was late in the morning. For them it was like an ordinary stop. But the next day we saw the women were already busy working on their thatch roofs. Some had not been re-thatched for three years.

The following day, most of the women began carrying back calabashes full to the brim with all sorts of objects from Djohong or other small villages. They also had tied-up cartons and trunks on their heads. Everything that would have burdened them or would have been useless during the months they were away had been kept for them by the Fulbe and the Gbaya in the surrounding villages.

A week later everyone was back to his old habits. The women left every morning with calabashes on their heads, offering milk to their usual customers. The men gathered in the square of the neighbouring village to spend the day in endless discussions.

This is the great time for invitations among the Mbororo: a name-giving ceremony for a newborn, an engagement, a marriage, a remarriage, a feast celebrating the end of Koranic studies and the awarding of the title 'mallam', a feast offered by a pilgrim who'd gone to Mecca, a feast of friendship in the honour of a relative who has come from far away ... .

Each week, and often several times a week, the young boys and girls have occasion to get together. As soon as they come back from one feast, they think about the next one. They run to it! Some gatherings last three days.

I knew a young *suka* who spent his time going from right to left. In the evening he could be seen leaving to spend the whole night with his friends. Coming back in the morning, he'd drink his milk, swallow the gruel which had been left aside for him and go to bed.

The Card-Players

Among these young men, there are some who go to all the festivities, not for the meat or for the girls but just for the cards. The card-players know each other very well; as soon as they arrive, they get together and disappear behind the bushes. Consumed by their passion, they hardly have time to nibble the bits of grilled meat which their accomplices bring secretly to them. Often they do not even touch the meat because the game absorbs them so.

The game is played for money. The stakes are never under a thousand francs. Fights break out, knives are drawn to intimidate the cheaters. Some new players who mix into the group are afraid of those young, quick-tempered Mbororo who are always ready to unsheathe their knives.

The great players arrive at these encounters with their pockets stuffed with bills. They've each sold a cow and they now have fifty thousand francs and more. For big occasions, cattle merchants – often Hausa – follow them and stay nearby. They open what they call a 'bank'. In a minute, an unlucky player can have all the money he wants by promising to sell an animal. 'I'm selling you my little fawn-coloured cow.'

'How much are you asking? . . . Too much! . . . OK. Here's the money. Your cow is mine.' And the game continues.

It should be noted that not one of those indebted Mbororo players would dream of going back on his word. In fact, nothing would be easier for him if he wanted to because such a contract has no value in court. But I've never heard of a ruined player who refused to face up to his debt.

These card games are often occasions for drinking binges, which are organised by prostitutes who attend. People also smoke a tobacco that makes you drunk, called *sade* in Cameroon and *wi-wi* in Nigeria.

Mutual Insults

I did not have much trouble adapting to my cousins in Adamawa who I nevertheless felt were so different from us, the Jafun from the North. But sometimes there were clashes: I did not hesitate to tell them how shocking their habits seemed to me. I criticised them while imitating them at the same time! And they got malicious pleasure out of boasting of their alleged superiority over us who came from north of the Benue. They considered us to be 'savage' and backward.

Here's what I heard one day from the mouth of one of my cousins when he returned from a trip to the North. 'Ah! You can't imagine greater misery than that of the Mbororo around Garoua. When you see their herds walk past, you can't tell the heifers from the old cows. They all look alike – so thin you're afraid for them. You can't distinguish castrated steers from pack-oxen!' And he added, 'They're so dirty, these Jafun from Garoua! The boys, until they're fairly old, have their hair braided like women. And all the metallic spangles they wear on their heads! And those ostrich feathers they wear in their hair on certain days! And their clothes! They wear short tunics, open on the sides, which let you see their ribs. You'd think they were farmers. As for their favourite game, the *soro*, let's not talk about it. What pleasure do they get out of hitting each other like that? And between brothers! It's a game of madmen! And to think that our fathers did that, "the good time of the *soro*" as they say!'

The young man who was talking like that either had not noticed me or did not know who I was. I shouted furiously at him, 'Have you finished talking about the Mbororo of the North? Now would you like to know what they think of you who live in the South? You're nothing but bastards and cowards, weaklings with tender skin! You boast about this or that, but you've never proven what you're really worth. However, among us Jafun, a man is measured by the *soro*: the stick reveals a man's worth.' And I added, 'Do you know what they say about you? They say you don't deserve to be called "herder", you who spend your time washing your clothes. You want your clothes to be whiter than milk! Clothes? You have at least ten sets! Those Mbororo from the South – they add – coat their bodies with perfumed creams. When they go to the hairdresser, they say they want their hair arranged in this way or that. They love to show off by pronouncing French words they've learned in the markets, which they haven't learned the meanings of! It's sad to see them dance with bottles of beer in their hands! Their friends make fun of them and they let them do it!'

I could tell them they're scorned in many other ways: the young mothers who smile at their first-born and the fathers who play with him; these illegitimate children who are more and more numerous; the marriages between pagan women and Mbororo. There are a few such marriages now, but they're certainly on the increase. There's something else they do which we consider intolerable: they pay money to the former husband of a divorced woman whom they want to marry. I've even heard one of the Jafun say about them, 'Those Mbororo from the South have no virility in those cold mountains. They only regain their virility by squatting in front of their braziers.'

Such reproaches are mutual between us Jafun from north of the Benue and those Jafun who emigrated two generations ago into the Adamawa Mountains. You must realise our words are often very exaggerated!

I spent this new rainy season in the midst of my cousins, but it would be my last.

Then came an event which would transform the course of my life: meeting the Para. He had just arrived at my uncle's camp with the intention of living there, in the midst of our herds. He wanted to share our life and watch from close-up the work of Alhaji Ori, the younger brother of my uncle Ardo Gauja and a famous healer.

The Para had already erected the posts for his future hut when I met him. He frequently visited me in my hut, which was open to all the winds. Hardly knowing him, I was surprised and also flattered when he said he'd noticed I was particularly good at explaining things to him. He'd never heard such things from his many Mbororo friends in the big Ringimaji clan that he'd had contact with nearly every day for many years.

He offered to take me with him to his home in Djohong. He would find me a house and would give me what I needed to live on. His offer intrigued me. 'Right away,' I said to him. 'Beginning today, if you want.' In fact, I was in a hurry to leave the village of my uncle who had never really accepted me. I had always felt a little like a stranger there.

That year many families left the region between Fada, Djohong and Ngaowi. They went further south and often closer to the Central African Republic border. My uncles Ardo Gauja and Alhaji Ori decided to follow the movement and to leave the hill of the Fig Tree, where they'd spent so many years, for good. The pastures were exhausted. The tsetse fly was doing more and more damage. Manioc was becoming hard to get and more expensive. There were conflicts with the farmers. They thought it was time to go somewhere else.

I'd decided not to follow my uncles for the reason I've just explained to you. I'd stay in Djohong where the Para Mbororo had invited me to live. He'd found a house for me near his, a mud house with a thatched roof. The roof leaked and the door was half eaten by termites, but that was not important; I had a house. Several bundles of straw on the roof and some nails were enough to put the house in good condition. I had the big advantage of finding myself a short distance from the dispensary, where I could go every day so the sores which were reappearing on one of my hands could be cared for.

My grandmother Jebu cried when I bid her my goodbyes. I learned later that during the long trip toward the Central African Republic border, she caused a lot of trouble. My uncles had realised that by making a very great detour, she could travel most of the way by truck. When she got in the first truck, she agreed – but not without difficulty – to ride in the cabin. But as soon as the motor started, she got scared. They tried every possible way to reason with her. Impossible! She had to get out.

They tried a donkey. She did not want that either. The only means left was on a man's back. And that's how she went – from Gbaya village to Gbaya village, by little steps – until she arrived at the prearranged site. That's where she died shortly afterwards, the day that God had decided her life would end. May God pardon her!

CHAPTER 26

Settled at Djohong

My Apprenticeship in Writing

So here I was living in Djohong, which is also called Doumba in memory of one of its great chiefs who died twenty years ago. It's called Doumba-Djohong too. I felt at home there since I'd been accustomed to living among many sorts of pagans. I knew the Tangalé, the Yanguru, the Ntabo, the Bata, the Nabiri, the Bura, the Mbula, the Kanakuru and the Firé, to name only those I knew in Nigeria.

The day after my arrival in Djohong, the Para Mbororo put a ballpoint pen between my fingers and a little book in front of my eyes. For me, it was an amusement of no importance. I didn't see anywhere it could take me. If only that book had been in French! But no, it was in Fulfulde, the language of the Fulani, which is not a written language. During the first days I was convinced I'd quickly get tired of this fastidious work, which seemed useless to me. But the Para was there, pushing me a little further each day. He knew where he was leading me!

At the same time, I helped him understand our language better. He'd recorded many stories and rapid conversations, which he only understood half of, or sometimes none at all. He had me listen to a sentence and then stop the recorder. I'd repeat the sentence slowly and distinctly on a second tape recorder and then play some notes on my *garaya*. Then he'd have me listen to another phrase. I'd repeat it in the same way, and so on. Later, when he was alone, he'd listen to the sentence I'd recorded. When he'd hear the guitar, he'd stop the tape recorder and try to write what he understood. I did not need to be with him while he did that work.

I admit there were days when we argued. Why deny it? We'd be reconciled the next day. And today this is the result: I can write the recorded history of my life without making mistakes!

At that time we made many trips so we'd get to know other Mbororo who lived far away: those of the Central African Republic, of Chad and especially of Nigeria. It was always a great pleasure for me. We even were supposed to go to Niger at the time the great drought hit that country, when the Wodabe were obliged to come look for work even here in Cameroon.

In fact, it was when we went to get a visa at the Nigerian Embassy in Yaounde that the Para Mbororo became ill. They put him into the hospital there and then onto an airplane for France. Our separation lasted three years.

So I was alone in Djohong. Alone, but not abandoned. The Para asked his brothers in the Catholic Mission to give me a hundred francs a day. Besides, in Yaounde he'd bought me a new sewing machine which allowed me to earn my living, even in his absence.

A New Matrimonial Adventure

I was not completely alone for a second reason. Before leaving Djohong, the Para had helped me get married. I'd lived for a while with a Gbaya girl. But I did not have the means of facing up to the expenses of marriage. Finding out about my embarrassment, the Para offered me the necessary money. He hesitated, however, asking himself what would happen in a marriage between an authentic Fulani and a Gbaya girl who'd already been married. He hesitated but did not refuse what I asked for: money for the trousseau, that is, for some cloth, a blanket, a mat and some toiletries. I also had to buy a sheep, called *sadaka*, for the occasion. And I had to buy two calabashes of kola nuts. As for the money for the entry house of the *sare*, where the exchanges would be made between the representatives of the husband and wife, the Para gave it to one of our friends – an American, Filip B, an important professor in London, who was studying the Gbaya and Mbororo peoples. When he came back from the *mallam*'s compound, he said to me, 'Ndudi, it's done. You're married, before Allah and before me too!'

I kept drawing lines and circles on my slate. Since I'd been living with that woman for several months, marriage did not change much in my life. Now she could just come to my house without doing it in secret, and she could bring her belongings there in daylight. From now on, she was my legitimate wife.

She was a Gbaya, the daughter of a Gbaya mother and a Gbaya father. Her father was a Muslim, himself the son of a Muslim father. She herself practised Islam very little. When I was with her, she agreed to make an effort, but I had to insist!

The first days of our life together, everything went well. But soon she showed herself to be jealous, like all Gbaya women are. She made scenes. Things reached such a state that she hit me. She even bit me on the arm so badly that I had to go to the Sister's dispensary. In spite of all that, I did not send her away. I preferred to continue my life with her as best as I could. She continued to gather wood, carry water and cook for me. I had to admit that, in spite of an old illness which made her limp, she was very active. It was not so bad between us.

But one thing really irritated me about her behaviour. Here it is. I had imagined that a Gbaya woman who'd become a Muslim would abandon those foods which we abhor: caterpillars, termites, worms, rats and other little dirty things. But no! It was soon evident she could not leave them alone; the desire was too strong for her. Like all Gbaya women, I now know, she used every trick so she could eat such repugnant and forbidden food secretly. No religion has succeeded in preventing the Gbaya from continuing to eat those foods.

I have to add that she never tried to fight against her habit of intoxicating drinks. But I do not know any Gbaya Muslim – man or woman – who's been successful in passing up alcohol. And this alcohol is found in the smallest villages, even right in the middle of the bush, all year long, starting with *argi*, which is made from fermented manioc. There's also *hamba*, which is like millet beer; *afuku*, also made with millet but it's more of a spirit than a beer; and *kuri*, a very alcoholic drink found everywhere at the time of the honey harvest. *Argi* is the worst; it burns when it comes in contact with a match! When I was in Djohong, there was talk of six people dying because of this *argi*.

Any woman can – when she wants to – sell these alcoholic drinks. To attract customers, she puts a flower in an empty bottle and sets it in front of her door or on the edge of the path. In general, these women arrange not to compete with each other, and they each earn a little money in turn.

A 'Cosmopolitan' Village

There were not just Gbaya in Doumba-Djohong. It's true this is first of all the land of the Gbaya, but they are no longer the only inhabitants of this region. Many others have come to live there. There are the Fulbe from Maroua, some Hausa and the non-Muslims from the Central African Republic that we call the Kongo or the Congolese.

At first the inhabitants were mixed together. But, realising how numerous they were, the Congolese quickly established their own section of town. And we also now have a Fulbe quarter, a Gbaya quarter . . . Each section has its own chief. But the Gbaya, the most numerous, have formed subdivisions, five or six of them; each one is under the responsibility of a chief. The Hausa, who are less numerous, are mixed in with the Fulbe. Sometimes it's really difficult to distinguish between them because they look so much alike.

Many Fulbe have small businesses. They also do a little farming and have some cattle. Little by little, they've invaded the centre of the village, buying up houses from the Gbaya at low prices; the Gbaya have been pushed to the edges of the village. The Gbaya rarely resist the five or ten thousand francs which the Fulbe offer them for their houses. On one side there's astuteness; on the other, the appetite for quick money.

What I'm describing for Doumba-Djohong could be said for Meiganga (the capital town of the subdivision, which has since become a division) and for other villages all along the road which goes for two hundred kilometres from Meiganga to Yamba, on the border near the Lancrenon Falls. There are no longer any Gbaya in the town centres, not even one who has a shop. You cannot actually call their little businesses in matches, cigarettes and candy – sold piece by piece – a 'shop'. Their merchandise is offered to customers on wobbly, portable tables.

More than the others, however, the Gbaya are on their own territory. The *lamido* is one of them. However, they find themselves in last place. Why? Laziness and drunkenness are enough to explain it.

But this does not prevent the Gbaya from scorning those they call the Kongo. The Kongo are people from the neighbouring country who came to make use of the land left free by the Gbaya. Their real name is the Pana or the Kare.

These Kongo are very active. They have beautiful fields: millet, manioc, peanuts. The men are indefatigable. They work fast and well. Both the Fulbe and the Mbororo prefer to use the Kongo for building mud houses or for repairing roofs. You feel they're in a hurry to finish the work so they can take on another task. They want to make as much money as possible. In this way they're very different from the Gbaya who have no ambition, no competition among themselves and therefore no passion for work.

However, the Gbaya consider the Kongo to be less than nothing. They reproach them for having ragged clothes, for being dirty and for speaking a language which irritates them. They're foreigners who must take care not to act proud. And they don't; they keep quiet, living in peace in their own section of the village.

The *Lamido*

The *lamido* holds an important place in the life of the Mbororo. He's the one who gives them authorisation to pasture their herds and who sometimes determines where they can place their camp. However, the headmen and the Mbororo *ardos* do not bring their annual taxes to him; they take their taxes to the *gomna* (governor) at the *bariki* (barracks).

I've had the opportunity of spending many years in the neighbourhoods of several *lamidos*. I saw the importance they held in the lives of the people who lived on their land. I amused myself by watching what happened in their homes and around them. I'm speaking now about the *Lamido* of Doumba.

Every morning about eight o'clock, the *lamido* comes out of his personal rooms to sit under the thatched veranda of his *sare* (compound) with its many houses. These houses are surrounded by a big mud wall which is as thick as it is high. He sits in an armchair which is placed there for him, to the left of the big door of the entry house.

He always finds people there who've been waiting a long time for him: some dignitaries, but also many of his servants, who are called 'slaves' by those who speak a little French. Little by little other people come to join the first group; they form his council.

When he's seated, each person greets him, repeating the traditional phrases: 'May God bless you! May God give you long days! May God look with favour on what you do!' He thanks them, but it's especially one of his courtiers seated near him who responds for him, 'The *Lamido* hears you. He thanks you. The *Lamido* hears you!'

The *lamido* is never alone. There are always people around him. The *kaygama* is often there. The *kaygama* is the most important of the dignitaries. In the absence of the *lamido*, he's the one who takes the *lamido*'s place and handles current business. He also exercises the functions of judge, in the same capacity as the *alkali*.

But all complaints are not made to the *lamido*, his *kaygama* or his *alkali*. Many little problems are dealt with by the simple village chief, the *jaoro*, or the chief of a town section (who is also called the *jaoro*). Everyone realises it's always in their best interest to straighten out problems at the lowest level. And it's preferable to do it in front of the *lamido* rather than before the *gomna*, who is the *sepdedisterik* (*chef de district*, the head of the district, as in Doumba) or the *sufrefet*, (the sub-prefect, as in Meiganga).

The *lamido* can take the initiative and summon anyone he wants to his court if a plaintiff asks him to do it. It's the *lamido*'s personal guards, his *dogari*, who deliver the summons. Those men – his policemen – always do their jobs rapidly, almost running. Their heads are always uncovered, their hats in their hands. When they arrive at the home of the man they're looking for, they say curtly, 'The Lamido calls you. Come! Follow me immediately!' The *dogari* take off. They turn around from time to time to make sure the man is following them. Sometimes when the matter concerns a person who has no particular respect due him, the *dogari* seize the man by the arm and do not let go of him. They do that when they've been given the order to bring him 'with their hands on his arm'.

Another order can be given to two *dogari*: 'Go get him; bring him quickly. May his feet never touch the ground!' So the *dogari* seize the man and transport him like a package to be thrown at the feet of the *lamido*. 'Whip him!' the *lamido* begins by saying. 'Give him five strokes!' The *dogari* carry out the orders. 'And now can you explain to us why you stirred up such trouble with your neighbour that he came here to make a complaint?'

'It's not true! He's lying! I didn't do what he says!'

'Whip him five times more!'

'And do you still say you didn't sleep with your neighbour's wife?'

'He's lying! I've never touched his wife!'

'That's not true!' the plaintiff answers back. 'I caught them in the act! Here's the proof – the clothes, his and my wife's. Do you dare deny these are your shorts?'

'Yes, those are my shorts, but you came to my house and took them. What would be easier than wrapping them up with your wife's wrapper-skirt?'

If the accused is judged guilty in spite of his denials and his facile explanations, he's condemned to pay a fine of two thousand francs to the husband who's been wronged. He's whipped again and sent back to his house. By the time he arrives home, he's decided to make his wife sell a few extra basins of manioc so he can pay his debt. Prison awaits anyone who says he cannot pay. And it's prison with hard labour during the day: rebuilding the thick mud wall, making bricks, cutting straw and transporting it to repair roofs, going to gather bales of grass for the *lamido*'s horses.

During the good season, the season when it doesn't rain, it is the tradition that the canton chief (another name for the *lamido*) should visit all the villages in his territory. This is a big event. It's called the *laturney* (the tour).

On the eve of the journey, all of Doumba is buzzing. Everyone wants to be part of the escort. It's a great honour to accompany the chief. And you can look forward to days when you can eat until you're full, stuff yourself with meat – indeed, you feast.

When moving between villages, everyone travels in procession. Four or five big drums precede the horse on which the chief is mounted. The *lamido*'s head is covered with a voluminous turban so that only his two little eyes peek out. He's clothed with several thick, scarlet robes. A huge parasol, held at arm's length by one of the servants, twirls over the *lamido*'s head. The voices of praise-singers compete with the rolling of the drums and the sombre tone of the long trumpets. 'You are the greatest! It is you who has inherited the throne, you, so-and-so, son of so-and-so. You are a lion. You are a leopard. You have no one to fear but God! You are the greatest *lamido*, the most just and the best. You are the one and only!'

When the chief arrives at the next village, he's received in front of the entry house of the *jaoro*. The 'servants' hurry to put an armchair on a carpet while others, taking infinite precautions, help the chief – who's tangled up in his robes – get off his horse and put his feet on the ground.

The chief sits down. He begins to talk. As soon as he opens his mouth, everyone in his entourage bends down, their backs broken in two, listening to his orders: 'So-and-so will be received at the home of so-and-so. So-and-so will go to the house of so-and-so.' For the people in his escort, the feast begins.

The chief who receives the *lamido* feels practically obliged to present him a cow. He solemnly presents it to the *lamido*. 'This is the meat for your people, Chief.' Sometimes he offers two cows. The porters say among themselves, 'Did you hear that; he said two!'

Many farmers come from the surrounding bush. No one comes with empty hands. Often they bring chickens. The young men in the *lamido*'s entourage introduce themselves to the farmers as the ones responsible for receiving gifts in the name of their chief. They take the chickens in their hands, but more than one chicken will never arrive at the feet of the *lamido*. A little way from the village, some accomplices have already prepared a fire so they can grill the chickens over the embers.

Bolder young men venture into the tiny villages of only two or three houses which are lost in the bush. They say to the old people they find there, 'The Lamido said we should come and get two sheep. You must give them to him right away.' How can someone with such great confidence be refused? Before leaving with their gift, they're careful to say, 'The Lamido told us to thank you. If you see him, you must not remind him of this gift which you just gave him. The Lamido doesn't like being reminded of good deeds. Take the advice of friends.'

'Of course,' says the old man. 'I know well enough that you shouldn't remind Important People about the good gestures done for them.'

One sheep will be grilled; the other sold in order to buy *argi*.

The next day the parade forms again and goes further on. All that was presented the evening before is left in the hands of the *jaoro*: chickens, sheep, goats, etc. and also sacks of manioc . . . Now there's a new triumphal reception. The warbles of the women greet the arrival of the chief. Everyone in the escort lifts up his head, including those who wear only rags around their waists which pass for shorts. All this rag-tag lot think they have special privileges, and they look down on the bush people who are gathering along their route.

The tour is finished and it's time to return to their village. The evening before their return, the news is passed to all the houses in Doumba: the *lamido* is arriving. He will be there the next day. And then he arrives. Although he is sitting on his horse, he can hardly be seen. He is lost in the crowd of people who are carrying all the sheep and goats on their shoulders and long baskets full of chickens, bundles of goods, bunches of bananas and bowls on their heads. Quite far behind, following as well as they can, are the cows, heifers and steers that the *lamido*'s herders pull along at the ends of long ropes. The praise-singers sing until they're hoarse, competing with the trumpets whose sounds are nearly obliterated by the drums whose stretched skins are still holding out against the drum sticks – though no one knows how.

But that is undoubtedly a thing of the past. It won't be seen any longer. Things have changed in Doumba. The *gomna* has installed a *sepdedisterik*[1] there. And everything has changed in a few months. This new chief of Doumba does not like idlers and people who drink alcohol. When he hears the drums playing in the evening somewhere in the village, he goes, accompanied by his guards, to see what's happening. Arriving unannounced, the guards jump on the drunkards, thrashing them, chasing them, forcing them to run to the office of the *sepdedisterik*. Prowling in the night and observing everything, the *sepdedisterik* is not duped. And he does not believe the old chief when he says there are no more *argi* drinkers in his village and that if he finds one, he'll arrest him immediately.

After several months, it's not surprising the drums are quiet in the village. The drums are not heard any more, not even when there's a full moon.

The Doctor-Sister

Another centre of interest in Doumba-Djohong is the dispensary. People come from far off to be cared for there. They're attracted by the great renown of the healer, this woman called *Ser-docta*.

Ser-docta is well organised. When people come to the door of her dispensary, she makes sure everything is in good order: men sit on one side, women on the other. She loves her hospital and is always improving it. There's absolutely no dirt, neither inside nor around the building. Anyone she finds spitting on the ground had better watch out!

The house where she lives with the other sisters is just as clean. She has great devotion. People have complete confidence in her and know that she'll do everything to heal them. Often she succeeds.

How different from some dispensaries I know where there are hardly ever any medicines and the surroundings are covered with rubbish. *Ser-docta* will not even put up with a dog turd!

The Mbororo are difficult people for her. They know that. They have to be really sick before they agree to go to the dispensary. And when they go there, many of them take the precaution of bringing their own 'medicines' with them. You can never be too careful!

The patient is often brought in a blanket which has been suspended from a big pole and carried on the shoulders of two men. Watch out if *Ser-docta* smells the odour of smoke or sees something that resembles bush medicine when she comes unexpectedly into a patient's room. She raises her voice. She threatens to throw the patient out the door: 'Go back where you came from if you want to keep using your own medicine!'

The Mbororo do not protest. They act like they're sorry. 'We won't do it again!' But that doesn't stop them, taking advantage a little while later of *Ser-docta*'s absence at noon, from bringing a healer to the room. He quickly makes poultices, gives the patient a liquid to drink, spits on his body and leaves as discretely as he came.

Often the Mbororo are not reasonable. How often they flee from the dispensary because they feel better after a few days of injections – but the treatment has only begun. The whole family is in agreement. 'Yes, you're healed! You'll be better off at home. We'll come get you tomorrow.' You can imagine the anger of the *Ser-docta* when she finds the bed empty! If the patient who was supposedly healed gets worse and has to come back as a last resort, she will not find enough words to insult him.

But her heart is good. Like the Fathers, she works first of all for heavenly recompense. And in the end she takes pity on the patient. She gives him another bed. She starts the series of injections again. She repeats once again what she tells all Mbororo when she hospitalises them: 'Listen! You Mbororo, I know you! If ever you leave secretly before you're cured, you can be sure I won't take you back again. You can go where you want. There are other dispensaries in the area besides mine. Ah, these Mbororo don't have two pennies worth of brains!'

It's true; she does all she can to educate us. But although she may say what she wants in any tone she pleases, the Mbororo are very determined to do only what's in their heads. All her words pass by their ears. They seem like they're listening to her, but they remain determined to leave the dispensary when they want to.

The *Ser-docta* pays special attention to the women who come to have their babies at her dispensary. You sense that she avoids annoying them. She gently cares for the mothers and the babies which have just been born.

On the other hand, she's pitiless toward boys and girls who come to her with venereal diseases. 'Where did you catch this? Go get treated by those who gave you the illness!' Those men, those women, she knows them well; and when it's necessary, she does not hesitate to hit them!

One day a middle-aged Mbororo came to her and showed her his illness. I happened to be there. 'Look, *Ser*,' he said. 'Look!'

'Will you please get that out of here!' the *Ser* said to him. Everyone laughed.

'Look, *Ser*, touch it. You'll see!'

That's how she is. She wants to heal us, but she also wants to educate us. She's a good woman. May God bless her! May God help her in her good works!

Religions

I cannot end this description of the village of Doumba-Djohong without talking about a subject to which everyone, everywhere, attaches the greatest importance: religion.

In Doumba, there are three religions: that of the Muslims, that of the Fathers and that of the Americans.

There are many Gbaya who've followed the religion of the Whites for a long time. By comparison, there are few Gbaya who have become Muslims.

When you look closely, you see the religion of the Fathers is easy to practise: there is no big fast and no prayers five times a day, which oblige you to have water always within reach; you can eat whatever you like. No food is forbidden, not termites, not caterpillars, etc. This religion does not forbid drinking wine; if you drink some, that does not count as a sin. You can say the same for beer and *argi*.

The Fathers have brought many Gbaya into their houses of prayer. But not all of them remain faithful. I know more than one who goes six months or more without entering the church. I'd like to know what the sermons they hear are about. Do the sermons enter one ear and go out the other? I think the Fathers teach them what they must do to be saved from something which I do not know about. They never repeat what they've heard from the Fathers' mouths. All I know is that they continue to drink and commit adultery. When they join the mission, they give up none of their former habits. It seems to me they are not very faithful to their religion which, I suppose, could help them a lot. They do not seem to feel the need for it.

One day the Fathers gathered the Gbaya of the mission together so they could elect a president. A woman was chosen. She lives with a relative who is a leper. She talks a lot about God. She always pays attention to giving alms. When she learns that someone has had a misfortune, she says, 'Doesn't that also come from God?' Is there an illness? For her, that too is something from God. In that way, her thoughts are far from those of her Gbaya brothers and sisters. For them, all illnesses come from someone who 'made the medicine'. If a sick person dies, they say he was 'eaten', and they try to find out who did it. In order to find the guilty one, they'll go to the point of beating the husband or wife of the dead person. These old customs are pagan, but the Gbaya who've become Christians do not abandon them. Those Gbaya who've become Muslims are no better. Neither the Christian religion nor the Muslim religion can eradicate these customs. On the other hand, that woman I spoke about always said, no matter what happened, 'That's what God planned! That's what God wanted!'

There is another religion of the Whites like the religion of the Fathers: the religion of the Americans. It's said the religions are similar. In Doumba, it's particularly the Kongo who follow the religion of the Americans. There you find true believers, people who really pray. They gather often to pray. But that does not prevent them from drinking wine and eating anything they want.

When I was in Doumba, their mission was directed by an old American and his wife who was just as old. They were well liked. He was called Baba (father), and she was called Dada (mother). They got along well with the Fathers and the Sisters. They invited each other for meals from time to time, first at one house and then at the other. I was there when the old couple finally returned to America. The man was replaced by a black pastor. That's not the same. This new pastor has nothing to offer, no free rides in the mission jeep, no old clothing, no this, no that . . . He does not seem to be very useful to the converted Gbaya. In their eyes, he does not have any prestige! Anyway, since he's been there, there's less coming and going to the mission. That's how it is, and not otherwise.

Within one family there are often people who follow a religion and others who are called 'pagans'. They are not Muslims and they have not chosen another religion, neither that of the Fathers nor that of the Americans. They're nothing; they're only 'pagans'. I do not know if there's a Great One who unites the pagans. People I know like that are usually young people. You cannot say they haven't ever heard about God because they certainly see some of their relatives and friends going to the houses of prayer. But religion does not interest them. They have no desire to go along.

The life of a family is not simple when some children are Muslims and others belong to another religion. There was a boy of the mission whose older brother was a Muslim. The younger boy came to his brother's house for food because he was hungry. One day I saw the older brother refuse to give his younger brother food. 'No, I won't let you eat with me; I'm a Muslim and you're not. You no longer have anything in common with me; even if I die, you'll inherit nothing from me, and from this time on I refuse to inherit anything from you. If you're hungry, go to the mission to get your food!' More than one Christian cannot resist and, so life will be less complicated, he decides it's better for him to practise the religion of Mohammed. From that point on, everyone knows he's become a Muslim . . . but everyone also knows that nothing will be changed in his life!

The Fulbe are always praising their religion. For them, it is the greatest, the only truth. 'Those who go to the mission should be pitied!' they say. 'They're lost people, condemned to the fire of hell. There's only one true religion, the religion of Mohammed. Only he who believes in it has his salvation assured. Issa (Jesus) will come back to earth, like the Christians say. He'll re-establish his kingdom. But he'll only do it after he's become a Muslim and has gone to Mecca. And he'll have no pity on those people of the mission. They'll be treated like the pagans; he'll slaughter them mercilessly!' At least that's what Muslims around me say.

But in the end, to understand the relationship between Issa and Mohammed, you must ask those who've studied the religions.

The Muslims I know have not had a lot of instruction; they cannot accept a Muslim becoming a Christian. They reject him. His family renounces him. For everyone, he is like carrion.

Among ourselves, we often talk about Allah. Opportunities are not lacking. Here's an example of a discussion I just had. There were several of us seated under a thatched shelter which shades the vendors on market day. Our conversation was suddenly diverted when a woman passed on the road. Someone said to his neighbour, 'Hey, my friend! Stop looking at the bottom of that woman who's passing! That's bad. It's a sin.'

Another started to respond, 'Hasn't God said that . . .'

But while he was searching for words, a third man – one of those who thinks he knows more than the others – interrupted. 'God said: "When you see someone else's wife pass in front of you, don't look any longer than one minute. That would be bad; that would be a sin. If you prolong your stare at her, you're committing adultery in your heart." That's what it says in our Book. And do you know what God said to do in such a case? If that happens – look at the woman, watch her well and then turn away. Look at her again; observe her well. Do that a third time.

Why? It's also God who told us this: "When you act in this way, you're only think-ing about her height, the colour of her clothes, the kind of shoes she has on." Who knows? Maybe it's a woman running away whose husband is looking for her. And it could happen that the husband, following her footsteps, would ask you, "Haven't you seen a woman go by?" "Yes, I saw a woman passing by. This is what she looked like . . ." "Thank you, that's my wife." And thanks to you, he quickly catches his wife and takes her back to the house!'

When he'd finished his long discourse, I heard someone – who knew nothing – say, 'That's rubbish, all of it! Where have you heard someone preach like that?'

'I heard it was in the Book.'

'No, that's not true! It's not in the Book. Give me the name of the *mallam* who told you that!' And finally everyone started talking, including a Gbaya near me whose breath stank of alcohol!

It seems to me that we Muslims, when we're together, talk about God more often than Christians do.

Figure 26.1: Ndudi Umaru and one of his brothers

Figure 26.2: Ndudi Umaru and Henri Bocquené

CHAPTER 27

Family Visits

In Garoua: Various Incidents

During my long stay in Doumba-Djohong, I had occasion to visit my family whose herds moved with the seasons here and there around Garoua. I'd try to find a ride to Meiganga or to Ngaoundere. But from there on, I had to take a bus in order to get to Garoua. When I'd get there, I'd have no trouble finding my family's whereabouts. Sometimes I'd arrive at their camp the same day, after a walk of an hour or two.

On one of these visits, I was involved in a sad incident: the accidental death of a young Mbororo about twenty years old. He'd fallen dead, killed outright, when hit by a *suka* during a clandestine *soro*, a *soro* which was more like a stick fight than a game played according to the rules. This had happened near my relatives' village.

The victim's family immediately considered this to be the result of sorcery perpetrated by the opposing clan. There was talk about a stick which had been treated with magic. And so, to avenge the death and to make trouble for the murderer's family, the victim's family decided to turn the affair over to the police. They refused to bury their dead son until the affair had been straightened out.

What an idea! I could not help telling them, 'You're very wrong to have the police come. They only have contempt for us Mbororo. Let's bury our dead. Don't let his body rot in the sun!' I argued insistently, trying to get them to agree with me. Wasted time!

'What do you know about our business, Ndudi?'

'The police are hard on the villagers; they'll be even harder on us. Just wait and see how they'll take your wealth, as well as the wealth of the murderer's family!' No matter how many times I said the police would have no pity on them, they did not listen to me. Some people even looked at me like I was crazy.

The next morning, before the sun was too high, I decided to shave the dead man's head. It would not be right to bury this Mbororo with his *suka* braids. Then the cadaver began to bloat; it quickly decomposed because of the heat. I was sitting beside the body, along with the young man's father who had been summoned.

During that time some men from the man's clan visited all the surrounding villages, offering money to anyone who held any authority. Some others had already gone to the *lamido* to offer him cattle. The members of the family who stayed behind – all the women – were mourning.

Two men on horseback appeared. They were the *lamido*'s horsemen. They took away the two fathers, the father of the dead man and the father of the murderer. Then we did not see anyone further.

It was the next day before the police arrived. They came in a car because this all happened near a bush road, which was passable in that season. Unaccustomed to the odour, they stopped a long way off and took care to park their car upwind. They quickly said, 'Bury him!' without even asking to see the cadaver, which was covered by a mat.

Then, while standing off to one side, they signalled for one Mbororo after another to come speak with them. They avoided talking to two witnesses at the same time. They exchanged a few words with each one and then asked him to go back to his place. You could quickly guess the gist of the conversation; it was said the police received a lot of money. All this for what? For nothing. The father of the murderer – against whom the parents of the dead man were seeking revenge – was not even imprisoned. He had been free to move around the *lamido*'s village. Two days later he came back to his family.

A few days later, Ardo Jalel, one of my paternal uncles, reflected on what had happened in the presence of all the men assembled. 'Remember what Ndudi told us: "Let's not get involved with the police, who think we're worthless. Let's quickly bury our dead before he rots." Wasn't Ndudi right? But you didn't want to listen to him. Look at what happened: we buried our dead without the purification rites which our religion requires, without prayers. We did nothing for him that should be done for the dead.' Then, turning toward the victim's father, he said, 'How much money did you spend? I'm told it was more than ninety thousand francs. To one sad event – the loss of your son – all you did was add another – the loss of your wealth. And that didn't prevent the father of the one who killed your son from coming back to his home without even spending one day in prison!' He ended by saying, 'We should have listened to Ndudi. He's travelled a lot. He knows the world better than we do.'

That same year an old Mbororo woman was hit by a motorcyclist in the middle of Garoua. I was a witness. It was the day I was returning to Ngaoundere with my new wife Alima, the daughter of my maternal aunt.

The old woman's head had struck the pavement violently. She seemed dead. A little girl was crying and lamenting near her. People gathered. A car took her to the hospital.

When she'd gone, someone regretted not having called a policeman who would have made an *anket* (*enquête*, investigation). Someone else immediately responded, 'An investigation for whom? Why have an investigation? Isn't she a Mbororo? What are those people? Less than nothing! They're like wild animals.'

I was there and I was listening. These words made my blood boil. I stepped in front of the man who'd just insulted us. 'Dear Mallam, pardon me ... Do not leave, please. I have a few words to say to you.' He did not move. He never imagined the person talking to him was a Mbororo. 'Concerning what you just said, I believe the fear of God does not live in your heart. That old woman who you just ranked with the wild animals, isn't she a child of Adam like yourself? Doesn't she have life like you do? The same life you have? Why despise her? She said nothing to you. She did nothing to you, nothing bad! It isn't that woman, the Mbororo, who will throw you on the fire of hell. It is God himself.' The man could not respond.

A witness to the scene agreed with what I'd said. 'What you said is true.'

I continued, 'Please, don't speak any more about the Mbororo in words of contempt like you just did. Don't forget to have pity on every son of Adam who suffers, especially when his life is threatened. For all of us, whoever we may be, there's nothing more precious than life. Are you the only son of Adam who will not die?' The man left without opening his mouth.

Strangers, Everywhere and for Always

No matter where we are, no respect is given to us Mbororo. How can that be explained? We are people without a village and without a country; we are illiterates who know little about our religion and nothing about things of the world. People fear us only because of our knowledge of magic.

What if a Mbororo presents himself at the door of a *sare*? He politely announces himself with the usual phrase: *Salam aleykum!*[1] Alerted by that greeting, the master of the house sends his son to see who's there. If the boy comes back saying, 'It's a Mbororo!' he'll hear this response, 'Forget it! A Mbororo? Who receives a Mbororo?'

That's our curse, we people of the bush, nomads without education. We're just good for being exploited in all places and by everyone! Wherever we are, we're strangers. Wherever one nomad sets up camp, he's one too many. He comes from somewhere else; he should have stayed there!

Is there a 'homeland' for the Mbororo? Where is this Mali which the Mbororo often consider to be the country of their most ancient ancestors? They have only a vague idea. But they know in olden times there was only one race of Fulani. It was later they split into different clans.

I've heard it was the great Shehu Usumanu who organised the Fulani in order to conquer the pagans for Islam. He gave his banners to the Fulani to be used in the countries they subdued. It's said a large group of those Fulani refused to be recruited; they were the Mbororo. They did not participate in the holy war. They loved their cattle more than religion. That's the reason some Fulbe have an irrational scorn for us.

Go to School?

What should we do? Increase the number of Koranic schools? That isn't enough. We have to try to combine in ourselves knowledge of God and knowledge of the world. If knowledge of God assures us of happiness in the other life, knowledge of the world can save us from the miseries which are the common lot of people on earth. Therefore we should go to the school of the Whites so we can acquire their knowledge. That school is open to everyone without discrimination.

But up to this point, the Mbororo have always run away from that school. For them, there's practically no difference between the government school and the mission school. One is just as bad as the other. All Mbororo have it in their heads that their children who go to school will be lost because they'll quickly lose interest in the life they have been leading, the life their fathers have always led. They would never be herders again! And if they were at school, who would replace them? Who would remove ticks from the animals, tie up the calves, lead the herd to the watering hole, guard the cattle and render those thousand-and-one services which we count on them doing?

The Mbororo add, 'Don't you see what's happening around us? All those little Gbaya who go to school, what becomes of them? They look down on their parents too much to stay with them. They think it's better to look for work in the towns when they aren't lucky enough to find a post as a government official!'

The elders know all this. They also know their children want to go to school so they can learn to drive a truck or a bus, play football – and who knows what else? They would often say as much to the Para who, in a sense, agreed with them, but always ended his remarks by saying, 'Yes, what you say is true, but the world is changing.'

'Ah, yes,' they concluded, nodding their heads, 'the world is changing!'

However, the Para tried to prove to them that their children could learn to read and write very well – at least that – without leaving their homes, without mixing with those Gbaya they were afraid of. One day he called some Kongo men who, in return for a thousand francs, built him a shelter: a thatched roof on posts. This was the school of the Mbororo, the freest school in the world, the Para said. He chose its location at an equal distance between many camps, in the middle of the bush, right in the midst of the pastures and the herds.

Some boys arrived. They came out of curiosity. The Para began by asking them if they would not prefer to read and write their own language rather than French, which they did not understand at all. They all refused. 'How would that help us when we go to the towns?' They were certainly thinking about their drivers' licenses!

That attempt did not go very far. The parents, encouraged by the Fulbe, could never get rid of their mistrust of the Para. 'It is,' they said, 'a way to win our children over to the mission!' No matter how much he said he would not touch their religion or their customs, they did not believe him. So in the end, he let the termites eat the posts.

'When you want a school,' he let them know, 'tell me so by giving me a list of the children you want taught. If you refuse, that's your right. Let's not talk about it any more. You're free.' Today they understand better and they know that he did not come to their camp to 'have' them!

But the result is that the Mbororo of Djohong and its surrounding area still do not go to school. Outwardly, they seem more advanced today with their clean clothes, sunglasses and salamander.[2] But they are not any less ignorant than they've always been. That's what they're considered by the farmers' sons who go to the three schools in Djohong (the Protestant school, the Catholic school and – now – the government school). And that's how they're treated by people in offices.

Recently a Mbororo complained to the Para that he'd been forced to pay four thousand francs to a policeman because he could not show his identity card; he'd never had one! 'How much did you pay?' the Para asked him.

'Four thousand francs! Look at the paper he gave me.' The Para took the paper and read it: 'Two thousand francs.'

Just recently I myself suffered from my lack of knowledge. I'd become acquainted with a Mbororo from Bamenda who lived near me. He spoke English very well, but not French; besides that, he was a complete stranger in Ngaoundere. He'd been foolish enough to loan fifty thousand francs to a butcher. When he understood that he would never retrieve that money, he decided – on my advice – to make a formal complaint. I accompanied him to the police.

As soon as I'd said two words in Fulfulde,[3] I was curtly interrupted. 'We speak French here. If you aren't capable, go away!'

'Ah, good!' I said to them – still in Fulfulde, which some of them certainly understood. 'I hear what you say. Anyone is authorised to steal from someone who doesn't speak French! Should I let myself be killed because I don't speak French?' And with that, I left them, ashamed to have been turned away like that before the eyes of my friend.

The Para and I

I could have told them I wasn't illiterate – I can read and write – but what good would it have done? That day I wanted to ask the Para why he had not taught me French during the ten years I've lived with him. How does it help me today to read and write in my own language?[4] How does it help me to know there are rules to be followed for speaking correctly – rules which are called grammar, with nouns and verbs?

It is a fact that the Para and I have never exchanged a single word in French. He certainly has not forbidden me to learn his language, but I would have to learn it by myself. But in my neighbourhood, only Fulfulde is spoken. However, those who know me know that my gift of imitation allows me to speak the way the French do, without really understanding what I'm saying; the way the British do too; and even like the Indians, whose accent – according to the films I've seen at the cinema – is very close to that of the Mbororo.

It's also a fact that our relationship concerning our religious feelings – mine as a Muslim and his as a Catholic missionary – has never changed.

It pleases me to end this long story – where I've said some pleasant things and some sad things, but everything I've said is true – with the following declaration.

The people of the section of Ngaoundere where I've lived for several years now think I belong to the mission (that is, they think I've converted to Catholicism). Nevertheless they see me regularly praying like a Muslim. I let them talk. It amuses me to see them shake their heads pensively, as if they were saying, 'The poor man! He's lost!' The truth is just the opposite. Never, a big never – I repeat it – the Para has never tried to make me join the mission. He has never once directed our conversation to that subject. He knows very well it's in someone's heart that such a resolution must be born.

So what touched the heart of my friend Pita, a Mbororo from Nigeria, a leper like me? What touched the heart of Ibrahim, a Jafun from near Djohong? Both of them are married, they have children and they live at the Protestant Mission in Ngaoundere. They are announcers for the radio programme 'Sawtu Linjila', 'the Voice of the Gospel', which transmits in the Fulani language all over Africa.

What touched the hearts of Zae and his wife? I met this Zae two years ago here in Ngaoundere, and we've become good friends. Each time we meet, we argue, calling each other 'hypocrites'. Zae wants me to do what he did: stop praying like a Muslim so I can pray with him like a Christian. Zae says Jesus spoke to him in the midst of a great light which made him invisible. Jesus asked him to learn about the Path of Christians. For many years, he resisted that call. Then one day, he 'surrendered', as he says. After many years of studies in a Bible school in Nigeria, he has become a pastor. And now with his wife and a young woman from France, he's trying, as he says, to 'share the joy of following Jesus with the Mbororo'.

But according to what people tell me, the Mbororo of the Central African Republic – where Zae's pasturing his herd – do not want to hear anything about that. He was even beaten until he was nearly dead and imprisoned in an isolated place from which he escaped.

Zae knows very well that I do not want to follow him either. I've always told him I'm happy and proud to listen to Mohammed. For the long time I've lived with Christians, I've never thought of asking them questions about their religion. How do they pray? What do they think about sin? Do they have a heaven and a hell?

The little I know about them I've learned from Christian books written in the Fulani language: *Alkawal Kesal* and *Alkawal Kidngal* (the New Testament and the Old Testament). I practised my reading with those books. There weren't any others! I admit I've read them with pleasure and that I'll continue to do so.

This is my witness. All that is contrary is pure invention.

In this account of my life up to this point, I've always tried to be faithful to the truth. If I've twisted anything, it's been in spite of myself. May God pardon me.

All along the path which comes to an end today, God has helped us, the Para and me. May He be thanked!

My first words were: *Bissimillahi*![5] May my last words be: *Alhamdu lillahi*! *Amina*![6]

End Notes

Chapter 1

1 Termites build mounds of dirt which can be up to two meters in height. For the Mbororo, termite hills are places where spirits dwell. Parents warn their children not to play on these mounds.

2 The rhythm of a Muslim's liturgical day is determined by the five prayers. The following list of these prayers gives the approximate prayer times in the Adamawa area, where the hours of sunrise and sunset vary little throughout the year:

subaha	about 5 a.m.
jura	about 1:30 p.m.
asiri	about 3:30 p.m.
mangariba	about 6:30 p.m.
esa'i	from 7 p.m. to 5 a.m.

3 *Jabbi: Tamarindus indica.* The wood of the tamarind tree is often used for carpentry. Its bark contains a dye. An infusion made from the bark cures diarrhoea.

4 The *dado* is a place set a little apart where the men meet to take their meals in common and hold their evening discussions.

5 Until recently, the only containers used by the Mbororo were calabashes. These gourds are made from the fruit of a plant in the pumpkin family. Their pulp cannot be eaten. When cleaned out, dried and sometimes artistically decorated, they are traded from northern Nigeria toward the more remote cattle-herding areas in neighbouring countries like Cameroon. Mbororo women carefully look after them, especially those which are intended for selling milk. Because they are used for milk, these calabashes are highly valued.

6 Ndudi employs the term *Fulbe* here to refer to sedentary Fulani in contrast to the pastoral Fulani, or Mbororo. The Fulbe are viewed as being more committed to the practice of Islam than the Mbororo.

7 This term *pulaku* appears over and over in Ndudi's story. It is an abstract term, based on the root *Pul-* (Fulani). *Pulaku* refers to the essence of the Fulani way of life, the epitome of their cultural values. Ndudi devotes a whole chapter to a discussion of this quality.

8 The word *Kado* (plural *Habe*) denotes first of all a non-Fulani: that is, anyone who does

not have the honour of being subject to the code of *pulaku*. *Kado* is also synonymous with 'pagan' and 'animist'. In certain contexts, it can be translated as 'farmer' or even 'clodhopper'. In that case, it carries a pejorative meaning which is scarcely disguised. There are many conflicts between these *Habe* and the Mbororo, between the farmers and the cattlemen. Ndudi has amused himself by depicting for us their mutual distrust.

9   Parallel cousins are children whose fathers are brothers or whose mothers are sisters. If the mother of one cousin and the father of another cousin are brother and sister, these cousins are called cross cousins. Note that the singular of parallel cousin is *derdirawo* and the plural is *derdirabe*. It follows the same pattern for cross cousins; the singular is *dendirawo* and the plural is *dendirabe*.

Chapter 2

1   This staple porridge is a stiff doughy mass made from the flour of millet, manioc, or maize and shaped into a ball.

2   *Barkehi: Piliostigma reticulata*. The bark of this bush is used for making cord; the bark of the roots has a reddish-brown colour and is used for medicinal infusions.

3   This passage offers an example of the oral style of the Fulani. There are a number of such examples in this story.

4   For a Muslim, an animal is unfit for consumption unless it has been killed by having its throat cut, accompanied by a ritual invocation. When this has not been done, the meat is considered carrion. The owner cannot sell it, give it away, or exchange it. The meat belongs to the first non-Muslim who comes along, although he would not take it before the owner had acknowledged the death. This is true for any Mbororo, no matter what his degree of Islamisation.

5   The clan may be thought of as a large patrilineal kinship group under the responsibility of a leader, called the *ardo* (the one who walks ahead). In the Adamawa region, there are three large groups of clans: the Jafun, the first to arrive at the beginning of the century; the Aku, who followed nearly a half a century later; and the Wodabe (different from those of Niger, though they have a common origin). Each of these groups is made up of a large number of clans that are not geographically localised. It is at the level of each clan that an *ardo* exercises his authority as leader. There is no *ardo* whose authority is superior to the rest.

6   The *soro* is a contest among adolescents that is intended to display their qualities of *pulaku* – in particular, their courage and endurance. Chapter 13 is devoted to a description of the *soro*.

7   The word *suka* refers to the youth who, as Ndudi says, only worry about their braids and about girls at this stage of life.

8   To ask for the thing' is synonymous with the expression Ndudi uses later on: 'to ask a girl for her favour'. At this age, he tells us, 'It is only an amusement without consequence.' He will have occasion to explain this further.

9   *Bakurehi: Nauclea latifolia*, (cf. *Sarcocephalus esculentus*). This tree resembles a fig tree; the leaves are shiny; the flowers are white and spherical; the fruit is also spherical and has many seeds. Its hard wood is good for making mortars. The fruit, which is edible, cures haemorrhoids and female illnesses.

10 *Alali: Securidaca longipedunculata*. This bush has a thin trunk and branches; the leaves are dark green; the flowers are purple and have a scent; the oil-producing seeds look like parachutes; the roots are purgative.

Chapter 3

1 For those who are not content to divide the year into two seasons – the dry season (from mid-November to mid-March) and the rainy season (from mid-March to mid-November) – the annual cycle is as follows:

> *ndungu*: the rainy season;

> *yamnde*: the harvest at the end of the rains;

> *dabunde*: the first part of the dry season - sunny with cold mornings;

> *sedu*: the second part of the dry season - sunny and very hot;

> *guleli*: the third part of the dry season - stormy;

> *seto*: the first rains.

In the Adamawa area, this annual cycle is very consistent. In the North near Garoua, there is a great variation in this calendar.

2 *Yafi* is a form of magic that is used for many purposes. A Muslim who practises it does so with a bad conscience because he must work with unclean objects. He must also believe in the efficacy of the words and of the gestures themselves, without reference to God. However, some try to justify themselves by saying, 'This will only work if God wants it to.'

3 There will be many references to *karfa* in the first chapters of this story. This powder is mixed with salt and used to make the cattle wild, nervous and difficult to control. This word also designates the magic process used to provoke a quarrel between two lovers or a disagreement between a man and his wife. Cf. Chapter 14, Note 4.

4 Measures of millet are sold in a small cup of a standard size. It equals about 800 grams (1.75 pounds).

5 Here are some figures on Mbororo milk production. They are derived from a report on 'The production and sale of milk in the Meiganga region' by Dr Albert Doufissa, head of the Animal Husbandry Unit for the Department of the Mbere at Meiganga. 'The cattle numbers per herd varied from 10 to 144, with an average of 59 head. In this average herd, there were only six cows in milk on average, four of which were milked per day to give an average total yield of 9.79 litres or 1.54 litres per cow.' The price of milk (in 1987 prices) was 150 CFA francs per litre (approximately $0.45) and the price of butter was 1,500 CFA francs per kilogram ($4.50).

6 *Barka* comes from the Arabic word *baraka* (blessing) and is synonymous with it.

7 According to the meticulous study done in 1987 by Dr Albert Doufissa, veterinarian in Meiganga, the quantity of milk produced per cow is about 1.54 litres per day, with an average of 6.4 milk cows per herd. Therefore, a woman selling milk has about 10 litres which she uses as follows: 80% for butter, 7% for whipped yogurt, 7% for sour milk and 3% for fresh milk.

8   When a young man leaves the *suka* age group, he enters the *kori* age group. The first group is between 15 and 25 years of age; it is the time of hair braids and the *soro*. The second group, which ends at about age 30, is particularly known for the rude behaviour which they display at their big gatherings.

9   To have recourse to 'black medicines' is to use plants, leaves, bark and roots - anything from the vegetable kingdom. 'Tree' and 'medicine' are the same noun in Fulfulde: *lekki* (*ledde* in the plural).

Chapter 4

1   The phrase 'to swallow a tooth' means to display an intense admiration, right up to the point of swooning.

2   Favours: See Chapter 2, Note 8. It would be more accurate to translate this as: Will you and I have … ?

3   See the legend of 'The Black Bull', in Chapter 10.

Chapter 5

1   *Bobori: Sterculia setigera*. This is a small tree with thin, reddish bark; the leaves are light green; the fruit is in long, pointed pods which are covered with greenish down; the seeds are reddish; the bark produces a gum.

2   *Sadaka*: In the religious context of the Koran, this word corresponds to our almsgiving. The person giving such a gift always does so with a more or less explicit religious intention. In any case, *sadaka* is always different from a simple gift.

3   A *lamido* is a paramount Fulani chief or emir.

Chapter 6

1   There are many forms of leprosy; Ndudi's is called lepromatous leprosy. It requires care for life.

2   *Gabdi: Acacia scoprioides, arabica* or *nilotica*, (cf. *Mimosa egyptica*). A small tree with spiny trunk and branches. Its pods are used for dyeing and tanning leather.

3   *Sabuli gorki: Ximenia americana*, the wild cherry-plum tree.

4   Boys are circumcised around the age of seven. In spite of appearances, circumcision has a certain religious significance, serving to distinguish the boys from the uncircumcised pagans.

5   *Sobal* is millet dough shaped by hand into balls. The balls are eaten after being broken up into the sour milk.

6   *Buteru* is the name given to the hut of the head of the family.

Chapter 7

1   The bush is nature in its wild state. Its unknown and mysterious character always causes a certain concern, even for those who - like the Mbororo - decide to live there. There is always a deep-bush which the Mbororo imagine is populated by evil spirits (*ginaji*). Before going there, the Mbororo feel a need to protect themselves by using magical charms. One such practice involves having a *mallam* spit his saliva on their bodies as he recites verses or other phrases.

     The appearance of the African bush is quite varied. For Ndudi and the nomadic cattle-men he describes, particularly those from Adamawa, it is a semi-wooded savanna. The land is covered by tall grasses in the wet season, which are burned by the hot sun and by bush fires in the dry season. In this monotonous terrain, it is very difficult to find landmarks.

2   Vulgar carrion: See Chapter 2, Note 4.

3   *Pam*: Under British influence, the Nigerian currency was the pound (which became '*pam*'). One pound was then worth 1,000 CFA or 20 French francs (about $3). Later, the present-day money was introduced, based on the *naira*. Three or four naira were exchanged at that time for 1,000 CFA (20 French francs or about $3).

4   *Nassara* refers to the Christians and, by extension, the 'Whites', without doubt because it is assumed they follow Jesus of Nazareth.

5   That is, wild pigs or – more precisely – wart hogs.

Chapter 8

1   *Karehi*: *Butyrospermum parkii*, the shea butter tree, whose nuts makes a well-liked oil.

2   '*Mallam*' is the title which is awarded to a student at the end of his Koranic studies. These studies vary in length according to the diligence and capabilities of each student. The best end their study after three years. Finishing school is the occasion for a family assembly, the *doa*. Guests are extremely generous and, at the end of the day, the young *mallam* is given many head of cattle and sometimes a large sum of money. Many students stop their studies at that point and 'put down their slates'. Some teach themselves to be teachers. Others will try to earn money from their knowledge through different practices which are more or less orthodox.

     A few students will continue their studies, deepening their knowledge of the Arabic language. After a number of years of individual study and schooling with respected teachers, these men become the experts of Koranic knowledge and, naturally, accede to the prestigious title of *modibo*. It is the *modibo* who is asked for interpretations of certain Koranic passages and solutions to legal and ethical cases. It is from this same circle of learned men that is chosen the *imam*, who is responsible for leading prayers in the mosque and commenting on Koranic verses.

3   Baptism: This word is sometimes used by certain Christians who live near the Mbororo.

4   *Alfatiya*: This is the title of the first chapter (*sura*) of the Koran, which is pronounced here as a final invocation.

5   Names: In the course of his life, each Mbororo is endowed with four names:

The name of the Book (Koran): this is called the 'big name'. It is given by the *mallam* on the day of the name-giving ceremony: Musa (Moses), Yusufu (Joseph), Adamu (Adam), Hawa (Eve), Mayrama (Mary).

The birth name: this is related to circumstances of the time or place of the birth – Sippi (a child born while milk is being sold), Veti (born at dawn), Eggi (born during the seasonal migration), etc.

The *suka* name: Silal (a fish net), Lewrujo (the face of the moon); for girls: Jabire (morning star), Inndia (beautiful as an Indian), Alijabet (Elizabeth, the Queen of England).

The *kori* name: this is a coarse nickname, always dealing with sex. Decency does not permit citing even one example.

6   Ndudi was given his name to honour a passer-by named Ndudi. This name evokes the idea of the wind which precedes the storm.

7   *Makama*: This is a Hausa title which designates the leader of the food distribution in such circumstances.

Chapter 9

1   The Ibo, who numbered eight million, were grouped in south-eastern Nigeria, in the region which was called Biafra during the Nigerian civil war. They were also numerous in the North where they were called the Nyamiri. The name Nyamiri has no particular significance.

2   The reader may recognise certain italicised words as sounding like French. Ndudi uses them, even though he does not speak the French language.

For example: *nivakin* (Nivaquine, a common brand of quinine), *garmofon* (gramophone), *tourne-disque* (record player), *missio* (mission), *singa* (Singer sewing machine), *koudata* (coup d'état), *bomb*, *boy*, *telefon* (telephone), *colonel*, *batalya* (battalion), *gouroup* (group), *gernet* (grenade), *lespor* (sports), *marto* (hammer), *persidan* (president), *nuvote* (novelty), *ler* (air), *bank*, *sepdedisterik* (chief of the district), *sufrefet* (sub-prefect, government administrator of a part of a state), *ser-docta* (Catholic nursing-sister), *tourne* (tour), *anket* (inquiry), *katasit* (catechist), *ampul* (vial) and often heard is *para* (priest).

3   Within a few lines in this section, there is a double meaning to the word 'begging'. The first, practised by the Koranic school students (*almajiri*), is more or less a ritual. Certainly it is very much appreciated by the teacher because the cost of the food he must give his students is therefore diminished. But it is also meant to remind rich people of their duty to share with those who are hungry: 'Do not forget to give alms.' This begging is practised without shame.

The second type of begging is that of a really poor man who has nothing to eat. Ndudi, as a Fulani, is ashamed of this, at least to begin with.

Chapter 10

1   Musical instruments are not numerous among the Mbororo. Aside from flutes and reed pipes (*dudandu*), which are made from plant stems and are short-lived, you can say there are only two instruments: the armpit drum and the monochord guitar. The armpit drum (*mbagu*) is deeply concave in the middle, which allows the drummer to press with his elbow, using varying degrees of tension, the strings that are attached to the stretched antelope skin head, to modify the drum's resonance. The *garaya*, a type of guitar, is made from half of a small oblong calabash that has been cut lengthways and covered with a skin. It is equipped with a single nylon string. The tension is regulated by loosening or tightening the string, which runs along a stick that protrudes from the calabash. At the end of the arm of the *garaya* hang pieces of light metal which make a rattling noise. The player plucks the string with the tips of his fingers, or sometimes with his knuckles. Ndudi plays exceptionally well.

2   I asked Ndudi to give a commentary about these spirits, which seem so strange to us and which are so familiar to him. See the appendix at the end of this chapter.

We already know that these *ginaji* are the *jinns* of the Arab tradition. We can also translate this as 'genies'. All animists tend to turn to such spirits when they try to explain why things happen, especially things which are surprising. Termite hills, as we have seen, are the habitation of spirits because of a strange phenomenon which must be explained: how can termites build their hills with wet earth when they are sometimes working in earth that is completely dry, without the least drop of water in the vicinity?

3   Ndudi's description of Yunusa's and Gogo's illnesses, and especially of their healing through dance and music therapy, strangely recalls the phenomenon of tarantism, in which the desire to dance is contagious. Seeing a sick person in a state of crisis encourages the spectators to dance. The illness is treated by music.

4   Ndudi explains elsewhere that the *boka* are people who have been possessed by the spirits, as his brother Yunusa was. Once 'exorcised', the possessed are freed from that which was evil in them. Only the good is left: the gift of divination, the art of conjuring, the knowledge of medicinal plants and the ability to chase away the evil spirits.

5   Parents prefer to choose a wife (the word used is *debbo*) for their son from one of the following categories of relatives:

The daughter of his paternal uncle, *bappanyo*, i.e., his father's brother,

The daughter of his paternal aunt, his father's sister (*gogo*),

The daughter of his maternal uncle, his mother's brother (*kao*)

But never the daughter of his maternal aunt, his mother's sister (*yapendo*).

6   When asked about the places he had stopped during the migrations he had made since he was born, Ardo Seni, a Jafun from the Autanko clan, listed without hesitation all the villages near which he had spent one or more rainy seasons. I made a list: Tignere (2 years), Tibati (1 year), Banyo (2 years), Ngaoundere (4 years), Tignere (7 years), Ngaoundere (10 years), etc. Long ago he had told me his age, which corresponded exactly with the number of years he had enumerated. He was 77 years old.

7   *Bariki* and *gomna* are terms borrowed from Hausa, which in turn had borrowed them from the English words 'barracks' and 'governor'.

8   The word 'to eat' is frequently used to mean exploit, deceive or dupe. It is also the most adequate term to describe the action of a sorcerer who 'eats' the 'double' of his victim. This meaning of 'eat' is so strong that its usage in the normal sense is avoided. Some people prefer to say they 'drink' their meat.

Chapter 11

1   This word *wuro nagge* is the name of a place: 'town' (*wuro*) and 'cow' (*nagge*). It is the 'town of the cow'.

Chapter 12

1   Among the Fulbe, the *sare* is the family space which is surrounded by a circular or rectangular fence. The fence, which is about as tall as a man, is made of woven straw or mud. A modern *sare* has thick walls with cement plastering. Inside this wall there are as many houses as the owner has wives. A single entrance gives access. This is the *jauleru*, the entry house where visitors are received. A Mbororo habitation does not have a fence.

2   This compound Hausa word means 'prevent from sleeping'. *Anabarsi* is a pharmaceutical product, the effects of which are close to those of amphetamines.

3   *Kabihi: Commiphora* sp. (*africana?*). This is a small, thorny tree with spherical, green fruit that have a sour pulp.

4   This condiment occupies an important place in the diet of the Mbororo. It improves sauces, giving them a particular taste which resembles that of bouillon (Maggi) cubes, to the point that the words 'Maggi' and *daddawa* have become synonymous. *Daddawa* is shaped like a small cake about the size of the palm of the hand. This condiment is laboriously made from the seeds of the *narehi*, a tree with pods. Its scientific name is *Parkia filicoides* or *P. clappertoniana*.

5   *Serip*, also pronounced *serif* or *cherif*, is a kind of superior marabout who claims descent from the Prophet and, on the basis of this title, claims special honours.

Chapter 13

1   *Dingali: Gardenia triacantha*. This is a small tree with strong, short branches with leaves at their tips; it has fragrant, creamy-white flowers and yellow, egg-shaped fruit; its ashes are used for medicine.

2   This Hausa word means 'young beard'. *Sabon-gemu* is the age at which the *koraku* ends, about thirty years old. By that age, a man is supposed to have become conscientious about his responsibilities toward family and clan. Coming next is the class of the *ndottaku*, the full blossoming of personality. This comes just before the first signs of old age, *dayeku*, which is considered by the Mbororo to be the age of grandeur.

3　This refers to Indian hemp.

4　Shehu Usumanu is better known as Usman dan Fodio. Originally from the Senegalese Futa-Toro, he was born in 1754. He first led the life of a wandering preacher. Then, after 1804, he sent twelve of his most faithful disciples, his 'standard bearers', to conquer the Hausa states. In 1814, Adama, one of the most famous 'standard bearers', settled in Yola, which is considered to be the origin of the Fulbe emirates, the lamidates, of Adamawa. Many Wodabe tend to consider Shehu Usumanu to be 'the Prophet'.

Chapter 14

1　*Mangariba*: See Chapter 1, Note 2.

2　*La Illa Illa'llah*: 'There is no other god than Allah!'

3　*Kurkuku* or *kurkutu* is the name of an insect that lives in the ground in a hole which seems smaller than the insect's body. Some call it the 'ant-lion'.

4　*Karfa*, cf. Chapter 3, Note 3.

Chapter 15

1　The *kori* play on the phonetic resemblance of these two verbs: *min puuti* and *min tuubi*. The first, *min puuti* means 'we farted' and the second, *min tuubi*, means 'we're sorry'.

2　These specialists in *boka* and *burda* are both magicians. But while the former are supposed to be in connivance with the spirits, the latter are scholars whose magical skill is acquired from books.

3　The Nigerian War, called the Biafran War, lasted thirty months, from 6 July 1967 to 15 January 1970.

4　The Sardauna was a political personality from the Northern Province. He was assassinated by an Ibo officer at the time of the coup d'état of 15 January 1966. To revenge his death, the Hausa Muslims waged a pogrom during which many tens of thousands of Ibo were killed.

5　'Wart hogs' refers to bulldozers, those huge machines which the Mbororo saw excavating the land and pushing the earth in front of them on road and building sites in Nigeria. When the Mbororo saw bulldozers working, they compared them to wart hogs which move the earth with their snouts.

6　Ironsi was the general who, after the bloody coup d'état of 15 January 1966, instituted a predominately Ibo military regime. On 24 May of that same year, he formed a unified state. Riots followed. General Ironsi was captured on 29 July and shot by his Northern officers.

7　After the tragic death of General Ironsi, Lieutenant-Colonel Ojukwu proclaimed himself Supreme Chief of State of Nigeria on national radio. That was 1 August 1966. Then, after a period of great disorder, he proclaimed the Republic of Biafra. He took over the presidency of Biafra and, by doing that, began the war against the rest of Nigeria. The war ended in 1970 with the defeat of the Biafran separatists and the flight of their chief.

8   For the Mbororo, 'knowledge', par excellence, is that which permits a person to have an effect on things, or on the course of events, by means of certain procedures that are often secret. They call this knowledge; we call it magic.

9   See Chapter 13, Note 4 for a discussion of Shehu Usumanu.

Chapter 16

1   The Wojabe form a particular group within the Wodabe clans.

2   *Anabarsi*: see Chapter 12, Note 2.

3   Do not take all Ndudi says about the Wodabe from Niger literally. His opinion is obviously exaggerated. This accumulation of faults and reproaches is a beautiful illustration of the universal phenomenon of ethnic prejudice, even within a human group which seems uniform. 'The smallest differences sustain rivalry between men,' writes Joseph Vendryes in *Le langage* (Albin Michel, p. 226). He continues: 'One might say that once people have formed a group, they look for the most trivial occasions to support their group while opposing others.'

Does Ndudi know that what he criticises about the Wodabe, the town Fulbe extend to all Mbororo in general, and thus to the Jafun, the group Ndudi is a member of? To the town Fulbe, all the Mbororo (without distinction) are descendants of an incestuous origin. The town Fulbe charge them all – Wodabe or not – with all the vices: lying, stealing, casting evil spells, infidelity, impiety … Since recounting this chapter on the Wodabe, Ndudi has had occasion to get to know many Wodabe; some of them – victims of the Sahelian drought – are real refugees from misery. Some pass by fairly regularly each year to sell their medicines. They never fail to come greet their good friend Ndudi, whose company they always enjoy. In spite of these ties of mutual respect, Ndudi holds to all he has said about them. 'They are just the way I judged them in the past. That's still the way my Mbororo brothers judge them and, in general, the way town Fulbe think too.'

Chapter 17

1   Guitar: Cf. Chapter 10, Note 1.

2   *Bambahi* or *babambi: Asclepias gigantea* (Soubko), cf. *Calotropis procera*.

3   *Dakel*, an unidentified snake.

4   *Mai Kura*: This is a compound Hausa word: *mai* (owner, boss) and *kura* (hyena).

Chapter 18

1   As a salary in those days, a herder received a two-year-old cow, a sack of millet or man-

ioc and an outfit of clothing every five months. He could drink all the milk he wanted from the herd, but he and his wife could not sell the cows' milk. Today the salary is paid in cash: 50,000 CFA every five months, 10,000 CFA for food and 5,000 CFA for clothing.

2   The calabash is a unit of measure: 100 kola nuts at an average price per nut of 50 CFA (1 French franc or about $0.15).

3   The title 'mother of the *sare*' is given to the wife who first crossed the threshold of her husband's house. In principle, this first wife has no privileges over the co-wives. Islam demands that a husband avoid all signs of favouritism in his relations with his wives. This obligation is considered by some men to be impossible; some men deliberately choose monogamy for this reason.

4   The *nangaru* is the first stage in Mbororo marriage. The successive stages are discussed in the next chapter.

Chapter 19

1   See the note on preferential marriage, Chapter 10, Note 5.

2   5,000 CFA is 100 French francs (about $15).

3   500 CFA is 10 French francs (about $1.50).

4   See Chapter 8, Note 4.

5   See the note on cross cousins, Chapter 1, Note 9.

Chapter 20

1   The Nigerian pound was worth about 1,000 CFA. Ndudi received 40,000 CFA, equivalent to 800 French francs (about $130).

2   *Hitila*: This nickname was given at that time to a famous bandit. As you see, it comes from the name of Hitler.

3   The phrase in question, repeated endlessly in a rhythm like a litany, is *La Illa Illa'llah* (There is no other god but Allah).

4   This custom, called the levirate, conforms to the Biblical tradition. See Deuteronomy 25:5-10. It recognises the perpetuity of patrilineal descent and the conservation of family wealth.

Chapter 21

1   Ndudi often returns to the subject of religion. The only part of his account given here is that which concerns his personal life history and the impact of Islam on the Mbororo, and on his family in particular. He is obviously preoccupied with trying to understand the world view of his ancestors who did not know Islam, and their concepts of life and death.

What religious value should be attributed to the *ginaji* who inhabit their universe and who the Mbororo try to manipulate with potions and magic words - nowadays with a Koranic veneer - which 'will work, if God wants it to'? There is no reference to a superior *ginaji*, at least not unless it is identified with the heavenly vault (*asama*) toward which they point their finger when they answer the question: 'Where is God?' They hurry to add, 'He looks down on me from up there (*e mo tiima yam*).' As for Ndudi, he considers the existence of God to be self-evident. But does his response come down from the ages or from his Muslim training?

In the course of Ndudi's story, each time we come across the word Allah, we have usually translated it as 'God'. This is no place to have a polemical discussion on this subject because it is clear that in the mouth and the heart of Ndudi, Allah has the same sound as 'God' does for us.

2   This invocation begs for God's pardon: May God pardon me!

3   *Imanaku* is a degree of piety which surpasses simple submission to the will of God (Islam).

4   'Drinking the Scriptures' is a common practice in Africa. A text taken from the Koran or another formula is written on a slate (*alluha*) with ink made from burnt corn thickened with resin. This slate, when covered with writing, is washed. The water is collected in a basin and given as a drink to the client, who is seeking a certain effect relating to the text and conforming to his own expressed intentions. Some write the same phrase up to a thousand times. Others want to drink the whole Koran. They have a *mallam* come to their house; they offer him their hospitality for all the time required, which is about a month. The *mallam* writes assiduously, slate after slate, collecting the water in a bottle which is always at the disposition of his client. For such a 'writing', the honorarium is about 200,000 CFA, that is, 4,000 French francs (about $700).

5   See Chapter 13, Note 4.

6   This phrase can only be fully appreciated by those who know the Fulani language.

Chapter 22

1   Kola nuts, which are fruit of a tree in the Sterculia family, are grouped in clusters of five or six nuts. Each nut can have up to ten seeds, which contain caffeine and theobromine. As medicine, the kola nut is used as a tonic and a stimulant for the nervous system.

In the social life of African people, this nut plays a major role. Its distribution is symbolic of sharing, union and reconciliation. Chewing it habitually produces effects similar to that of a drug.

2   The distinction between parallel cousins and cross cousins is discussed in Chapter 1, Note 9.

Chapter 23

1   *Anabarsi*: See Chapter 12, Note 2.

2   Ndudi often plunges us into a world of magic and sorcery. As much as we feel close to him at a deep psychological level, we nevertheless feel strange in this world of spirits (*ginaji*), magicians (*gardijo*) and sorcerers (*karamajo*) where he seems very much at ease.

As I have already explained, I always abstained from having a frank conversation with him about this chapter, preventing myself from contradicting him in the least bit. I was worried that I might make him self-conscious and might detract from the spontaneity of his words. The scepticism which he sometimes displayed was particularly directed toward certain *mallams* whose practices he thought were dishonest.

3   'To eat': See Chapter 10, Note 8.

Chapter 24

1   The presence of the Germans on the Cameroon coast dates to about 1800. But it was only in 1884 that the German–Douala treaty was signed. It was during the conquest of Gbaya country, in the course of their expedition toward the North (about 1900) that the Germans opened the road which Ndudi travelled between Laka and Batoua.

2   The 163,000 square kilometres of Adamawa in the north and extreme north of Cameroon are populated by more than 2.7 million cattle and 2.4 million people. The herds are essentially composed of long-horned zebus of the Mbororo breed in the north and extreme north and of short-horned zebus of the Fulbe breed in Adamawa. Their very great sensitivity to trypanosomes (sleeping sickness), transmitted by tsetse flies, has restricted their migration southwards toward more equatorial zones.

The herds are regularly decimated by epidemics of rinderpest or bovine pleuropneumonia against which vaccination campaigns have been instituted. The animals are also susceptible to illnesses transmitted by ticks and are affected by tuberculosis, black quarter and anthrax. Hoof-and-mouth disease, brucellosis, dermatophilis and cutaneous nodular disease are endemic. These diseases all carry Fulani names which vary according to region and clan.

Each animal has a name. This name is passed on in the following way to its descendants. If the heifer has the name Bale (the Black One), all its calves will also be called Bale. But to this principal name, which recalls the colour of the mother's coat, a nickname is added relating to a physical peculiarity of the new calf. So you can have Bale-Njotte (Black One – Short Tail). Very quickly this new calf will lose its first name and will only be called Njotte (Short Tail). With this system, it's easy to understand how, at any particular time, there's not necessarily an agreement between the name and the physical characteristics.

Many names relate to the colour of the cow's coat: Ole (Fawn-coloured), Bale (Black), Rane (White); other names describe the spots on the coat (their placement, shape, colour), the shape of the horns, the length of the tail, etc. The ending '-e' is feminine, while the masculine is '-i.' However, when naming a steer, the feminine ending '-e' is used. It's only when you talk about the steer that the masculine ending '-i' is used.

3   *Kelli: Grewia mollis.* This is a small tree with its leaves in separate bushy bunches; it has lacy leaves, small yellow flowers and spherical fruit, which are edible; its bark is rough and black; its leaves are used to bandage wounds.

4   Cattle need mineral salts with their fodder. When there's no salt springs in the area, it is provided by slabs of natron, weighing about twenty kilos, which are traded southward from around Lake Chad. In many areas, salt from the sea, packed in eighteen-kilo bags, has replaced the natron.

5   This refers to the traditional practice of loaning a cow as required by custom, which is intended to bind friendships. This system of loans is called *habbanaye*.

6   That is to say, this animal must not be killed at the time of a feast (a name-giving ceremony, a marriage, etc.). A Mbororo would never use his herd simply to satisfy his family's desire for meat.

7   *Dundehi: Ficus platyphilla* (gutta percha for the British). This is a big tree with aerial roots; it has rough, reddish-yellow bark, milky sap, large leaves and fruit which grows in clusters at the ends of the branches.

Chapter 26

1   *Sepdedisterik*: The office of the district head is a fairly recent creation in Cameroon. It is a territorial administrative authority beneath that of the sub-prefect. This new level of administration is supposed to make government action more effective in those regions where long distances and poor roads and paths make communications difficult. The old traditional political structure is still in place, but it is losing its importance daily.

Chapter 27

1   *Salam aleykum* is a greeting which means 'Peace be with you'. A person must announce himself this way when he arrives at someone's house.

2   'Salamander' is a brand name of imported European shoes. Perhaps the word makes Ndudi think of a particular kind of shoes which the Mbororo like. Cf. Chapter 9, Note 2.

3   Fulfulde is the term the Fulani use to designate their own language.

     This language is common among all the Fulani of Africa, from the East or the West, sedentary or nomadic, socially dominant or socially dominated – depending on where they live. Some censuses estimate their number at six million but who can really judge? Fulfulde has many dialectical forms, with differences in morphology and syntax. In addition, certain words have been acquired by some dialects but not by others. Those words, which have been more or less integrated into the language, come from the many ethnic groups with which the Fulani have had contact over the course of centuries. Although some literate Fulani have resorted to Arabic characters (which they learned from the Koran) in order to commit their language to paper, Fulfulde remains basically a language of oral tradition. The work of linguists in this century has opened the path to a literature, which is still in its beginnings. Readers interested in this problem are invited to consult the excellent bibliography of Christiane Seydou: *Bibliographie Générale du Monde Peul*, 1977, (*Etudes nigeriennes*, no. 43).

4   Today Ndudi could add, 'Is it worth it to write this account of my life in my own language? Encouraged by the Para, I have already done some pages.' I think this question would be answered in the affirmative by many Africans who are increasingly interested in their national languages and who desire to create a written literature.

5   *Bissimillahi*: This is the invocation of the name of God which is uttered before starting to do something.

6   *Alhamdu lillahi! Amina!* This is an expression of thanks to God when something is finished.

Glossary

Adamawa – 'the Country of the Mountain'; a high plateau region in northern Cameroon and adjacent parts of Nigeria

afel – first-born child

afuku – a type of beer made by the Gbaya people

Aku – a major sub-group of the Mbororo

alali – a tree, *Securidaca longipedunculata*. See Endnote 10, Chapter 2

alfalu – magical techniques, especially aimed at promoting fertility and well-being

Alfatiya – the opening verse of the Koran, often said as a prayer

Alhaji – title for a man who has made the pilgrimage (*hajj*) to Mecca

alhamdu lillahi – 'praise be to Allah'; an expression of thanks

alkali – a Muslim judge

Alkawal Kesal – the New Testament

Alkawal Kidngal – the Old Testament

alluha – a wooden slate for writing Koranic verses

almajiri – students of a Koranic school

amina – 'amen'; exclamation at the end of a prayer

ampul – a cupping horn for medical treatments

anabarsi – amphetamines

anket (cf. French *enquête*) – an investigation, usually by the police

ardo – a Mbororo leader

argi (cf. English alcohol) – an alcoholic drink distilled from grain or manioc

asama – the sky, the location of Heaven

asiri – the mid-afternoon prayer, the third of the Muslim daily prayers

Autanko – a Mbororo clan

Ba – a major sub-group of the Mbororo

baba – term of address for one's father

babambi (cf. *bambahi*) – a tree, *Asclepias gigantea* (cf. *Calotropis procera*)

babaya ayifu – a cry of alert shouted by the *kori* age class

bakurehi – a tree, *Nauclea latifolia* (cf. *Sarcocephalus esculentus*). See Endnote 9, Chapter 2

bale – a black cow

bambahi – see *babambi*

bangal – the ceremonial stage of a Mbororo marriage when the bride's trousseau is brought to the groom's village. See Chapter 19

bangtal – the ceremonial stage of a Mbororo marriage when the bride rejoins her husband after the weaning of their first child. See Chapter 19

bappanyo – paternal uncle

baraka – blessings or spiritual power of a holy person

bariki (cf. English barracks) – government office building or headquarters

barka – an expression wishing blessings upon you

barkehi – the sacred bush of the Mbororo, *Piliostigma reticulata*. See Endnote 2, Chapter 2

Bata – a Nigerian people

batalya (cf. English battalion) – battalion

biri jam-jam – holy water from a spring in Mecca

bissimillahi – an invocation of the name of Allah before starting to do something

bitiri – poor quality; said of a *mallam* who is poorly educated or a charlatan

bobori – a tree, *Sterculia setigera*. See Endnote 1, Chapter 5

Bodi – a major sub-group of the Mbororo

boka – specialist in magical techniques. See Endnote 2, Chapter 15

bokki – the baobab tree, *Adansonia digitata*

Bori – a spirit possession cult of the Hausa people, adopted by some Mbororo

borkonno – a hot pepper

Borom – a Nigerian people

Bororo – See *Mbororo*

Bura – a Nigerian people

burda – specialist in magical techniques. See Endnote 2, Chapter 15

bushin – a magical technique which allows the user to escape attacks by becoming invisible

buteru – house of male head of a Mbororo family

cherif – see *serif*

dada sare – the 'mother of the house', particularly referring to the senior wife in a polygamous household

dabunde – the first part of the dry season

dado – sitting place for adult men in a Mbororo encampment

dakel – an unidentified poisonous snake

Danagu – a Mbororo clan

Daneeji – a major sub-group of the Mbororo

dayeku – customary behaviour associated with the oldest Mbororo age class; old age

debbo – woman or wife

deetawal – a marriage by abduction

dendirabe – plural of *dendirawo*

dendirawo – a cross cousin; see Endnote 9, Chapter 1

derdirabe – plural of *derdirawo*

derdirawo – a parallel cousin; see Endnote 9, Chapter 1

Didimanko – a Mbororo clan

Diganko – the Mbororo clan of which Ndudi Umaru is a member

dingali – a tree, *Gardenia triacantha*. See Endnote 1, Chapter 13

doa – a Muslim prayer ceremony

dogari – a native-policeman of a superior chief

dogoleya – a dance

dudandu – a flute

dundehi – a tree, *Ficus platyphilla*. See Endnote 7, Chapter 24

esa'i – night-time Muslim prayer

Firé – a Nigerian people

fiyaou – exclamation referring to something good-tasting

Fulbe – settled Fulani people, in contrast to the pastoral Mbororo

Fulfulde – the language of the Fulani people, including the Mbororo and the Fulbe

gabay – Indian hemp, *Cannabis* sp.

gabdi – a tree, *Acacia scoprioides*, *arabica* or *nilotica* (cf. *Mimosa egyptica*). See Endnote 2, Chapter 6

gafara – expression used to announce one's presence on entering a house

galbal – wooden rack used for grilling meat at Mbororo feasts

garaya – the one-stringed guitar

gardi – a magician; an initiate into esoteric magical knowledge

gardijo – singular of *gardi*

garmofon (cf. English gramophone) – record player

gaude – large reeds used to make Mbororo beds

Gbaya – a Cameroonian people

gerewol – the courtship dance of the Wodabe

gernet (cf. English grenade) – grenade

Geroji – a Mbororo clan

gettile – the ceremony in the Mbororo marriage process when the parents of the future spouses, who have been promised to each other during their infancy, confirm their intentions to carry through with the marriage. See Chapter 19

ginaji – jinns; minor spirits in Islamic belief

Girka – see *Bori*

gogo – paternal aunt

gogue – toy cows made from forked sticks

gomna (cf. English governor) – government administrator

Goranko – a Mbororo clan

gouroup (cf. English group) – group

gri-gri – an amulet

guleli – the third part of the dry season, a stormy period before the rains

habbanaye – the loan of a cow by one Mbororo to another

Habe – non-Fulani pagan peoples

hakkilo – intelligence; one of the key qualities associated with the *pulaku* code

hamba – a type of beer brewed by the Gbaya people

Hausa – major ethnic group of northern Nigeria

Ibo – major ethnic group of eastern Nigeria

imam – religious head of a mosque

imanaku – Muslim piety

inderi – naming ceremony for a new-born child

inna jomba – the chorus of a traditional Mbororo marriage song

irde – a type of magical charm used to cause misfortune

istijin faru – a religious invocation asking Allah's pardon

jabbi – the tamarind tree, *Tamarindus indica*. See Endnote 3, Chapter 1

Jafun – the major sub-group of the Mbororo of which Ndudi is a member

janaba – in Islamic belief, a state of sexual impurity

jaoro – a chief of a village or residential quarter

jauleru – the entry hut of a Fulbe compound

Jetanko – a Mbororo clan

jikiri – a religious litany. See *la illa illa'llah*

jinadire – a fire-lighting kit containing flint and steel

jire – a squirrel

jura – first Muslim prayer of the afternoon, about 1:30 p.m.

kabidowu – a rain cape

kabihi – a tree, *Commiphora* sp. See Endnote 3, Chapter 12

Kado – singular of Habe

kai – exclamation of amazement or disbelief

Kanakuru – a Nigerian people

Kananku – a Nigerian people

kanko – him/her; an indirect way to refer to a person without mentioning their name, especially used in the context of Mbororo name-avoidance taboos

Kanuri – a people from the Bornu region of north-eastern Nigeria

kao – maternal uncle

karamajo – a sorcerer

Kare – a people of the Central African Republic

karehi – a tree, *Butyrospermum parkii*. See Endnote 1, Chapter 8

karfa – magical medicines used for treating cattle to render them energetic and preserve them from attacks

kata – onomatopoeia expressing the sound of animal hooves on a bridge

katasit (cf. English catechist) – Christian religious teacher

kaygama – the title of the second-in-command in a chiefdom

kebal – a 'favour', especially referring to securing a romantic liaison with a woman

kelli – a tree, *Grewia mollis*. See Endnote 3, Chapter 24

kerma – a magical medicine to increase one's dancing skill and attractiveness

Kessu – a major sub-group of the Fulbe people

kindirmo – unwhipped sour milk

kirankasko – an evil magical practice used by a sorcerer to attack a victim

Kiri – a major sub-group of the Fulbe people

kiring – onomatopoeia expressing the sound of a drum

Krisimet (cf. English Christmas) – Christmas

Kitaku – a major sub-group of the Fulbe people

kobgal – a feast that forms part of the Mbororo marriage process, held during the
    future spouses' childhood. See Chapter 19

Kongo – labour migrants to Cameroon from the Central African Republic

koraku – the customs of the *kori* age class

kori – a member of the Mbororo age class of early adulthood, which is particularly known for its ribald and
    outrageous behaviour

kori soro – the *soro* contest, which is presided over by the kori age class

koudata (cf. French *coup d'état*) – a political coup

kuri – an alcoholic beverage made from honey by the Gbaya people

kurkuku – a small burrowing insect, the ant-lion

kurkutu – see *kurkuku*

la illa illa'llah – an exclamation: 'There is no other god than Allah!'

lamidate – the chiefdom of a *lamido*

lamido – a superior chief

laturney (cf. French *la tournée*) – an administrative tour by a chief or official

ledde – plural of *lekki*

lekki – generic noun for tree and for medicine

Lelewaji – a Fulbe clan

ler (cf. French *l'air*) - air

lespor (cf. French *le sport*) - sport

Lungundu – a Nigerian people

maccudo – a slave

mai kura – a hyena trainer

makama – the title of the man who presides over distributing grilled meat at Mbororo celebrations

Maké – an initiated member of the Hunters' Society

mallam – a man who has attended Koranic school

Mandinka – a people of Mali and neighbouring countries

mangariba – the Muslim prayer at sunset

marabout – a Muslim holy man

marto (cf. French *marteau*) – a hammer

mbagu – a drum

mbordam – a thin porridge made from millet

Mbororo – nomadic pastoral section of the Fulani people

Mbula – a Nigerian people
missio (cf. English or French *mission*) – a Christian missionary station
modibo – a specialist in Koranic knowledge
munyal – patience; one of the key qualities associated with the *pulaku* code

Nabiri – a Nigerian people
naira – a Nigerian unit of currency. See Endnote 3, Chapter 7
nangaru – infant betrothal, the first stage in Mbororo marriage. See Chapter 19
narehi – a tree, *Parkia filicoides* or *P. clappertoniana*. See Endnote 4, Chapter 12
Nassara – Muslim term for Christians or white people, cf. Nazarene
ndottaku – customary behaviour associated with the Mbororo age class of mature adults; the prime of life
ndungu – the rainy season
nivakin – Nivaquine anti-malarial medicine
njabordi – a ceremonial food dish, prepared to welcome newcomers
njotte – a short-tailed cow
Ntabo – a Nigerian people
nuvote (cf. French *nouveauté*) – a novelty
Nyakanko – a Mbororo clan
Nyamiri – colloquial name for the Ibo people, used in northern Nigeria

pam (cf. English pound) – former monetary unit of Nigeria. See Endnote 3, Chapter 7
Pana – a people of the Central African Republic
para (cf. French *père*) – a Catholic priest
Para Mbororo – Ndudi's name for Père Henri Bocquené
pasto (cf. English pastor) – a Protestant pastor
perlimpinpin – talcum powder
persidan (cf. English president) - president
pulaku – the Fulani code of values. See Chapter 22

rane – a white cow
Ringimaji – a Mbororo clan
ronga – a type of sorcery
rubu – brideprice money given to the bride by the groom

sabon gemu – literally 'young beard'; young men leaving the *kori* age class
sabuli gorki – a tree, *Ximenia americana*. See Endnote 3, Chapter 6
sadaka – alms
sadaki – heifer given to the bride by the groom as part of the marriage settlement
sade – cannabis, a narcotic plant
salam aleykum – 'peace be with you', a Muslim greeting
Sambo – one of the *Bori* spirits
Sardauna – the traditional title of Alhaji Sir Ahmadu Bello, a prominent northern Nigerian political leader.
    See Endnote 4, Chapter 15
sare – a walled or fenced family compound, particularly characteristic of Fulbe households
saruandu – a species of bird
Sawtu Linjila – the 'Voice of the Gospel', a Christian radio programme broadcast in Fulfulde
sedu – the second part of the dry season, sunny and very hot
semtende – shame; one of the key qualities associated with the *pulaku* code
sepdedisterik (cf. French *chef de district*) – administrative head of a district
ser (cf. French *soeur*) – a Catholic sister
ser-docta (cf. French *soeur docteur*) – a Catholic nursing sister
serif – a person claiming descent from the Prophet Mohammed and reputed to possess special religious
    gifts

serip – see *serif*

seto – the beginning of the rainy season

shea butter – an edible oil from the seeds of the karehi tree

Shehu Usumanu – Fulani Muslim religious leader, better known as Usman dan Fodio, who declared a holy war in 1804 against the Hausa states of northern Nigeria and established the Sokoto Caliphate. See Endnote 4, Chapter 13

sidabaru – magical tricks based on sleight-of-hand

singa – a Singer sewing machine

sobal – millet dough shaped into balls, which are broken up into sour milk to form a thin gruel

soro – a ritualised stick-beating contest between youths of the suka age group

subaha – the Muslim dawn prayer

sudu – a house

sufrefet (cf. French *sous-préfet*) – sub-prefect, government administrator of a part of a province

suka – a member of the Mbororo adolescent age class, particularly associated with the *soro* contest

sukaku – the customs of the Mbororo *suka* age class; the age of adolescence

sura – a verse or chapter of the Koran

sureji – the part of a cattle herd left behind during the dry season migration

tafsiru – commentary on the Koran

Tambu – a Nigerian people

Tangalé – a Nigerian people

Tarbiya – a Muslim Sufi sect

Targui – a Saharan people

tegal – the stage of a Mbororo marriage when the spouses are officially married according to the Muslim marriage rite. See Chapter 19

telefon (cf. English telephone) – telephone

tourne (cf. French *tournée*) – an administrative tour by a chief or official

tourni-diski (cf. French *tourne-disque*) – a record player

Usman dan Fodio – see *Shehu Usumanu*

Wawa – a Nigerian people

Witi – a major Fulbe group

wi-wi – cannabis, a narcotic plant. See sade

Wodabe – a major sub-group of the Mbororo

Wojabe – a Wodabe clan

Wolof – a Senegalese people

Wuaduganko – a Mbororo clan

wuro – a village

yadiri – a variety of millet

yafi – magical practices considered to be paganism by orthodox Muslims

yamnde – the harvest season at the end of the rains

Yanguru – a Nigerian people

yapendo – maternal aunt

yarindo – an acrobatic dance

ye kwa – 'hear ye, hear ye!'; an exclamation uttered at the beginning of a public proclamation.